D1563642

Patterns of Destiny

Patterns of Destiny

*Narrative Structures of Foundation and Doom
in the Hebrew Bible*

Diane M. Sharon

Eisenbrauns
Winona Lake, Indiana
2002

Library of Congress Cataloging-in-Publication Data

Sharon, Diane M.
    Patterns of destiny : narrative structures of foundation and doom in the Hebrew Bible / Diane M. Sharon
        p. cm.
    Revision and expansion of the author's thesis (doctoral), The literary function of eating and drinking in Hebrew Bible narrative with reference to the literatures of the ancient Near East—Jewish Theological Seminary of America, New York, N.Y., 1995.
    Includes bibliographical references and index.
    ISBN 1-57506-052-3 (cloth : alk. paper)
    1. Dinners and dining in the Bible.   2. Drinking in the Bible.   3. Bible as literature.   4. Bible. O.T.—Structuralist criticism.   5. Bible. O.T.—Criticism, Narrative.   I. Sharon, Diane M. Literary function of eating and drinking in Hebrew Bible narrative with reference to the literatures of the ancient Near East.   II. Title.

BS1199.D55 S52 2001
221.6—dc21

               00-067210
               CIP

Contents

Acknowledgments

וההחכמה מאין תמצא ואי זה מקום בינה

This book is a reworking and expansion of my doctoral dissertation, "The Literary Function of Eating and Drinking in Hebrew Bible Narrative with Reference to the Literatures of the Ancient Near East," accepted with distinction in May, 1995, by the Jewish Theological Seminary of America. In the acknowledgements for my dissertation I thanked those who enabled me to complete that project. Here I would like to thank again some of those whose efforts on my behalf made possible the underlying dissertation, and hence this book.

With great love and respect I honor my teachers and colleagues at the Department of Bible and Ancient Semitic Languages at JTS whose many gifts enabled me to complete this task: Dr. Stephen P. Garfinkel, Dean of the Graduate School; Dr. Stephen A. Geller, my dissertation adviser and advocate; Dr. David Marcus, Department Chair; and Dr. Yochanan Muffs, Rapaport Distinguished Service Professor of Bible and Religion.

I would like to honor publicly the members of my dissertation committee who were not members of the Bible Department: Dr. Zvia Ginor ז״ל, Assistant Professor of Jewish Literature at the Jewish Theological Seminary; Dr. Edward L. Greenstein, Professor of Bible at Tel Aviv University, Israel, who was my second reader; and Dr. Anne Golumb Hoffman, Professor of English and Comparative Literature at Fordham University. I am also grateful to Dr. Susan Niditch, Professor of Religion at Amherst College, who generously lent her scholarly perspective.

I would like to acknowledge two scholars who were particularly helpful at the initial stages of this project: Dr. Mary Douglas, for her anthropological expertise, and Dr. Yehoshua Gitay, of the University of Cape Town, for his guidance in rhetorical analysis and oral traditions. I also remember with gratitude the encouragement of Dr. Baruch M. Bokser, ז״ל, when I began my doctoral studies. I honor, as well, the teachers at other institutions whose desire to teach inspired mine to study. They taught me graciousness and generosity along with Sumerian, Akkadian, and Kabbalah: Dr. William W. Hallo of Yale University; Dr. Åke Sjöberg of the University of Pennsylvania; Reb Zalman Schachter-Shalomi, founding Rabbi, ALEPH/Center for Jewish Renewal.

אם אין קמח אין תורה

The dissertation was made possible in part by funds granted to me through a fellowship program sponsored by the Charles H. Revson Foundation. Its completion was supported by a dissertation fellowship from the National Foundation for Jewish Culture and a grant from the Memorial Foundation for Jewish Culture. I am honored to acknowledge financial support from these institutions; I take full responsibility for the contents of this study, for its accuracy, and for the views expressed herein.

כי אם יפלו האחד יקים את חברו

Academic studies rely on the logistical support of many. I am particularly indebted to the staff of the library at the Jewish Theological Seminary, especially to Ms. Annette Muffs Botnick, and also to Anne-Marie Whitfield for her ongoing research assistance. I acknowledge with great appreciation NotaBene® word processing software and its technical assistance team, without whom this project would never have been completed, and Elisheva Urbas, who brought her considerable editorial skills and cogent questions to the task of reshaping the dissertation into a real book. Thanks, also, to Janice Meyerson and to Michelle Kwitkin-Close for their meticulous copy editing, and to Beverly Fields of Eisenbrauns for her patience, care, and professionalism.

In loving gratitude I salute particularly the friends who listened, read, cheered, warned, counseled and sympathized, in person and electronically, far above and beyond the call of duty: Yocheved Herschlag Muffs, whose artwork is the basis for the cover of this book, Ada Hannah Citron, Sarah Diamant, Tamara M. Green, Bonnie R. Grosz, Tikva Frymer-Kensky, Robert Harris, Ora Horn Prouser, Jane L. Rockman, Marian S. Rothenberg, Claudia Setzer, Dorothy G. Weiss, Helene Bergman Witt, and Ilene S. Zatal. It is a pleasure to offer thanks here as well to Mrs. Cyrilla Alexander for her loyalty and energy on behalf of our household.

שימני כחותם על לבך כחותם על זרועך כי עזה כמות אהבה

Most of all I cherish with great love and devotion two generations of my family, to whom this work is dedicated: my parents, Rebecca Menaged Sharon ז״ל and Gabriel Sharon ז״ל, and my children, Susannah Rebecca Sharon Nadler and Reena Evelyn Sharon Nadler.

ברוך ה׳ שההחיינו וקיימנו והגיענו לזמן הזה

Abbreviations

AB	Anchor Bible
ABD	*Anchor Bible Dictionary*
AnBib	Analecta biblica
ANET	*Ancient Near Eastern Texts Relating to the Old Testament*
AOAT	Alter Orient und Altes Testament
BA	*Biblical Archaeologist*
BAR	*Biblical Archaeology Review*
BASOR	*Bulletin of the American Schools of Oriental Research*
BHS	*Biblia Hebraica Stuttgartensia*
Bib	*Biblica*
BJS	Brown Judaic Studies
BKAT	*Biblischer Kommentar, Altes Testament*
BO	*Bibliotheca orientalis*
BR	*Biblical Research*
BTB	*Biblical Theology Bulletin*
BZAW	Beihefte zur Zeitschrift für die alttestamentliche Wissenschaft
CAD	*The Assyrian Dictionary of the Oriental Institute of the University of Chicago*
CADIR	Centre pour l'Analyse du Discours Religieux
CBQ	*Catholic Biblical Quarterly*
CTA	*Corpus des tablettes en cunéiformes alphabétiques découvertes à Ras Shamra-Ugarit de 1929 à 1939*
EncJud	*Encyclopaedia Judaica*
ErIsr	*Eretz-Israel*
FOTL	Forms of the Old Testament Literature
GOTL	*Greek Orthodox Theological Review*
HSM	Harvard Semitic Monographs
HSS	Harvard Semitic Studies
HTR	*Harvard Theological Review*
HUCA	*Hebrew Union College Annual*
ICC	International Critical Commentary
IDB	*Interpreter's Dictionary of the Bible*
IEJ	*Israel Exploration Journal*
Int	*Interpretation*
IRT	Issues in Religion and Theology
JANES	*Journal of the Ancient Near Eastern Society*
JAOS	*Journal of the American Oriental Society*
JBL	*Journal of Biblical Literature*

JCS	*Journal of Cuneiform Studies*
JECS	*Journal of Early Christian Studies*
JNES	*Journal of Near Eastern Studies*
JSOT	*Journal for the Study of the Old Testament*
JSOTSup	Journal for the Study of the Old Testament: Supplement Series
KAI	*Kanaanäische und aramäische Inschriften*
KAR	*Keilschrifttexte aus Assur religiösen Inhalts*
KB	*Keilinschriftliche Bibliothek*
KTU	*Die keilalphabetischen Texte aus Ugarit*
LCL	Loeb Classical Library
NJPSV	New Jewish Publication Society Version
OBO	Orbis biblicus et orientalis
OLA	Orientalia lovaniensia analecta
Or	*Orientalia*
OTS	Old Testament Studies
OtSt	*Oudtestamentische Studiën*
RB	*Revue biblique*
RHA	*Revue hittite et asianique*
RlA	*Reallexikon der Assyriologie*
RThom	*Revue thomiste*
RSV	Revised Standard Version
RTP	*Revue de théologie et de philosophie*
SBLRBS	Society of Biblical Literature Resources for Biblical Study
SBLSP	*Society of Biblical Literature Seminar Papers*
SBLWAW	Society of Biblical Literature Writings from the Ancient World
SJLA	Studies in Judaism in Late Antiquity
ScrHier	Scripta hierosolymitana
TAPA	*Transactions of the American Philological Society*
TQ	*Theologische Quartalschrift*
TS	*Theological Studies*
TZ	*Theologische Zeitschrift*
UF	*Ugarit-Forschungen*
VT	*Vetus Testamentum*
VTSup	Vetus Testamentum Supplements
ZA	*Zeitschrift für Assyriologie*
ZAW	*Zeitschrift für die alttestamentliche Wissenschaft*

CHAPTER ONE

Introduction

In this book, I seek to demonstrate how a structuralist tool may be used to discover patterns in many stories in biblical narrative. The patterns I found define genres that were understood in the ancient world but were lost to our modern understanding. The insights made possible by this analysis illuminate ways of thinking about God and human purpose in the Hebrew Bible—and perhaps in other ancient literatures as well.

The Bible has been revered as a sacred text for millennia by succeeding generations in a variety of communities. The meanings taken from reading biblical texts are thus theological in nature. Biblical narrative tells of human interactions with God and understandings about divine will that arise from those interactions. A tool that gives us a new way to understand ancient conventions encoded in the text can be valuable in enlarging our understanding of cultures from biblical times and the evolution of their thinking about the relationships between the human and the divine.

As I read episode after episode in the Bible that portrayed eating and drinking, I was struck by how often major encounters seemed to occur at gatherings around food. This was not surprising, I rationalized, since a big banquet was an opportunity for people to get together and for conflicts or interactions of other sorts to arise. But as I read further, it became clear to me that this rationalization was not sufficient to account for what I was seeing.

For example, I was struck, at first, by the considerable emphasis on food in the story of Isaac's blessing of Jacob and Esau in Genesis 27. Isaac sends Esau out to hunt and prepare the venison he loves—the patriarch plans to eat the venison and bless his elder son. This meal did not seem to be necessary for Isaac's blessing of his sons; Jacob blesses Joseph's children in Genesis 48, for example, and his own children in Genesis 49, without any mention of a meal. I thought that perhaps sending Esau out to hunt food for a meal might be tied to the plot of

1

this story, to get Esau out of the way. But other biblical figures are dispatched in contexts where food is completely absent—Saul is sent searching for his father's lost asses in 1 Samuel 9, and Joseph is sent to convey his father's greeting to his brothers in Genesis 37.

I wondered, if eating and drinking are not necessary in order for Isaac to bless his children (the purpose of the story) or in order to get Esau out of the way (the plot of the story), why is food made so much of in this story? Could there be other levels of significance to this emphasis on a meal?

From my study of Isaac's blessing, I realized that it was not enough to assume that encounters would "just naturally" follow on occasions where eating and drinking take place. I also realized that looking at the narrative plot and purpose is not enough to answer the questions I had. I needed to look more deeply at episodes where eating and drinking occurred. I began to look at the structure of these stories for clues.

I needed a research tool to examine the structural level of the text, and I found it in Vladimir Propp's model of morphological analysis. Early in the twentieth century, this Russian literary critic, folklorist, and philologist had studied a corpus of about 100 Russian fairy-tales and concluded that they followed a specific structural pattern, in spite of a surface appearance of colorful variety. Propp concluded that the underlying structural pattern, or morphology, that he had identified defined the genre of Russian fairy-tales and that other genres could be defined by applying his methodology to other corpora. These other genres need share none of the elements defining Russian fairy-tales: the *mode* that emerged from other corpora might be completely different, even though the *methodology* applied to these corpora was the same.

Stated briefly, Propp's literary approach works on the surface structure of a text, on the level of plot. First, it describes and charts the linear sequence of elements in a text, seeking to recognize the constant sequential pattern of types of actions in the narrative without being distracted by the specific variable forms the type of action may take. Second, once a morphology of such narrative events is isolated, where they occur in a story and what their function might be can be analyzed and interpreted.

The first major point Propp makes is to differentiate between what is constant and what is variable in comparing narratives. A main character—prince or princess, craftsworker, farmer, servant, entertainer, or other person—secures a spouse by winning a contest, slaying a monster, sewing, weaving, overcoming geographical obstacles, answering riddles, or passing some other trial. Each of these ways a main character may secure a spouse is a *variable*, as is the gender, status, or occupation of that character. The *constant* elements are that a hero succeeds in a trial and wins a spouse.

The second central insight of Propp's is the idea that the function of a motif in a story depends on where it occurs in the story sequence. At the time Propp wrote, folklorists were focused on collecting motifs that occurred in a variety of narratives and a variety of cultures, without any concern for where the motif occurred in the sequence of the story or how it functioned differently in different narratives.[1] A major contribution of Propp's study is the idea that the meaning of any motif depends as much upon where it occurs in a sequence as upon what it is.

An anecdotal illustration may clarify how important this insight is. When my daughter Reena was nine years old, she loved to read fairy-tales, and she once observed to me that there is a difference between someone falling off a boat at the beginning of a story, and someone falling off a boat at the end of a story. I asked her what she meant. "Well," she said, "if someone falls off the boat at the beginning of the story, then it's probably the hero and the story will probably be about his adventures. If someone falls off the boat at the end of the story, then it's probably the villain, and he will probably drown." This insight that the same motif can mean different things depending on where it occurs in the story may be self-evident today, but it was revolutionary when Propp discovered it.

Propp published his findings and his methodology in a slim volume, *Morphology of the Folktale*. It was published in Russian in 1928, but an English translation was not published until 1958, in an edition riddled with editorial problems. A revised edition was published in 1968. With this publication, Propp's substantial contribution to folklore and literary studies was finally available to scholars in the West.

I describe Propp's method and my initial application of it in chapter 2. More specifically, chapter 2 addresses my decision to analyze the function of eating and drinking on a structural level in Hebrew Bible narrative, and why I identified Vladimir Propp's model of morphological analysis as the appropriate tool for this analysis: *because it works*. In this chapter, I describe Propp's method in detail and show

---

1 The classic example is Antti Aarne's *Verzeichnis der Märchentypen*, later edited by Stith Thompson and published in 1928 under the title *The Types of the Folktale: Antti Aarne's Verzeichnis der Märchentypen, Translated and Enlarged* (Folklore Fellows Communications 74; Helsinki: Suomalainen Tiedeakatemia / Academia Scientiarum Fennica). A recent English edition was published in six volumes by Indiana University Press in 1969 as *Motif Index of Folklore Literature*.

how productive it can be in biblical study in general and in addressing the questions I am raising in particular.

The essential part of this book, what I discovered by applying Propp's method to biblical narrative, is the substance of chapters 3–7. To be applied successfully, Proppian analysis must account for all examples in my corpus, whether or not they fit my hypothesis. In chapter 3, I use Proppian analysis to examine a wide range of stories that include eating and drinking in a variety of ways. These are cases where eating and drinking function as a variable element in biblical narratives in which some other function operates as a constant element. I continue in chapter 4, where I look at cases in which the unexpected absence of a structural element, here eating and drinking, can be examined for its significance.

In chapters 5 and 6, I focus much more closely on one particular pattern within the structure of many stories where eating and drinking appear in biblical narrative—a pattern that consists of a series of elements that occur in a recognized sequence: an act of EATING or DRINKING, followed by an ENCOUNTER of some kind, in which is embedded an ORACLE (either positive or negative) that is presently AFFIRMED. When the oracle is positive, the subject of the oracle is divinely established (and blessed); when the oracle is negative, the subject of the oracle is divinely doomed (and condemned). In chapters 5 and 6, I discuss the more obvious examples, and in chapter 7, I focus on the more subtle occurrences of this genre.

In this book I take one of the most modern Western tools, literary analysis, and apply it to some of the oldest texts from the cultures of the ancient Near East. I also assume throughout that these ancient Near Eastern literary works have something to contribute to biblical scholarship. The lands of Mesopotamia, Egypt, Anatolia, and the Levant produced rich, thriving cultures that preceded the Bible, in some cases, by millennia. "Until the mid-twentieth century, to speak of the 'Ancient Near East' was also to speak of the 'Lands of the Bible.'"[2] Since then, these cultures have been studied for themselves. The more we learn about these cultures, the more we discover the vast extent of their interactions with one another and the complex interchange of material, intellectual, and cultural artifacts. In the years since these ancient languages were first deciphered, beginning about a century and a half ago, the profound influence of these cultures on biblical development has become a commonplace in biblical studies.

---

2. Jack M. Sasson (ed.), *Civilizations of the Ancient Near East* (4 vols.; New York: Scribner's, 1995).

Many of my insights were triggered first by reading the literatures of Sumer, Akkad, and Egypt and then confirmed by discovering them in the biblical narrative as well. Among the significant findings I report in this book is the fact that the roots of the patterns I uncovered can be found in some of the earliest written texts we have, from Mesopotamia in the third millennium B.C.E. That is why throughout this book I view the structural analysis of biblical narrative within the context of the ancient Near East.

In chapters 5 and 6, I show that the pattern of destiny that I find in biblical narrative occurs beginning with Sumerian texts from the third millennium B.C.E. and even earlier, that it can be found throughout the Hebrew Bible, and that it even shows up in the New Testament and in Homeric literature of the Classical Greek period. Having identified such a widespread pattern, I conclude that it was widely recognized within its cultural context; that hearers of this pattern would have recognized it in all of its variations, perhaps in the same way that we recognize the expression *once upon a time* as signaling a genre of narrative; and that they would have understood the cluster of implications behind any use, reuse, or transformation of this pattern. Identifying and recognizing this pattern today, therefore, can unlock levels of meaning in the text that were obvious to ancient audiences and that were invisible to modern readers until now.

A Note to the Reader about Typestyle in This Volume

In this book, I distinguish patterns, constants, initial situations, and constant elements that do not always occur, from variable elements in the following ways:

- Patterns and genres appear in uppercase and lowercase letters (example: Foundation Pattern). See pp. 17 and 70 for definition.
- Constants, discussed in their function as a regular part of a pattern, are set in small capital letters (example: EATING). See p. 86 for definition. However, when these words are used to describe generic actions or are not part of a pattern, they are set in lowercase letters (example: eating). See p. 29 for further clarification.
- Initial situations are formatted in italic type (example: *Initial Situation*). See pp. 122–26 for definition.
- Constant elements that do not always appear are typeset in small capital letters within brackets (example: [JOURNEY/PILGRIMAGE]). See p. 128 for definition.
- Variable elements are noted in normal typeface (example: war, poverty, famine). See pp. 28–29 for definition.

CHAPTER TWO

Structuralism, Proppian Analysis, and Biblical Narrative

My insights into the destiny patterns of Foundation and Doom arise from a structuralist reading of the biblical narrative. Before observing these structures as they emerge from the biblical text through a Proppian structural analysis, I find it helpful to review the emergence of structuralism and to examine the ways that Propp, especially, applied it to corpora of literature that are analogous to the Hebrew Bible narratives that I examine later on.

A Brief History of Structuralism

Most scholarly approaches that are termed *structural*, whether linguistic, literary, anthropological, or in some other discipline, derive from or demonstrate the impact of the thinking of the great Swiss scholar of language and linguistics, Ferdinand de Saussure. His *Course in General Linguistics*, compiled from student notes on his lectures and published posthumously in 1916, changed the course of linguistic scholarship and had a broad interdisciplinary impact. Like many scholarly disciplines in the last century, linguistics was historically oriented.[1]

---

1. Although this is common knowledge today, it is sometimes useful to follow the evolution of a scholarly perspective from one paradigm to another. Some interesting reflections on this process within the disciplines of linguistics, anthropology, and biblical studies include: Hermann Gunkel, *The Legends of Genesis* (New York: Schocken, 1974); idem, "Introduction," *The Folktale in the Old Testament* (trans. M. D. Rutter; introduction by J. W. Rogerson; Sheffield: Almond, 1987) 10; Stith Thompson, "Introduction," *The Folktale* (New York: Dryden, 1946); Alan Dundes, *The Morphology of North American Indian Folktales* (Folklore Fellows Communications 195; Helsinki: Suomalainen Tiedeakatemia / Academia Scientiarum Fennica, 1964) 32–34, 36, 38–39; and also Richard M. Dorson, "The Eclipse of Solar Mythology," in *The Study of Folklore* (ed. A. Dundes; Englewood Cliffs, N.J.: Prentice-Hall, 1965) 57–83.

Scholars in all fields were preoccupied with identifying the origins of whatever they were studying, approaching their subjects atomistically rather than systemically. This focus on individual fragments prevented scholars from seeing the structural whole and noting the relationship of the individual parts to that larger system.[2] Among the major distinctions made by de Saussure was the distinction between diachronic (historical, evolutionary, comparative) and synchronic (punctive, static, descriptive, labile)[3] studies of language. De Saussure's notion that language is a self-contained system, just one of many conventional systems of signs within a culture, and that any such system can be studied in terms of its surface structure (*parole*, words, signs, units of the system) and metastructure (*langue*, grammar, the system of signs, rules of the system) gave rise to the science of semiology.[4] Semiologists seek to uncover the internally coherent system underlying the surface level of signs.

Two Main Approaches to Structural Analysis:
The Syntagmatic and the Paradigmatic

This uncovering of the underlying structure is the task taken on by structuralists in all disciplines. Where many differ from one another is in defining the *kinds of relationships* that link the signs within the structure. De Saussure identified two kinds of relationships operating among signs in a system: syntagmatic and associative. De Saussure's term "associative" has been replaced by the term *paradigmatic* in most discussions of structuralist theory.[5] Each of these two primary approaches in structuralist analysis is represented by a major scholar who articulated the basics of his respective school. The syntagmatic approach to structuralist analysis is represented by Vladimir Propp, whose intellectual roots are among the philologists, linguists, literary historians, and folklorists known as the Russian Formalists.[6]

---

2. Dundes, *North American Indian Folktales*, 34, 39.

3. A. Stender-Petersen, cited in ibid., 41.

4. Ferdinand de Saussure, *Course in General Linguistics* (ed. Charles Bally, Albert Sechehaye, and Albert Riedlinger; trans. Roy Harris; La Salle, Ill.: Open Court, 1983) 16–17.

5. Pamela J. Milne, *Vladimir Propp and the Study of Structure in Hebrew Biblical Narrative* (Bible and Literature Series 13; Sheffield: Almond, 1988) 274 n. 12.

6. The standard introduction to this approach is Victor Erlich, *Russian Formalism: History–Doctrine* (3d ed.; Slavistic Printings and Reprintings 4; The Hague: Mouton, 1969). See also Dundes, *North American Indian Folktales*, 50; Milne, *Vladimir Propp*, 26–29.

The paradigmatic approach is represented by Claude Lévi-Strauss, the French anthropologist, who based his initial observations on kinship systems.[7]

Syntagmatic relationships, like the syntax of a sentence, follow a linear order that is identifiable, predictable, and replicable. A term derives its meaning from its position in the sequence. Studies of syntagmatic relationships are concerned with form or structure. Morphological studies fall within this category.

Paradigmatic relationships are associative, reaching below the surface structure that is the concern of morphological studies to the "deep structure" or "mythic level" of analysis.[8] As Lévi-Strauss writes, "If there is a meaning to be found in mythology, this cannot reside in the isolated elements which enter into the composition of a myth, but only in the way those elements are combined."[9] He calls these combined elements "bundles of relations" and writes, "It is only as bundles that these relations can be put to use and combined so as to produce meaning."[10]

Syntagmatic or morphological analysis of the "surface level" adheres to the diachronic order in which constants occur in a pattern. Paradigmatic analysis of the "deep" or "mythic level" may reorganize elements on the basis of their belonging to the same "bundle of relations," ignoring the diachronic order in which they occur. "Relations pertaining to the same bundle may appear diachronically at remote intervals, but when we have succeeded in grouping them together, we have reorganized our myth according to a time referent of a new nature. . . . To put it in even more linguistic terms, it is as though a phoneme were always made up of all its variants."[11] Lévi-Strauss uses the analogy of a musical score that is to be read "diachronically along one axis—that is, page after page, and from left to right—and also synchron-

---

7. Ibid., 40–41; Dundes, *North American Indian Folktales,* 42–43.

8. De Saussure, *Course,* 123–27; Jonathan Culler, *Structuralist Poetics: Structuralism, Linguistics and the Study of Literature* (Ithaca, N.Y.: Cornell University Press, 1976) 13; Dundes, *North American Indian Folktales,* 41–42; Robert Scholes and Robert Kellogg, *The Nature of Narrative* (New York: Oxford, 1966) 18–19; Milne, *Vladimir Propp,* 26.

9. The classic C. Lévi-Strauss essay, "The Structural Study of Myth" (1955), has been reprinted many times. For the reader's convenience, citations will be made to Lévi-Strauss's own paragraph numbers. This quotation is taken from his §2.6, item #1, on p. 86 of the reprint. The translation here and in all citations from this essay in this chapter is taken from the essay as it is reprinted in *Myth: A Symposium* (ed. Thomas A. Sebeok; Bloomington, Ind.: Indiana University Press, 1972) 81–106.

10. Ibid., 87, §3.4.

11. Ibid.

ically along the other axis, all the notes which are written vertically making up one gross constituent unit, i.e., one bundle of relations."[12]

The differences between the approaches of these two scholars have been discussed in other works.[13] They are often presented in opposition to each other, as an "either/or" proposition.[14] In fact, however, the focus of each addresses entirely different questions about the same text, and both may offer valuable insight at different points of analysis and interpretation.[15]

These two structuralist approaches can be summarized briefly. The major difference between them is the level of text upon which each operates. Propp's approach is syntagmatic. Propp works on the surface structure of a text, on the level of plot. He describes the linear sequence of elements in a text and charts it, noting its form or morphology. His goal is to recognize sequential patterns of actions in the narrative. Lévi-Strauss's approach is paradigmatic. Working on the deep structure, he seeks patterns by examining and charting the

---

12. Ibid.

13. Milne, *Vladimir Propp*, 35–36; A. Dundes, in his introduction to Vladimir Propp, *Morphology of the Folktale* (ed. L. A. Wagner; trans. L. Scott; Austin: University of Texas Press, 1968), especially p. xii; see also Dundes, *North American Indian Folktales*, 42–52 and passim; and B. Nathhorst, *Formal or Structural Studies of Traditional Tales* (Stockholm: Acta Universitatis Stockholmiensis, 1969); among others.

14. Unfortunately, this situation was exacerbated by the scholars themselves. Lévi-Strauss praised Propp's "many intuitions" that "compel our admiration" (C. Lévi-Strauss, "Structure and Form: Reflections on a Work by Vladimir Propp," in *Structural Anthropology II* [Chicago: University of Chicago Press, 1976] 127) but was critical of Propp's approach (pp. 115–45), accusing Propp of "formalism," an apparently formidable charge at the time. Lévi-Strauss has been accused of not understanding what Propp was doing (Milne, *Vladimir Propp*, 89, 96–104), and Propp himself was very defensive of the structuralist (versus formalist) nature of his approach in response to Lévi-Strauss's criticism (Vladimir Propp, "Structure and History in the Study of the Fairy Tale" [trans. Hugh T. McElwain; *Semeia* 10 [*Narrative Syntax: Translations and Reviews*; Chico, Calif.: Scholars Press, 1978] 57–83). Although Lévi-Strauss is recognized as "definitely a standard-bearer for a structural approach to anthropology" (Dundes, *North American Indian Folktales*, 42), his own work has been criticized for "serious methodological and theoretical errors, not to mention a general lack of lucidity in presentation" by the folklorist Alan Dundes, who espouses a methodology based firmly on Propp (ibid., 43; details and discussion, 43–44; see especially pp. 121–22 n. 62 for citations of similar criticism of Lévi-Strauss by other scholars).

15. I am especially indebted to Dr. Jack M. Sasson, formerly Kenan Professor of Religious Studies, University of North Carolina at Chapel Hill, for the clarification that resulted from our discussion of this issue. See also William O. Hendricks, "Methodology of Narrative Structural Analysis," in *Essays on Semiolinguistics and Verbal Art* (The Hague: Mouton, 1973) 179–95.

"bundles" of elements that occur in a text, sorting them into opposing pairs such as life/death, male/female, and so on, without reference to their linear sequence on the level of plot.[16] In Lévi-Strauss's view, important sets of oppositional relations will occur repeatedly beyond the surface sequence of a text. The significance of a text is determined more by the prominence of a particular relational set than by the sequence of elements in the narration.

Structuralism and Biblical Studies

Structural analysis is not new to biblical studies. The astounding variety of approaches that are characterized as "structuralist" has been applied to the Hebrew and Christian Bibles no less than to the literature of other genres and periods. Pamela Milne, whose book conveniently and thoroughly summarizes structural approaches to biblical studies up to 1988, comments on this variety. She writes that "the great diversity which characterizes structural investigations makes it extremely difficult to compare and classify them."[17] Robert C. Culley, Jack Sasson, David M. Gunn, Robert Alter, David Jobling, Albert B. Lord, Alan Aycock, Roland Barthes, Edmund Leach, and Claude Lévi-Strauss have each applied his particular structural approach to segments of the biblical corpus, although none has addressed eating and drinking events systematically.

So many scholars have applied structural approaches to biblical narrative because they sensed its potential for producing important insights not otherwise available to the reader. In as highly structured a text as the Hebrew Bible, replete as it is with repetitions and variations of theme and motif, an approach that operates on the structural level is bound to be productive. Although later on in this chapter I discuss some of the ways these earlier structural analyses may have fallen short of their goals, these scholars nonetheless pioneered an important methodological approach. In my own work, I found that by applying structural methods to the group of biblical narratives that incorporate eating and drinking events I was able to uncover the genre of narratives that is the subject of this book: narratives containing Patterns of Destiny featuring ORACLES of Foundation or ORACLES of Doom.

---

16. See most conveniently Dundes in his introduction to Propp, *Morphology* (1968) xii.

17. Milne, *Vladimir Propp*, 35.

The Relationship between Structuralism and Poststructuralism

A word is in order here on the relationship between structural and poststructural studies. Structural analysis is out of fashion in some quarters, replaced for some by poststructural readings of narrative texts. Poststructural analyses emerged in the 1960s, in part a reaction to the pretension to objectivity and other claims by structuralists. While any definition of poststructuralism is controversial, in general, poststructuralists favor the idea that there is no absolute, final meaning possible for any text. Meaning arises out of the cultural contexts of author and reader, and since these contexts differ with every reader and every reading, poststructuralists insist upon a free play of meaning for any text, with no final arbiter of what a text ultimately means. Poststructuralism is at the same time an evolution from structuralism and a "deconstruction" of its contradictions.[18]

In its insistence that there can be no ultimate authority in textual interpretation, poststructuralism has had a major impact on literary studies and also on biblical studies that take a literary approach to the text. I welcome the multiplicity of readings opened up within the biblical text by poststructural influence on biblical studies. Nevertheless, it is my experience that structural approaches can be productive of important levels of meaning when applied to biblical narrative. I do not claim for these either exclusivity or ultimate truth, but I do claim the value of airing and discussing them as one way to illuminate what has heretofore, perhaps, remained obscure.

Syntagmatic Approach and Morphological Analysis as the Methodology for This Study

I undertook a syntagmatic approach based on Propp's method for several reasons. First, the applied method addresses the most accessible level of text in a corpus, the surface level of plot. The degree of abstraction demanded by Propp's method remains very close to this surface structure. Propp's method has the advantage of being concrete and linear, with results that are verifiable by referring back to the text under analysis.

---

18. See Chris Baldick, *The Concise Oxford Dictionary of Literary Terms* (Oxford: Oxford University Press, 1990) 109 and 175–76; and Jeremy Hawthorn, *A Concise Glossary of Contemporary Literary Theory* (London: Edward Arnold, 1992) 137–38.

Second, the narrow focus of Propp's method is appealing, especially for an investigation as circumscribed as the present one must necessarily be.[19] Morphological analysis has as its anticipated outcome the description of a specific genre or subtype by means of the identification of predictable patterns that a text falling within that particular category may be expected to follow. Propp's applied method seeks to develop a morphological model for only one genre or type at a time within a body of texts, allowing a clear focus on a single objective during the analytic process.

Third, from a methodological point of view, syntagmatic analysis often precedes paradigmatic analysis, although both are ultimately necessary.[20] In literature, as in language, morphological study of forms as they are actually found precedes the construction of paradigms.

Morphological analysis, like all literary readings, is based on working hypotheses that are checked and rechecked in the process of reading.[21] Applied with rigor, morphological analysis can be an empirical, replicable method of analyzing stories from the Bible and from ancient Near Eastern literatures on a common basis. It can also be used to measure a story's variation from the expected pattern. These variations are important for what they reveal about the texts themselves and about their cultural contexts, as well as for what they represent in

---

19. This point is appreciated by Robert Scholes in his *Structuralism in Literature: An Introduction* (New Haven: Yale University Press, 1974) 102 and passim. Scholes is a supporter of Propp's approach and seems to understand the method and objectives of later literary studies based upon Propp's work.

20. See Hendricks, "Methodology of Narrative Structural Analysis."

21. On this issue of the role of the reader in the act of reading, and hence the reader's participation in determining the meaning of a text, there is an enormous volume of literature. See, for example, Wolfgang Iser, *The Act of Reading: A Theory of Aesthetic Response* (Baltimore: Johns Hopkins University Press, 1978); idem, "The Reading Process: A Phenomenological Approach," in *Reader-Response Criticism* (ed. Jane P. Tompkins; Baltimore: Johns Hopkins University Press, 1980) 50–69. In biblical scholarship, see, for example, Edward L. Greenstein, "Reader Responsibility: Making Sense and Non-Sense of Biblical Narrative," *The Aaron-Roland Lecture* (Stanford: Stanford University Press, 1992), who differs from Iser in some respects. To illustrate the subjective nature of even the most surface-structure examination of a text, there is an article by Monique Schneider ("La Maîtrise de la temporalité: Un Combat mythique," *Le mythe et le mythique* [Cahiers de l'Hermétisme / Colloque de Cerisy; Paris: Albin Michel, 1987] 29–40), in which she asserts that "a curious effect of reflection or inversion occurs if one attempts to apply to analytical texts the method of analysis that they (themselves) propose. The narrative thus doubles. It resides equally in the text under analysis and in the theoretical texts engaged in the pursuit of that which represents the key to the narrative" (pp. 29–30; the translation is my own).

terms of the conventions and expectations of the literature of a region. By means of the constructs underlying morphological analysis, the text under discussion is broken into its component parts, which are labeled and compared with other texts similarly analyzed and with a template derived from comparing many previously analyzed texts. The result of morphological analysis is descriptive. It tells us where our text stands with respect to other texts and with respect to an abstract pattern.[22]

Differentiating Propp's Method from His Model

Propp's corpus was a group of about 100 Russian folk stories, part of a collection of tales selected and cataloged according to "tale-type" by the Russian folklorist Aleksandr Afanas'ev.[23] Propp undertook his study largely in reaction to the inadequacies of this type of tale classification by "tale-type" or "motif." He sought to arrive at a systematic and methodologically valid way of defining the "genre" of a tale.[24] Propp was looking for categories that would be mutually exclusive and exhaustive, in which examples would only occur once and in which every case could be accounted for.

A differentiation must be made between Propp's *method* and Propp's *model*. Propp's *method* consists of three fundamental steps: first, to identify the component parts of each item in a given corpus; and second, to compare the sequence of component parts in each story with that of every other item within the corpus.[25] The desired result of these first two steps is the definition of a genre. The third step is to compare the sequence of functions in a particular narrative with the sequence defining the genre. The result of this is to determine

---

22. Propp writes, "We shall insist that as long as no correct morphological study exists, there can be no correct historical study. If we are incapable of breaking the tale into its components, we will not be able to make a correct comparison. And if we do not know how to compare, then how can we throw light upon, for instance, Indo-Egyptian relationships, or upon the relationships of the Greek fable to the Indian, etc.? . . . This resemblance cannot be explained if we have wrong conception of character. The historian, inexperienced in morphological problems, will not see a resemblance where one actually exists; he will omit coincidences which are important to him, but which he does not notice. And conversely, where a similarity is perceived, a specialist in morphology will be able to demonstrate that compared phenomena are completely heteronomous. We see, then, that very much depends upon the study of forms" (Propp, *Morphology*, 15–16).

23. Propp used Aleksandr Afanas'ev, *Narodnye Russkie Skazki* (3 vols.; 6th ed.; ed. Vladimir Propp; Moscow: Gosudartvennoe Izdatelbstvo Xudozestvennoj Literaturi, 1957).

24. Propp, *Morphology*, 10–12.

25. Ibid., 19.

whether a particular narrative fits the genre-specific pattern defined by the first two steps of Propp's method. A genre-specific pattern is conventionally called a *model* by folklorists employing Propp's method and will be used this way for the purposes of this study.[26]

An illustration may be useful. In a typical fairy-tale, a princess is abducted (VILLAINY), and her absence results in the king's desire for her return (LACK/DESIRE). The king makes it known far and wide that a reward will go to the man who rescues his daughter (MEDIATION), and the hero takes on the challenge (COUNTERACTION) and departs on his quest (DEPARTURE). The hero encounters a magical helper (DONOR) who challenges him (TEST) and, upon the hero's successful performance (REACTION), who grants him a boon to help him in his task. The hero is magically transported to the realm of the king (TRANSFERENCE), where he is challenged by the villain (STRUGGLE) and prevails (VICTORY). The princess is returned to her father (LACK LIQUIDATED) and the hero receives the hand of the rescued princess (REWARD).

The *model* for this example consists of 13 of Propp's functions, each of which he designates with an abstract noun: VILLAINY, LACK/DESIRE, MEDIATION, COUNTERACTION, DEPARTURE, DONOR, TEST, REACTION, TRANSFERENCE, STRUGGLE, VICTORY, LACK LIQUIDATED, and REWARD. Propp found that there were a maximum of 31 of these common categories that were stable across all of the 100 or so tales in his particular corpus, the Afanas'ev collection. These 31 stable elements, or constants, make up the *model* Propp identified, a model that holds only for the Russian fairy-tale.

The method Propp employed may be used on any corpus: to analyze each individual tale in a corpus, to compare it with each of the others, and to identify the common elements. The resulting pattern(s), however, would not necessarily fall into the specific pattern that defines the model of the Russian fairy-tale but, depending on the corpus chosen, might define some other genre.

Vladimir Propp identified the morphology defining the genre that he called the Russian fairy-tale. Subsequent scholarship has refined this definition somewhat, calling Propp's Russian fairy-tale the "heroic fairy-tale" and defining other genres of fairy-tale by applying Propp's method in order to derive models for genres he does not address directly.[27]

---

26. See Milne, *Vladimir Propp*, 12.

27. Heda Jason, "The Lion Slayer and the Clever Princess: Case Study of a Multigenre Folktale," in *Studies in Turkish Folklore in Honor of Pertev N. Boratav* (ed. I. Basgoz and M. Glazer; Turkish Studies 1; Bloomington: Indiana University Press, 1978) 117.

The need to distinguish Propp's method from his model has been articulated by other scholars of folklore. Steven Swann Jones criticizes Dov Noy for relying on Propp's "Procrustean" morphology.[28] Jones faults Noy and other scholars who do not "advance structural typologies for those individual tale types" that they are analyzing. Jones's call for specific structural typologies for other tale-types has already been anticipated by such folklorists as Heda Jason, Rina Drory, Ilana Dan, and Alan Dundes himself. Each applies Propp's method to derive models for additional folklore genres other than the Russian fairy-tale.

Jason, for example, proposes a model based on Propp's method for the active-heroine fairy-tale. She notes that other models based on Propp's method have been worked out for the reward-and-punishment fairy-tale by Rina Drory, and for the persecuted-heroine fairy-tale by Ilana Dan.[29] Jason herself has worked out another proposed model based on Propp for the narrative structure of an epic struggle.[30] Alan Dundes develops his model for the analysis and classification of morphology of North American Indian tales using Propp's method, though the North American model Dundes identifies differs significantly from the one isolated by Propp.[31] Other scholars in the fields of both literature and anthropology show considerable finesse and comprehension in applying Propp's method to the development of new models and the refinement of genre definitions.[32]

---

28. See Steven S. Jones, *New Comparative Method: Structural and Symbolic Analysis of the Allomotifs of "Snow White"* (Folklore Fellows Communications 247; Helsinki: Suomalainen Tiedeakatemea, 1990) 127–81, in which Jones terms Propp's model for the Russian fairy-tale "Procrustean."

29. Heda Jason, "The Fairy Tale of the Active Heroine: An Outline for Discussion," in *Le conte: pourquoi? comment? Actes des Journées d'Études en Littérature Orale* (ed. G. Calame-Griaule, V. Görög-Karady, and M. Chiche; Paris: Centre National de la Recherche Scientifique, 1984) 81. See the essays by Rina Drory, "Ali Baba and the Forty Thieves: An Attempt at a Model for the Narrative Structure of the Reward-and-Punishment Fairy Tale," in *Patterns in Oral Literature* (ed. H. Jason and D. Segal; The Hague: Mouton, 1977) 31–48; and by Ilana Dan, "The Innocent Persecuted Heroine: An Attempt at a Model for the Surface Level of the Narrative Structure of the Female Fairy Tale" (in the same volume) 13–30.

30. Jason, "Ilja of Murom and Tzar Kalin: A Proposal for a Model for the Narative Structure of an Epic Struggle," in *Slavica Hierosolymitana: Slavic Studies of the Hebrew University* (ed. L. Fleishman, O. Ronen, and D. Segal; Jerusalem: Magnes, 1981) 47–55.

31. Dundes, *North American Indian Folktales*, 1964.

32. Among the excellent applications of Propp's method and refinements of genre, see Alexandra Hennessey Olsen, "Loss and Recovery: A Morphological Reconsideration of Sir Orfeo" (*Fabula* 23/3–4 [1982] 198–206), in which the author defines a subgenre using Propp's method; as does Satu Apo, in "The Structural

Failure to distinguish Propp's method from his model can, however, result in unnecessary confusion. Propp's fairy-tale model has been pressed upon such diverse works as Beowulf, ancient Greek romances, the Epic of Gilgamesh, and even the television series *Mission Impossible*. These studies focus on forcing the material into Propp's fairy-tale model without any attempt to modify it and without any attempt to derive new genre models from the application of Propp's methodology to the material.[33]

Issues of Terminology:
Genre, Tale-Type, Theme, and Motif

A word is in order about the difference between categorizing texts by *tale-type* or *motifs*, and categorizing texts by what Propp calls "genre."

Schemes of a Repertoire of Fairy Tales: A Structural Analysis of Marina Takalo's Fairy Tales Using Propp's Model," in *Genre, Structure and Reproduction in Oral Literature* (Bibliotheca Uralica 5; Budapest: Akademiai Kiado, 1980) 147–58; see also idem, "The Variability and Narrative Structures of Wondertales: From Universal Models to Describing the Differences between Tales" (*Studia Fennica: Review of Finnish Linguistics and Ethnology* [Helsinki: Suomalaisen Kirjallisuuden Seura, 1989] 33.151–60), reprinted as "The Variability and Narrative Structures of Magic Tales from Universal Models to Describing the Differences between Tales," in *D'un Conte . . . à l'autre: La Variabilité dans la littérature orale* [From One Tale . . . to the Other: Variability in Oral Literature] (ed. V. Görög-Karady and M. Chiche; Paris: Centre Nationale de la Recherche Scientifique, 1990) 487–501. David Buchan ("Propp's Tale Role and a Ballad Repertoire," *Journal of American Folklore* 95 [1982] 159–72) elaborates on Propp's concept of tale-role or character in his examination of certain ballad types, using this aspect of Propp's method to clarify relationships among ballad categories, enabling him to classify "subtypes" not previously noted. See also idem, "Talerole Analysis and Child's Supernatural Ballads," in *The Ballad and Oral Literature* (ed. Joseph Harris; Harvard English Studies 17; Cambridge: Harvard University Press, 1991) 60–77.

33. Folklorist Kent Gould's essay "*Beowulf* and Folktale Morphology: God as Magical Donor" (*Folklore* 96/1 [1985] 98–103) features careless application of Propp's fairy-tale model to *Beowulf* and misstatements about both Propp and Dundes, whom he asserts work on the "deep structure" of narrative (p. 100); Consuelo Ruiz-Montero, in "The Structural Pattern of the Ancient Greek Romances and the *Morphology of the Folktale* of V. Propp" (*Fabula* 22/3–4 [1981] 228–38), fails to understand that differences in morphology signal differences in genre and struggles mightily to account for the variations from Propp's fairy-tale morphology that she finds in her corpus; Bruce A. Beatie ("The Myth of the Hero: From 'Mission: Impossible' to Magdalenian Caves," in *The Hero in Transition* [ed. Ray Browne and Marshall W. Fishwick; Bowling Green, Ohio: Popular Press, 1983] 46–65) demonstrates considerable confusion regarding Propp's functions and also misses the genre-defining role of morphology.

The term *genre* is an imprecise term, applied simultaneously to different levels of literature, from the most general to the most specialized subcategories. Genre definitions have been based on form, on content, on means of presentation, or on some combination of qualities.[34] Discussion and resolution of issues surrounding genre definition are beyond the scope of this work. For purposes of this study, the term *genre* will be used in Propp's sense, to designate a category of narrative defined by a common structural pattern featuring specific, recognizable elements in a predictable sequence. Propp's proposed structural definition of genre was an attempt to begin to clarify the ambiguity of multiply-defined or never-defined terms used in the description and discussion of literary narrative.[35] Among these terms are "tale-type," "motif," and "theme."

Historically, the dominant school of folklore until the last third of the 20th century was the Finnish school. This approach advocated the geographical-historical method modeled on the philological-historical approach to language current in nineteenth-century scholarship.[36] The Finnish approach is atomistic: folktales are dissected into their

---

34. Biblical scholarship has historically used the term *genre* as it relates to the Sitz im Leben of a text: how it might have been used originally by the people. This approach is associated with Gunkel and the form-critical school of biblical scholarship, which is concerned with the origin or source of biblical traditions. Anthropological, sociological, and other social-science approaches to biblical scholarship have also been concerned with these issues. The present study, however, takes a literary approach to the material and so is concerned with a literary definition of the term *genre*. In this, as in all aspects of this discussion, lucidity is hampered by terminological limitations. Baldick (*Concise Oxford Dictionary of Literary Terms*, 90–91) attributes the confusion surrounding the term *genre* to "the fact that it is used simultaneously for the most basic modes of literary art, . . . for the broadest categories of composition, . . . and for more specialized sub-categories." Discussions of genre in literary criticism suffer from the limitations of their time and place. Classically, Aristotle and Plato distinguish *genres* by "manner of imitation" (or "representation"; see Rene Wellek and Austin Warren, *Theory of Literature* [3d ed.; New York: Harcourt, Brace, Jovanovich, 1984] 227). Neoclassically, *genre* is assumed but never defined: "Neo-Classical theory does not explain, expound, or defend the doctrine of kinds or the basis for differentiation" (ibid., 230). Wellek and Warren propose, "Genre should be conceived, we think, as a grouping of literary works based, theoretically, upon both outer form (specific metre or structure) and also upon inner form (attitude, tone, purpose—more crudely, subject and audience)" (ibid., 231). By this definition, Propp's method results in the identification of a genre (or subgenre) of narrative. Since Propp himself uses the term "genre," so shall I, bearing in mind its lack of precision.

35. See, for example, Propp's discussion in *Morphology*, 6–7 and passim.

36. Ibid., 8–9; see also Dundes, *North American Indian Folktales*, 38–39.

component motifs, and a hypothetical original archetypal form of the folktale is posited. The emphasis is on the individual motifs, based on the underlying assumption that "a folktale is equal to the sum of motifs in it."[37] The classic work produced by this approach is Antti Aarne's collection, translated and enlarged by Stith Thompson.[38] Thompson followed this with the first edition of the still-basic resource, the *Motif-Index*, termed by Dundes "a mammoth source-book for atomistic analysis."[39]

This approach has come under considerable criticism from Dundes and Jason, among others.[40] Milne summarizes the objections to Aarne's division of tales into types: "Genres were never fully worked out or adequately defined and, hence, his categories failed to be mutually exclusive. Aarne's use of terms such as 'type,' 'plot,' and 'motif' also went undefined and, as a result, the work was seriously lacking in clarity."[41]

Propp raises similar objections. He praises Aarne's work as a necessary listing of themes, an essential preliminary to the work of folklore study, but cautions that it also presents grave limitations. He says of Aarne,

> His list entered into international usage and rendered the study of the tale an enormous service. Thanks to Aarne's index, a coding of the tale has been made possible. Aarne calls themes *types*, and each type is numbered. A brief, conventional designation of tales (in this instance: by reference to a number in the index) is very convenient. . . . But along with these commendable features, the index also reveals a number of real insufficiencies.[42]

---

37. Ibid., 39.

38. S. Thompson, *The Types of the Folktale: Antti Aarne's Verzeichnis der Märchentypen, Translated and Enlarged* (Folklore Fellows Communications 74; Helsinki: Suomalainen Tiedeakatemia, 1928).

39. Dundes, *North American Indian Folktales*, 39, commenting on Stith Thompson's *Motif Index of Folklore Literature* (6 vols.; Bloomington: Indiana University Press, 1969).

40. See Dundes, *North American Indian Folktales*, 38–40; and Heda Jason, "Structural Analysis and the Concept of the Tale Type," in *ARV: Journal of Scandinavian Folklore* 28 (1972) 36–54; see especially p. 53; also p. 39, where she asserts that "Aarne's 'type' disintegrates under Propp's analysis."

41. Milne (*Vladimir Propp*, 22), referring to Heda Jason's article "Russian Criticism of the 'Finnish School' in Folklore Scholarship," *Norveg* 14 (1970) 285–94. See also Alan Dundes, "From Etic to Emic Units in the Structural Study of Folktales," *Journal of American Folklore* 75 (1962) 97–99, 101, and passim.

42. Propp, *Morphology*, 10. Italics are his.

Propp notes especially that Aarne's categories are not mutually exclusive, nor do they allow for stories containing more than one theme. These deficiencies could lead different scholars to categorize the same tale in several different categories, reducing rather than increasing clarity of reference. Imprecision in terminology, especially in differentiating among *type*, *motif*, and *theme*, only added to the potential confusion.[43]

Propp notes that

> themes (especially the themes of fairy-tales) are very closely related to each other. In order to determine where one theme and its variants end and another begins, one must first have made a comparative study of the themes of the tales, and have accurately established the principle of the selection of themes and variants. However, nothing of the kind exists. . . . At the same time, the fully objective separation of one theme from another and the selection of variants is by no means a simple task. . . . There are no completely objective criteria for the separation of one theme from another.[44]

Propp concludes, "Thus we see that the problem of classification of the tale finds itself in a somewhat sorry state. Yet classification is one of the first and most important steps of study."[45]

Proppian Analysis and the Biblical Canon

Vladimir Propp's methodology is a powerful tool when applied to a corpus of texts, even with its terminological and other drawbacks. It is useful to review Propp's pioneering work with a collection of Russian fairy-tales, since it establishes the methodology that I apply in my Proppian analysis of biblical narrative and that results in my identification of the genre of Patterns of Destiny.

Vladimir Propp and Structuralism:
Approach, Method, and Model

In contrast to the prevalent atomistic approach of the Finnish school, Propp and his colleagues turned their attention to the tale as a unit. Propp and the Russian formalists pioneered an approach to narrative focusing on the formal aspects of folktales, particularly through structural studies undertaken to identify the universal principles by which all tales are constituted.[46] They believed that "a tale is composed

---

43. Ibid., 10–12.
44. Ibid., 9.
45. Ibid., 11.
46. Propp, "Structure and History in the Study of the Fairy Tale," 66.

from a lexicon of content units organized according to a set of compositional rules."[47] Propp's approach addresses the surface structure of
the narrative.[48] As Milne notes, "It is not necessary to abstract very far
from the individual fairy-tales to reach the structure Propp studied.
Thus the structure for which he constructed a model is, indeed, an abstraction, but one which remains close to the surface of the texts in his
corpus."[49] Propp's concern is to identify the rules by which a system
operates on the level of plot.[50]

At the time Propp began his *Morphology*, there was no formal definition of the fairy-tale as a genre. Propp proposed to prove the existence
of this genre in his study. He writes of his approach, "The existence of
fairy-tales as a special class is assumed as an essential working hypothesis. By 'fairy-tales' are meant at present those tales classified by Aarne
under numbers 300 to 749. This definition is artificial, but the occasion will subsequently arise to give a more precise determination on
the basis of resultant conclusions." Propp set out to identify and label
the fundamental component parts of fairy-tales, list them, and compare the tales in his corpus according to their components. "The result
will be a morphology (i.e., a description of the tale according to its
component parts and the relationship of these components to each
other and to the whole)."[51]

Propp's analysis distinguishes between what is constant and what is
variable in a group of tales.[52] Propp finds that the effects of the actions
of the characters of a tale are remarkably constant, even though the actual means by which the actions are realized varies considerably.[53] It
may be helpful to look at Propp's analysis of VILLAINY, identified by
Propp as one of three complication constants, any one of which must
be present in a tale in order to get things moving.[54] The other two are
LACK and DESIRE.[55] Propp lists the ways VILLAINY is perpetrated in his
corpus in all its amazing variety: abduction, seizure, pillage, plunder,

47. Milne, *Vladimir Propp*, 23.
48. Dundes, "Structuralism and Folklore," *Essays in Folkloristics* (Kirpa Dai Series
in Folklore and Anthropology 1; New Delhi: Folklore Institute, 1978) 189.
49. Milne, *Vladimir Propp*, 12.
50. "Propp's analysis is concerned with narrative structure and is confined to
surface-level narrative structure" (ibid.).
51. Propp, *Morphology*, 19.
52. Ibid., 20.
53. Ibid. "Definition of a function will most often be given in the form of a noun
expressing an action (interdiction, interrogation, flight, etc.)" (ibid., 21).
54. Ibid., 36.
55. Ibid., 102.

bodily injury, sudden disappearance, expulsion, enchantment, substitution, murder ordered or committed, imprisonment or detention, forced matrimony, threat of cannibalism, torment at night, or declaration of war.[56] Despite the variability of its representation, the function of VILLAINY is a constant in these stories: each of these actions has the same effect in a tale. Propp terms constant elements, such as VILLAINY in this example, "functions."

Propp defines "function" based on the significance of that element for the course of the action in a tale. Different acts can have the same meaning by serving the same function in a story. The function of VILLAINY can be served in a variety of nefarious ways, but the train of consequences, the significance of the villainy for the course of the action in the tale, is constant no matter what form the villainy takes. A corollary of this idea is that the same act can have different meanings depending on where it occurs in the sequence.

For Propp, the definition of a function is not at all dependent on the one who carries out the action. Rather, the definition of a function is wholly dependent on the impact that an action has on the outcome, as is the case for VILLAINY in this example. Propp uses the element of "transference of money" as an example of this phenomenon. The literary significance of "transference of money" differs depending on whether it occurs in the beginning of the tale (the hero receives the money from his father and purchases a wise cat with it, thus precipitating the action of the plot) or at the end (the money is received by the same hero from the hand of the queen as a reward for an act of bravery, at which point the tale ends).[57] Who is distributing the money is less important to the significance of the transference than at what point in the narrative the transference occurs.

Propp finds that "the number of functions is extremely small, whereas the number of personages is extremely large. This explains the two-fold quality of a tale: Its amazing multiformity, picturesqueness, and color, and on the other hand, its no less striking uniformity, its repetition."[58] Tales that share an identical sequence of functions all belong to one type or "genre." Propp proposes that an index of genres can be created, based not on theme or motif but on exact structural features such as a sequence of constants. Propp also finds that, even though not every tale exhibits every possible constant belonging to that pattern, the constants that are present nonetheless occur in the

---

56. Ibid., 30–34.
57. Ibid., 21.
58. Ibid., 20–21.

proper sequence. "The absence of certain functions does not change the order of the rest."[59]

Propp analyzed each of his tales according to the series of functions that he generalized from the specific sequences he extracted from the collection of tales in the corpus of tale-types categorized by Afanas'ev. This analysis resulted in the identification of a model for a particular genre of fairy story within this corpus, the Russian fairy-tale.[60] Thus, Propp followed his own dictum that "the study of the tale must be carried on strictly deductively, i.e., proceeding from the material at hand to the consequences."[61]

Key to Propp's analysis are the following points:

1. Functions performed by characters remain the stable, constant elements in a tale no matter how or by whom they are fulfilled. Propp identified these constants as the fundamental components of a narrative.
2. The number of functions in a particular genre is limited.[62]
3. The sequence of functions is always identical.[63]

Propp concluded from his analysis that all Russian fairy-tales are of one type, based on their structure, and thus belong to the same genre.[64] He identified a generalized, invariable sequence of up to 31 functions for the structure of Russian fairy-tales. Although not every function was present in each example, the functions that did occur followed a strict, predictable sequence in each example. Propp's model for the Russian fairy-tale provided the first objective definition of the Russian fairy-tale as a specific genre having recognizable, predictable elements in a constant, predictable sequence. "Tales with identical functions can be considered as belonging to one type. On this foundation, an index of types can then be created, based not upon theme features, which are somewhat vague and diffuse, but upon exact structural features."[65]

---

59. Ibid., 22.

60. Ibid., 23–24. Although the model Propp identified was for a specific genre of folktale and is not identical with the model identified in this study, a summary of his functions, with brief definitions or examples, is appended to this study for illustrative purposes for the convenience of the reader.

61. Ibid., 23. Scholars today might prefer to call Propp's method *inductive* rather than *deductive*, since he moves from the particular to the general. We are dependent on Propp's translator for the term used in the text.

62. Ibid., 21.

63. Ibid., 22.

64. Ibid., 23.

65. Ibid., 22.

Criticism of Propp

Propp's major work, *The Morphology of the Folktale*, was published in Russian in 1928 but had little direct impact on emerging structural theory until it was translated into English in 1958.[66] In most quarters, it was hailed as a theoretical breakthrough.[67] The first English edition, however, was riddled with editorial and copy errors, making it difficult to follow in places. Milne comments on the editorial and copy problems of the first English edition: "These criticisms of *Morphology* of the Folktale appear to be well-founded. Such problems are bothersome and lamentable and have, no doubt, contributed to the misunderstanding of parts of the book by some readers. However, these problems are not unsurmountable and do not seriously affect the substance of Propp's work."[68] The second English edition, which came out in 1968, corrected almost every error of this kind. Still, the work was sometimes misunderstood and, partly as a result, did draw some criticism.[69]

There are valid criticisms to be made of Propp's methodology. Several of these are rooted in the conciseness of Propp's *Morphology of the Folktale*, which was meant to be preliminary to studies on other genres of folklore and which itself represents a distillation of voluminous underlying work.[70] As a result of these limitations, many clarifications

---

66. A French edition was published in 1965.

67. See, for example, Dundes, *North American Indian Folktales*, 50–55; Milne, *Vladimir Propp*, 89–90.

68. Ibid., 91.

69. Bertel Nathhorst, *Formal or Structural Studies of Traditional Tales: The Usefulness of Some Methodological Proposals Advanced by Vladimir Propp, Alan Dundes, Claude Lévi-Strauss and Edmund Leach* (Stockholm Studies in Comparative Religion 9; Stockholm: Acta Universitatis Stockholmiensis, 1969). Nathhorst's publication was based on his dissertation, translated into English by Donald Burton. Nathhorst, who misunderstood all aspects of structuralism, directed his disdain not only at Propp but also at Alan Dundes, Claude Lévi-Strauss, and Edmund Leach. Nathhorst subscribes to the view that the task of science is to set up theories that can be tested empirically. By this measure, Nathhorst is critical of structural analysts in general and Propp in particular for imagining that their "reasoning" constitutes "proof in the proper sense of the term" (p. 19), and faults their proposals for being "badly formulated." Ironically, in the light of modern literary critical sensibilities, it is Nathhorst whose formulations are faulted for adhering to the perspective that "scientific" objectivity is possible.

70. Propp, *Morphology*, in the author's foreword, pp. xxv–xxvi, and p. 115. The impact of these shortcomings on the study of literature is also discussed by Patricia Carden, in "Fairy Tale, Myth and Literature: Russian Structuralist Approaches," in *Literary Criticism and Myth* (ed. Joseph P. Strelka; Yearbook of Comparative Criticism 9; University Park, Penn.: Pennsylvania State University Press, 1980) 179–97.

that students of morphological analysis would prefer to have explicitly from Propp's own pen instead must be inferred from the material that we have before us.

One of these deficiencies centers on Propp's axiom that the sequence of functions in any genre is always identical.[71] Scholars have noted inconsistencies in the structural sequences in Propp's own examples. Some of these inconsistencies in the sequences of functions (which are usually designated by letter or symbol) may be due to the checkered printing history of Propp's work and the many editorial and copy errors that have beleaguered the text.[72] Other variations, however, are more substantive.

Critics have pointed out that some paired or grouped functions can appear in reversed or inverted positions.[73] This is indeed sometimes the case and contributes to the variety observable in Propp's corpus.[74] For Propp, an inversion or reversal of a function served the same role as the function in its original position.[75] Milne notes that Propp was able to tolerate these variations without violating his sequence hypothesis, and she does the same in her Proppian analysis of Daniel 1–6.[76] Significantly, she notes that "there is some regularity to the ways in which the sequence is disrupted."[77]

This insight is important. Drawing on the analogy of literature and language, it is possible to view explicable variations in the expected structural sequence of a text just as grammarians view the attestation of a variation from the expected word order in different languages and even for the same language in different kinds of discourse. The variation of actual occurrences from the predictions of grammatical rules does not invalidate the general applicability of the grammatical rules, nor does it negate the value of grammatical studies for comprehension of a language.

---

71. Propp's third point, elaborated in his *Morphology*, 22–23.

72. Noted in the preface to the second edition of ibid., ix–x.

73. See Milne, *Vladimir Propp*, 282 n. 25.

74. Propp provides for the designation of negative functions with an asterisk before the letter or symbol associated with that function. Thus, *victory* is designated by the letter I; *defeat* by the symbol *I. Propp also notes that "a large number of functions are arranged in pairs (prohibition-violation, reconnaissance-delivery, struggle-victory, pursuit-deliverance, etc.). Other functions may be arranged according to groups. Thus villainy, dispatch, decision for counteraction, and departure from home (ABC↑), constitute the complication" (Propp, *Morphology*, 64–65).

75. Ibid., 107–8.

76. Milne, *Vladimir Propp*, 96.

77. Ibid., 94.

The same may be true of variations from the expected order of elements in a text classified within a certain genre, when these variations from the expected pattern of that genre occur according to regular, predictable rules. For this reason, perhaps *predictable* is a more apt description of the sequence of functions than *identical*. Notably, Propp himself explicitly groups inverted or reversed sequences with their orthodox originals and perceives the sequences of tales that exhibit these variations as essentially identical with them.[78]

Another criticism involves Propp's terminology. It has been faulted for being vague and imprecise, failings shared by much of the terminology used for literary criticism of all kinds.[79] One of the problems in isolating the component units of narrative or folklore is that they are infinitely divisible. Dundes has suggested the use of heuristic units of analysis based on Propp's method and the work of Kenneth Pike, among others.[80] Dundes and several other scholars have proposed alternatives for key terms,[81] but none has yet been widely accepted. The problem is compounded as structuralist scholarship

---

78. Propp writes (italics are his): "The assertion concerning absolute stability would seem to be unconfirmed by the fact that the sequence of functions is not always the same as that shown in the total scheme. A careful examination of the schemes will show certain deviations. . . . Does this not break the rule? No, for this is not a new but rather an *inverted* (*obraščënnyj*) sequence. The usual tale presents, for example, a misfortune at first and then the receipt of a helper who liquidates it. An inverted sequence gives the receipt of a helper at first and then the misfortune which is liquidated by him (elements DEF before A)" (Propp, *Morphology*, 108). In addition to negation and inversion, Propp also accounts for transposition of functions and other variations within the larger scheme. These are discussed in his *Morphology* in chapter 9, entitled "The Tale as a Whole," 92–117. One critic unconvinced by this element of Propp's argument is Archer Taylor. See his article "The Biographical Pattern in Traditional Narrative," *Journal of the Folklore Institute* 1 (1964) 114–29.

79. Dundes, "From Etic to Emic," and Heda Jason, "The Narrative Structure of Swindler Tales," *ARV, Journal of Scandinavian Folklore* 27 (1971) 141–42 and passim. See, conveniently, Baldick, *Concise Oxford Dictionary of Literary Terms*, 90–91.

80. Alan Dundes, "Structuralism and Folklore," 178–200. This suggestion is made on p. 179. Dundes is heavily influenced by Kenneth L. Pike, *Language in Relation to a Unified Theory of the Structure of Human Behavior* (The Hague: Mouton, 1967).

81. Dundes ("From Etic to Emic") proposes a scheme based on the linguistic model suggested by Kenneth L. Pike in his book *Language in Relation to a Unified Theory*. Jason (in "Narrative Structure of Swindler Tales," 141–60 and passim) proposes her own terminology, as does Stephen Swann Jones in his article "Structural and Thematic Applications of the Comparative Method: A Case Study of 'The Kind and Unkind Girls,'" *Journal of Folklore Research* 23/2–3 (1986) 147–61.

evolves. Narratology, which builds on de Saussure, Propp, and the work of other syntagmatic scholars, proposes its own terminology that in some cases renames units that Propp named and in other cases identifies new ideas or nuances not accounted for by Propp. This state of affairs requires the student of structural methodologies to master several different vocabularies in order to comprehend a variety of structural analyses. This state of affairs cannot be laid at Propp's feet but illustrates a larger problem that is the result of the amorphous and evolving nature of the field. In this book, I will not resolve these complex terminological issues, but, having acknowledged the problem, I shall attempt to define key terms in the way they will be used here.

A considerable limitation of Propp's methodology is that it does not offer an interpretive hermeneutic. Once one has isolated a morphology for defining a "genre" of text, one is left to find another construct within which to interpret the multiplicity of meanings implicit in that distinction, whether literary, sociological, psychological, or otherwise. Propp's focus was still the 19th century's concern with the origin of folktales and with the history of their dispersion and evolution.[82]

Propp's method is aimed at the accurate categorization of tales in order to facilitate that investigation. Our concerns at the beginning of the 21st century are somewhat different. We would like to shed light on what these stories mean to us and, perhaps, to speculate on what significance they might have had to the audiences of their times. As the anthropologist Alan Dundes has commented, it is insufficient to identify or describe, though description is often the first step.[83] "It is not enough to say that folklore is a mirror of culture. We must try to see what it is that folklore reflects."[84]

This lack of an interpretive hermeneutic as an outcome of Proppian analysis was noted and criticized by Propp's fellow structuralists. Although Lévi-Strauss acknowledges Propp's major contribution, he accuses Propp of being concerned with form to the exclusion of content. Lévi-Strauss is critical of Propp's remaining at the surface structure of narrative and of not delving more deeply below the surface as he him-

---

82. In fact, when Propp resumed his study of the folktale some twenty years after the original 1928 publication of *Morphology* in Russia, it was to address the question of the history of folklore. His work was published in English as *Theory and History of Folklore* (trans. Ariadna Martin and Richard P. Martin; ed. Anatoly Liberman; Theory and History of Literature 5; Minneapolis: University of Minnesota Press, 1984).

83. Dundes, "Structuralism and Folklore," 196.

84. Ibid., 199.

self did. Propp replies at great length in his own defense, and many of his partisans join him.[85] They claim that Propp is in fact a structuralist, primarily concerned with the interplay between form and content.[86] Lévi-Strauss appears to have been expressing his legitimate discomfort with the lack of a built-in interpretive hermeneutic in Propp's approach when he criticizes Propp for being a "formalist."[87]

Followers of Propp have noted his failure to provide an interpretive component in his methodology and have incorporated various interpretive hermeneutics into their own work to compensate for this lack. Alan Dundes chooses the psychoanalytic/sociological model, as does his student Stephen Swann Jones.[88] Dundes suggests, for example, that for the Russian fairy-tale, the marriage of the hero at the end of each tale suggests a preoccupation of the tale-tellers with the socialization process of leaving one's natal home and forming a new one with an appropriate partner.[89] Jones makes a similar suggestion for the tale of "Snow White."[90]

The approach of Lévi-Strauss offers another interpretive option, once morphological analysis has been done. One advantage of paradigmatic structuralism as practiced by Lévi-Strauss and his adherents is that the outcome of the repeated dialectic of polarity and mediation is, by definition, an interpretation of a text or body of texts.

William O. Hendricks is a literary critic who synthesizes both Proppian analysis and the methodology of Lévi-Strauss into a single model based on symbolic logic. He has taken Proppian analysis into the realm of symbolic logic in order to arrive at a theoretically justified methodology for synopsis: the "leveling" of rhetorical devices, descriptors, and other literary figures that occur in differing degrees in different kinds and styles of literature, in order to permit the derivation of the morphology of a text in controlled degrees of abstraction. His approach also accounts for texts analyzed in translation. Hendricks's

---

85. Propp, "Structure and History in the Study of the Fairy Tale," 10, 57–83.

86. Ibid., 77. See, for example, Dundes, *North American Indian Folktales*, 37, 50; A. Liberman in his introduction to Propp, *Theory and History of Folklore*, esp. pp. xli and xliv; and Milne, *Vladimir Propp*, 104–5, 284 n. 10, and passim.

87. In C. Lévi-Strauss's essay, "Structure and Form: Reflections on a Work by Vladimir Propp," in *Structural Anthropology* (trans. Monique Layton; ed. C. Lévi-Strauss; Chicago: University of Chicago Press, 1976) 2.115–45.

88. See Steven Swann Jones, *The New Comparative Method*; and idem, "Structural and Thematic Applications of the Comparative Method."

89. In Dundes's introduction to Propp, *Morphology*, xiii.

90. Jones, "Structural and Thematic Applications of the Comparative Method," 152–53.

procedure lends precision to aspects of analysis that are treated intuitively by other structuralists, including both Propp and Lévi-Strauss.[91] In his global model, Hendricks places Proppian morphological analysis at a level preceding the interpretive task for which he adopts a Lévi-Straussian paradigmatic approach.[92] Hendricks's graphic explication of the interrelationship of paradigmatic and syntagmatic structural approaches is extremely useful.

Application of these three steps helped me to define the destiny pattern that can be seen throughout my discussion: using these three tools revealed a relationship between the individual constant elements of EATING and DRINKING and the larger Pattern of Destiny that is defined when the constant element of ORACLE is also present in the text.

*Utility of Propp's Method for Defining Genre
in Biblical Narrative*

Looking at the biblical corpus through the lens of Propp's methodology, I concentrated on three of his structural tools for defining genre: (a) identifying when an element is variable and when it is constant in the biblical corpus; (b) understanding the nature of apparent "reversals" of constant elements and their structural relationship; and (c) defining the narrative unit itself.

*Identifying When an Element Is Variable and
When It Is Constant in the Biblical Corpus*

My first step in the genre analysis was to define every case where eating or drinking is mentioned anywhere in Hebrew Bible narrative. This corpus consisted of more than 150 examples. Once these stories were identified, I analyzed them morphologically in order to identify and chart the sequence of action events in each individual text. In most of the cases, the sequence of action events, or constants, did not include eating and drinking in that narrative. Eating and drinking were variables within some other constant category that I tried to define by means of Proppian analysis. However, in a significant number of other cases, EATING and DRINKING did appear to be constant func-

---

91. See especially Hendricks's study, "Methodology of Narrative Structural Analysis," 175–95, on the importance of a systematic approach to synopsis and an outline of his method.

92. See, for example, the collection of studies by Hendricks in ibid. His other works on literary analysis, narrative style, and linguistics include *Grammars of Style and Styles of Grammar* (North-Holland Studies in Theoretical Poetics 3; Amsterdam: North-Holland, 1976); and idem, "The Notion of Style," *Language and Style* 13/1 (1980) 35–54.

tions. I charted the pattern of these constants and compared the sequence of functions in individual texts with each of the others to see if any was identical to another. When the sequences matched each other, I attempted to abstract a general model to account for the genre or category of story these examples might constitute.

First, I needed to distinguish between what is variable and what is constant in the biblical narratives I had identified. Propp identified the variables as the ways that constant elements, or functions, are expressed in a particular tale or version of a tale. Thus, variable expressions of the constant of MISFORTUNE may be war, poverty, famine, and the like.[93] My task was to distinguish the constant function of EATING and DRINKING from its variable occurrences, those cases where eating and drinking can just as easily change places with other characteristics that together are the variable elements within some other constant category.

Just like the elements Propp identified that make up the Russian fairy-tale constant VILLAINY, such as abduction, seizure, or pillage, in biblical narrative eating and drinking are variable when they are only two of many possible options that may fill a constant slot. In the Bible, a miracle, for example, may involve eating and drinking, but it may just as well involve, among other variables, sprinkling, stretching, or touching. Miraculous escape, miraculous guidance, and miraculous appearance or disappearance may occur just as readily as miraculous eating and drinking and the corollary variable, miraculous food and drink. Thus, the constant element is MIRACLE, while the nature or content of the MIRACLE is variable. In this example, eating and drinking are simply variable options among others within the constant function of MIRACLE.

EATING and DRINKING operate as constants, on the other hand, when they are stable elements across different narratives and fall in the same sequence with respect to other constants in a morphological pattern. I did indeed find that EATING and DRINKING events may serve as a stable element in certain cases, operating as a constant in a limited number of morphological patterns. These patterns occur in a variety of narratives throughout the biblical corpus. Each of the patterns I identified shares the distinction that whenever it occurs (1) it contains an EATING or DRINKING event as a stable element, or constant, and (2) the EATING and DRINKING event follows a fixed sequence with respect to the other functions making up that pattern. In chapters 5 and 6 of this book, I discuss these findings in detail.

---

93. Followers of Propp have termed these variables "allomotifs." See Dundes, especially his article "From Etic to Emic."

Understanding the Nature of Apparent "Reversals" of Constant Elements and Their Structural Relationship. Propp considers reversals of variable elements to be another variable occupying a function slot within the sequence of a pattern. Propp also considers reversals of constant elements to be identical morphologically to the constant element itself, marking the place of that function in the sequence of elements that defines genre. He includes these without comment in his charts of story elements, designating reversals with a minus sign (–).[94]

It may be helpful to look at examples of these from the fairy-tale corpus. For Propp, examples of variables might include forcible imprisonment or its reverse, forcible exile. Both of these would be variables of the constant function VILLAINY and thus identical as far as their role in the underlying structure of the tale. Another set of examples would be leaving home to seek one's fortune or its reverse, returning home after a long absence. These would be variables of the function Propp labeled REACTION OF THE HERO, which follows VILLAINY. Reversals occurring as constants or functions would include a REACTION OF THE HERO to the VILLAINY or LACK that sets the tale in motion—a reaction that is either positive or negative. At the end of a tale, the constant might be a WEDDING, which either takes place or is refused or thwarted.[95]

For purposes of discussion, I would like to designate both constant and variable elements as *direct* and *reverse* to mark these distinctions, which, although they have identical functions morphologically, may nevertheless affect the meaning of a text. In examining my biblical corpus, direct EATING and DRINKING events would include hospitality offered and accepted, or successful cultic, royal, or military provisioning. Reversals include hospitality withheld or refused, provisioning absent or withheld, famine, and fasting. I shall also use a broader understanding of reversal as more than mere negation, further including in this category elements or circumstances that appear contrary to the usual manner or expectation.[96]

In general, direct EATING and DRINKING events correlate with well-being, bonhomie, even celebration, and the reversals—famine, fasting, hospitality withheld or refused—correlate with the opposite. However, this equation does not hold universally. Under certain circumstances,

---

94. Ibid., 135–44, 151–53, 155, and passim.

95. Ibid., 141, 151.

96. See *Shorter Oxford English Dictionary*, 1727. Propp treated the phenomenon of reversal as understood and accounted for it in his morphology by using the minus sign (–) as the symbol for the negative result of a function. See, for example, his *Morphology*, 134–55. Propp never defines *reversal* explicitly.

as I find in my analysis of the category of PERFIDY in chap. 3, disaster can and often does follow a direct EATING and DRINKING event. These reversals of expectation, embodied in such perfidious actions as deception, betrayal, treachery, and coercion, often occur, for example, in proximity to hospitality offered and accepted.

Even more complex is the finding that a reversal of the expected EATING and DRINKING behavior can foreshadow a reversal in the anticipated narrative outcome: if a positive outcome is expected, the reversal, naturally enough, would suggest that a negative outcome may be forthcoming, and vice versa. For example, if a reversed EATING and DRINKING event (such as a fast or famine) suggests that a negative outcome is expected, a reversal of that reversal (abundance during a famine, as when Joseph feeds his father and brothers in Gen 45:21–24 and 47:1–12) implies a reversal of the negative expectation to a positive one instead. Reversal of the expected outcome appears to be the operative element in this case, rather than whether an outcome is in absolute terms positive or negative.[97]

Because they can occur at all structural levels, reversals operate as powerful and subtle literary devices that convey significant meaning within the structural framework of biblical narrative.

Defining the Narrative Unit Itself.   Propp was working with discrete tales that were clearly marked with a beginning and an end, so defining his narrative unit would appear to have been relatively straightforward. In fact, however, Propp struggled with the task of defining narrative blocks within tales, wrestling with ways to classify tales that appeared to contain more than one story line or to have complete tales embedded within the larger narrative.[98]

Ultimately, Propp defined his tales morphologically, according to the nature and sequence of the functions making up the tales. He wrote, "Morphologically, a tale may be termed any development proceeding from villainy or a lack, through intermediary functions to marriage, or to other functions employed as a dénouement."[99] Propp termed this type of development a "move," explaining that "each new act of villainy, each new lack creates a new move. One tale may have several moves, and when analyzing a text, one must first of all

---

97. Propp accounts for reversal in his schema, although he refers to this phenomenon as the "negative outcome" of a function and does not use the word *reversal*. Note in this regard Propp, *Morphology*, 46, 152, and especially p. 155, where he defines *reversal* in terms of the negative outcome of a function.

98. Ibid., 92–117.

99. Ibid., 92.

determine the number of moves of which it consists."[100] Propp acknowledged that singling out a move is not always easy, since moves may interweave and literary devices such as repetition, assimilation, and transposition of morphological elements may interfere with straightforward analysis.

Propp raised the question of how to recognize when a single tale is composed of multiple moves as opposed to when two or more tales are present. Propp outlined seven or eight parameters that indicate when the subject is a single complex tale. For example, a single tale occurs even when entire moves are doubled or tripled, as when three brothers try to vanquish a dragon. The first two fail in the first two moves, and the last brother succeeds in the final move. A single complex tale is also present when a magical object won in the first move (magical horses, perhaps) is used successfully (to rescue a princess, perhaps) only in the second move.

Even with all of its complexity, defining moves was easier for Propp's corpus of tales than it is for the Hebrew Bible. Biblical narrative is large and continuous, with chapter breaks that were imposed many centuries after the composition of the text. Even though a reader might be tempted to treat chapters as units for the purpose of defining pericopes, this is not always appropriate or desirable in identifying structural units that may cross such artificial boundaries. Several of the examples I discuss in chapters 5 and 6 contain structural patterns that go beyond chapter designation. Unlike historically late surface-level designations, the underlying morphology emerges out of the internal framework of the text itself.

Applicability of Propp's Method to a Biblical Corpus

This book is based on expanding the application of Propp's method to a preclassical, non-European, non-fairy-tale corpus.[101] I have found

---

100. Ibid.

101. Propp's method has been deemed applicable to non-oral genres and to non-folkloric materials as well. On the applicability of Propp's method to other genres and other cultures beyond Propp's own, Claude Brémond comments in his essay "The Narrative Message": "The method which he used seems to us capable of being extended to other literary or artistic genres" (*Semeia* 10 [*Narrative Syntax: Translations and Reviews*; 1978] 5). Dundes writes:

> To what extent is Propp's analysis applicable to forms of the folktale other than the fairy tale? . . . There is also the question of whether Propp's analysis might be applicable to non-Indo-European folktales. . . . [Studies done using Proppian analysis on other cultures] suggest that parts of Propp's *Morphology* may be cross-culturally valid. . . . And what of the structure of nonfolkloristic materials? If there is a pattern in a culture, it is by no means necessary that it

Propp's proposed methodology impressively applicable to biblical narrative, confirming Dundes's comment in his introduction to the 1968 edition of Propp's *Morphology*, where he suggests that Propp's analysis of the fairy-tale may well prove applicable cross-culturally, and to other forms of folklore as well.[102]

An important task in beginning this project was to determine whether biblical narrative is an appropriate corpus for Proppian analysis. In selecting a corpus, Propp was concerned less with its size than with the quality of the analysis applied to it. He thought that a small sample corpus may be just as reliable as a larger one. Propp claimed that the degree of repetition in a corpus is more significant than its size: "If repetition is great, then one may take a limited amount of material. If repetition is small, this is impossible. . . . Consequently, it is theoretically possible to limit oneself to a small body of material. . . . We are not interested in the quantity of material, but in the quality of its analysis."[103] Propp also insisted that the analysis should be applied to a standing corpus and that individual examples should not be hand-picked by the researcher: "But just because material can be limited in quantity, that does not mean that it can be selected at one's own discretion. It should be dictated from without."[104] The narrative corpus of biblical literature would appear to meet Propp's criteria of sample size and integrity, and degree of repetition.

Today, the issue of corpus size has come in for some discussion. Milne believes that development of the models themselves should be left to folklorists and literary critics who have large corpora of work on which to base their models.[105] On the other hand, two of the models

---

be limited to only one aspect of that culture. Quite the contrary. Culture patterns normally manifest themselves in a variety of cultural materials. Propp's analysis should be useful in analyzing the structure of literary forms (such as novels and plays), comic strips, motion picture and television plots, and the like. In understanding the interrelationship between folklore and literature, and between folklore and the mass media, the emphasis has hitherto been principally upon content. Propp's *Morphology* suggests that there can be structural borrowings as well as content borrowings (Dundes in Propp, *Morphology*, xiv–xv).

Dundes himself applied Propp's method to the analysis of nonverbal folklore such as games. See Alan Dundes, "On Game Morphology: A Study of the Structure of Non-verbal Folklore," *New York Folklore Quarterly* 20 (1964) 276–88.

102. Dundes in Propp, *Morphology*, xiv–xv.

103. Ibid., 24.

104. Ibid., 23.

105. Milne, *Vladimir Propp*, 12. Milne also prefers to reserve the development of Proppian models to corpora outside the Bible. This approach carries with it the risk that it would preclude the possibility of identifying genres unique to biblical

posited by the folklorist Heda Jason are based on corpora containing very small numbers of tales, even though a wide cross-section of cultures is represented. Jason, by her own account, used only 12 examples to come up with her tentative model for the narrative structure of the "epic struggle" tale[106] and only 37 texts from multiple cultures for her proposed model for the "active heroine" fairy-tale.[107]

The sample I surveyed for this study included 100% of the standing corpus, Hebrew biblical narrative. Within this corpus, texts containing references to eating and drinking were isolated, amounting to more than 150 examples. These were then systematically compared with one another and with biblical narratives that do not contain references to eating and drinking, as well as to examples from ancient Near Eastern literature. The result was the emergence of Patterns of Destiny that tell us what was divinely established or divinely condemned in Hebrew Bible narrative.

Proppian Literary Analysis of Hebrew Bible Narrative

Many scholars have applied structural analysis to biblical texts since the middle of the twentieth century. Structural analysis of biblical literature falls into the same two categories as structural analysis in general: paradigmatic studies, those primarily based on the approach advocated by Lévi-Strauss; and syntagmatic studies, those primarily based on the ideas articulated by Propp. Historically, the influence of Lévi-Strauss has been more widely felt than the influence of Propp in biblical studies, perhaps in part because of the unavailability of Propp in English translation before 1958[108] and perhaps in part because of the origin of the Lévi-Strauss approach in social anthropology, a field traditionally in dialogue with biblical scholarship. Propp's approach, on the other hand, originated in folklore studies, a discipline within anthropology that until recently had little contact with biblical studies.[109]

---

and ancient Near Eastern literature that would not be found by models built on Turkish or other collections. These potentially unique genres could be recognized only by applying Propp's method to the narratives of the Bible and the ancient Near East. In addition, combining the corpus of ancient Near Eastern texts with the corpus of biblical narrative increases both the number of relevant examples and the size of the total corpus.

106. Jason, "Ilja," 48.

107. Idem, "Fairy Tale of the Active Heroine," 81.

108. See Dundes's introduction to the second edition in Propp, *Morphology*, xi.

109. An exception is Gunkel's work from the first decades of the 20th century, recently reissued as Hermann Gunkel, *The Folktale in the Old Testament*. This work appeared after his still-influential *Legends of Genesis*, published in 1910, and although the later work modified somewhat the earlier, Gunkel's original formulation is still

I think it may be useful to note some of the major scholars who apply paradigmatic analysis to biblical texts. Very briefly, major contributors to biblical scholarship writing from the structuralist perspective influenced by Lévi-Strauss are Edmund Leach, Alan Aycock, and David Jobling.[110] In addition, semiotic studies of biblical texts operate

---

the most widespread (see Rogerson's introduction to the reissue of *The Folktale* [1974] for further discussion). For the most part, folklore scholarship ignored the Bible until the 1970s.

A pioneer in the examination of the folklore issue of orality in biblical texts is Robert C. Culley. See, for example, Robert C. Culley, "An Approach to the Problem of Oral Tradition," *VT* 13 (1963) 113–25. Among his other early structural studies (none of which relies on Proppian analysis) are: "Some Comments on Structural Analysis and Biblical Studies," in *Congress Volume: Uppsala, 1971* (VTSup 22; Leiden: Brill, 1972) 129–142; idem, "Oral Tradition and Historicity," in *Studies on the Ancient Palestinian World* (ed. J. Wevers; Toronto: University of Toronto Press, 1972) 102–16; idem, "Themes and Variations in Three Groups of OT Narratives," *Semeia* 3 (*Classical Hebrew Narrative*; 1975) 3–13. Most recently, he has acknowledged Propp's indirect influence on his work. See *Themes and Variations: A Study of Action in Biblical Narrative* (Society of Biblical Literature Semeia Studies 23; Atlanta, Scholars Press, 1992).

Biblical scholar Susan Niditch also focuses on the role of folklore in biblical narrative. See "Legends of Wise Heroes and Heroines," in *The Old Testament and Its Modern Interpreters* (ed. Douglas A. Knight and Gene M. Tucker; Chico, Calif.: Scholars Press, 1985) 167–200; idem, *Underdogs and Tricksters: A Prelude to Biblical Folklore* (San Francisco: Harper & Row, 1987); and, most recently, idem, *Folklore and the Hebrew Bible* (Minneapolis: Fortress, 1993).

Folklorists like Dundes, and even Lord, have also turned their attention to oral traditional traces in the biblical text. See Alan Dundes (ed.), *Sacred Narrative: Readings in the Theory of Myth* (Berkeley: University of California Press, 1984); idem, *The Flood Myth* (Berkeley: University of California Press, 1988); Albert B. Lord, "Formula and Non-narrative Theme in South Slavic Oral Epic and the OT," *Semeia* 5 (*Oral Tradition and Old Testament Studies*; 1976) 93–105; for the Christian Bible, see idem, "The Gospels as Oral Traditional Literature," in *The Relationships among the Gospels: An Interdisciplinary Dialogue* (ed. William O. Walker, Jr.; San Antonio, Tex.: Trinity University Press, 1978) 33–91. Also see, most recently, the many essays in Susan Niditch (ed.), *Text and Tradition: The Hebrew Bible and Folklore* (Society of Biblical Literature Semeia Studies 20; Atlanta: Scholars Press, 1990).

110. See especially Edmund Leach, *Genesis as Myth and Other Essays* (London: Jonathan Cape, 1969); also, for example, Edmund Leach and D. Alan Aycock (eds.), *Structuralist Interpretations of Biblical Myth* (Royal Anthropological Institute of Great Britain and Ireland; London: Cambridge University Press, 1983); and David Jobling, *The Sense of Biblical Narrative, II: Structural Analyses in the Hebrew Bible* (JSOTSup 39; Sheffield: Sheffield Academic Press, 1987); a chapter of this book was originally published as "'The Jordan a Boundary': A Reading of Numbers 32 and Joshua 22," *Society of Biblical Literature 1980: Seminar Papers* (SBLSP 19; ed. Paul J. Achtemeier; Chico, Calif.: Scholars Press, 1980) 183–207.

paradigmatically on a similar deep or mythic structure, although the development of semiotic models, most notably by A. J. Greimas, has evolved well beyond the structural models proposed by Lévi-Strauss. Biblical studies of this nature include those by the CADIR group, whose principles are articulated by Jean Calloud and Olivette Genest, among others.[111] Roland Barthes, in this as in so much else, is in a class by himself, participating in the approaches of Greimas and Lévi-Strauss at different times and to a greater or lesser extent. As we shall see, he was also one of the first to attempt an application of Propp's morphology to a biblical text.[112]

Among syntagmatic applications to biblical scholarship, Pamela Milne's recent work stands out.[113] The greater portion of Milne's book is a thorough review of the history of structural analysis and its proponents, including controversies and differences in structural approaches. Milne also devotes a chapter of her book to a thorough examination of eight scholars whose work on biblical texts is based even partially on Propp's morphological approach.[114] In addition, sev-

---

111. CADIR is an acronym for scholars from the Centre pour l'Analyse du Discours Religieux, in Lyon, France, termed by Milne "the most influential and highly developed of the approaches based on Greimas" (Milne, *Vladimir Propp*, 50). The bulletin *Semiotique et Bible* is published by CADIR. Articles are presented as a product of the work of the group and are not signed by individuals. A collection of articles from this bulletin was published as *Analyse semiotique des textes: Introduction, theorie, pratique* (Lyon: Presses Universitaires de Lyon, 1979), including an application of semiotic approach to Gen 11:1–9, the story of the Tower of Babel.

Jean Calloud has analyzed literary texts from the Christian Bible using a semiotic approach, notably in *Structural Analysis of Narrative* (trans. D. Patte; Philadelphia: Fortress, 1976), in which he addresses the desert temptations of Jesus. Olivette Genest has addressed texts in the Hebrew Bible, for example, in "Analyse semiotique de Gn 22, 1–19," in *Science et Esprit* 33/2 (1981) 157–77. Daniel Patte has demonstrated the application of Greimas's approach to biblical exegesis in his recent book, *The Religious Dimensions of Biblical Texts: Greimas's Structural Semiotics and Biblical Exegesis* (Society of Biblical Literature Semeia Studies 19; Atlanta: Scholars Press, 1990).

Roland Barthes briefly analyzes a biblical text using two structural approaches, that of Propp and that of Greimas, in "The Struggle with the Angel: Textual Analysis of Genesis 32:23–33," in *Structural Analysis and Biblical Exegesis: Interpretational Essays by R. Barthes, F. Bovon, F.-J. Leenhardt, R. Martin-Achard, and J. Starobinski* (trans. A. M. Johnson, Jr.; Pittsburgh: Pickwick, 1974); reprinted and retranslated in Roland Barthes, *Image–Music–Text* (ed. and trans. Stephen Heath; New York: Farrar, Strauss and Giroux, 1977).

112. Barthes, "Struggle with the Angel."

113. Milne, *Vladimir Propp*.

114. Ibid., chap. 5, pp. 125–73.

eral articles applying Propp to the Hebrew Bible have been published since Milne's book.[115] While it would be redundant to duplicate her thorough examination, a survey of what she found to be either positive or lacking is illuminating and instructive for this study. Although none of those scholars refers to eating and drinking except in the most cursory way, my examination of Patterns of Destiny benefits from their work and also from the cautionary lessons that Milne derives from these earlier efforts.

Milne examines the work of several scholars, some of whose fields are primarily literary criticism rather than Bible, who have used Propp's approach to analyze the same biblical text.[116] Among these are Roland Barthes, Robert Couffignal, and Xavier Durand, each of whom addresses Gen 32:23–33, Jacob's struggle at the Jabbok.[117] Wolfgang Roth, a scholar of Bible, is also considered a part of this group since he "used Gen. 32:23–33 as a sample text to illustrate four types of structural analysis: the sequential analysis of Barthes, the functional analysis of Propp, the actantial analysis of Greimas, and the analysis of mythical structure of Lévi-Strauss."[118]

---

115. Will Soll, "Misfortune and Exile in Tobit: The Juncture of a Fairy Tale Source and Deuteronomic Theology," *CBQ* 51 (1989) 209–31; Carole R. Fontaine, "Folktale Structure in the Book of Job: A Formalist Reading," in *Directions in Biblical Hebrew Poetry* (ed. E. Follis; JSOTSup 40; Sheffield: JSOT Press, 1987) 205–32. While these are worthwhile studies, they do not add to the methodological or cautionary considerations relevant to this study that are summarized at the end of this section. In another article relevant to our topic, Adele Berlin has applied the structural poetics of Heda Jason to an ancient Near Eastern text, in "Ethnopoetry and the Enmerkar Epics," *JAOS* 103 (special issue dedicated to Samuel Noah Kramer; 1983) 17–24.

116. Milne, *Vladimir Propp*, 128–41.

117. Barthes, "Struggle with the Angel"; Robert Couffignal, "'Jacob lutte au Jabboq': Approches nouvelles de Genese, xxxii, 23–22," *Revue Thomiste* 4 (1975) 582–97; Xavier Durand, "Le combat de Jacob: Gn 32,23–33," in *L'ancien Testament: Approches et lectures* (ed. A. Vanel; Le Point Theologique 24; Paris: Institut Catholique de Paris, 1977) 99–115.

118. Milne, *Vladimir Propp*, 130–31, discussing Wolfgang Roth, "Structural Interpretations of 'Jacob at the Jabbok' (Genesis 32:22–32)," *Biblical Research* 21 (1976) 51–62. See also Roth's article, "You Are the Man! Structural Interaction in 2 Samuel 10–12," *Semeia* 8 (*Literary Critical Studies of Biblical Texts*; 1977) 1–13. In addition to her comments in *Vladimir Propp*, see also Pamela J. Milne, "Folktales and Fairy Tales: An Evaluation of Two Proppian Analyses of Biblical Narratives," *JSOT* 34 (1986) 35–60. In *Vladimir Propp*, Milne also addresses the structural work of Jack Sasson and Joseph Blenkinsopp. See Jack M. Sasson, *Ruth: A New Translation with a Philological Commentary and a Formalist-Folklorist Interpretation* (Baltimore: Johns Hopkins University Press, 1979); Joseph Blenkinsopp, "Biographical Patterns in

Milne is critical of the poor understanding of Propp exhibited by these scholars. As Milne suspects, the fault does not lie with Propp's work but "primarily in the way Propp's model has been used. All four authors appear to assume that the model is a general one for all types of folktales rather than a specific model for the surface structure of heroic fairy tales."[119] Milne's analysis highlights a significant pitfall to be avoided, that of failing to differentiate Propp's method, which is general and may be applied to a variety of corpora, from his model, which is specific and describes only the genre of the Russian fairy-tale.

Another important caution for all biblical applications of Propp's method is raised by Milne, who finds that the texts in each study were never adequately delimited.[120] Authors would claim that they were analyzing a specific pericope and would then insert actions from verses that lie outside that pericope. Studies that purported to treat the same narrative would define that narrative by specifying boundaries that differed one from the other. As a result, Propp's model was not always applied to the same text in each essay. Even Heda Jason, the ground-

---

Biblical Narrative," *JSOT* 20 (1981) 27–46. For another Proppian analysis, this one of the book of Tobit, Will Soll's recent article does a thorough job of this text, demonstrating a sensitive reading of Propp. See his "Misfortune and Exile in Tobit." While I appreciate his application of Propp's method, I do not agree with his conclusions that hypothesize about the origins of the sources he sees coming together in this text.

119. Ibid., 141. In *Vladimir Propp*, Milne criticizes Sasson on two counts: "Firstly, Propp's model in its original form does not seem to be very suitable for application to this particular biblical text. Secondly, Propp's model does not seem to have been applied to the text properly" (pp. 152–53). Other scholars, such as Greenstein and Niditch, have also evaluated Sasson's effort. See Edward L. Greenstein, "Biblical Narratology," *Prooftexts* 1 (1981) 201–8; Niditch, "Legends of Wise Heroes and Heroines," 167–200. In *Ruth* (p. 201 and passim), Sasson attempts to apply Propp's model of the Russian fairy-tale directly to the book of Ruth, both to show its folklore affinities and to define the form of this Bible story more precisely as a folktale. It is not an easy fit. If Sasson had better understood the limitations of Propp's defined genre, he might have felt freer to conclude that the book of Ruth does not appear to fit precisely Propp's model of the "heroic fairy-tale," and he might have been able to define another kind of folktale category to which the book of Ruth does belong. Sasson himself notes that Propp's *method* might be useful when applied to material that does not share the folklore form, although, as Milne notes, Propp's folklore *model*, which Sasson applied to Ruth "without any adaptations or amelioration, will eventually have to be refined, perhaps even restructured, in order to better suit tales from both the Ancient Near East and the Bible" (Milne, *Vladimir Propp*, 214).

120. Ibid., 141.

breaking Israeli folklorist who appears to have influenced Milne pro-foundly, is criticized by Milne for not strictly delimiting her text.[121] As Milne correctly points out, "the question of the limits of the text is es-pecially important in the analysis of biblical narrative where individual stories are part of larger contexts."[122]

It should be clear from this discussion that Propp's methodology is a tool, not a panacea. As such, it can be only as effective as the way in which it is applied. Certain cautions must be observed: first, Propp's method must be distinguished from the specific model that he derived from the corpus under his examination; second, great care must be taken to understand Propp's methodology thoroughly and to apply it consistently to an appropriate corpus; third, the boundaries of each text under discussion must be explicitly delimited, and the analysis must be contained entirely within these bounds.

In the following chapters, I examine the biblical texts themselves through a Proppian lens, isolating morphologies to define a genre that I am calling the Pattern of Destiny, a narrative pattern that occurs whenever something is divinely established or divinely overturned in the Hebrew Bible. First, in chapters 3 and 4, I focus on eating and drinking when they occur as variable elements within other constant functions, in order to confirm that Propp's methodology can indeed account for all instances of eating and drinking, whether the narratives they belong to fit into my sequential pattern or not. This examination will lead to brief reviews of a number of genres in biblical narrative newly defined morphologically by Proppian analysis. Then, in chap-ters 5 and 6, I identify cases where EATING and DRINKING function as constants, looking in much greater depth at one particular, powerful, and persuasive genre pattern in which EATING and DRINKING become a figure in the Pattern of Destiny, whether for good or for ill.

---

121. Heda Jason's only work directly in Bible studies to date is an article ana-lyzing the story of David and Goliath, "The Story of David and Goliath: A Folk Epic?" *Bib* 60 (1979) 36–70. Only part of her article deals with a Proppian analysis of the plot structure of 1 Samuel 17. In this article, Jason also applies a model for a type of Russian national epic. In addition to Jason's article, see Milne, *Vladimir Propp*, 154.

122. Ibid., 156.

CHAPTER THREE

Eating and Drinking
as Variables in
Biblical Narrative

Eating and Drinking as Meaningful Literary Elements

Literary criticism is an undertaking fraught with peril. There are an infinite number of ways to find meaning in any text, and the selection of an analytic methodology is intrinsically arbitrary. In many ways, the method itself may determine the outcome of an investigation.[1] In spite of these hazards, I profess an approach that is primarily literary, and

---

1. That no field of study is wholly objective, and that every discipline includes important uncertainties has been recognized recently even in the "hard" sciences and mathematics by Karl Popper, Thomas Kuhn, Morris Kline, and Stephen Hawking, among others. For a summary of these philosophical shifts and an evaluation of their effect on religious studies, see Frederick W. Norris, "Black Marks on the Communities' Manuscripts," *Journal of Early Christian Studies* 2 (1994) 443–66.

The understanding that the act of reading necessarily involves presuppositions that may be challenged and reformulated in the process of reading is part of a process known as the "hermeneutic circle." This process was originally suggested by the theologian Friedrich Schleiermacher in the early nineteenth century and, in its most recent formulation, has influenced the development of "reception theory," an approach to reader-response criticism. See Chris Baldick, *The Concise Oxford Dictionary of Literary Terms* (Oxford: Oxford University Press, 1990) 97 and 185; Terry Eagleton, *Literary Theory: An Introduction* (Minneapolis: University of Minnesota Press, 1983) 54–90, especially pp. 74–80. For discussions of the role and limitations of the hermeneutic circle and its modern applications in Bible studies, see Stephen A. Geller, "Through Windows and Mirrors into the Bible: History, Literature and Language in the Study of Text," in *A Sense of Text: The Art of Language in the Study of Biblical Literature* (Supplement to JQR; Philadelphia: Dropsie, 1983) 3–40, especially pp. 14–18; and Robert M. Polzin, *Biblical Structuralism* (Semeia Supplements 5; Missoula, Mont.: Scholars Press, 1977) 21–23.

begin with the premise that eating and drinking events serve a meaningful literary function when they occur in the Hebrew Bible.

Recent literary approaches to the Bible—in particular, those of Conroy, Bar-Efrat, and Sternberg[2]—have drawn attention to the spareness of Hebrew narrative and to the fact that all reported events, even the most apparently ordinary, are of literary significance when they occur in the Hebrew Bible. Eating and drinking, sleeping, excretion, and sexual intercourse are all commonly performed human activities necessary to sustain life, but when they occur in biblical stories, their function moves beyond the mundane. The Bible is selective about reporting these daily functions; not every possible instance is noted in the biblical text. What is it, then, that determines which are included and which are not?[3]

Within the literary context of the Bible, ordinary bodily functions are always germane to plot or message. For example, consider the importance of sleep for Adam when Eve is created in Genesis 2, for Abraham during the Covenant between the Pieces in Genesis 15, for Jacob at Bethel in Genesis 28, for Sisera in Yael's tent in Judges 4, for Solomon at Gibeon in 1 Kings 3: in each of these cases, the sleep is no ordinary slumber but operates to manifest the will of God. Regard the significance of excretion by a vulnerable Saul, who relieves himself as David, his enemy, hides and watches in 1 Samuel 24, and by a dead Eglon, whose bowels are sliced open by Ehud, misleading his courtiers

---

2. Charles Conroy, *Absalom, Absalom! Narrative and Language in 2 Samuel 13–20* (AnBib 81; Rome: Pontifical Biblical Institute, 1978); Shimon Bar-Efrat, *Narrative Art in the Bible* (JSOTSup 70; Sheffield: Almond, 1989); Meir Sternberg, *The Poetics of Biblical Narrative: Ideological Literature and the Drama of Reading* (Bloomington: Indiana University Press, 1985).

3. Sternberg (ibid.) uses the terms "gap" and "blank" to designate the selectivity of the biblical text, places where the text skips from one incident to another without denoting all intervening events. Sternberg reserves the term "gap" for lacunae that are literarily significant according to his understanding of authorial intention, provoking the reader to questions that are usually resolved later in the text in such a way as to emphasize the divine plan. These "gaps" thus result in purposeful ambiguities that must influence any reading of the text.

Sternberg contrasts "gaps" with "blanks," which he terms omissions in the text of irrelevant details or information, lacunae in the narrative text that are not literarily significant according to his understanding of authorial intention. Although the arbitrariness of these distinctions has been criticized by other scholars (notably, Naomi Segal in her review of Sternberg's *Poetics*, *VT* 38 [1988] 243–49, where she correctly points out that one reader's gap is another's blank), both "gaps" and "blanks" must be recognized for their acknowledgment that the biblical text is selective and not exhaustive.

into respecting what they believe is his privacy in Judges 3: in both cases, the weaker outmaneuvers the stronger, and the circumstances surrounding the most personal of human necessities function to confirm a shift in the political status quo. Review the consequences of fornication for David and Bathsheba in 2 Samuel 11 and for Judah and Tamar in Genesis 38; for Amnon with Tamar in 2 Samuel 13 and for Shechem with Dinah in Genesis 34: the repercussions of these private acts of fornication and rape reverberate through the history of Israel.

Each of these events, though it treats of ordinary bodily functions, is of crucial significance to any reading of the text because of the context in which it is embedded. The same is true for eating and drinking accounts in the biblical narrative.

Realizing that literary meaning may be encoded in the mundane details in biblical stories, I return to my questions about the episode of Isaac's blessing of Jacob and Esau in Genesis 27. When I first read this text, I was struck by the focus on eating and drinking—the acts themselves, the preparation, the serving. The fact that eating and drinking are not germane to either the plot of the story or the stated purpose of the narrative suggested to me that I was missing some elusive kernel of meaning in this text. Could I use Propp's methodology to uncover this elusive meaning?

With this question, I embarked on an investigation that led me through more than 200 biblical and ancient Near Eastern episodes that contained references to acts of eating or drinking. First I studied these examples, reading and rereading in accord with the accepted hermeneutic method and charting the action sequences and their consequences, as Propp had done for his corpus of Russian fairy-tales. Then I read the secondary literature to see whether the work of other scholars would bear fruit for my examination of eating and drinking.

The first insight I had was that, from Osiris to Isaac, the ancient Near Eastern literature I looked at is full of occasions when people gather to eat and drink. On these occasions, an encounter among the participants—discord, contest, or other challenge—often results in a pronouncement, positive or negative, of enormous significance to the unfolding story. I formed the hypothesis that EATING and DRINKING are functioning in these cases as a Proppian constant, part of a recurring sequence making up a structural pattern that in its simplest form appeared to me to consist of an EATING or DRINKING event followed by an ORACLE. If the ORACLE is positive, a positive outcome ensues; if the ORACLE is negative, the outcome is Doom. Before I was finished, I had found more than fifty examples of this Destiny Pattern in biblical literature and several dozen examples in the other literatures of the ancient Near East.

Finding these examples was not enough. In order to define a genre using Propp's methodology, distinctions must be made between an element operating as a constant, as EATING and DRINKING appear to do in the pattern I identified, and an element operating as a variable within other constants. According to Proppian analysis, the cases that do not fall into the category of constant must be variable elements within some other constants. To confirm or discredit my hypothesis that on occasion EATING and DRINKING do function as a constant in biblical narrative, I needed to be able to account for the examples of eating and drinking that do not.

I needed to look at eating and drinking in every case that did not fit my pattern to determine whether in those examples eating and drinking operated as variable elements within some other constants that I had yet to identify. Unless Proppian analysis could account for the cases that did not fit my hypothesis, my hypothesis that these other cases do indeed form a Destiny genre must fall, and Proppian analysis must fail.

In this endeavor, the work of other scholars was invaluable. Many scholars have noted acts of eating and drinking within their larger studies of biblical phenomena. These scholars are situated intellectually within the structuralist framework, but their work does not directly invoke or depend upon either Propp's method or his model. Although these scholars were not analyzing their subjects within Proppian parameters, many of them had in fact described the subjects of their studies in ways that made it clear to me that these subjects were operating in a way that Propp would describe as constant functions.[4] Although these scholars can shed little light on specific ways Propp's

---

4. A special word is in order about scholars whose work deals with orality in folklore. Milman Parry and his student Albert B. Lord revolutionized the study of epics in their examinations of the Homeric tradition and the living Slavic bards in the early part of the twentieth century. The most influential of these studies is Lord's major work in the field of oral-formulaic theory, *The Singer of Tales*, in which he builds and expands on Parry's foundation. Although a complete bibliography of studies on orality and tradition in Greek, Hebrew, and other literatures is beyond the scope of this work, a foundational bibliography may be found in John Miles Foley's *Oral-Formulaic Theory and Research: An Introduction and Annotated Bibliography* (New York: Garland, 1985). Major scholars with a structuralist orientation who have made contributions to these fields or who have edited important collections are cited in the bibliography appended to this book. The most important include Dan Ben-Amos, David Buchan, Ira R. Buchler, Jesse Byock, Alan Dundes, Ruth H. Finnegan, John Miles Foley, Béla Köpeczi and Gyögy M. Vajda, Veronika Görög-Karady and Michele Chiche, Clyde Kluckhohn, Burke O. Long, Pierre Maranda and Elli Kongas Maranda, Susan Niditch, Axel Olrik, Lord Raglan, C. W. von Sydow, and Archer Taylor, among many others. Of special note is Robert Culley, who

method or model may be applied, they are nevertheless important observers of structures in biblical narrative, and their works have much
to contribute to our understanding here.

For these scholars, eating and drinking appear as variables within
the phenomena they examine, such as CULT, MIRACLE, COVENANT,
DREAMS, and other elements that function as constants in Proppian
terms. Within these constants eating and drinking occur, but so do
other constituents in impressive variety. It became clear to me as I investigated these examples that, in the cases that do not fit my proposed genre of Destiny Patterns, eating and drinking do indeed
operate as variables within other phenomena that function as constants in other narrative patterns. My hypothesis—that when EATING
and DRINKING are followed by an ORACLE, they constitute elements in
a Pattern of Destiny—was validated. Also validated was the applicability
of Proppian analysis as a tool. In this section of the book, I briefly review examples of eating and drinking as they occur as a variable element within other constants and briefly examine some of the patterns
within which those constants function.

Eating and Drinking as Variable Elements within Other Constants

In this section I consider the constant functions of CULT, MIRACLE,
SYMBOLIC ACTION, DREAM, ETIOLOGY, MILITARY LEADERSHIP, PERFIDY
(deception, treachery, and coercion), SUPPLICATION, MOURNING and
MISFORTUNE.[5] These categories of constants emerged as part of the
process of applying Proppian morphological analysis to the corpus of
150 biblical texts containing references to eating and drinking. Each
example was sorted into categories that emerged from the identification of the elements making up that example.[6] In my discussion of
each of these categories, I note its constant function within biblical
narrative and then show that eating and drinking, when they occur
within these constants, are just two among many other possible variables that may also occur within these constants.

---

is an important scholar of structures in biblical narrative and a pioneer in the study
of folklore and the Hebrew Bible.

5. Hospitality is briefly surveyed below within the constant category of PERFIDY.

6. Due to the literary richness of the biblical text, in which multiple functions
overlie one another, examples may appear in more than one category and so may
be mentioned in more than one context in this study (see Vladimir Propp, *Morphology of the Folktale* [ed. L. A. Wagner; trans. L. Scott; Austin: University of Texas
Press, 1968] chap. 9).

Following my discussion of these categories of constants, I discuss two categories in which readers might expect EATING and DRINKING to be constants but in which eating and drinking are in fact variables of other elements. These categories are: (1) life-cycle events; and (2) other celebrations in Hebrew biblical narrative.

The groundwork of other scholars has enabled me briefly to identify here in chapter 3 the outlines of many patterns in addition to the key morphology that I explore in great detail in chapters 5 and 6. The patterns suggested by the constants identified in this chapter represent rich sources for scholarly examination in the future. Throughout each of these chapters, I take the opportunity from time to time to examine in detail particularly interesting or problematic texts to illustrate the productivity of this literary approach.

Constants within Which
Eating and Drinking Are Variables

Cult

Most spheres of life in ancient Israel have the potential of coming within the cultic purview, which may be defined as the institutionalized system of official Israelite rituals for organized service to the deity. Anyone familiar with the theocratic orientation of the Hebrew Bible has noticed that cult for the Israelites encompasses much to do with eating and drinking (the food prohibitions in Leviticus 11 are the parade example)[7] but also much to do with other aspects of the sacred and the secular. For example, beyond rules governing eating and drinking, the cultic commands making up a substantial portion of the book of Leviticus govern such items as expiation (Leviticus 4), sin and

---

7. For a discussion of aspects of this significance in Leviticus 11, see Mary Douglas, "The Abominations of Leviticus," reprinted in *Anthropological Approaches to the Old Testament* (ed. Bernhard Lang; Issues in Religion and Theology 8; Philadelphia: Fortress, 1985) 100–16. This essay was originally published as part of her book *Purity and Danger: An Analysis of Concepts of Pollution and Taboo* (London: Routledge and Kegan Paul, 1969) and was expanded in two chapters in her volume of collected essays, *Implicit Meanings: Essays in Anthropology* (London: Routledge and Kegan Paul, 1975), entitled "Deciphering a Meal" (pp. 249–75) and "Self-Evidence" (pp. 276–318). For a cogent evaluation of the strengths and errors of Douglas's reading of the text, as well as his own discussion based in some measure on Douglas's insights, see Jacob Milgrom, *Leviticus 1–16: A New Translation with Introduction and Commentary* (AB 3; New York: Doubleday, 1991) 718–36. See the discussion of Douglas's views by Edwin Firmage, "The Biblical Dietary Laws and the Concept of Holiness," in *Studies in the Pentateuch* (ed. J. A. Emerton; VTSup 41; Leiden: Brill, 1990) 177–208.

reparation (Leviticus 5), healing (Leviticus 13 and 14), sexual behavior (Leviticus 18 and 20), priestly regulations (Leviticus 21 and 22), the sacred calendar (Leviticus 23), and regulations for the transfer of property and real estate (Leviticus 25).

The Constant Element of Cult. In each of these examples, the constant element is the cultic command. It does not matter to a morphological reading of the narrative whether the cultic command consists of eating and drinking elements or whether it concerns the condition of one's skin or the location of a corpse. From a literary point of view, the elements making up these commands are equivalent to one another as variable components, even if they are not interchangeable from a ritual perspective. Literarily, eating and drinking are variables of CULT along with each of the other possible constituents of cultic command.

The constant of CULTIC COMMAND may be defined by the sequence consisting of a promise followed by a command to be implemented once the promise is fulfilled. In some cases, an actual fulfillment follows the promise and command, often with a textual comment that the command was fulfilled according to God's word. Sometimes, the promise and command are asyndetic, not connected to one another explicitly but only by rhetorical juxtaposition.[8] Such a reading may be

---

8. This insight has long been understood intuitively by many commentators who have sought a relationship between the nature of the narrative and the nature of the command in texts so juxtaposed. This is the rabbinic exegetical principle of סמיכות פרשיות, juxtaposition of sections, implicit in several rabbinic exegetical prescriptions. The earliest of these are the thirteen principles of rabbinic exegesis listed in the introduction to *Sifra*, an extensive rabbinic commentary on the book of Leviticus focusing primarily on the Temple cult and dating from the Mishnaic period of rabbinic thought (through the second century C.E.). These principles, attributed to Rabbi Ishmael, are basic to an understanding of how the words of the Torah may be read in order to derive law, מדרש הלכה. The second of these principles, designated by the technical term גזרה שוה 'equivalent commands', suggests that two independent laws or cases may shed light on each other based on similarities in language and/or subject. A later formulation extends the application of exegetical principles from derivation of law, מדרש הלכה, to the derivation of other kinds of homiletical meaning, מדרש אגדה. The ל״ב מדות '32 Principles' of exegesis were formulated in a Gaonic era work (8th–9th century C.E.) pseudepigraphically attributed to the second century C.E. Rabbi Eliezer ben Yossi Hagalili. On R. Eliezer, see H. G. Enelow (ed.), *The Mishnah of Rabbi Eliezer, or the Midrash of Thirty-Two Hermeneutic Rules* (New York: Bloch, 1933) [Heb.], and Moshe Zucker, "Towards a Solution to the Problem of the Thirty-Two Rules and the 'Mishnah of Rabbi Eliezer,'" in *Proceedings of the American Academy for Jewish Research* 23 (1954), Hebrew Section, pp. 1–39 [Heb.]. For a summary of scholarship on the issue of the thirty-two principles, see Yonah Frankel, *The Ways of Aggadah and Midrash* [Heb.]

made for the juxtaposed texts of Numbers 13–14 and Numbers 15.[9] The people of the Exodus generation had just been condemned to die in the wilderness for their lack of faith in God expressed in their reception of the account of the spies. The juxtaposition of a text prescribing rules that must be followed when their children ultimately do inherit the land and benefit from its abundance serves as a reassurance that the divine promise will ultimately be kept with the next generation.

In other cases, the command itself implies a commitment by God to fulfill the promise. Thus, the Passover commands of Exod 12:1–28 deal not only with the present situation but also look forward to the future. The cultic command is for future observance of the Passover as a memorial for posterity of what has not yet taken place at the time it is commanded.[10] This anticipatory placement of the directive implicitly reinforces the promise that, just as what had been predicted in the past has already come to pass, so what has been promised for the future will also be fulfilled. This promise is fulfilled when Israel crosses the Jordan and camps at Gilgal, where the men are circumcised as a sign of the covenant and the people observe the first Passover in the promised land (Joshua 3–5).

Once the pattern has been set, consisting of promise leading to fulfillment associated with the Passover, Exodus, and return to the land, it can be invoked in other instances. For example, this juxtaposition of promise and fulfillment is also intrinsic to the dedication of the Second Temple in Ezra 6:15–22, where the Temple dedication and resumption of Temple service abut the account of the observance of the Passover feast by the people. The text makes a point of connecting this Passover celebration to the first, explicitly associating the return of these exiles from captivity to the Exodus from Egypt (6:21). In so doing, it analogizes this second occasion of Exodus and return to the first, which preceded an independent (and sometimes glorious) history of Israel in its own land. The morphology of promise and command occurs in other cultic contexts where the ritual activity is in

(Jerusalem: Massada, 1991) 501–3 and his notes and bibliography. For a discussion of the value of סמיכות פרשיות, juxtaposition of sections, and other rabbinic exegetical approaches to modern biblical scholarship, see Kalman P. Bland, "The Rabbinic Method and Literary Criticism," in *Literary Interpretations of Biblical Narratives* (ed. K. R. R. Gros Louis; Nashville: Abingdon, 1974) 16–23. I am grateful to Dr Robert Harris of JTS for his guidance with these references.

9. See Rashi's commentary on 15:2 and 19.

10. The technical literary term for this kind of anachronism, sometimes also referred to as foreshadowing, is *prolepsis*, the Greek term for 'anticipation'. On the literary nuances of this term, see, for example, Baldick, *Concise Oxford Dictionary of Literary Terms*, 178. This concept is an important one for reading texts in general and for morphological analysis in particular.

acknowledgment of the promise fulfilled: Jethro, Moses, and the elders offer burnt offerings and sacrifices (זבח) to God in acknowledgment of the delivery of the Israelites from Egypt (Exod 18:12); the inauguration of Saul as monarch is celebrated at Gilgal with well-being sacrifices (זבח, 1 Sam 11:15); Nehemiah and the people dedicate Jerusalem's wall with offerings (זבח) and rejoicing (Neh 12:43).

These readings have in common that they see each cultic prescription in syntagmatic terms, taking into account its position relative to what precedes it and what follows it. The salient feature, the constant in these readings, is the CULTIC nature of the text: that it communicates the word of God commanding the future behavior of God's people. The message of the cultic command embedded in the narrative is precisely this divine concern for Israel; what that command consists of is almost incidental to this reading. God's concern for Israel, God's special affinity with the people, God's intention to fulfill divine promises are all expressed in the fact that a cultic prescription has been given that applies to the Israelite people who will in the future inhabit the land of promise, dwelling in unique relationship to the God who brought them there.

Eating and Drinking as a Variable of Cultic Ritual.   Cultic commands often include, among many other variables, specifications for cultic rituals. These cultic rituals may contain eating and drinking activities along with other prescribed actions. When a cultic ritual arises within the constant of CULT, the business at hand may have to do with eating and drinking but may also involve acts of washing, anointing, scraping, cutting, cleansing, blood sprinkling or pouring, and the like. Each of these fills the same role, acting as variable components within the constant of CULTIC RITUAL. Like eating and drinking, these other acts may be prescribed or proscribed by divine command communicated by Moses to all of the people, as they often are in Leviticus, or undertaken by them under the inspiration of leader (Joshua 24), judge (Gideon, in Judges 6), or king (Josiah, in 2 Kings 23). Many other actions, gestures, or events may take the place held at times by an eating or drinking event, although the nature of the textual morphology, CULT, remains constant. In these cases, eating and drinking are variables of the constant function of CULTIC command expressed within the morphology of CULT in the form of cultic ritual.

The cultic act of consecration or dedication illustrates the variable nature of these elements.[11] In the instructions for priestly consecration

---

11. On the act of cultic consecration in ancient Near Eastern religions, see, for example, R. D. Barnett, "Bringing the God into the Temple," in *Temples and High*

commanded in Exod 29:1–35 and performed in Leviticus 8,[12] the description of Aaron's food portion to be boiled and eaten with unleavened bread at the entrance to the Tent of Meeting (Lev 8:31–36) occurs only following other actions also classifiable as cultic variables: priestly washing, changing of clothes, and anointing with oil and blood. The fat, the liver, and other portions of the sacrifice making up the priestly meal have already been completely burned on the altar as a pleasing odor for God (Lev 8:25–28), and the blood has already been smeared on the priests during their ordination. The constant function of CUL-TIC RITUAL contains many variables besides eating and drinking.

Although the context is cultic and the boiled meat is part of a sacred meal that is taken during the week of dedication, in the strictest sense the meal may not be part of the morphology of consecration at all. Many of the sacrifices associated with the actual performance of consecration in Leviticus 8 are never even eaten. Instead, other variables fill the slots within the constant of CULTIC consecration: sacrifices are wholly burned, or portions are waved, turned into smoke upon the altar, or the remains are burned outside the camp (Lev 8:14–21). The command specifying the priests' meal is structurally outside the ritual acts of ordination and dedication, and a meal is apparently not a requirement for these rituals. The text proclaims that the consecration of the priests is complete (Exod 29:9), before any eating or drinking has taken place. The command for this meal occurs at the very end of the prescriptions for the dedication ceremonies in a context that suggests that one reason for prescribing a sacred meal is to provide for the practical reality of feeding the priests during the seven days they are confined to the Tent of Meeting for their ordination.

In support of this observation, I found three other accounts of cultic consecrations that exhibit many variables of cult without ever mentioning eating and drinking explicitly. The parallel accounts of Solomon's dedication of the First Temple in 1 Kings 8 and 2 Chronicles 5–6[13] and the description of Hezekiah's Temple rededication in

---

Places in Biblical Times (ed. A. Biran; Jerusalem: Hebrew Union College and Jewish Institute of Religion, 1981) 10–20.

12. The text in Exodus represents the "command" portion of a two-part "command-performance" convention common in the Bible and ancient Near Eastern literature. The final chapters of Exodus appear to assume a completed priestly consecration, even though the final consecration is not performed until Leviticus 8–9. For a discussion of the common literary device in ancient Near Eastern and other literatures of the repetition of command/performance passages, see Murray H. Lichtenstein, *Episodic Structure in the Ugaritic Keret Legend: Comparative Studies in Compositional Technique* (Ph.D. diss., Columbia University, 1979) 60–97.

13. 2 Chr 5:12–13 adds Levitical singers, musical instruments, and a hymn fragment to the account in 1 Kings; each of these elements is a cultic variable.

2 Chronicles 29 include blood rituals, music, burnt offerings, prostration, supplication, and praise. Thanksgiving and well-being sacrifices traditionally eaten by priest and offerer are also noted,[14] though eating and drinking are neither described nor mentioned explicitly in any of the three accounts.

Neither does either of the two accounts of David's installation of the ark in Jerusalem (2 Sam 6:1–19 and 1 Chr 13:5–14, 15:1–16:3) mention eating and drinking explicitly. In both accounts, David's first attempt to bring up the ark is accompanied by dancing and music but no sacrifice or food. This attempt ends in disaster when Uzzah reaches out to stabilize the ark as it threatens to topple. The second, successful, attempt in both accounts adds to rejoicing the element of sacrifice and food distribution to the people,[15] although the text does not refer specifically to eating and drinking, and it is unclear whether the food is to

---

14. The sacrificial term שלמים is translated here as 'well-being', along with Jacob Milgrom, who notes that in Leviticus, "the well-being offering is brought solely out of joyous motivations: thanksgiving, vow fulfillment, or spontaneous free-will (7:11–17)" (*Leviticus 1–16*, 49). The exact definition of the Hebrew term is a matter of dispute. These sacrifices are taken by some scholars to be greeting or peace offerings, as they may be interpreted on the basis of Ugaritic usage. See Baruch A. Levine, *In the Presence of The Lord: A Study of Cult and Some Cultic Terms in Ancient Israel* (SJLA 5; Leiden: Brill, 1974) 1–52. On the understanding of זבח as always involving an eating and drinking event, Jacob Milgrom has said in a private communication that wherever the term זבח is used in the Hebrew Bible, "it is safe to assume" that eating and drinking take place. This term denotes a well-being sacrifice, or שלמים, in the eating of which the offerer and his guests participate. See, for example, Leviticus 3 and 2 Chr 30:22, which will be discussed in greater depth in chapter 4. L. Koehler and W. Baumgartner (p. 262) note that the noun זבח connotes a communal sacrifice.

15. The account in 1 Chronicles focuses on the contribution made by sanctified priests and Levites to the second, successful attempt. 1 Chronicles also elaborates on the musical elements of the celebration performed by Levites, listing the names of the players and their instruments (15:16–24). For an examination of the differences in the roles of the Levites in 1 Chronicles 15–16 compared with the parallel account in 2 Samuel 6, see Paul D. Hanson, "1 Chronicles 15–16 and the Chronicler's Views on the Levites," in *"Sha'arei Talmon": Studies in the Bible, Qumran, and the Ancient Near East Presented to Shemaryahu Talmon* (ed. Michael Fishbane, Emanuel Tov, and Weston W. Fields; Winona Lake, Ind.: Eisenbrauns, 1992) 69–91.

The sacrificial element in 1 Chronicles is more subdued than in 2 Samuel, where sacrifices of an ox and a fatling are offered every six paces (2 Sam 6:13); in 1 Chronicles, the Levites bearing the ark, grateful for the safe completion of their task, sacrifice seven bulls and seven rams (1 Chr 15:26). The Qumran scroll 4QSamuel[a] seems to harmonize both traditions, noting there that seven oxen and seven rams are sacrificed every six paces.

be eaten at the public event or taken home to be consumed (2 Sam 6:19, 1 Chr 16:3).

Still, eating and drinking are significant variables of CULT; many cultic directives do concern what may and may not be eaten and drunk, when and where.[16] In addition to the Passover commands of Exod 12:1–28, also included in this category are the cultic commands in Num 15:17–21 regarding the setting aside as an allocation to God of חלה, first yield of baking, and בכורים, first yield of produce in Exod 23:19. Both of these commands, like those concerning future Passover rituals, are to take effect once the Israelites have reached the promised land and participated in its divinely granted bounty. Each of these texts exhibits the morphology of CULT, divine promise (Israelites dwelling in the fruitful land, implicit in the context) followed by divine command (involving first yields of the land's bounty). In CULTIC contexts, eating and drinking occur often, two among many other variables within the constant function of CULTIC COMMANDS and RITUALS.

"Direction" in Cultic Contexts.   Above, I discussed the idea of "direction" in reading both variables and constants within the Proppian framework. I noted that both constants and variables may occur in direct or reverse forms and that reversal may refer either to the negation of the direct element or to an element operating contrary to the usual or expected manner. Cultic contexts are a rich source of supporting illustrations.

The constant element itself may be reversed—in this case, the CULTIC function. The direct function of CULT is divinely commanded Israelite practice, with reversal a deviation from this paradigm. Thus, a reversal of orthodox Israelite cultic practice might be a pagan festival, as with Samson in the Temple of Dagon (Judg 16:23–31),[17] or an episode of apostasy, as with the golden calf at Sinai (Exodus 32) or at Baal Peor (Numbers 25).

Eating and drinking occur as variables in cases of cultic reversals as they do in cultic contexts that are direct. Eating and drinking are explicitly mentioned among other festive activities—notably, sexual impropriety suggested by the Hebrew root צחק surrounding the reverse

---

16. The listing of clean and unclean foods in Leviticus 11 does not occur in a strictly narrative setting, but it certainly represents an example of eating and drinking in association with cultic commands.

17. This single reversal of cult is just one of many anomalies in the Samson story; for an outstanding examination of the reversals, inversions, allusions, paradoxes and riddles, and multiple levels in the story of Samson, see Edward L. Greenstein, "The Riddle of Samson," *Prooftexts* 1/3 (1981) 237–60.

cultic event of worship of the golden calf (Exod 32:6).[18] At Baal Peor, another reverse cultic event, no eating or drinking is mentioned at all in the account in Num 25:1 and 8, and only sexual impropriety (צחק) is adduced. In the retelling of the Baal Peor episode in Ps 106:28–29, cultically improper (hence reversed) eating and drinking is the indictment on that occasion; sexual impropriety and the root צחק are completely absent.[19] Thus, eating and drinking occur among a range of variables in biblical contexts where the constant function of Cult is reversed. In interpreting such texts, clearly, cultic direction is germane to any reading, whatever the nature of the variables that fill the variable slots.

Reversal as Refusal to Eat. Variables as well as constants may occur in both direct and reverse configurations. An example of reversal of the variable within a direct cultic context occurs in Leviticus 10.[20] In this case, an expected ritual meal is not eaten. In the aftermath of the deaths of Nadab and Abihu, Aaron makes a burnt offering out of the cultically prescribed priestly offering that he and his fellow priests are meant to eat (10:16–20). When Moses challenges him, Aaron gives the reason that he was wary, in the aftermath of the day's disaster, of making an unintentional error and so took what he perceived to be the safer course of making a burnt offering to God out of the priestly repast. This surface reading is sufficient, but dimen-

---

18. For a discussion of the meaning of צחק in this passage, see Jack M. Sasson, "The Worship of the Golden Calf," in *Orient and Occident: Essays Presented to C. H. Gordon on the Occasion of His Sixty-Fifth Birthday* (AOAT 22; ed. H. A. Hoffner; Neukirchen-Vluyn: Neukirchener Verlag / Kevelaer: Butzon & Bercker, 1973) 151–59. Note that this root is also associated with the festivities in the Temple of Dagon in Judg 16:23–31, in another instance of cultic reversal, where Israel's God acts in an explicitly pagan cultic environment. For a discussion of the relationship between the destruction of the golden calf and the death of Mot in Ugaritic literature, see three related articles in Samuel E. Loewenstamm, *Comparative Studies in Biblical and Ancient Oriental Literatures* (AOAT 204; Neukirchen-Vluyn: Neukirchener Verlag / Kevelaer: Butzon & Bercker, 1980): "The Making and Destruction of the Golden Calf," 236–45; "The Killing of Mot in Ugaritic Myth," 426–32; and "The Making and Destruction of the Golden Calf: A Rejoinder," 503–16.

19. Ps 106:28 reads: ויצמדו לבעל פעור ויאכלו זבחי מתים 'and they joined to Baal Peor and ate the sacrifices of (to? for?) the dead'. For a fuller discussion of directionality as it affects the reading of a text on the structural as well as on the surface level, see the discussion below of the golden calf episode of Exod 32:6 as part of my examination of covenant.

20. For an expanded discussion of this example and others, see my forthcoming article "When Fathers Refuse to Eat: The Trope of Rejecting Food and Drink in Biblical Narrative," *Semeia* 86 (2001) 135–48, edited by Athalya Brenner.

sions may be added to our understanding of this text by focusing for a moment on the direction of the eating and drinking event and reading the reversal, Aaron's abstention from a cultic meal, in light of other such abstentions in the Hebrew Bible.[21]

Three other instances of cultic meals refused are Hannah's abstention from the family sacrifice during the pilgrimage festivals (1 Sam 1:1–8);[22] David's abstention from Saul's table during the Feast of the New Moon (1 Sam 20:5–7, 24–29); and Jonathan's abstention from eating during the same event (1 Sam 20:34). In each case, the person holding back from participation is doing so in a distressed state of mind: Hannah is brought to tears by Peninah's nasty teasing about her barrenness; David feels persecuted by his king; and Jonathan storms away from the feast in a rage after a murderous attack by Saul.

Aaron is likewise in a distressed state of mind: his sons have just been consumed by the God he serves, and he has been prohibited from expressing his grief (Lev 10:6–7). Aaron, who must sublimate his personal feelings so as not to desecrate the seven-day consecration, is silent.[23] He does express his intense distress nonetheless in his tersely

---

21. See Michael Fishbane, *Text and Texture: Close Readings of Selected Biblical Texts* (New York: Schocken, 1979) xii, 12, and passim, where he defines this approach to reading texts as "intertextual." Among other modern studies of biblical texts applying an intertextual approach, see Daniel Boyarin, "Old Wine in New Bottles: Intertextuality and Midrash," *Poetics Today* 8 (1987) 539–56; H. Cazelles, "Connexions et structure de Gen XV," *RB* 69 (1962) 321–49; J. Cheryl Exum and David J. A. Clines (eds.), *The New Literary Criticism and the Hebrew Bible* (Sheffield: Sheffield Academic Press, 1993); Danna Nolan Fewell (ed.), *Reading between Texts: Intertextuality and the Hebrew Bible* (Literary Currents in Biblical Interpretation; Louisville: Westminster John Knox, 1992); Michael Fishbane, *Biblical Interpretation in Ancient Israel* (Oxford: Oxford University Press, 1985); Geoffrey H. Hartman and Sanford Budick (eds.), *Midrash and Literature* (New Haven: Yale University Press, 1986); Jacob Neusner, "Intertextuality in Judaism: The System and the Canon, the Word and Words," *Conservative Judaism* 45 (1992) 53–66; and George Savran, *Telling and Retelling: Quotation in Biblical Narrative* (Indiana Studies in Biblical Literature; Bloomington: Indiana University Press, 1988). This literary approach is important to our approach to interpretations, and other works on intertextuality will be cited throughout this work.

22. The Hebrew syntax of this section describes an ongoing or repeated event: they would go up to worship, Peninah would afflict Hannah, Hannah would cry and not eat. The transition to the occasion that is the focus of the story in 1 Sam 1:9 does not state explicitly that Hannah again abstained from this ritual meal, but the notation in 1:18b that she left (Eli's presence) and ate implies that she had not done so before but, her heart eased by the old priest's blessing, she does so now.

23. This is the traditional interpretation of the verbal root דמם in the Hebrew text of 10:3. For an alternate suggestion, see Baruch A. Levine, "Silence, Sound, and the Phenomenology of Mourning in Biblical Israel," *JNES* 22 (1993) 89–106.

reported gesture: he abstains from the meal, even the ritually important, divinely commanded cultic meal of priestly consecration. His gesture is twofold: he does not eat, and he also chooses not to share a
meal with the God whose fire consumed his sons.[24]

The ancient idea that sacrifice is a meal for the deity resonates in
Num 28:2: צו את־בני ישראל ואמרת אלהם את־קרבני לחמי לאשי ריח ניחחי
תשמרו להקריב לי במועדו 'Command the Children of Israel and say to
them, "My offerings, the food (לחם) for my fire-offerings, my pleasing
aromas, take care to offer to me in the appointed time"'. A sacrifice
such as the חטאת prescribed in Leviticus 10, in which part of an offering is eaten by the priest and part is reserved for the deity, may thus be
said in some sense to be a meal "shared" by the priest with the deity.
An עלה, or burnt offering, the sacrifice actually offered by Aaron, is
completely consumed by fire and thus devoted entirely to God and not
shared at all by the human participant(s).

Aaron's emotions legitimately may be imagined also to reflect those
of Hannah, David, and Jonathan in their respective instances: bereavement over missing progeny; wariness in the face of subversion by a
trusted sovereign; rage at the treachery of a beloved guardian. Reading this reversal of variable in terms of other similar reversals thus may
add poignant dimensions to the spare characterization of Aaron in
this text.

In narratives exhibiting cultic contexts, eating and drinking occur
frequently, operating as variables within the constant function of
CULT. This constant is defined by the morphology of a divine promise
that may be explicit or implied in context, followed by divine command that often incorporates one or more cultic rituals. This morphological relationship holds true whatever the direction of the constant
or the variable. The essential morphology of the constant CULT is divine promise followed by divine command. Both promise and command may take many forms; eating and drinking are only two among
many possible variables.

---

24. For the ancient idea underlying sacrifice in the Near East, namely, that the
offering is a meal for the divinity, see, for example, A. L. Oppenheim, *Ancient Mesopotamia: Portrait of a Dead Civilization* (Chicago: University of Chicago Press, 1964);
see especially the section entitled "Care and Feeding of the Gods," 183–98; G. van
Driel, *The Cult of Assur* (Assen: Van Gorcum, 1969), especially pp. 159–62; William
W. Hallo, "The Origins of the Sacrificial Cult: New Evidence from Mesopotamia
and Israel," in *Ancient Israelite Religion: Essays in Honor of Frank Moore Cross* (ed. P. D.
Miller, P. D. Hanson, and S. D. McBride; Philadelphia: Fortress, 1987) 3–14; and
idem, "Cult Statue and Divine Image: A Preliminary Study," in *Scripture in Context
II: More Essays on the Comparative Method* (ed. W. W. Hallo, J. C. Moyer, and L. G.
Perdue; Winona Lake, Ind.: Eisenbrauns, 1983) 1–18.

Miracle

MIRACLE, like CULT, is a constant that may include eating and drinking as variables but need not. A thorough treatment of MIRACLE in the Hebrew Bible is far beyond the scope of this study,[25] but an examination of miracle texts in which eating and drinking occur reveals some insights into the constant function of MIRACLE. Earlier, I noted that MIRACLES in the Hebrew Bible involve, among other variables, miraculous escape, miraculous guidance, and miraculous appearance or disappearance, along with miraculous eating and drinking and the corollary variable, miraculous food and drink. Thus, the nature or content of the constant function MIRACLE is diverse, and eating and drinking are but two of its variables.

The Constant Function of Miracle. In every case, MIRACLE serves a constant function of divine (re)assurance, with the variable content slot of MIRACLE filled sometimes by eating and drinking (or elements of food and drink) and sometimes not.[26] Sometimes the divine reassurance is aimed at a single individual, as when Elijah or Samson is reassured by divine providence of God's continued protection. Sometimes it is for the benefit of a group, as when Israel is shown God's grace, and sometimes for the benefit of individuals, as when the authority of Moses and Aaron is upheld by means of a variety of miraculous special effects in Numbers 16 and 17. In the narrative account of the plagues and the Exodus, epitome of the divine miraculous, we are told explicitly that signs and wonders will be displayed precisely in order to demonstrate God's guardian presence to the faithful and God's punitive potency to the unbelieving (Exod 7:3–5, 10:1–2, 14:4), and that they were in fact successful in this purpose (Exod 14:31).

The morphological pattern of MIRACLE appears to consist of the elements of CHALLENGE, miraculous REASSURANCE, and AFFIRMATION. The constant function of MIRACLE seems to be an especially dramatic reassurance by God to friend and foe alike: "I AM HERE."[27]

---

25. See, for example, Heda Jason's suggestive categorization of the miraculous "mode" as a category of tale in *Ethnopoetry: Form, Content, Function* (Forum Theologiae Linguisticae 11; Bonn: Linguistica Biblica, 1977) 4–20. See also Yair Zakovitch, *The Concept of the Miracle in the Bible* (trans. Shmuel Himelstein; Tel Aviv: MOD, 1990).

26. See ibid., 130 and passim, where Zakovitch emphasizes that the function of miracle in the Bible is to arouse faith.

27. See especially Edward L. Greenstein's comment on Exod 3:14, on p. 83 of "Exodus," in *The Harper Collins Study Bible* (ed. Wayne A. Meeks; New York: Harper Collins, 1993) 77–150.

Eating and Drinking as Variables of Miracle.   There are sixteen biblical texts in which the constant of MIRACULOUS REASSURANCE is filled by the variables of eating and drinking.

Twice Hagar is vouchsafed miraculous water in the wilderness, in Gen 16:6–15 and again in 21:17–20. When she raises her eyes and beholds the first miraculous well, Hagar is reassured that the divine promise regarding her son will be fulfilled, which it is. The text includes an etiology, as she names the well after the God who saved her. A similar pattern occurs in the second text, although the etiology is absent. Similarly, Samson calls upon God as he is dying of thirst in Judg 15:18–19 and is graced by the appearance of a miraculous well at En-hakkore.[28] A place-name etiology is associated with this watery epiphany, as it is with Hagar's. Eating and drinking as variables of ETIOLOGIES are discussed in greater detail later in this chapter.

The Children of Israel are the beneficiaries of miraculous water in the wilderness on several occasions, each associated with a place-name etiology: at Marah (Exod 15:22–26), at Massah and Meribah in Rephidim (Exod 17:1–7), and again at Meribah in Kadesh (Num 20:2–13). The Bible also contains two accounts of the provision of miraculous manna and quail, one in Exodus 16 and the other in Numbers 11. In both cases the food is divinely provided at the request of the Children of Israel, and in both cases the people are adjured to have faith in God's providence. Ps 78:15–31, a poetic recapitulation of this miracle of food from heaven, emphasizes the issue of stubborn Israelite skepticism in spite of overwhelming evidence of divine faithfulness. In Numbers 11, their punishment for this lack of faith is immortalized in a

---

28. For a discussion and analysis of the correspondences between this incident about Samson and the incident about miraculous water in the wilderness for the Israelites, see pp. 251–52 of Greenstein, "The Riddle of Samson." In this text, as in the wilderness texts discussed next, a pattern recognized by Propp and Dundes applies, which, in its simplest form, consists of the functions of LACK and LACK LIQUIDATED. See, for example, Propp, *Morphology*, 34–35 and passim; and Alan Dundes, *Morphology of North American Indian Folktales* (Folklore Fellows Communications 195; Helsinki: Suomalainen Tiedeakatemia / Academia Scientiarum Fennica, 1964) passim. A complete story may be recognized and defined by the bracketing of these paired functions. The same is true of the pattern defined by INTERDICTION, INTERDICTION VIOLATED, and PUNISHMENT, sometimes followed by AMELIORATION of punishment, which underlies so much of biblical narrative, including the murmuring motifs discussed just below, and may even be said in many ways to be the macropattern for Israelite history in the land of promise. See Propp, *Morphology*, 26–28 and passim. Unfortunately, I cannot give these patterns the comprehensive treatment they deserve. Here I can only acknowledge the existence of these patterns in the Hebrew Bible.

place-name etiology. The patterns of these stories are so similar, whether they have to do with lack of food and water in the wilderness or with some other complaint, that they have been recognized as constituting a genre alliteratively termed "the murmuring motif."[29]

Miracles punctuate the careers of the prophets Elijah and Elisha. One of the earliest appearances of Elijah in the biblical text concerns his communication of an ORACLE to Ahab of an impending drought, divinely decreed as a scourge for Ahab's faithlessness.[30] The prophet is forced to flee for his life to the remote wilderness after delivering his imprecation, and divine protection for the prophet is manifest as Elijah is miraculously fed by ravens, though he is watered by a naturally occurring wadi in the vicinity. The language of this text speaks of bread and meat morning and evening (1 Kgs 17:6): וְהָעֹרְבִים מְבִיאִים לוֹ לֶחֶם וּבָשָׂר בַּבֹּקֶר וְלֶחֶם וּבָשָׂר בָּעֶרֶב וּמִן־הַנַּחַל יִשְׁתֶּה 'The ravens would bring him bread and meat in the morning and bread and meat in the evening, and from the brook he would drink'. This allusion is reminiscent of the reference in Exod 16:8 to meat at night and bread in the morning, בָּעֶרֶב בָּשָׂר לֶאֱכֹל וְלֶחֶם בַּבֹּקֶר לִשְׂבֹּעַ 'In the evening meat to eat, and bread in the morning to satiety', echoed in 16:12: בֵּין הָעַרְבַּיִם תֹּאכְלוּ בָשָׂר וּבַבֹּקֶר תִּשְׂבְּעוּ־לָחֶם 'At twilight you shall eat bread and in the morning you shall be replete with bread'.

---

29. For just a brief sampling of the many resources available on this topic, see Shemaryahu Talmon, "The 'Desert Motif' in the Bible and in Qumran Literature," in *Biblical Motifs: Origins and Transformations* (ed. A. Altmann; Cambridge: Harvard University Press, 1966) 31–64, repr. in Talmon, *Literary Studies in the Hebrew Bible: Form and Content* (Jerusalem: Magnes / Leiden: Brill, 1993) 216–54; George W. Coats, *Rebellion in the Wilderness: The Murmuring Motif in the Wilderness Traditions of the Old Testament* (Nashville: Abingdon, 1968); Robert C. Culley, *Studies in the Structure of Hebrew Narrative* (Philadelphia: Fortress / Atlanta: Scholars Press, 1976) 83–87, 101–6; W. H. Propp, *Water in the Wilderness: A Biblical Motif and Its Mythological Background* (HSM 40; Atlanta: Scholars Press, 1987); Mary Douglas, *In the Wilderness: The Doctrine of Defilement in the Book of Numbers* (JSOTSup 158; Sheffield: Sheffield Academic Press, 1993) 130–32 and 246–47.

30. This complex text is discussed here only in terms of the miraculous food supplied to Elijah after his flight. However, it must be noted that three LACKs are present in the text and are LIQUIDATED in three Proppian "moves": (1) Lack of rain is the first, the prediction of which precipitates Elijah's flight/PILGRIMAGE. This LACK is not LIQUIDATED until 1 Kings 18, and so technically the "move" or episode is not completed until then. (2) Lack of water is second, when the wadi dries up, precipitating another PILGRIMAGE for Elijah, this time to the widow of Zarephath. This LACK is LIQUIDATED in his initial encounter with her. (3) Her lack of sufficient food for her family and Elijah is miraculously LIQUIDATED and confirmed in 17:13–16.

Later, when the wadi dries up because of the severity of the drought, Elijah is directed to a widow in Zarephath who will feed him. When Elijah discovers that she, too, is a victim of the drought and is down to the last of her flour and oil, he works a miracle in God's name and assures the widow that God will provide flour and oil for her, her son, and Elijah until rain breaks the drought (1 Kgs 17:12–16). When the widow's son falls ill and dies, Elijah reproaches God for repaying the woman's kindness with this calamity, and God responds by returning the boy's soul to his body (1 Kgs 17:17–24). The conclusion is a reassuring restoration of the widow's faith in Elijah and in his reliable transmission of the word of God (17:24). This series of miracle stories, exhibiting the morphology of CHALLENGE, miraculous REASSURANCE, and AFFIRMATION, attests to divine protection of Elijah, Elijah's ability to predict accurately what God has willed, and the prophet's ability to intercede successfully for human beings with God in matters great and small.

Elisha's career echoes Elijah's experience of the miraculous,[31] but more numerous and more varied miracles have come down to us concerning the disciple. Some of these concern eating and drinking, or at least food and water, as when Elisha provides the entire army of Israel with water while simultaneously tricking the army of Moab into jumping to deadly conclusions (2 Kgs 2:16–24) or when he heals a spring of tainted water by sprinkling salt upon it (2 Kgs 2:19–22) or heals a pot tainted by a poison gourd by sprinkling meal upon it (2 Kgs 4:38–44).

Some miracles consist of other variables besides eating and drinking, such as when Elisha, like Elijah, generates miraculous oil for a poor widow (2 Kgs 4:1–7). However, Elisha supplies not the makings of oil cakes, as Elijah does, but rather a capital-generating commodity for the poor widow to sell in the market. Later, Elisha rewards his benefactor, the otherwise anonymous woman of Shunem (2 Kgs 4:8–37), with the miraculous birth of a son. And, like Elijah, Elisha resurrects the woman's dead child after she reproaches him for his faithless dealing with her, in first granting her a son and then letting him perish.[32] The series of miracles in 2 Kings 2–4 establish Elisha as successor to Elijah. Initially, his miracles are private, for his own prophetic circle

---

31. See Kenneth R. R. Gros Louis, "Elijah and Elisha," in *Literary Interpretations of Biblical Narratives* (Nashville: Abingdon, 1974) 177–90; and Robert B. Coote (ed.), *Elijah and Elisha in Socioliterary Perspective* (Atlanta: Scholars Press, 1992).

32. This pattern of PROMISE/SKEPTICISM/PROMISE FULFILLED in the granting of a son is reminiscent of the situation in Genesis 18, Isaac's annunciation, perhaps even to the extent of a later miraculous rescue from death, with the Shunemite boy's death and resurrection parallel to Isaac's binding and release in Genesis 22.

(2 Kings 2); then Elisha establishes his public reputation, with the po-
litical/military miracles of 2 Kgs 3:9–27. The stories in 2 Kings 4 reca-
pitulate those in Elijah's career and may even "go the elder prophet
one better."

Eating and drinking are two among a wide range of variables that
may occur within the function of MIRACLE. Whatever the variable content, the function of MIRACLE is a constant: it is reassurance of divine
presence. Miracles appear to function either as a bolster to flagging
faith and waning morale or as a dire consequence for the absence of
proper faith or respect for God or for God's agent(s). These texts follow the morphology for MIRACLE: challenge, miraculous reassurance,
and affirmation.

Symbolic Action

The subject of symbolic actions has a long history of interpretation,
both homiletic and scholarly. Symbolic actions have been defined as
functioning magically (Fohrer), as an especially potent form of the "divine word,"[33] or emblematically (the rabbis), as foreshadowings of
what will actually come to pass.[34] I limit my examination of symbolic
actions to those that take place in the world of narrative reality, where
it is within the expectations set by the narrative that the action will
yield immediate effects within that narrative reality. I am not treating
actions occurring in a dream or vision,[35] nor those expressed as poetic
discourse or literary metaphor. In this discussion, I will first identify
the constant function of SYMBOLIC ACTION in the Hebrew Bible, and
then I will check whether eating and drinking occur as variable elements within that constant function.

The Constant Element of Symbolic Action.   I begin by defining *symbolic*
as that which "bridges two realities, bringing them into relationship

33. Georg Fohrer, *Die symbolischen Handlungen der Propheten* (Zurich: Zwingli,
1953), especially pp. 88–107, 121–24, and passim. See Isaac Rabinowitz, *A Witness
Forever: Ancient Israel's Perception of Literature and the Resultant Hebrew Bible* (ed.
R. Brann and D. I. Owen; Bethesda, Md.: CDL, 1993) 1–25.

34. See the comment of Nachmanides (רמב"ן) on Gen 12:6, where he articulates
the principle מעשי אבות סימן לבנים 'the deeds of the fathers are significant for their
children'. Nachmanides analogizes these deeds and their fulfillment to the symbolic actions of the prophets, which foreshadow the certain fulfillment of their oracles in the history of the people.

35. See Susan Niditch, *The Symbolic Vision in Biblical Tradition* (HSM 30; Chico,
Calif.: Scholars Press, 1980).

with one another."[36] A symbolic gesture is a visual representation "of that which is unseen and invisible."[37] As the numerous examples discussed throughout this section suggest, the act of implementing the symbolic gesture appears to concretize such abstract ideas as *relationship*, or *commitment*, as in symbolic actions enacted in the making of interpersonal or divine-human covenants; *omnipotence*, as in miracles initiated by symbolic actions; *judgment*, *providence*, or *redemption*, as when punishment, healing, sustenance, or salvation are initiated by the enactment of a symbolic gesture. The morphology of SYMBOLIC ACTION is generally that a COURSE OF ACTION IS DETERMINED, a SYMBOLIC ACTION IS ENACTED, after which the action is CONCLUDED or CONFIRMED.

Symbolic gestures may occur in interpersonal contexts or in human-divine interactions but, even when the context appears superficially to be civil or political, the enactment of the symbolic gesture invokes the presence of the divine in the situation at hand. For example, in the symbolic gestures enacted in the interpersonal covenants that I discuss later on in this section, a covenant is agreed upon, followed by a symbolic action through which divinity is invoked as witness and, if necessary, as judge against violators, even though the subject of the covenant may be the human concerns of a geographical boundary or ownership of a water source. The constant function of SYMBOLIC ACTION in the Hebrew Bible in every case where it occurs is to underscore dramatically the interplay between human action and divine actuation.

The literature on symbolic gesture is too extensive to review fully here, but I begin by discussing the occurrence of symbolic actions comprehensively in one important setting: covenant contexts in the Hebrew Bible.[38] I selected this area because the idea of a *covenant meal*

---

36. See J. A. Ross Mackenzie, "Symbol," *Harper's Bible Dictionary*, 1003–7.

37. V. H. Kooy, "Symbol, Symbolism," *IDB* 4.472.

38. The literature on covenant in general is voluminous. I note here only a selection of references that deal with the covenant meal. See W. T. McCree, "The Covenant Meal in the Old Testament," *JBL* 45 (1926) 120–28; J. Muilenburg, "The Form and Structure of the Covenantal Formulations," *VT* 9 (1959) 347–65; V. Korošec, "Les Hittites et leurs vassaux Syriens à la lumière des nouveaux textes d'Ugarit," *Revue Hittite et Asiatique* 66–67 (1960) 65–79; R. Martin-Achard, "La Nouvelle alliance selon Jérémie," *Revue de théologie et de philosophie* (1962) 81–92; C. F. Fensham, "The Wild Ass in the Aramaic Treaty between Bargaʾayah and Matiʿel," *JNES* 22 (1963) 185–86; D. J. McCarthy, "Hosea XII 2: Covenant by Oil," *VT* 14 (1964) 215–21; idem, "Three Covenants in Genesis," *CBQ* 26 (1964) 179–89; K. H. Deller, "Šwmn bll (Hosea 12,2): Additional Evidence," *Bib* 46 (1965) 349–52; E. Kutsch, " 'Bund' und Fest," *Theologische Quartalschrift* 150 (1970) 299–320; Moshe Weinfeld, "The Covenant of Grant in the Old Testament and in the Ancient Near East," *JAOS* 90 (1970) 184–203; idem, "Covenant Terminology in the Ancient Near

has long been a commonplace in biblical scholarship,[39] and the nature of that "meal" is an important topic in any exploration touching upon eating and drinking in the Hebrew Bible. My goal in this discussion is to explore whether eating and drinking—the "covenant meal"—are constant elements in covenant contexts, or whether they act instead as just two of many different variables that fill the "slot" of the constant element of SYMBOLIC ACTION. Following this investigation, I will examine cases of symbolic gestures that involve eating and drinking in settings other than covenants. Throughout, it will be evident that SYMBOLIC ACTIONS are constants, or functions, in many biblical contexts, although the contents of these symbolic gestures are rich in their variety.

Symbolic Actions as a Constant Element in Covenant Contexts.   Keeping in mind my definition of symbolic action as a bridge between human action and divine actuation, I begin to examine SYMBOLIC ACTION as a constant element in the making of covenants. The morphology of SYMBOLIC ACTION is only slightly modified in covenant contexts. In a covenant context, the constant element DETERMINATION OF A COURSE OF ACTION is filled by the content of the covenant. This is followed by the constant element of SYMBOLIC ACTION that in covenant contexts often includes an oath as part of this function. The CONCLUSION/CONFIRMATION constant is filled by the culmination of the covenant ceremony.

Interpersonal Covenants.   When Abraham makes a COVENANT with Abimelech in Gen 21:22–34, there are two SYMBOLIC GESTURES. In the first, Abraham gives sheep and oxen to Abimelech, and they "cut" a covenant with each other, ויכרתו שניהם ברית (Gen 21:27). The specifics of how this is done are absent from this text, but other contexts in the Bible and in ancient Near Eastern literature make it possible to conjecture that the animals are cut into pieces, and the covenanters pass between the pieces, thus swearing symbolically that they themselves shall be so cut up should the covenant be violated.[40] In a second symbolic

---

East and Its Influence on the West," *JAOS* 93 (1973) 190–99; Klaus Baltzer, *The Covenant Formulary in Old Testament, Jewish, and Early Christian Writings* (Philadelphia: Fortress, 1971).

39. See W. Robertson Smith (*The Religion of the Semites: The Fundamental Institutions* [original pub., 1889; New York: Meridian, Appleton, 1956] 300–302), who is extremely cautious in his discussion of the connection between Israelite covenant and sacrifice/communion; and McCree ("Covenant Meal," 120–28), who sees in every biblical meal a type of covenant.

40. Note the covenant between God and Abraham in Genesis 15, often referred to as the Covenant between the pieces, ברית בן הבתרים, and the reference in Jer 34:18. We note here among the earliest to point out the symbolic practice of cutting

act, Abraham sets apart seven ewe-lambs as a sign that he dug the well. In CONFIRMATION, a place-name etiology is extrapolated by the text from this gesture.

When Abraham and Abimelech are cutting this covenant, there is no shared meal or sacrifice. There is no eating or drinking in this covenant narrative. The constitutive acts of making this interpersonal covenant appear to be swearing an oath, here expressed via the verbal root שבע, accompanied by one or more symbolic actions.

In a later interpersonal pact, 1 Sam 18:3–4 reports laconically that Jonathan and David make a COVENANT with each other, an event that is alluded to in 1 Sam 20:8 and CONFIRMED in 1 Sam 20:14–17. In the first account, a SYMBOLIC ACTION immediately follows the cutting of the covenant (ויכרת יהונתן ודוד ברית, 18:3): Jonathan removes his cloak and tunic and gives them to David, along with his sword, bow, and belt. No swearing is mentioned here, though in 20:17 Jonathan is said to swear once again his loyalty to David (ויוסף יהונתן להשביע את־דוד באהבתו אתו), implying that loyalty had been sworn before.[41] Taking these accounts together, swearing an oath (שבע) plus symbolic action are both present with reference to this interpersonal covenant, though they are dispersed in separate references.

When Abraham adjures his servant to find a wife for Isaac among Abraham's kin (COVENANT, Gen 24:1–9), Abraham asks the servant to place his hand under Abraham's thigh and swear an oath (שבע, Gen 24:2–4), which the servant eventually does (Gen 24:9) before undertaking the mission. This SYMBOLIC GESTURE plus the oath-swearing constitute the symbolic actions representing the servant's commitment to Abraham's wishes. No eating or drinking accompanies this interpersonal covenant.

Other interpersonal covenants, on the other hand, do include eating and drinking events that appear to fall alongside of or in the same position as symbolic actions in the above-cited instances. Isaac's covenant with Abimelech in Gen 26:26–33 includes eating and drinking

---

up an animal in the making of a covenant: G. Mendenhall, "Puppy and Lettuce in Northwest Semitic Covenant Making," *BASOR* 133 (1954) 26–30; and Fensham, "The Wild Ass in the Aramaic Treaty," 185–86; and see the correctives of Moshe Held in his "Philological Notes on the Mari Covenant Rituals," *BASOR* 200 (1970) 32–40. See also Theodor H. Gaster, *Myth, Legend and Custom in the Old Testament: A Comparative Study with Chapters from Sir James G. Frazer's* Folklore in the Old Testament (New York: Harper & Row, 1969) 140–55.

41. On the technical use of the root אהב as 'loyalty' in treaty contexts, see William L. Moran, "The Ancient Near Eastern Background of the Love of God in Deuteronomy," *CBQ* 25 (1963) 77–87.

followed by swearing (שבע), with no other symbolic action; Jacob's covenant with Laban in Gen 31:43–46 includes two symbolic actions preceding the eating and drinking: the setting up of a pillar (מצבה) and of a mound of stones (גל).[42] This section of text is separated from the next by a place-name etiology (יגר שהדותא in Aramaic, גלעד in Hebrew, both meaning 'place of witness') and is followed by the formal designation of the pillar and stone heap as witnesses, by swearing an oath (שבע), then by sacrifice and another meal. The first meal may be a variable of symbolic action in a covenant context; the second may be a general meal, since Laban and his retinue spend the night with Jacob's family. In the morning, Laban blesses his children before the departure of his retinue.

Divine-Human Covenants.   Besides occurring in every interpersonal covenant, symbolic actions appear to be a part of every divine-human covenant in the Hebrew Bible as well. Again, the symbolic actions in these covenants sometimes involve eating and drinking but often do not. There is an absence of any eating and drinking event in Genesis 15, where the solemnization of the divine-human covenant binding God to Abraham is embodied by the smoking furnace, the תנור עשן, representing God, passing between the severed pieces (Gen 15:17–18).[43] This passage constitutes the symbolic gesture of covenant-binding; a meal does not appear to be required to seal the compact.

Another divine-human covenant, the covenant between God and Noah described in Gen 8:20–9:18, appears to exhibit two symbolic actions. The first of these consists of Noah's burnt offerings (עלת) to God when he disembarks from the ark. The second is God's placing of the divine bow in the heavens as a sign of God's promise never completely to destroy the earth again by flood. Instead of using the verb form שבע for swearing an oath, God uses the syntactic formula 'As for me, here I establish (מקים) my covenant with you' ואני הנני מקים את־בריתי אתכם

---

42. For a discussion of these interpersonal patriarchal covenants in light of treaty practices in the ancient Near East, see McCarthy, "Three Covenants in Genesis."

43. See Jer 34:18. It has been noted that in this text God is the party bound to the stipulations of the covenant, as the party (symbolically) moving between the cut halves. See, for example, E. A. Speiser, *Genesis* (AB 1; New York: Doubleday, 1963) 113–14; Nahum M. Sarna, *Genesis: The Traditional Hebrew Text with the New JPS Translation* (Philadelphia: Jewish Publication Society, 1989) 117; Loewenstamm, *Comparative Studies*, 273–80; and Yochanan Muffs, *Love and Joy: Law, Language and Religion in Ancient Israel* (New York: Jewish Theological Seminary of America, 1992) 135 n. 29.

(Gen 9:9). Although the burnt offering may be an allusion to a divine eating event, it is certainly not an explicit sacrificial meal shared by the bringer of the offering. The sacrifice is not structurally part of the covenant at all, since God does not determine to make the covenant until he smells the aroma of the offering.[44] The symbolic gesture associated with this covenant is the setting of God's bow in the heavens, an action that has nothing to do with eating or drinking.

Classical Covenants. The pacts between God and Noah and between God and Abraham are the only two divine-human covenants that occur before the covenant between God and Israel at Sinai. The Sinai covenant itself (Exod 24:1–8) is the paradigmatic covenant between God and the Children of Israel, and when covenant patterns are discussed in biblical scholarship, this classical covenant is the reference.[45] Among the symbolic actions represented in the Sinai covenant are the writing of the scroll, the offering of sacrifices, public eating and drinking, public reading of the scroll on which the terms of the covenant are inscribed, and the sprinkling of blood from the sacrifices (Exod 24:4–8).

Only two other covenant accounts in the Hebrew Bible include a sacrificial meal among the symbolic actions, and both of these appear to be modeled on the Sinai covenant in establishing a commitment between God and the Children of Israel. Asa's covenant in 2 Chr 15:9–15 evokes the pattern of Moses at Sinai. Asa assembles the people in Jerusalem, where they offer many sacrifices of oxen and sheep and enter into a covenant to seek the God of their ancestors with all their heart and spirit. Any who do not comply are to be put to death. The covenant concludes with the people's swearing to God in a great voice and with a great noise of trumpets and rams' horns. The symbolic actions here are the offering (זבח), the swearing (שבע), and the great noise (בקול גדול ובתרועה).

---

44. See a further discussion of the morphological function of the EATING and DRINKING allusions of Noah's sacrifice in chapter 5 below.

45. See A. H. J. Gunneweg, "Sinaibund und Davidsbund," *VT* 10 (1960) 335–41; W. Zimmerli, "Sinaibund und Abrahambund: Ein Beitrag zum Verständnis der Priesterschrift," *TZ* 16 (1960) 268–80; H. B. Huffmon, "The Exodus, Sinai and the Credo," *CBQ* 27 (1965) 101–15; H. Cazelles, "Alliance du Sinai, alliance de l'Horeb et renouvellement de l'alliance," in *Beiträge zur Alttestamentichen Theologie: Festschrift für Walther Zimmerli zum 70. Geburtstag* (ed. H. Donner, R. Hanhart, and R. Smend; Göttingen: Vandenhoeck & Ruprecht, 1977) 69–79; Eduard Nielsen, "Moses and the Law," *VT* 32 (1982) 87–98; Norbert Lohfink, "Poverty in the Laws of the Ancient Near East and of the Bible," *TS* 52 (1991) 34–50.

When the Israelites gather at Gilgal in Joshua 5 upon their entry into the land of promise, the symbolic actions consist of circumcision and a sacrificial meal, the Paschal sacrifice. Joshua has been equated with Moses from the time of his designation as Moses' successor in Numbers 27 and Deuteronomy 31, and the events of Joshua 1–5 reinforce this equation.[46] In Joshua 5, Abraham is added to Joshua's spiritual predecessors: the covenanting event described in this chapter evokes God's pact with the patriarch as well as the events at Sinai. God's covenant with Abraham (Genesis 15) is invoked in the sign of that covenant (Genesis 17), the act of circumcision that here precedes the making of the Paschal sacrifice (Josh 5:2–9).

Upon their circumcision, the Israelites enter into the covenant of Abraham; upon their eating of the Paschal sacrifice in Josh 5:10, the divine promise to Abraham, reiterated at Sinai, is redeemed: to bring the people into the promised land. The circumcision is the symbolic action, as they enter the land of promise, that links Abraham's descendants to the divine promise made to Abraham in Genesis 15. The Paschal sacrifice is the symbolic action that links the events at Gilgal with the Exodus and the Sinai covenant of Exod 24:1–8. The sign that this is so is the cessation of manna, the wilderness food of the people, the day after the Paschal sacrifice when the Children of Israel eat the produce of the promised land (Josh 5:11–12). This cessation demonstrates that the people are no longer wilderness wanderers but have been delivered to the land of promise and are able to sustain themselves on its produce. The promise made to Abraham and reiterated at Sinai has been realized: God has fulfilled the role of divine redeemer and deliverer; the people must now keep their part of the covenant.

Classical Covenant Reversed.   Exodus 32, the episode of the golden calf, is clearly a cultic reversal. Because of the smashing of the tablets, it may also be interpreted as a reversal of the covenant between Israel and God that was just made at Sinai. This reading is reinforced on the structural level: the expected classical covenant-making sequence of assembly followed by symbolic action is reversed in this text.

---

46. Many of the actions and miracles associated with Joshua are evocative of the leadership of Moses. Joshua, like Moses (Num 13:17), sends spies into enemy territory (Josh 2:1), and both lead the people over a body of water that divides miraculously to reveal dry land, Moses at the Reed Sea (Exod 14:16–18) and Joshua at the Jordan (Josh 4:23–24). The leadership equation between Moses and Joshua is made explicit in Josh 4:14: "On that day YHWH exalted Joshua in the sight of all Israel, and they stood in awe of him, as they had stood in awe of Moses, all the days of his life."

The narrative begins with cultically reversed sacrifices, eating and drinking, and other activities, and Moses' symbolic actions of smashing the covenant tablets (Exod 32:19), pulverizing the cultic image, strewing it on water, and giving it to the people to drink (Exod 32:20).[47] These symbolic actions are followed by the assembly of the Levites, who are summoned to punish the transgressors. The classical covenant-making sequence of assembly / symbolic action is reversed here to symbolic action / assembly. The narrative of the golden calf thus encodes within the very structure of the text the undoing of the covenant expressed in the narrative by the symbolic action of Moses' smashing the tablets of the covenant.

Covenant Renewals.   Symbolic actions also appear consistently in a group of texts that may be classified as covenant renewals but with a significant difference in the nature of the symbolic actions represented. Among the texts in this group are the accounts of the second set of tablets secured by Moses in Exodus 34, the covenant renewal at Shechem in Josh 24:1–28, and Josiah's covenant as it is recorded in parallel accounts in 2 Kgs 23:1–3 and 2 Chr 34:29–32. These covenant renewal narratives share in common that in every case at least one of the symbolic actions consists of the reading aloud of a covenant that already exists. This act of reading may be preceded by some expression of repentance or supplication on the part of the people or the leaders and may be followed by the acceptance and recording of the recommitment to the covenant.

Other symbolic actions may also be included. In Josh 24:26–27, for example, in addition to reading the covenant aloud, Joshua, like Moses, writes the covenant on a scroll and, like Jacob, he sets up a great stone of witness. But whether or not reading occurs alone or in combination with other symbolic actions, any references to eating or drinking are absent from each of these covenant renewal narratives. Only the public reading of the covenant commitment appears in these texts. This is in contrast to the sacrifices and public eating and drinking that are frequent variables of the Sinai-type covenant.

Postexilic "New" Covenant.   The sole postexilic covenant in the Hebrew Bible, in Neh 8:1–12, differs from both the Sinai pattern and the

---

47. See the parallel Ugaritic accounts of Anat's destruction of Mot, CTA 6:II:30–37 and CTA 6:V:12–15; and the discussion in Loewenstamm, *Comparative Studies*, 238–40, part of a larger discussion in that volume entitled "The Making and Destruction of the Golden Calf," 236–45, and two other related articles in that volume, "The Killing of Mot in Ugaritic Myth," 426–32, and "The Making and Destruction of the Golden Calf: A Rejoinder," 503–16.

covenant renewal pattern, while retaining some characteristics of each. This narrative exhibits the symbolic action of a public reading that is common to both the Sinai and covenant renewal texts. However, unlike the other covenant renewals, this covenant account does exhibit an eating and drinking event, although this is not the sacrificial meal of the Sinai pattern. In this text, the public sacrificial meal of the Sinai covenant is transformed into a private meal at the homes of individual families following the dispersal of the assembly (Neh 8:10–12). No reference to any sacrificial offering occurs in this account. The public gathering of the people, the public reading, and the dispersal to private meals in individual households may be a pattern for a new covenant, a postexilic compact that stands firmly in the tradition of earlier covenants but that signals its difference through transformations in the nature of the eating and drinking variable associated with it.[48]

One or more symbolic actions appear to be necessary to the sequence making up a covenant pattern, based on the evidence of these examples of interpersonal, human-divine, and renewal covenants. However, the variables of eating and drinking do not occur in every covenant situation; a "covenant meal" is not a required component of the covenant sequence. Once a covenant is proposed, a verbal response such as swearing an oath by the other party does not always follow; it appears that one sign of acceptance of a covenant may be the immediate taking of a symbolic action: making a sacrificial feast, piling up stones, setting up a pillar, exchanging a sheep, or the like. Symbolic action is therefore a constant function in covenant narratives, and eating and drinking appear to be two of many different variables that may be included in the category of symbolic actions.

Eating and Drinking as a Variable of Symbolic Action. Eating and drinking are just two variables of symbolic action within covenant contexts. Symbolic actions are associated with many other contexts as well, and eating and drinking are variables that may occur in these other situations, just as they do within covenant contexts.[49] In this section, I examine all cases of symbolic action, whether covenantal or not, where eating and drinking are the variables, and selected examples of SYMBOLIC ACTIONS that contain other variables.

---

48. This pattern is very similar to that of modern synagogue worship, where public assembly to hear the reading of the Torah is followed by dispersal to individual households for a private meal.

49. For a comparative treatment of gesture in ancient Near Eastern literature, see Mayer Irwin Gruber, *Aspects of Non-verbal Communication in the Ancient Near East* (Studia Pohl 12; Rome: Pontifical Biblical Institute, 1980).

Symbolic actions figure heavily in cultic ritual. Some have nothing to do with eating and drinking: blood is sprinkled, oil is poured, people and objects are bathed in water. Some do involve eating and drinking: food and drink offerings are heaved or waved or poured or burned.

Symbolic actions often initiate miracles. This is so whether or not the miracle concerns eating and drinking. Among the symbolic actions in which no eating or drinking is involved are several of the plagues that are initiated following symbolic gestures on the part of Moses or Aaron: Aaron's rod smites the water of the Nile, turning it to blood (Exod 7:20); the same rod stretched out over the fresh waters of Egypt is followed by the plague of frogs (Exod 8:2); Moses and Aaron sprinkle ashes toward heaven, followed by the plague of boils (Exod 9:10); Moses' rod stretched toward heaven heralds the plague of hail (Exod 9:23); divine protection is invoked when blood is smeared on Israelite doorposts on the night of the tenth plague (Exod 12:7); and so forth.

Keeping in mind the definition of symbolic action noted at the beginning of this section, we see that the symbolic actions that do concern eating or drinking invoke, as do all other symbolic actions, the implicit participation of God in the action of the human agent. The bridge between the human and divine in the transmutation of the toxic into the sustaining is often expressed as the gesture of a prophet of the Lord, often employing in his gesture objects or elements associated with life and preservation. Moses sweetens the bitter waters at Marah by throwing a tree into the spring (Exod 15:22–26); Elisha heals bad water by sprinkling salt (2 Kgs 2:19–22);[50] Elisha neutralizes the poison gourd in the stew by sprinkling meal (2 Kgs 4:38–41).

Truth that is beyond the ken of the human community to determine is ascertained by the drinking of the potion in the ordeal of the suspected adulteress in Num 5:11–31.[51] Dissolved in the water of this potion is dust from God's holy sanctuary and ink from God's holy words.[52] These symbols of God's truth pass without harm through a

---

50. For a fascinating discussion of the symbolic values embodied in salt in biblical contexts, including that of preservation, see the structural analysis by Alan Aycock, "The Fate of Lot's Wife: Structural Mediation in Biblical Mythology," in *Structuralist Interpretations of Biblical Myth* (ed. E. Leach and D. A. Aycock; London: Cambridge University Press, 1983) 113–19.

51. See Tikva Frymer-Kensky, "The Strange Case of the Suspected Sotah (Numbers v 11–31)," *VT* 34 (1984) 11–26.

52. The act of dissolving powder in water to be drunk echoes Moses' actions in the episode of the golden calf in Exodus 32. Though the dust here is from the

woman who is innocent but with dire consequences for the woman
who has transgressed. God, represented by the symbols of divine habi-
tation and divine commandment, can find and reveal truth hidden
from mortal eyes, but the means for revealing that truth is symbolic action undertaken by human beings.

Certain life-cycle events are expressed in symbolic gestures, such as
spreading one's robe upon a woman as a symbol of espousal, whether
literally, as when Ruth exhorts Boaz to do so in Ruth 3:7–11, or metaphorically, as in the divine espousal of Jerusalem evoked in Ezek 16:8.

Symbolic actions are employed in the Hebrew Bible as striking illustrations of present or future conditions. The prophets especially ex-
ploit the dramatic power of the symbolic gesture. On the one hand,
Hosea is directed to choose his wife and name his children in a manner that illustrates Israel's transgression and her fate (Hosea 1–2); on
the other hand, Jeremiah is forbidden to take a wife or father children
for similar reasons (Jer 16:2), to dramatize the dire fate in store for the
wives and children of Judah. These symbolic acts do not involve eating
and drinking, although many others do. As with the variety of variables filling any constant, the function of SYMBOLIC ACTION in the biblical text is the same whatever the variable filling it: the symbolic
human gesture is a bridge to divine actuation.

Of all the prophetic books, the book of Ezekiel is most extravagant
in the number and nature of symbolic gestures. His call in Ezek 3:1–9
includes the symbolic eating of the word of God:[53] Ezekiel eats the
scroll as commanded by God, and he finds the word of God to be
sweet. The poignancy of this moment is counterpointed by the actual
message that the prophet will have to convey: bitter tidings of the fate
of Judah and the destruction of Jerusalem; and by the personal suf-
fering that the prophet will have to undergo: indignity (4:4–6, 9–17),
paralysis (3:25–27, 4:8),[54] and bereavement (24:16–18).[55] Eating and

---

sanctuary and therefore holy and the dust of the pulverized golden calf is worse
than profane, the symbolic gesture links the two.

53. For a literary treatment of Ezekiel, see Ellen F. Davis, *Swallowing the Scroll:
Textuality and the Dynamics of Discourse in Ezekiel's Prophecy* (Bible and Literature Series 21; Sheffield: Almond, 1989).

54. On the subject of Ezekiel's disabilities, see Stephen Garfinkel, "Another
Model for Ezekiel's Abnormalities," *JANES* 19 (1989) 39–50; and Moshe Greenberg, "On Ezekiel's Dumbness," *JBL* (1958) 101–5. Both of these studies rely on
comparative material from Akkadian literature to clarify the nature of Ezekiel's
impairment.

55. For a discussion and illustration of this phenomenon, termed by Wolfgang
Iser "advance retrospection" as it is applied in the Bible, see, most recently, Edward
L. Greenstein, "The Firstborn Plague and the Reading Process," in *Pomegranates and*

drinking participate in an even more dramatic gesture, when God commands Ezekiel to mix a dough of many grains and bake it in human excrement to illustrate the dire straits of Judah under siege (4:9–17). The beleaguered prophet, descendant of priests, begs to be excused from this ritually defiling act; God accedes, and the bread is to be baked in animal dung instead.

Many of Ezekiel's dramatic actions have nothing to do with eating and drinking. In Ezekiel 4, just before he is commanded to prepare the above-noted bread, the prophet is directed to perform an elaborate charade in which he inscribes a brick to represent Jerusalem and surrounds it with a siege model complete with fort, mound, and battering ram, with an iron pan to symbolize the obdurate nature of the siege.

In many prophetic writings, the boundaries blur between symbolic action and poetic metaphor.[56] The wickedness of the people and the rigor of the coming punishment, for example, are expressed in metaphors that are as dramatic as are gestures. In 24:1–13, Ezekiel is commanded to tell the rebellious people a detailed parable (מָשָׁל) involving the image of a stewpot. The prophet is to describe setting a pot (on a fire), pouring in water, filling it with choice bones of the flock, the shoulder and thigh, and letting it burn and boil dry. Ultimately, the pot is to be heated until the polluted scum from the cooking is melted in it, symbolizing the impossibility of purging Israel's wickedness. This parable is as vivid as any symbolic action performed by the prophet, but as a visionary metaphor it falls outside of the definition of symbolic action that I specified at the beginning of this section.

Also excluded by this definition are many other graphic images related to food and drink abundant in prophetic literature: Jeremiah speaks of two baskets of figs, one fine and one too rotten to contemplate eating (Jer 24:3); the cup of wrath drunk to the dregs is almost a commonplace of prophetic discourse (Jer 25:15–17, among many

---

Golden Bells: Studies in Biblical, Jewish, and Near Eastern Ritual, Law, and Literature in Honor of Jacob Milgrom (ed. D. P. Wright, D. N. Freedman, and A. Hurvitz; Winona Lake, Ind.: Eisenbrauns, 1995) 555–68. Note there in n. 1 Greenstein's difference with Iser and alliance with Stanley Fish's criticism of Iser, cited with appropriate references.

56. Several comparative studies have been done touching upon the uses of metaphoric gesture and figurative language in a variety of written genres, beginning with the classic by Yochanan Muffs, *Studies in the Aramaic Legal Papyri from Elephantine* (Leiden: Brill, 1969); and the supplementary essays in idem, *Love and Joy: Law, Language and Religion in Ancient Israel*. See also M. Mindlin, M. J. Geller, and J. E. Wansbrough (eds.), *Figurative Language in the Ancient Near East* (London: University of London, 1987).

other instances). The variety and richness of the content of these devices demonstrates that eating and drinking are two of many possible
variables occupying the content slot of poetic metaphor. A morphological analysis of symbolic action in poetic metaphor and prophetic
rhetoric is beyond the scope of this study, which is limited to narrative; but even from this brief glance, it is clear that such an examination promises fruitful results.

Dream

In the Hebrew Bible, DREAM exhibits but one constant function: it is
an expression of divine intent. Sometimes this expression is sought,
and sometimes it is not; sometimes it is expressed in a manner that requires interpretation, and sometimes it is fully understood by the
dreamer. The basic morphology associated with the category of DREAM
consists of three elements: a statement of CIRCUMSTANCES, the DREAM
itself, and a REACTION to the dream. The CIRCUMSTANCES may be drawn
tersely or elaborately; the DREAM may be reported in great detail and
repeated or only referred to in passing; the REACTION may be that of
the dreamer or the audience and may be explicitly stated or inferred
from subsequent action. The contents of each of the constant categories within the function of DREAM are as varied and multifarious in biblical narrative as they are in real life.

The Constant Element of Dream. As I noted in chapter 2, Propp used
the term *genre* to delineate a category of narrative based on a shared
structural pattern featuring a series of specific, recognizable, constant
elements that occur in a predictable sequence. This structural pattern
can also be referred to as the *morphology* of the genre. According to this
definition, there is a genre of Wisdom Dreams in the Hebrew Bible
that shares a structural pattern, or morphology. The element of DREAM
is a constant element in the pattern making up this genre.

The constant elements making up this genre of Wisdom Dreams
are a CIRCUMSTANTIAL STATEMENT, a DREAM, and a REACTION. The CIR-
CUMSTANCE preceding a dream is often a journey, as in Jacob's flight
from Esau in Gen 28:10 or his later move to Egypt in Gen 46:1–4. In
many other cases, the CIRCUMSTANCE of the dream is introduced by
nothing more than a temporal clause fixing the dream or vision according to regnal year (Daniel 2, Daniel 10) or relative to earlier
events: in Genesis 40 the butler and baker are put into prison some-
time after Joseph's incarceration, ויהי אחר הדברים האלה. Pharaoh's
dreams in Genesis 41 occur two years after the butler is released from
prison and forgets Joseph. Samuel's dream in 1 Sam 3:1–15 opens with

a more elaborate description of the circumstances that obtained in Israel at the time of Samuel's vision. Joseph's dreams in Genesis 37 are preceded by a report on Joseph's age and family dynamics.

In the content of the DREAM itself, God may begin by introducing the divine self to the dreamer and may also present new information. Most often dreams foretell what will befall in the near or more distant future. The rest of the dream may take the form of an audible or visual warning, promise, prescription, reassurance, or punishment, all relating to the new information presented earlier in the dream.

The REACTION to the dream may be as simple as the dreamer awakening to the realization that it was a dream (Pharaoh in Gen 41:4, 7; Solomon in 1 Kgs 3:15), but the dreamer may also be agitated (Dan 2:1 and 10:7–8), wakeful (1 Sam 3:15), or awe-inspired (Gen 28:16–17). In other cases the REACTION is more elaborate, including reporting the dream in great detail or taking an action specified in the dream. The dream may already be understood by the dreamer upon waking, or it may require interpretation. Besides the dreams in the Joseph cycle, only the dreams occurring in Daniel 2 and Daniel 10 require interpretation.[57] Whatever the variety of its expression, the morphology of DREAM is constant: CIRCUMSTANCE, DREAM, REACTION.

Eating and Drinking as Variables of Dream. The contents of biblical DREAMS are diverse in subject and action: they may consist of animals, plants, people, the word of God, heavenly bodies and so forth, serving, pecking, swallowing, warning, making obeisance, or taking other action. In biblical narrative, eating and drinking are variables within the constant function of DREAM.[58]

Eating and drinking are explicit elements of only two different sets of DREAMS in biblical narrative, each consisting of two accounts. The

---

57. Scholarly attention has focused in the past on similarities between key elements of Daniel and the Joseph cycle, as well as comparisons of both with late-period Egyptian "wise man" literature. Just a few references from the many works on this subject: Nili Shupak, "Egyptian Phrases in Biblical Wisdom Literature," *Tarbiz* 54 (1985) 475–83 [Heb.]; W. S. McCullough, "Israel's Eschatology from Amos to Daniel," in *Studies on the Ancient Palestinian World* (ed. J. Wevers; Toronto: University of Toronto Press, 1972) 86–101; Niditch, *Symbolic Vision in Biblical Tradition*. Issues of genre and classification raised by these observations are beyond the scope of this study.

58. The classic work on dreams in the ancient Near East is A. L. Oppenheim, *The Interpretation of Dreams in the Ancient Near East* (Transactions of the American Philosophical Society n.s. 46/3; Philadelphia: American Philosophical Society, 1956). On the Joseph story and Egyptian cultural elements, see Donald B. Redford, *A Study of the Biblical Story of Joseph (Genesis 37–50)* (VTSup 20; Leiden: Brill, 1970).

first concerns the respective fates of the butler and baker as expressed in their dreams in Genesis 40, and the second foreshadows the seven years each of abundance and famine in the dreams of Pharaoh in Genesis 41.

The butler and baker meet Joseph as he languishes in prison after Potiphar's wife has falsely accused him of sexual harassment. Each has a dream that involves his professional role: the butler serves Pharaoh a cup filled with juice pressed from grapes that grow from three branches of vine; the baker carries three baskets of baked foods on his head, and birds pluck at the contents. The butler tells Joseph his dream first, and Joseph interprets it positively as an indication that in three days the butler is destined to return to his accustomed position serving Pharaoh. Emboldened by the promising fate predicted for his fellow, the baker tells his dream to Joseph. Alas, in his case the dream represents a dire fate: in three days he is to be executed, and the birds will pluck his flesh. Later, Pharaoh's dreams of seven skinny cattle consuming seven fat cattle and seven skinny ears of grain consuming seven fat ears are interpreted by Joseph as seven years of famine following seven years of plenty.

The variable components of biblical dreams are consistent with the concerns of the larger narrative context. For example, four out of the six dreams in the Joseph cycle are concerned with consumption, and even Joseph's first dream of bowing sheaves is concerned with grain, a food commodity. The two sets of dreams in Genesis 40 (butler and baker) and Genesis 41 (Pharaoh) are each a paired set expressing direct and reverse polarities: life and death for the individuals, plenty and famine for the polity. These variables are fully appropriate in light of the concern of the Joseph stories with these same issues of life and death, abundance and famine. In other contexts, other variables may occur that have no relationship to eating and drinking.

Two other examples consist of dreams juxtaposed to eating and drinking contexts, but the contents of the dreams themselves contain no such references. In the first, Samuel's night vision (מראה) in 1 Sam 3:1–18, the warning in the dream concerns the sins of Eli's sons and describes the fate of Eli's house. The oracle in the night vision alludes to the iniquities of Eli's sons and the punishment they face only in the most general terms. This dream in 1 Samuel 3 follows the double condemnation of Eli's sons in 1 Samuel 2: once for violations of sacrificial procedure that are described at length (1 Sam 2:12–17), and a second time for sexual improprieties that are noted briefly in 2:22. Both kinds of sin involve transgressions of sacred boundaries, but only the first occurs in a context of eating and drinking. Samuel's night vision itself and its contents exhibit no relationship to eating or drinking.

In the second example in this category, Solomon's dream at Gibeon in 1 Kgs 3:4–15 is preceded and followed by extravagant eating and drinking contexts, though the night vision itself contains none. Solomon journeys to Gibeon, the largest shrine, and brings one thousand burnt offerings. As in the cultic contexts I noted earlier, these can be interpreted as food dedicated wholly to God. Solomon experiences a dream (חלום לילה) in which he asks for wisdom and receives that and many other blessings. Solomon awakens, realizes he has dreamed, and upon his return to the Jerusalem shrine again offers many sacrifices, some that are wholly burnt and others, termed well-being (שלמים), that may be eaten by everyone who participates. Solomon also throws a drinking party (משתה) for all who serve him.

Other dreams in biblical narrative do not involve eating or drinking at all, either in content or in context. Among many examples: Joseph's dream of stars bowing in Genesis 37 that foreshadows his glorious future; Abimelech's dream of warning in Genesis 20, in which God reveals to him Abraham's true relationship to Sarah; Jacob's night vision (מראת הלילה), in which God reassures him before his departure from Canaan to join his sons in Egypt, in Gen 46:1–4.

This is the briefest of surveys; the morphology of DREAM deserves a deeper analysis in another forum. For my purpose here, it is enough to recognize that there is a series of constants making up the morphology of DREAM accounts: CIRCUMSTANCE, DREAM, and REACTION; and that within this pattern of constants the elements of eating and drinking are variables.

Etiology

The Bible is replete with *etiologies*, a term that literally means the study of origins. Many of these tell the origin of place-names, others the origin of practices or other phenomena. Sixteen of the etiological accounts in the Bible occur in contexts involving eating and drinking. I have already reviewed several of these etiological texts under the headings in this section dealing with miracle and symbolic action. Although an exhaustive discussion of etiology in the Bible is beyond the scope of this study, here I consider etiologies that occur in eating or drinking contexts in the aggregate to see if they share a pattern or reflect a function that might also apply to stories of origin in general.[59] I

59. Summaries of tradition-historical approaches to etiologies may be found in B. O. Long, *The Problem of Etiological Narrative in the Old Testament* (BZAW 108; Berlin: Alfred Töpelmann, 1968) 1–4; Friedmann W. Golka, "Aetiologies in the Old Testament, Part 1," *VT* 26 (1976) 410–28; idem, "Aetiologies in the Old Testament, Part 2," *VT* 27 (1977) 36–47. For a form-critical approach, see John Van Seters, "The

shall assess whether etiologies serve a constant function in the Hebrew Bible and what this function might be, using as a sample corpus all etiologies involving EATING and DRINKING, plus a few illustrations from among the ones that do not. Given the limitations of the present study, I shall supplement my circumscribed sample with suggestive conclusions drawn from prior scholarship in this and related areas.

The Constant Element of Etiology.   Friedmann W. Golka has studied the phenomenon of biblical etiology extensively. He focuses on the tribal period as the time of formulation of the "etiological narratives" of the Hebrew Bible.[60] Most significant is Golka's insight that etiological references connect the individual to the larger group and the present to the past.[61] Typology, the present standing for the past, or the individual standing for the larger group, is not a new idea; it is expressed in the rabbinic principle of מעשי אבות סימן לבנים 'the deeds of the ancestors are archetypes for the descendants' and is employed in modern biblical scholarship as well.[62]

Place of the Yahwist in the History of Passover and Massot," *ZAW* 95 (1983) 167–82. It is unnecessary to reiterate that, unlike these, the present study is interested in literary issues and does not address historical, tradition, or form-critical questions.

60. See Golka's dissertation, *Die Ätiologien im Alten Testament* (University of Heidelberg, 1972). Golka distinguishes "aetiological narratives" from "aetiological motifs" and "aetiological notes"; see Golka, "Aetiologies, Part 1," 411. In this two-part form-critical summary of his larger survey of etiologies in the Hebrew Bible, Golka identifies "aetiological narratives" as stories in which "the aetiology is identical with the arc of tension" in the story.

61. Since this study is concerned with Propp's rigorous approach to genre definition, Golka's intuitive division of etiologies into narratives, motifs, and notes is not relevant here, but his insight that etiological references stand for national archetypes is important. See especially Golka, "Aetiologies, Part 2," 37, 40, 41.

62. This rabbinic idea is expressed by Nachmanides (רמב"ן) in his comments on Gen 12:6, 10–20, as I noted earlier (p. 59 n. 34), and, among other places, in the collection of rabbinic midrash *Genesis Rabbah*, where R. Phinehas quotes in R. Hoshaya's name that everything written in connection to Abraham is written in connection to his children (*Gen. Rab.* 40:6; for an English translation, see Jacob Neusner, *Genesis Rabbah: The Judaic Commentary to the Book of Genesis—A New American Translation, Volume II* (BJS 105; Atlanta: Scholars Press, 1985). The concept is noted by Golka without, however, citing the rabbinic maxim, in "Aetiologies, Part 2," 46. For two examples of the rabbinic idea cited in modern critical literature relevant to typology, see Stephen A. Geller, "The Sack of Shechem: The Use of Typology in Biblical Covenant Religion," *Prooftexts* 10 (1990) 1–15, noted explicitly on p. 2; and idem, "The Struggle at the Jabbok: The Uses of Enigma in Biblical Narrative," *JANES* 14 (1984) 37–60, noted explicitly on p. 51. Revised versions of these articles have been published most recently in idem, *Sacred Enigmas: Literary Religon in the Hebrew Bible* (London: Routledge, 1996).

Stephen Geller has drawn most clearly this double tier when he speaks of two strata of meaning, the individual/familial level and the national level, in his analyses of two biblical episodes: Jacob at the Jabbok in Genesis 32, and the sack of Shechem in Genesis 34. Both Golka and Geller also allude to another element of explicit etiologies that is important in defining their function in the biblical text: the self-consciousness of explicit etiologies. These step out of the frame of the narrative of which they are a part and consciously connect the past with the present, simultaneously in time, in space, in person, and in event.[63] This self-consciousness, coupled with the two-tiered references to the individual/familial and the tribal/national, point to the function of ETIOLOGY as a bridge joining past to present, individual to community.

The morphology for ETIOLOGIES consists of a description of a circumstance—event or action, human or divine—and its impact on the characters directly involved, followed by a "bridge," or statement linking the single event in the past to an ongoing phenomenon in the future and the individual involved in the initial circumstance to the wider tribal or national scope. The description of an etiological pattern would thus consist of an occurrence, a statement of its individual impact, followed by its archetypal impact.

A word is in order here distinguishing between an etiology and the structural phenomenon of the patterns of destiny that I describe in chapters 5 and 6 of this book. An etiology tells a story of the source or reason for something—how it came into being. It occurs on the most surface level of plot in a narrative and may often be given as an aside in a story whose major concern is with some other thread. Although etiologies are often part of miracle stories, there is no sense that divine protection or maintenance of the newly originated phenomenon is ongoing. Once the cause for a phenomenon has been put forth in an etiology, that phenomenon appears to be of no further interest to the narrative. Most often the main narrative does not concern the maintenance or further history of the phenomenon whose etiology has just been told.

In contrast, the morphologies that I call Patterns of Destiny tell more than just how something came into being. The Foundation Pattern, for example, communicates the foretelling of an entity,[64] confirms its actual establishment, and implies the permanent maintenance

---

63. See idem, "Sack of Shechem," 2; and Golka, "Aetiologies 2," 36–37.

64. Whenever I use the word *entity* in the context of either Patterns of Foundation or Patterns of Doom, I use it in the sense of social or national units: nation, people, city-state, family, object, individual, or other culturally significant element.

of the subject of the foundation account. Unlike an etiology, the Foundation Pattern occurs on the structural level of the narrative, once removed from the topmost surface level of plot. The establishment of the entity that is the subject of the foundation account is usually the central focus of the narrative in which it occurs, and the permanent maintenance and further history of that entity is a significant concern of the larger narrative. There is a focused sense of divine will and ongoing divine concern expressed in the foundation account that is not present in an etiology.

Eating and Drinking as Variables of Etiology. Some etiologies arise directly out of an eating or drinking event that is intrinsic to the subject of the etiology, and other etiologies occur in a context in which eating and drinking are wholly absent or completely tangential to the etiology under consideration. Thus, eating and drinking are variables within the constant function of ETIOLOGY.

There are twelve examples of etiologies where eating or drinking is intrinsic to the etiology under discussion, out of a total of 179 identified by Golka:

1. The naming of the place Beer-lahai-roi (Gen 16:6–15) by the pregnant Hagar in gratitude for the miraculous appearance of a well of water in the wilderness.
2. The origin of the tribes of Ammon and Moab (Gen 19:30–38) after an incestuous seduction by the scheming daughters of Lot, who has drunk too much wine.
3. The account of the restructuring of Egyptian landholding (Gen 47:13–26) as a result of Joseph's plan to exchange bread for title during the seven years of famine in Egypt.
4. The naming of the place Marah in the wilderness (Exod 15:22–26), for the bitter waters sweetened by Moses' throwing a tree into it.
5. The naming of the phenomenon of manna (Exod 16:31) for the people's puzzled query "What is it?" when it first appears.
6. The naming of the place Massah and Meribah in Rephidim (Exod 17:1–7) where the people "complain and contest" with Moses over the lack of water, which he redresses by smiting the rock with his rod
7. The naming of the place Kibroth-hattaavah (Num 11:34) in the second account of the deadly consequence of the people slaking their carnivorous desires with too much quail.
8. The naming of the place Naḥal Eshcol (Num 13:24) for the giant bunch of grapes brought back by the twelve spies following their reconnaissance of the Promised Land.

9. The naming of the place Meribah in Kadesh (Num 20:2–13), where the people "contest" again with Moses and Aaron over the lack of water and other delights, which Moses redresses again by smiting the rock with his rod.
10. The naming of the altar Adonai-shalom by Gideon (Judg 6:24), who is grateful for divine reassurance that he will not die even though the visitor, who calls Gideon to lead Israel and then turns his repast into a flaming offering, is divine.
11. The naming of the place En-hakkore (Judg 15:18–19) by Samson after God answers his "cry" for water following Samson's single-handed defeat of the Philistines.
12. A multivalent example is the naming of the place Peniel (Gen 32:31), where Jacob wrestles with the divine messenger "face-to-face." Although the reader discovers in the next verse that Jacob is marked in that struggle, which is the reason Jacob's descendants do not eat the sinew in the hollow of the thigh "to this day," it is the encounter with the divine "face-to-face" that is the focus of the place-name etiology. Three levels of etiology are operating in this account: Jacob as an individual names the place based on his subjective experience; the divine renames him Israel, as the link between the individual and the tribal; and the food taboo links all three to the national level, bridging past and future.

By far, the majority of these etiologies have to do with place-names: out of 12 examples, 8 are place-names and another 3 name objects such as manna, an altar, and the two ethnic clans of Ammon and Moab. For the Bible as a whole, by Golka's count (he excludes the "primeval history"), 60 etiologies concern names of places and tribes and 15 concern names of individuals, out of his total of 179 etiologies.[65]

One would expect to find proportionately more place-name etiologies in a list weighted, as mine is, with eating and drinking references than would be found in the Bible as a whole, since such etiologies naturally reflect the concerns of people living in the geographic area of Israel: many place-name etiologies arise out of the need for water and relate to specific watering places, whether miraculous or mundane in origin.[66]

---

65. Golka, "Aetiologies, Part 2," 42.
66. Similarly, Golka's listing in ibid., 36. For a discussion of the evolution of the well motif from the realia of ancient Israel through ancient Jewish thought, see Michael Fishbane, "The Well of Living Water: A Biblical Motif and Its Ancient Transformations," in *"Sha'arei Talmon": Studies in the Bible, Qumran, and the Ancient*

There are also many etiologies in which an eating or drinking event is nonexistent or else marginal to the main focus of the etiology. Five examples demonstrate the array of variables occurring within etiological patterns.

1. The naming of the place Beer-sheba (Gen 21:22–34), when Abraham and Abimelech make a nonaggression pact in which "seven" sheep are exchanged, and no eating, drinking, or sacrifice occurs at all.
2. The naming of the place Mitzpah (Gen 31:46–49) after the setting up of a stone mound and a pillar as "witness," followed by the eating of a symbolic meal by Jacob and Laban.
3. The naming of the place Gilgal (Josh 5:9) for the "rolling away" of divine reproach following the circumcision of the males at the "hill of foreskins" (Josh 5:3) in the promised land. No eating or drinking is noted in connection with the place-name etiology, although the first Passover in the land is celebrated shortly afterward.
4. The origin of practices regarding sharing spoils of battle (1 Sam 30:1–25), when David insists on distributing them equally with those who stay behind with the baggage. No eating or drinking is mentioned.
5. The naming of the place Perez-uzzah (2 Sam 6:8), after Uzzah is struck down by the "breaking forth" of the *mysterium tremendum* during the bringing up of the Ark to Jerusalem.[67] No sacrifice, eating, or drinking accompanies this first attempt at transportation.

It is obvious from even this brief survey that not all biblical etiologies include eating and drinking, whether marginally or intrinsically. Thus, eating and drinking operate as variable components within the constant function of ETIOLOGY.

Military Leadership

Fitness for military leadership and competent execution of leadership responsibilities are manifested in many different ways in the Hebrew Bible. One of the most important of these, although by no means the only one, is the provisioning of troops with food and water. Other expressions of leadership competence include acquiring and fairly

Near East Presented to Shemaryahu Talmon (ed. M. Fishbane, E. Tov, and W. W. Fields; Winona Lake, Ind.: Eisenbrauns, 1992) 3–32.
67. See Edward L. Greenstein, "Deconstruction and Biblical Narrative," *Prooftexts* 9 (1989) 43–71.

distributing spoils, mustering or dismissing troops, victory or defeat in battle, and wise judgment or keen discernment—or the reverse—when problems present themselves.

The Constant Element of Military Leadership.   God is the consummate military leader in the Bible, demonstrating divine fitness to lead by means of miraculous victory against all odds.[68] Time and again, the text tells of actions commanded by God of human warriors that appear counterproductive for victory but nevertheless lead to the sound defeat of Israel's enemies. The morphology of MILITARY LEADERSHIP appears to be threat, divine reassurance/instruction, battle against all odds, and outcome. If God's instructions have been followed, the outcome is victory. If not, the outcome is defeat.

God is often invoked as the ultimate warrior for Israel, including many instances where miraculous provisioning is not a factor:[69] victory over the pursuing Egyptians at the Reed Sea (Exod 14:30), Moses' victory against Amalek (Exod 17:8–16), Joshua's battle against Jericho (Josh 6:1–27), the second attempt against Ai (Joshua 8, especially vv. 18–26), and the defense of Gibeon (Josh 10:8–14) are just a few examples.

In each of these accounts, God is depicted as the competent, sure leader. Human leaders, on the other hand, are at best divine instruments and at worst incompetent: bewildered, desperate, unwise. Although military provisioning is not the only means of representing leadership capability, one important vehicle for conveying the impression of superior competence is God's unfailing provision for the mili-

---

68. Among recent studies on the role and ethics of war in the Hebrew Bible, see Claudia Camp and Carole R. Fontaine (eds.), *Semeia* 61 (*Women, War, and Metaphor: Language and Society in the Study of the Hebrew Bible*; 1993); Peter C. Craigie, *The Problem of War in the Old Testament* (Grand Rapids, Mich.: Eerdmans, 1978); and Susan Niditch, *War in the Hebrew Bible: A Study in the Ethics of Violence* (New York: Oxford University Press, 1993).

69. The idea of Israel's God as divine warrior has been widely noted by scholars of both text and iconography. See, for example, Millard C. Lind, *Yahweh Is a Warrior: The Theology of Warfare in Ancient Israel* (Scottdale, Penn.: Herald, 1980); Patrick D. Miller, *The Divine Warrior in Early Israel* (HSM 5; Cambridge: Harvard University Press, 1973); Othmar Keel, *The Symbolism of the Biblical World: Ancient Near Eastern Iconography and the Book of Psalms* (New York: Seabury; repr. Winona Lake, Ind.: Eisenbrauns, 1997); Frank Moore Cross, "The Epic Traditions of Early Israel: Epic Narrative and the Reconstruction of Early Israelite Institutions," in *The Poet and the Historian: Essays in Literary and Historical Biblical Criticism* (HSM 26; Chico, Calif.: Scholars Press, 1983) 13–40; and idem, "The Divine Warior in Israel's Early Cult," in *Biblical Motifs: Origins and Transformations* (ed. A. Altmann; Cambridge: Harvard University Press, 1966) 11–30.

tary needs of the people; human leaders are not as reliable as God, although they can be quite successful, and on occasion human leaders are acknowledged, even on the structural level, as successful military leaders.

Although a variety of circumstances provide the setting for proving MILITARY LEADERSHIP—divine and human—in biblical narrative, the underlying morphology is constant: threat, divine reassurance/instruction, battle against all odds, and outcome dependent on adherence to God's will.

Eating and Drinking as a Variable of Military Leadership. There are fourteen occasions on which the Bible remarks upon the provision of food or water in a military context or upon the division of military spoils within an eating and drinking context. In every instance, the provisioning (or lack thereof) of the troops or the nature of the distribution of spoil represents only one of several reflections upon the qualities and competence of the leader who is responsible for that provisioning or that distribution. First I will examine cases in which divine leadership is acclaimed and then examples in which human leadership is evaluated. In every case, eating and drinking operate as variables within the morphology of MILITARY LEADERSHIP.

In Patterns of Divine Leadership. Only one of these examples appears to represent the normal preparation for battle: in 1 Kings 20, when Ahab prepares to go against Ben-hadad of Syria. The season before, Ben-hadad had suffered a rout at the hands of Israelite troops during a surprise attack that caught him drinking with his royal colleagues, the worse for wear (1 Kgs 20:16). The return engagement is billed as a test of whether the God of Israel is indeed Lord of the plain as well as the mountains (1 Kgs 20:23 and 28).

That divine leadership is being venerated is apparent from the larger context. From the moment Ahab first decides to resist the coercion of Ben-hadad (20:7–11), prophetic messages reassure him (and the reader) that God is manipulating the chessboard and victory is assured. This first victory follows the pattern for MILITARY LEADERSHIP: the threat by Aram (1 Kgs 20:1–12), divine reassurance and instruction (1 Kgs 20:13–14), battle against all odds (1 Kgs 20:15–20), and victorious outcome based on following God's command (1 Kgs 20:21). This pattern—defining the constant function of MILITARY LEADERSHIP—is the most significant element of the narrative. The eating and drinking details are incidental, providing the setting for the surprise attack.

Following the miraculous first victory over Aram, the prophet warns that a second encounter is inevitable, and Israel duly prepares. Although the mustering and provisioning of the Israelites for this second encounter is reported matter-of-factly by the text, the context requires us to see these preparations as an act of faith in divine providence. Although Aram greatly outnumbers the army of Northern Israel (1 Kgs 20:27), God has instructed Israel to prepare for a second clash with Aram (1 Kgs 20:22), promising Israel victory. Faith in God requires acting upon that divine command, taking to heart that reassurance. The outcome is victory (1 Kgs 20:28), as the Israelites again miraculously wipe out the Arameans (1 Kgs 20:29–30). This narrative follows the pattern for MILITARY LEADERSHIP: threat, divine reassurance/instruction, battle against all odds, and, in this case, victorious outcome.

Miraculous victories are divine reassurances that external political alliances are unnecessary for a nation protected by God, the ultimate leader. Ahab, however, fails in the ensuing narrative to heed these lessons, attempting to grant his enemy's petition for mercy in hopes of formulating a favorable treaty with Ben-hadad. Ahab's leadership, in stark disregard of the divine directive implicit in the double victories over Aram, is roundly and explicitly condemned in the mouth of an anonymous prophet (1 Kgs 20:30b–43). Given the structural pattern for MILITARY LEADERSHIP, readers may expect Ahab to experience mortal defeat at the hands of Aram, an expectation fulfilled in 1 Kgs 22:34–37.

God's desire to demonstrate the divine origin of Israelite victories is the explicit reason for the winnowing of Gideon's troops (Judg 7:2, 4, 7). The final cut (Judg 7:5–8) is done by separating soldiers according to the way they drink water: those who lap water like dogs, about 300 troops, are chosen to fight. Those who fall on their knees to drink, about 9,700 men,[70] are sent home.

The divine hand is also evident in the enigmatic narrative of 2 Kgs 6:8–23, in which Elisha leads a confounded Syrian raiding party into the heart of Samaria and orders them fed and released after forbidding Jehoram to smite them. The outcome of this reversal of expected treatment of an enemy miraculously delivered into Israel's hands is that Syrian raiding parties cease to trouble Israel. This narrative is followed by another of Ben-hadad's full-scale attempts to intimidate Israel, but God is more than equal to this larger threat as well (2 Kgs 6:24–7:16).

Divine leadership is demonstrated in at least one other narrative of miraculous provision for a military host. In 2 Kgs 3:4–25, an allied army headed by the kings of Judah, Israel, and Edom marches against

---

70. Subtracting 300 from the 10,000 remaining after the first separation of troops, as noted in Judg 7:3.

a rebellious King Mesha of Moab. The three kings and their troops march for seven days, but they have not planned well, for they despair when they run out of water. Elisha is the agent through whom God waters the troops of Israel, Judah, and Edom, simultaneously confounding the Moabite enemy.

It may be suggested that God surprises the kings with a drought they do not expect and for which they could not have planned. Whether the lack of water can be ascribed to God's actions or to poor planning on the part of the mortal kings, the narrative clearly depicts the helplessness of the human leadership in the face of this lack and the power of God to remedy the situation and provide for the troops. Elisha's oracle continues with the promise (presently fulfilled) that God will assure the allies complete victory over the troops and settlements of Moab. This example is an indication that God's provision of water is a manifestation of divine leadership. God as provider of food and water is a variable operating within the constant pattern of MILITARY LEADERSHIP, consisting of THREAT, DIVINE REASSURANCE/INSTRUCTION, BATTLE AGAINST ALL ODDS, and OUTCOME.

In Patterns of Human Leadership. Not all human leadership is deprecated. The career of King David and, before him, of the patriarch Abraham demonstrate military prowess and worthiness to lead within contexts of military provisioning.[71] Even though successful provisioning is only one variable among many that demonstrate MILITARY LEADERSHIP, when it occurs it serves as a potent device for characterization, as a closer examination of David's experience will demonstrate.

David, military leader par excellence, is shown to provision his men (though almost always by means of gifts from loyal subjects or enemy booty) in all contingencies. His career is punctuated by accounts of military provisioning, and David's leadership judgment is showcased more than once within the context of military provisioning.

David is almost always on the receiving end of provisions supplied (by free will or under duress) by others. Only once is he the bringer of such provisions to the troops when, before his career begins, David is sent by his father, Jesse, with a gift of provisions for his brothers, who are camped with Saul's troops in the valley of Elah (1 Sam 17:17–19) and facing Goliath's twice-daily taunts (1 Sam 17:16).[72] For the rest of

---

71. For an examination of the less emphasized military aspect of Abraham, see Yochanan Muffs, "Abraham the Noble Warrior," *Love and Joy*, 67–95.

72. For a morphological study of this chapter, applying Propp's method to the biblical text, see Heda Jason, "The Story of David and Goliath: A Folk Epic?" (trans. Sara Mishan), *Bib* 60 (1979) 36–70.

David's career, even at its lowest point when he flees ignominiously before his rebellious son Absalom, provisions for his entourage are supplied by loyal followers (2 Sam 17:27–29)—as well as by those with axes
to grind (2 Sam 16:1–4).

As David's star begins to rise, his encounter with Nabal in 1 Sam
25:2–42 is an attempt to collect payment for protection services ren-
dered to (if not commissioned by) Nabal and his household. Nabal suf-
fers divine punishment for withholding these provisions, and his wife,
Abigail, is rewarded for the resourcefulness, alacrity, and grace with
which she makes them available.

Just as division of spoils is joined to the provisioning of troops as a
device for enhancing the perception of the prestige, nobility, and leadership qualities of David, so earlier the same combination strength-
ened the reputation of the patriarch Abraham. In Gen 14:11–24, Abraham caps his amazing victory over the coalition of the five kings and
the rescue of his nephew Lot with the humble refusal of even a sandal
strap of enemy spoil for his personal enrichment. He is careful, however, to provide for what his servants have eaten and for the shares of
his own men and of the men accompanying his fellow leaders, Aner,
Eshkol, and Mamre. This incident enhances Abraham's positive characterization as a reliable leader who can be counted on to take care of
his troops even as he exhibits unassailable personal integrity. David
performs a similar strategic marvel in his recapture of the goods and
inhabitants of his town of Ziklag in 1 Sam 30:1–25. This time, David's
insistence on an equitable division of the spoils among the rear guard
as well as the front line is adduced to his credit as a fair and innovative
military leader whose policy in this regard becomes the custom of Israel.[73] This incident marks David, too, as a reliable leader whose concern extends equally to all his troops.

During David's flight from Absalom, the gifts and provisions offered
to the retreating king provide a study in contrasts and a worthy background against which his wisdom may be evaluated. Three encounters
that occur upon David's retreat from Jerusalem are illustrative. These
encounters may be divided into two categories: (1) David's relationship
with the house of Saul and (2) David's relationship with his own loyal
followers.

---

73. For an ancient Near Eastern parallel in which a leader's qualities are reflected in his division of spoil, see Edward L. Greenstein and David Marcus, "The
Akkadian Inscription of Idrimi," *JANES* 8 (1976) 59–96. The correspondences
between David and Abraham in this context were seen already in a number of
studies on David and the ideology associated with him in the Hebrew Bible; see, for
example, Moshe Weinfeld's Hebrew commentary on *Genesis* (Tel Aviv: Gordon,
1975) 68 [Heb.].

The first category, David's relationship with the rival house of Saul, includes two incidents. Ziba, servant of Mephibosheth, the lame son of Jonathan, greets David with supplies to be eaten and drunk by David's retinue (2 Sam 16:1–4). David questions Ziba about his master's whereabouts, Ziba denounces Mephibosheth, and David accepts his accusation at face value, without investigation or verification: Ziba is granted all his master's property, and Mephibosheth is effectively dispossessed.

David's second encounter with Saul's loyalists is with Shimei ben Gera, whose offering, a reversal of Ziba's gift of provisions, is a negative one of hurled stones, dirt, insult, and execration (2 Sam 16:5–13). Calling David a man of bloodshed and a wicked man (איש הדמים ואיש הבליעל), his accusation concerns David's usurpation of the throne of Saul. Abishai ben Zeruiah offers to slay Shimei but David restrains him with the first of a two-part refrain connecting this text with 2 Sam 19:16–40, David's return to Jerusalem: "What has my (business) to do with you, son of Zeruiah?" (מה־לי ולכם בן צריה, 2 Sam 16:10a, and compare 19:23a). David does not feel in a position to take action against a partisan of his rival's house while he himself is fleeing from a mortal threat by his own son (2 Sam 16:11).

The second category concerns David's relationship with his own loyal supporters and includes a single encounter related in 2 Sam 17:27–29. As he reaches Mahanaim, David is greeted by a coalition headed by Barzillai the Gileadite. Beyond the minimum provision required for a fleeing troop, his loyal subjects present to the king foods and furnishings fit for a royal feast in a royal abode, thereby affirming their loyalty to David's kingship even in retreat.[74] Barzillai's name is cited last of the three listed benefactors in this citation, but in 2 Sam 19:32–40 he is the only one of the three mentioned, and the text is careful to note there that it is for his loyal generosity at Mahanaim that he is later offered a reward.

Taken together, these narratives illustrate the importance of military provisioning as a clue to the quality of the leader who is the subject of these texts. The resolution of each of these three incidents illuminates the leadership of David just past the zenith of his career.

These three incidents plus the final resolution make a pattern of contrasts: BETRAYAL (of Mephibosheth by Ziba) and loyalty (to David by Barzillai and his co-benefactors), conditional generosity (from Ziba) and unconditional generosity (from Barzillai), David's family

---

74. On banquet language in the Bible and in ancient Near Eastern literature, see Murray H. Lichtenstein, "The Banquet Motif in Keret and in Proverbs 9," *JANES* 1 (1968) 19–31; and idem, *Episodic Structure in the Ugaritic Keret Legend: Comparative Studies in Compositional Technique* (Ph.D. diss., Columbia University, 1979), especially pp. 145–56.

relationships (symbolized by his son's rebellion) and David's political heritage (exemplified by the two encounters with partisans of the house of Saul). The text in 2 Sam 19:16–40 directs the reader to read the encounters of David with Ziba, Shimei, and Barzillai in terms of one another by bringing all three together to form a literary inclusion with the narrative beginning in 2 Samuel 16.

First, Shimei pleads for forgiveness, Abishai makes his offer, and David gives his formulaic restraining response. David's retribution upon Shimei is, however, only postponed; David charges Solomon, upon his succession, to remember Shimei's slight (1 Kgs 2:8–9). A reading of Shimei and Ziba as public threats to David's house by partisans of the house of Saul is confirmed in 1 Kgs 2:36–46: Shimei's ultimate elimination is taken by the narrative as the final end to any threat to Solomon's security upon the throne (1 Kgs 2:45–46).

Next, the lame Mephibosheth counters Ziba's accusation, pleading incapacity to come out and greet David upon his earlier retreat. Forbearing to decide which of the two is faithful and which disloyal, David splits Mephibosheth's holdings between master and servant. Is David remiss in not investigating further? Is he wise in recognizing a no-win situation? David's ambivalent relationship to the house of Saul, even represented at its least threatening by the beloved Jonathan's lame heir, is epitomized by this episode.[75]

An intertextual reading of this narrative evokes two other biblical occasions when kings are asked to judge between two rivals: Solomon, in a case involving two women and a child to be nurtured in 1 Kings 3; and an unnamed Northern king, in a dispute involving two women and a child to be eaten in 2 Kings 6.[76] At one end of the spectrum is Solomon's wise judgment in the case of the two women claiming the same child (1 Kgs 3:16–28), in which Solomon's decision to split the child reveals the true mother. At the other end broods the horror of the unresolved Northern parody of the king's judgment, the case of the cannibal women (2 Kgs 6:26–30), in which the king makes no judgment at all. Instead, he walks away from the bizarre case in disgust, vowing angrily to get even with Elisha, whom he holds responsible for the drought that has brought the women to the point of cannibalism. Where on the spectrum defined by these extremes does David's judgment fall? Is he as wise as Solomon to effect this distribution of property, or is he as helpless as the hapless Northern king, who walks away

---

75. See David Marcus, "David the Deceiver and David the Dupe," *Prooftexts* 6 (1986) 163–71.

76. See Stuart Lasine, "Jehoram and the Cannibal Mothers (2 Kings 6.24–33): Solomon's Judgment in an Inverted World," *JSOT* 50 (1991) 27–53.

from judgment cursing the prophet whose pronouncements he blames for this unspeakable turn of events?

Barzillai's unadulterated loyalty is recognized next. Returning measure for measure, the king rewards Barzillai's gift of royal provisions with an offer of perpetual attendance at the king's table in Jerusalem (1 Kgs 2:7). Barzillai declines this reward in favor of his son, thereby anticipating the closing of the circle of fathers and sons implicit in this entire narrative, first with reference to David and Absalom in the need for flight at all, then to Saul and Jonathan implicit in the Ziba/Mephibosheth encounter and finally resolved in 1 Kgs 2:36–46 by Solomon's elimination of Shimei and the security of his rule over a united kingdom.

Reversal of Direction in Provisioning. As might be expected in light of the discussion of direction in other categories, negative judgments on leaders are conveyed by means of reverse provisioning, which can be expressed as the withholding of provisions, injunctions to the troops against eating, or inappropriate or inadequate military provisions. I have noted above the divinely instigated consequences of Nabal's withholding of provisions from the divinely appointed troops he terms escaped slaves (עבדים המתפרצים איש מפני אדניו) in 1 Sam 25:10.[77] In Judg 8:4–17, Gideon punishes the towns of Succoth and Penuel for a similar error. In both cases the leaders who seek the provisions are favored, and those withholding the provisions are punished.

Once again, the supplying of provisions is commended and the interdiction against them is condemned. Among all the ways of evaluating fitness to lead, successful military provisioning is just another variable, one that may reflect positively or negatively upon the competence of the leader, whether human or divine. Thus, military provisioning is a variable within the constant of MILITARY LEADERSHIP, operating within a pattern consisting of THREAT, DIVINE REASSURANCE/INSTRUCTION, BATTLE AGAINST ALL ODDS, and OUTCOME.

Perfidy

There is a genre of biblical narratives that involves the villainous pursuit of a goal that may either serve God's will or be at odds with it. As I have noted earlier, Propp defines a genre as narratives that share a pattern made up of a sequence of constant elements. Such a pattern is also called the morphology of a genre. Here I identify the genre of Perfidy, made up of a pattern that includes the constant element of

---

77. See above, p. 84.

VILLAINY. The full pattern, or morphology, consists of the sequence of constants VOLITION, VILLAINY, OUTCOME, and JUDGMENT. I begin discussion of this genre with an examination of the kinds of villainy that occur in biblical narrative.

I identify three major categories of VILLAINY as occurring in connection with eating and/or drinking: DECEPTION, BETRAYAL or TREACHERY, and COERCION.[78] Many acts of VILLAINY occur in eating and drinking contexts in the Bible, but many other acts of DECEPTION, TREACHERY, or COERCION occur in circumstances where no eating or drinking occurs. Eating and drinking are thus variable elements within the constant category of VILLAINY. I would like to suggest that there is a theological message that is embodied in every account of DECEPTION, BETRAYAL, and COERCION in the Hebrew Bible, an issue of faith: the will of God must be served, by fair means or foul. The outcome of events in the Bible depends on the relationship of the actors to divine will as it is explicit or implicit in the text.

Patterns of Perfidy follow a sequence that begins with an expression of will. If this VOLITION is divine and explicit, all means of achieving it are acceptable; if this volition is solely human or not explicitly expressed, villainous means for achieving the goal are not acceptable. The statement of VOLITION, expressed or implied, is followed by some human effort to secure the stated objective. This effort may include all forms of VILLAINY, including DECEPTION, COERCION, BETRAYAL, or TREACHERY. The final two constants are the OUTCOME and the JUDGMENT. The OUTCOME may be a successful achievement of the perpetrator's goal even if it is not God's will, as when David successfully sends Uriah to his death in 2 Samuel 11. But the JUDGMENT will be positive if explicit divine volition is served by the VILLAINY and negative if God's will does not explictly enter into the villainous narrative. David's BETRAYAL of Uriah, though successfully achieved, is roundly condemned in the following chapter.

Although in most of the cases I cite here, VILLAINY occurs in contexts of eating and drinking, this pattern holds in many other contexts as well: sexual, cultic, or military, for example. Eating and drinking are variables within the Pattern of Perfidy, which consists of the constant

---

78. There have been several recent studies of deception in the Hebrew Bible. See Ora Horn Prouser, *The Phenomenology of the Lie in Biblical Narrative* (Ph.D. diss., Jewish Theological Seminary of America, 1991); and Marcus, "David the Deceiver." For a comparative study of the strategy of deception in the Bible and in ancient Near Eastern literature, see Carole Fontaine, "The Deceptive Goddess in Ancient Near Eastern Myth: Inanna and Inaraš," *Semeia* 42 (*Reasoning with the Foxes: Female Within a World of Male Power*; 1988) 84–102.

elements expression of VOLITION, act of VILLAINY, OUTCOME, and JUDGMENT. In biblical narrative, Perfidy is not condemned if it serves the expressed will of God.

Deception. The Hebrew Bible often tells of the triumph of the younger or weaker over the elder or stronger, frequently as the expressed will of God.[79] Often this triumph is achieved by means of DECEPTION, as when Jacob, with his mother's help, deceives his father and triumphs over his elder brother in Genesis 27 as predicted in Gen 25:22–23, or when Joseph conceals his true identity from his brothers in Genesis 42–44. In Gen 45:5 and again in Gen 50:20, Joseph makes explicit that he and his brothers have been serving the will of God all along when he tells his brothers that although they may have intended harm, God intended it for good. Over and over, God chooses the weaker, the younger, the underdog. In cases where those who are less powerful deceive those who are more powerful, or when there is a "measure for measure" element in the DECEPTION,[80] there is no condemnation, and often the deceiver is rewarded. In these cases, the weaker is serving God's will. But in cases where the powerful deceive those less powerful, the narrative roundly condemns this abuse of their advantaged position.[81]

David, before he achieves the peak of his power, is frequently the beneficiary of this equation: for example, in 1 Samuel 20, David and Jonathan flush out Saul's murderous intentions against David by a deceptive ruse at the feast of the New Moon, and in 1 Sam 21:2–10, David secures the sacred loaves from the priest of Nob. Following his rise to kingship, David experiences the equation from its other perspective. As king, David is often duped by those less powerful.[82] He is also

79. See Frederick E. Greenspahn, *When Brothers Dwell Together: The Preeminence of Younger Siblings in the Hebrew Bible* (New York: Oxford University Press, 1994); Jon D. Levenson, *The Death and Resurrection of the Beloved Son: The Transformation of Child Sacrifice in Judaism and Christianity* (New Haven: Yale University Press, 1993) 55–169; William Syrén, *The Forsaken First-Born: A Study of a Recurrent Motif in the Patriarchal Narratives* (JSOTSup 133; Sheffield: Sheffield Academic Press, 1993); Ronald S. Hendel, *The Epic of the Patriarch: The Jacob Cycle and the Narrative Traditions of Canaan and Israel* (Atlanta: Scholars Press, 1987); Isaac Mendelsohn, "On the Preferential Status of the Eldest Son," *BASOR* 156 (1959) 38–40.

80. See Marcus, "David the Deceiver," 163–71; and Murray H. Lichtenstein, "The Poetry of Poetic Justice: A Comparative Study in Biblical Imagery," *JANES* 5 (1973) 255–65.

81. See Prouser, "The Phenomenology of the Lie," 182–83 and passim.

82. See Marcus's thorough discussion of this phenomenon (in his article "David the Deceiver," 163–71), especially his summary of "measure for measure" (p. 165).

condemned for deceiving those less powerful, as in 2 Samuel 12, when the prophet Nathan uses a parable to censure the king for his treatment of Uriah in 2 Samuel 11: David pronounces judgment on himself when he expresses outrage at the rich man who steals a poor man's lamb to prepare a feast for a guest. Kings who abuse their power by deceiving their subjects are condemned in the Northern Kingdom as well: David's condemnation here is echoed in Elijah's later accusation of Ahab in the matter of Naboth's vineyard (1 Kings 21).

Betrayal/Treachery.   In the cases of BETRAYAL or TREACHERY that occur during or following an eating or drinking event, the same pattern prevails: the key to whether or not the action is condemned depends on the will of God,[83] specifically on whether or not the text contains an explicit statement of divine will regarding the outcome of the BETRAYAL.

There are many instances in which the text explicitly notes that God desires the outcome achieved by BETRAYAL. Joseph's BETRAYAL by his brothers, who throw him into a pit and then sit down to eat (Gen 37:24–25), is specifically attributed to the will of God (Gen 45:7 and Gen 50:19–21). Jael's murder of Sisera while he believes himself protected by her hospitality (Judg 4:18–21) is divine will as foretold by Deborah to Barak (Judg 4:9).

The TREACHERY of Gaal ben Ebed begins at a drinking festival and results in the destruction of Shechem (Judg 9:44–45) and ultimately in Abimelech's demise (Judg 9:53–54). It is foreshadowed by Jotham's curse of Shechem and Abimelech (Judg 9:20) and explicitly declared as divine will in Judg 9:23–24. Marital TREACHERY motivates Samson's destruction of the Philistines in revenge for his Timnite bride's BETRAYAL by disclosing the answer to his riddle to the wedding guests (Judg 14:15–19). This episode is preceded by the narrative report that God is seeking a pretext against the Philistines (Judg 14:4).

God's will is expressed by prophetic prounouncements in many texts. Zimri murders Elah ben Baasha after Baasha has been drinking in 1 Kgs 16:1–14a and then destroys all members of his house, in accordance with the prophecy pronounced against him by the prophet Jehu ben Hanani in 1 Kgs 16:1–7. Jehu ben Jehoshaphat ben Nimshi

---

Although the examples cited by Marcus appear to fall into the pattern of relative power we are discussing here, they do not involve eating and drinking events, additional evidence that in the constant category of PERFIDY, eating and drinking are variables.

83. See Harry Hagan, "Deception as Motif and Theme in 2 Sm 9–20; 1 Kgs 1–2," *Bib* 60 (1979) 301–26, especially p. 303.

becomes king of Israel according to the word of God (2 Kgs 9:1–10) after betraying Joram ben Ahab (2 Kgs 9:14–24) and encouraging TREACHERY against Jezebel, wife of Ahab (2 Kgs 9:31–33). He then sits down to eat and drink (2 Kgs 9:34–37).

In every one of these cases, where the TREACHERY is in keeping with the stated will of God, the perpetrator is successful in enacting the TREACHERY and is not condemned. However, in those cases where divine volition is not explicitly stated, the perpetrator is condemned and often severely punished. Examples of this denunciation of unsanctioned BETRAYAL include: Cain's punishment for the murder of Abel in Genesis 4; Noah's curse of Canaan for uncovering his nakedness in Gen 9:18–29; David's condemnation of Joab (1 Kgs 2:5–6), for, among other things, Joab's murder of Abner (recounted in 2 Samuel 3); Nathan's condemnation of David for his murder of Uriah (2 Samuel 12); Amnon's murder by Absalom to avenge the rape of his sister, Tamar (2 Samuel 13); and the murder of Gedaliah after a meal (Jer 40:7–41:15).[84] In none of these does the text express divine license for the treacherous act, and in each one the text ultimately tells of the condemnation or punishment of the perpetrator.

Coercion.   In cases of COERCION, the Perfidy Pattern shows some variation. When it comes to COERCION in any form, case after case demonstrates that, explicitly stated or not, divine will demands resistance. As a rule, COERCION of any kind in the Hebrew Bible must be opposed. Individuals or groups that accede to COERCION are at best viewed with contempt and at worst are destroyed. In Gen 25:27–34, Esau sells his birthright under COERCION by Jacob. Jacob is never chastised for his unbrotherly behavior, but Esau is explicitly condemned for not resisting Jacob's COERCION and so despising his birthright as to sell it cheap. In Judg 14:15, Samson's Timnite bride is coerced by the Philistines into betraying her husband. She does not resist, and ultimately she and her father are burned by the Philistines (Judg 15:6), who are themselves destroyed by Samson (Judg 15:7–8).

Resistance to COERCION appears to be viewed in the Hebrew Bible as an expression of faith in God's power to save the faithful from the evils of mortal force or perhaps simply as an expression of confidence that right is better than might. Generally speaking, individuals who resist COERCION, even to the sacrifice of their own lives, are viewed favorably by the text, and the coercive perpetrators are condemned or

---

84. Note that the terse report in 2 Kgs 25:25 of the murder of Gedaliah omits all reference to the circumstances, only naming the perpetrator, Ishmael ben Nethaniah ben Elishama, and mentioning that he is of the royal seed.

roundly punished. For example, Ahab initially gives in to Ben-hadad's COERCION, and the Aramean demands escalate. Then Ahab resists, and God rewards him with victory over his drunken challenger (1 Kgs 20:1–13). Hezekiah has a similar experience (2 Kgs 18:13–19:37, parallel to the account in Isa 36:1–37:38) when, with the encouragement of Isaiah, Hezekiah's initial compliance with the COERCION of Sennacherib turns to resistance, and God's protection is promised and delivered. Elisha helps the king of Israel resist the might of the Aramean raiders with the help of God (2 Kgs 6:8–23).

Daniel resists COERCION several times. Against the orders of the Babylonian king, Daniel refuses to eat food from the king's table (Dan 1:5–16) and requests, instead, a vegetarian diet. He and his companions thrive to such an extent on this fare that they are among those singled out for special service to the king. Daniel becomes such a favorite of the king that he arouses the jealousy of others at court (Daniel 6), who try to coerce Daniel and all the people loyal to the God of Israel into worshiping foreign gods. Daniel resists and survives his ordeal in the den of lions with divine assistance, while the Babylonian king fasts in supplication for Daniel's well-being.

Even when they appear to lose the ground of battle, those who resist COERCION retain the moral high ground. Uriah, who resists strong COERCION by David to return to his home and spend the night with his wife (2 Sam 11:8–13), is ultimately killed, but David is condemned and punished for his actions (2 Sam 12:1–14); Vashti refuses to succumb to the COERCION of Ahasuerus (Esther 1), and even though she is eliminated as queen, her action raises questions about the soundness of the king's judgment. Job, too, is ultimately vindicated for resisting pressure to admit to transgression he had not committed (Job 42:7), even though the attempted COERCION begins with divine permission and includes the loss of his wealth, the deaths of his children, and his own bodily illness (Job 1 and 2).

In another troubling example (Judg 19:22–24), COERCION by the mob of Benjaminites is resisted by the Ephramite host, who refuses to release his Levite guest to them. However, in a measure of the world gone amok, two women are offered by the host in place of the male guest, and one is actually thrown out to the mob by the Levite, to be ravaged all night and expire by morning.[85] The text is silent in its evaluation of the Levite, but the tribe of Benjamin is decimated with

---

85. See Stuart Lasine, "Guest and Host in Judges 19: Lot's Hospitality in an Inverted World," *JSOT* 29 (1984) 37–59, and Phyllis Trible, *Texts of Terror: Literary-Feminist Readings of Biblical Narratives* (Philadelphia: Fortress, 1984) 65–91.

divine approbation (Judg 20:28–48) on account of their coercive role in this episode.

In this discussion of the Perfidy Pattern, every element demands deeper examination. I am currently working on an expanded study of the role and function of COERCION in Hebrew Bible narrative that will elaborate on these observations. However, even as superficial an examination as this supports my observation that the morphology associated with the Perfidy Pattern consists of the sequence of constants VOLITION, VILLAINY, OUTCOME, and JUDGMENT.

Eating and Drinking as a Variable of Perfidy. So far, I have reviewed examples of VILLAINY that have occurred in connection with an eating or drinking context, but by no means all villainous acts in the Bible are performed in connection with eating and drinking events. VILLAINY in the absence of eating and drinking may involve sexuality, as in the DECEPTION of Pharaoh by Abraham about Sarah in Gen 12:10–20, the DECEPTION of Abimelech by Isaac about Rebekah in Genesis 26, Tamar's DECEPTION of Judah in Genesis 38, the abduction of the women of Shiloh in Judg 21:15–25, the BETRAYAL of Potiphar by his wife in Genesis 39, Delilah's BETRAYAL of Samson in Judges 16, or Bathsheba's BETRAYAL of Uriah with David in 2 Samuel 11. It may involve testing of faith, as in Shadrach, Meshach, and Abednego's resistance of COERCION in the fiery furnace in Daniel 3. It may follow an incidence of sacrifice, offering, or other symbolic action, as in Cain's murder of Abel in Genesis 4, Hazael's murder of Ben-hadad after a consultation with Elisha in 2 Kgs 8:7–15, and Jehu's roundup of the priests of Baal in 2 Kgs 10:18–28.

All of these occur in the absence of an eating and drinking context, demonstrating that eating and drinking are variable elements within the constant category of VILLAINY. Nevertheless, the large number of villainous events that occur during or immediately following hospitality contexts in the Hebrew Bible suggests that this subcategory merits a closer look.

Perfidy in Hospitality Contexts. I have just shown that a constant element of VOLITION appears to run through positive as well as negative consequences of VILLAINY in Perfidy Patterns in the Hebrew Bible. This is also true when the VILLAINY occurs in connection with hospitality. When God's will is made explicit in the text, by means of narrative statement, prophecy, or oracle sanctioning the violation of hospitality, the outcome is positive in the eyes of the narrator. When such a statement of divine volition is absent, the villainous violation of hospitality is condemned. In hospitality contexts, as in other circumstances in which VILLAINY occurs, the expected pattern holds: VOLITION, VILLAINY, OUTCOME, and JUDGMENT.

It is a commonplace in biblical studies that hospitality is valued, that the relationship between guest and host is somehow sacrosanct; the violations of this relationship by murder, TREACHERY, deceit, or some other breach is viewed with greater than usual horror.[86] The textual evidence, however, suggests that, at best, the biblical attitude toward hospitality is ambiguous. I have identified 27 instances of hospitality in Hebrew Bible narrative. Negative instances in which hospitality is withheld, greeted by refusal, or followed by VILLAINY or disaster occur in 15 examples, the majority of cases. It is possible that this apparently equivocal testimony on the inviolability of the guest-host bond is less expressive of social values than it is inherent in the nature of narrative: without disequilibrium, there can be no plot movement.[87] At the same time, however, a theological message is also being conveyed: even in the sacred relationship of guest to host, ultimately, service to God must take precedence.

The best-known examples of hospitality violated are the stories of Lot's visitors in Sodom in Genesis 19, in which Lot's injury is prevented by supernatural intervention, and the story of the concubine of the Levite in Judges 19, whose situation appears to be attributed by the text to a social context in which there is no king in Israel, and every man does what is right in his own eyes (Judg 21:25).

In the first case, the divine intent to discover the extent of the wickedness of Sodom is stated explicitly, and messengers are dispatched on this mission, in Gen 18:20–22. Following the demonstration of

---

86. See T. Desmond Alexander, "Lot's Hospitality: A Clue to His Righteousness," *JBL* 104 (1985) 289–91; Anne Draffkorn Kilmer, "How Was Queen Ereshkigal Tricked? A New Interpretation of the Descent of Ishtar," *UF* 3 (1971) 299–309; J.-J. Glassner, "L'hospitalité en Mésopotamie ancienne: Aspect de la question de l'étranger," *ZAW* 80 (1990) 60–75; idem, "Women, Hospitality, and the Honor of the Family," in *Women's Earliest Records from Ancient Egypt and Western Asia* (Proceedings of the Conference on Women in the Ancient Near East; ed. B. Lesko; BJS 166; Atlanta: Scholars Press, 1989) 71–90; Lasine, "Guest and Host in Judges 19"; Victor H. Matthews, "Hospitality and Hostility in Judges 4," *BTB* 21 (1991) 13–21; Robert E. Meagher, "Strangers at the Gate: Ancient Rites of Hospitality," *Parabola: The Magazine of Myth and Tradition* 2/4 (1977) 10–15; Susan Niditch, "The 'Sodomite' Theme in Judges 19–20: Family, Community, and Social Disintegration," *CBQ* 44 (1982) 365–78; and H. L. J. Vanstiphout, "The Banquet Scene in the Mesopotamian Debate Poems," in *Banquets d'Orient* (Res Orientales 4; Bures-sur-Yvette, France: Étude de la Civilisation du Moyen-Orient, 1992) 9–21.

87. Propp, *Morphology*, 30–36.

Sodom's depravity when Lot's guests are threatened, the visitors protect themselves by supernatural means, and Sodom is duly punished for its VILLAINY. In the second case, the violation of hospitality is not preceded by any statement of divine will. The perpetrators are Benjaminites who, despite their VILLAINY, are protected by their fellow tribesmen; the entire tribe is punished by near-extinction when Israel seeks vengeance (Judges 20–21), an excessive reaction that is characteristic of the entire pericope of Judges 19–21. The focus of these texts is not human conventions such as the inviolability of the guest-host relationship or the value of offering and accepting hospitality. Rather, in these accounts, the context of hospitality is merely the setting within which the overriding value is conveyed that divine will must be the ultimate guide to human action, or the result will be social chaos on both personal and national levels.

Other examples of hospitality violated also fall within this pattern. A case of refuge violated occurs when Jael murders Sisera, who believes he has found safety and sustenance in her tent in Judges 4. Jael is not condemned for this flagrant violation of the conventions of hospitality, even though there was peace between her husband and her victim at the time (Judg 4:17). Instead, her action is perceived as the working of divine will: Jael's action confirms the prophetic word of Deborah that Sisera would be delivered into the hands of a woman (Judg 4:9).

On the other hand, VILLAINY in the absence of divine approbation is condemned, even if the context is one of hospitality. In 2 Samuel 11, David hosts Uriah several times, plies him with good food and wine, and urges Uriah to return home. The king wishes thus to legitimate Bathsheba's illicit pregnancy; resisting the king costs Uriah his life. David has acted out of his personal desires and not on the express will of God; thus his VILLAINY is condemned and punished (2 Sam 12:1–15).

Unwitting violation of divine will is also punished, even in the context of hospitality. When the Judean man of God heeds the deceit of the lying Northern prophet in 1 Kgs 13:11–34, their repast proves to be his last, for in going along with his human host's reassurance he has failed to heed his own experience of the word of God. In the middle of the meal, the Judean man of God is condemned for this failing (1 Kgs 13:21–22), and shortly afterward pays the price with his life (1 Kgs 13:24).

Several others die offering or receiving hospitality. Punishment or reward for these deeds depends not on the hospitality context but on the presence or absence of an expression of divine volition. The murder, at the hands of Zimri, of Elah ben Baasha after drinking himself drunk in 1 Kgs 16:1–28 confirms the word of God spoken against Baasha and his house. Zimri's role as merely an instrument for fulfilling divine will is emphasized as he himself is struck down when Omri seizes power only seven days after Zimri's accession (1 Kgs 16:15–19).

Gedaliah ben Ahikam, appointed governor of Judah by the Babylonians following the fall of Jerusalem, hosts a meal for Ishmael ben Nethaniah and ten of his henchmen. At the meal, Gedaliah is struck down by his guests, as described in Jer 41:1–3. His death results in a test of faith for the survivors in Jerusalem, who demonstrate that they fear reprisal from Babylon more than they fear the word of God. Although the will of God is that they remain in Judah under divine protection (Jer 42:10–12), expressly against God's will (Jer 42:13–22) they flee to Egypt (Jeremiah 43–44).

Hospitality figures in another test of faith. Job's children, feasting together at one of their homes, are struck down by an act of God (Job 1:18–19) in the culmination of the first of a series of divine trials to test Job's loyalty to God (Job 1:7–12). They are innocent, as Job proves to be; the operating factor is divine will.

Enemies of the crown are shown hospitality if it is God's will that they be protected. Solomon's enemies are shown hospitality and given refuge and protection by foreign powers in 1 Kings 11 because of the Lord's displeasure with Solomon (1 Kgs 11:11–14). The most significant of these for the Israelites is Jeroboam ben Nebat, who is hosted by Egypt until Solomon's death, at which time he returns, eventually to fulfill the word of God that he will head the kingdom of Northern Israel (1 Kgs 11:26–40).

Refusal of hospitality occurs in six cases. Supernatural beings refuse to share meals with Gideon in Judges 6 and with Samson's parents in Judges 13. In both cases, this refusal, followed by the transformation of the meal into a cultic burnt offering, is a clue to the mortal observers of divine volition. Nabal in 1 Samuel 25 initially refuses to host David and his men. His wife, Abigail, quickly assembles a royal feast, rushes after David to offer it to him, and is rewarded by being made David's consort after her husband is struck down—by the hand of God—following another feast. The Judean man of God obeys the divine interdiction not to eat or drink when he refuses the hospitality of Jeroboam in 1 Kgs 13:1–10; his demise only comes later, when he is deceived into violating that interdiction. Daniel refuses to eat the king's food at the royal court in Babylon in Dan 1:5–16, insisting instead on a vegetarian diet. His adherence to divine law is rewarded. Finally, Aaron, whose sons are struck down while ministering to God at the consecration of priest and sanctuary in Leviticus 10, refrains from eating the priestly portion of the sacrifice, treating it instead as a burnt offering in what may possibly be taken as a refusal to share a meal with the divinity.

Hospitality is straightforwardly offered and accepted, even after some hesitation, in twelve instances. Abraham's hosting of the three visitors in Genesis 18 is viewed by the rabbis as a model for hospitality.[88] Hospitality is offered to Abraham's servant by the family of Laban when a bride is sought for Isaac in Genesis 24, and though he postpones his meal until he has stated his business, eventually he partakes of the hospitality of his host. Hospitality may only be implied when Jacob flees to the same source when he seeks refuge from his brother Esau's ire in Genesis 29. Here there is no explicit statement of hospitality, no mention of food and drink, but the text notes that when Jacob has been in Laban's house a month, Laban suggests that Jacob might work for wages (Gen 29:13–16). Has Jacob been working for nothing until now? Is the host politely suggesting that it is time for the guest to earn his keep? The biblical narrative is ambiguous.

Moses flees to Midian, where he is offered food and shelter in Exod 2:15–22, and, like Jacob, eventually becomes a shepherd for his father-in-law. Moses in exile, like Jacob and Joseph before him, is divinely positioned to undertake the role God has planned for him. At the other extreme, the willing hospitality of the Levite's father-in-law in Judges 19 is so pressed upon the Levite that he has difficulty leaving. This fatal delay is, like so much else in the final three chapters of the book of Judges, an example of the unreasonable excess and poor judgment of human beings operating without higher guidance. Barzillai's generosity in provisioning the fleeing king in 2 Sam 17:27–29 and his unwavering support of God's anointed is rewarded by David on the return journey in 2 Samuel 19.

There are other examples of hospitality as the expression of divine will: Elijah is hosted by the widow of Zarephath in 1 Kgs 17:7–16, but God supplies the victuals; Elisha accepts the divine call to be Elijah's disciple in 1 Kgs 19:19–21 by slaughtering his plow-oxen and feeding his neighbors; Elisha rewards the hospitality of the woman of Shunem by interceding with God to give her a child in 2 Kings 4; the Aramean raiders of 2 Kgs 6:8–23 are fed and watered at the table of the Israelite king and sent on their way as a sign of divine power; Jehoiachin is rehabilitated from his long prison term and feted at the table of the Babylonian king, perhaps as a sign of things to come, in 2 Kgs 25:27–30 and

---

88. See *Gen. Rab.* 48:10–14 (Neusner, *Genesis Rabbah*, 2.184–89). This episode is a major focus of my discussion in chapter 5.

the parallel account in Jer 52:31–34; Job's restoration to divine protection is marked at a meal that he hosts for his friends and family in Job 42:11–17; and in Ruth 2, the protection and hospitality shown to the ancestress of David by Boaz is echoed in David's experience of the generosity of Abigail and Barzillai.

Facilitation of hospitality offered or condemnation for hospitality violated appears to follow the same principle active in the cases of the reward or punishment implicit in the Perfidy Pattern: hospitality, like integrity, must bow to the test of whether divine will is served by its preservation or violation. Even in cases where perfidy occurs within the context of hospitality, the morphology for the Perfidy Pattern remains constant: a pattern consisting of VOLITION, VILLAINY, OUTCOME, and JUDGMENT.

Misfortune

Propp, in his corpus, identifies MISFORTUNE as belonging to the constant functions of LACK or DESIRE, which, along with VILLAINY, get the tale rolling.[89] Both VILLAINY and MISFORTUNE may result in lack or desire, and, in Propp's morphology of the Russian fairy-tale, lack or desire is the primary trigger of the hero's adventures. MISFORTUNE serves the same functions in the Bible that it does in Russian fairy-tales. When it occurs at the beginning of a biblical narrative, misfortune moves the plot forward. At the end of an episode, misfortune may represent punishment at the conclusion of an episode, or it may signal the beginning of a new episode—or both, as it does repeatedly throughout the book of Judges. MISFORTUNE serves all of these functions in Propp's model as well.[90] In biblical narrative, misfortune comes by the will of God, although it may be a direct result of either human or divine action. MISFORTUNE is a constant element containing many variables, including war, plagues, fire, disease, drought, flood, and earthquake. MISFORTUNE may also take the form of famine, a variable that is a reversal of eating/drinking.

Famine.   Famine is a variable of MISFORTUNE when it occurs in the Hebrew Bible and is a variable within all of the functions of MISFORTUNE, whether misfortune occurs at the beginning or end of an episode. As a natural disaster, famine may be theologically neutral, serving the plot function as the impetus for a pilgrimage or journey: that of Abraham and Sarah in Gen 12:10, for example, or of Elimelech

---

89. Propp, *Morphology*, 35, 36, 102, and passim.
90. Ibid., 63, 92–115, 154.

and his family in Ruth 1:1. In other cases, FAMINE may function among many other natural and man-made disasters as a threatened or actual divine punishment for Israel's transgressions, as it does in 1 Kgs 8:35–40, Solomon's advance plea for divine aid to Israel in time of future need. I will discuss both of these functions of MISFORTUNE, in which famine operates as the variable.

Famine as Plot Impetus.   Famine is the theologically neutral instigator of plot in several narratives. In Ruth 1:1, Elimelech flees to Moab in order to avoid famine in his hometown of Bethlehem, initiating the action making up the book. The two missions of Joseph's brothers to Egypt in Genesis 42 and 43 are motivated by famine in Canaan, culminating in the descent of all of Jacob's sons to Egypt. Fear of famine sends the Shunemite woman away from her patrimony for seven years (2 Kgs 8:1–6); the occasion for her appeal to the king for the restoration of her holding is an opportunity for Elisha's miraculous deeds to be more widely recognized and admired and for the woman's association with Elisha to be rewarded yet again.

Each of the three wife-sister accounts in Genesis, two involving Abraham and Sarah and one involving Isaac and Rebekah, is initiated by a natural disaster.[91] Abraham and Sarah's journey to Egypt in Genesis 12 and the sojourn of Isaac and Rebekah in Gerar in Gen 26:1–11 are each instigated by neutrally reported famines. In the wife-sister narrative in Genesis 20, however, the plot is instigated by a natural disaster of a different kind: the punitive destruction of Sodom and

---

91. Much scholarship has been applied to this topic. A brief survey of recent works: Daniel H. Gordis, "Lies, Wives and Sisters: The Wife-Sister Motif Revisited," *Judaism* 34 (1985) 344–59; Jonathan Magonet, "Abraham and God," *Judaism* 33 (1984) 160–70; Harry S. Pappas, "Deception as Patriarchal Self-Defense in a Foreign Land: A Form-Critical Study of the Wife-Sister Stories in Genesis (Gen. 12, 20, 26)," *Greek Orthodox Theological Review* 29 (1984) 35–50; James G. Williams, "The Beautiful and the Barren: Conventions in Biblical Type-Scenes," *JSOT* 17 (1980) 107–19; Samuel Greengus, "Sisterhood Adoption at Nuzi and the 'Wife-Sister' in Genesis," *HUCA* 46 (1975) 5–31; John Van Seters, *Abraham in History and Tradition* (New Haven: Yale University Press, 1975); Robert Polzin, "'The Ancestress of Israel in Danger' in Danger," *Semeia* 3 (*Classical Hebrew Narrative*; 1975) 81–98; and David Berger, "On the Morality of the Patriarchs in Jewish Polemic and Exegesis," in *Understanding Scripture: Explorations of Jewish and Christian Traditions of Interpretation* (ed. C. Thoma and M. Wyschogrod; New York: Paulist, 1987) 49–62.

On the wife-sister tale as a type scene, in addition to Williams noted above, see Robert Alter, "Biblical Type-Scenes and the Uses of Convention," *Critical Inquiry* (1978) 355–68, reprinted in idem, *The Art of Biblical Narrative* (New York: Basic, 1981); and Culley, *Studies in the Structure of Hebrew Narrative*, 33–34.

Gomorrah, which Abraham witnesses from afar (Gen 19:27–28). In this case, the same misfortune functions to end an episode with a punishment and also as the motivation triggering a new episode.

Famine as Divine Punishment. Famine also often occurs as divine punishment in the Hebrew Bible. It is the signal that God is displeased, as in 2 Sam 21:1–14, when David redresses the bloodguilt incurred by Saul's house by delivering seven of Saul's sons to the men of Gibeon. Famine is also one of three penalties (along with war and pestilence) among which David is permitted to choose as punishment for his own transgression of ordering a census in 2 Samuel 24 and its parallel in 1 Chronicles 21. Famine as divine punishment may result from natural or human agency. Rain is withheld in punishment for the sins of the Northern Kingdom (1 Kgs 17:1, read along with 18:17–18), resulting in famine that is only alleviated after the affirmation of Yahweh as God and the slaughter of 450 priests of Baal by Elijah (1 Kgs 18:20–41). Famine is imposed by human means when Samaria is besieged by the Arameans led by Ben-hadad and is alleviated when the siege is divinely terminated (2 Kgs 6:24–7:20). Famine resulting from Babylonian siege is foretold for Jerusalem and expressed symbolically by God's command to Ezekiel to eat bread baked in excrement (Ezek 4:9–17). Famine, among other dire misfortunes, does in fact accompany the fall of Judah in the divine retribution predicted by prophetic oracle (2 Kgs 25:1–26 paralleled by Jer 52:1–29).

Mourning and Supplication

Mourning and supplication are related tropes in the Hebrew Bible. They share many characteristics, gestures, and contexts, and the boundary between the two is frequently blurred. When eating and drinking occur as variables among many other expressions of mourning and supplication, they are most often reversed and expressed as fasting.

Mourning. Mourning the passing of biblical figures takes many forms, among them weeping, lamentation, setting up memorials, and most often, some reference to burial.[92] Fasting is not a normative

---

92. Some deaths are noted as persons' being gathered to their kin (ויאסף אל־עמיו, Gen 25:8, Deut 32:50), part of the form of burial, and others as lying with one's fathers (וישכב and/or ויקבר עם־אבותיו, 1 Kgs 14:31, 2 Chr 12:16, etc.). See Elizabeth Bloch-Smith, "Burials," *ABD* 1.785–88; see also B. Alfrink, "L'expression *Ne'esap 'el 'Ammaw*," *Oudtestamentische Studiën* 5 (1948) 118–31; idem, "L'expression *Šakab 'Im 'Abotâw*," *Oudtestamentische Studiën* 2 (1943) 106–18; and K.-J. Illman, *Old Testament Formulas about Death* (Åbo, Finland: Åbo Akademi, 1979).

expression of grief in the Bible and is not associated with mourning at all until David becomes king after the death of Saul.

Sarah's death is reported in Gen 23:2, where Abraham is reported to mourn and lament for her (ויבא אברהם לספד לשרה ולבכתה). No fasting is mentioned. The death of Rebekah's nurse is reported in Gen 35:8, where weeping for her is suggested by the associated etiology for the name of her burial place: weeping oak (אלון בכות). No fasting is mentioned. Rebekah herself dies, is buried, and a pillar is erected for her, as noted in Gen 35:20. No weeping, lamenting, fasting, or other mourning practice is mentioned.

A mixture of Egyptian and patriarchal observances is noted upon Jacob's death in Gen 50:1–14, the most elaborately reported funeral in the Bible. When Jacob breathes his last, Joseph falls upon his father, weeps, and kisses him (ויפל יוסף על־פני אביו ויבך עליו וישק־לו, 50:1). Jacob is then embalmed for 40 days and bewailed for 70 days. With Pharaoh's permission, his body is carried back to Canaan by an entourage of family and Egyptian nobility and cavalry, where seven days of mourning are observed, and the impressed locals rename the place 'Egypt's Mourning' (אבל מצרים, 50:11). No fasting is mentioned. Joseph's death is reported much more laconically in Gen 50:26. He dies and is embalmed and encoffined.[93] No fasting is mentioned.

In Num 20:1b, Miriam is noted to have died and been buried; no other mourning practices are reported. Aaron (Num 20:28–29) and Moses (Deut 34:5–8) are each lamented for 30 days by the people. Moses' burial is noted enigmatically (who buries him?), and Aaron's is not reported. No fasting is mentioned for either. Samuel's death, noted twice, in 1 Sam 25:1 and in 1 Sam 28:3, results in public mourning, but there is no mention of fasting.

The first mention of fasting in connection with a death in the Hebrew Bible is the seven-day fast observed by the men of Jabesh-gilead after their daring rescue, cremation, and burial of the remains of Saul and Jonathan (1 Sam 31:13). No other mourning practice by them is mentioned. When David hears of Saul's death (2 Sam 1:11–12), he and his men rend their clothes, lament and weep, and fast until evening for Saul and Jonathan and all the fallen warriors. David then slays the messenger who claims to have killed Saul and Jonathan (2 Sam 1:15–16) and intones his famous lament, as reproduced in 2 Sam 1·19–27.

---

93. This is the only occurrence of the term "coffin" in the Hebrew Bible and probably reflects Egyptian practice; see David Marcus, "The Term 'Coffin' in the Semitic Languages," *JANES* 7 (1975) 85–94, especially pp. 89–90.

In biblical narrative, fasting as a mortuary practice appears to be associated exclusively with David's public acts of mourning for his political enemies:[94] Saul, Jonathan, and Abner, commander of the troops of Saul's house, in 2 Sam 3:28–39. David declares innocence in regard to his commander Joab's shedding of Abner's blood and utters an imprecation upon Joab and his house as a consequence. David orders all of the troops to rend their clothing, don sackcloth, and make public lament. David himself walks behind the bier and intones a lament for Abner, reproduced in 2 Sam 3:33–34. In spite of the urging of his men to eat after the funeral, David vows to fast until sundown in honor of the fallen Abner. In this case, at least, David receives the approval of the troops for this mourning practice, which also appears to be taken as evidence of David's innocence of the deaths (2 Sam 3:36–37). It is interesting to note that David's "innovation" of public fasting as a sign of mourning probably did not become regular Israelite practice. 1 Kgs 14:17–18 reports the death of the anonymous son of Jeroboam of the Northern Kingdom. The child dies, is properly buried, and is lamented by all Israel. No fasting, public or private, is mentioned.

---

94. It has been suggested that David's public attestations of innocence are politically motivated. Baruch Halpern reflected upon the polemical intention underlying David's behavior in these narratives in a paper delivered in Bethlehem, Pennsylvania, in May 1994, at a conference sponsored by the Philip and Muriel Berman Center for Jewish Studies at Lehigh University, published as "The Artifact and the Text: Two Monologues?" in *The Archaeology of Israel: Constructing the Past, Interpreting the Present* (ed. N. A. Silberman and D. Small; JSOTSup 237; Sheffield: Sheffield Academic Press, 1997) 311–34.

Halpern examines the defense of David offered in biblical texts dealing with political murder. He notes that such murders often occur after the victim-to-be shares a meal with David, meals dubbed by Halpern "forgive and forget banquets."

In these narratives, David is repeatedly exonerated by man or God for all murders, except that he is given responsibility for the slayings associated with Solomon's name: Uriah (Solomon's mother's first husband), Joab, and Shimei (David instructs Solomon to kill the latter two in his final charge to his son and heir in 1 Kgs 2:5–6, 8–9). Halpern suggests that these stories of David's self-exoneration from the deaths of his enemies are apologetics for Solomon at his accession, explaining how Solomon came to be king and not necessarily how his father gained the throne. Halpern suggests that these concerns could only have been contemporary to Solomon's time; he judges that they would not be of pressing importance to any other era.

A literary approach, in contrast to Halpern's historiographic perspective, is suggested by Stuart Schreiber in his unpublished dissertation proposal, "The Meaning and Use of Eating in the Biblical Narrative." He terms the phenomenon "violent hospitality." I am indebted to Mr. Schreiber for allowing me to benefit from his study and to Dr. Edward L. Greenstein for drawing it to my attention.

That fasting as a sign of mourning is part of David's public posture is supported by the fact that David does not fast for his many private griefs. When David's son Amnon is slain in vengeance by his half-brother Absalom (2 Sam 13:36–39), the priests, the court, and David weep bitterly, and the text reports that David recovers from his grief. No fasting is mentioned. When David's son Absalom is slain, so ending his rebellion, David is inconsolable. The text repeatedly reports in 2 Sam 19:1–5 that David wails, laments, covers his face, and cries out loud. No fasting is mentioned.

Later in the David narrative, there is an interesting variation on this idea of fasting as a sign of grief that is closely associated with the persona of David. It is worth pausing to examine this puzzling text in some detail to see how skillfully both literary directionality and social convention can be manipulated in the Bible. The narrative in 2 Samuel 12 builds on the customary role of fasting as an act of supplication, which is discussed later in this chapter, and uses the device of reversal—of eating and drinking, as well as of conventional expectation—in a very sophisticated way.[95]

One outcome of David's adulterous coupling with Bathsheba is her pregnancy (2 Sam 11:5). Concern for this child's paternity has been suggested as one reason for David's several attempts to trick Uriah into sleeping under his own marital roof in 2 Sam 11:6–13 and, upon David's lack of success, for his effectively signing Uriah's death warrant in 2 Sam 11:14–25.[96] After her husband's death and a suitable period of mourning, Bathsheba marries David and bears the child (2 Sam 11:26–27).

David's court prophet, Nathan, condemns David for this transgression, delivering an oracle in which David's private relationships are condemned to tragedy (2 Sam 12:1–14): the sword shall not depart from David's house, his concubines will be taken carnally by another in broad daylight, and, most immediately, the child of his adulterous union with Bathsheba will sicken and die. Before the end of David's story, every one of these predictions comes to pass.

When the baby falls critically ill, David fasts and sleeps on the bare ground, apparently in supplication for the child's recovery (see 2 Sam 12:22). When the child dies after seven days, the servants fear to inform David, concerned that he will react even more drastically to the baby's passing than he did to his illness. But instead of mourning even

---

95. This example is discussed in greater depth in my essay "When Fathers Refuse to Eat," *Semeia* 86 (forthcoming, 2001).

96. See Marcus, "David the Deceiver," 163–71.

more deeply at the death of the child, David astonishes his servants by washing and anointing himself and eating. He replies matter-of-factly to their exclamations of surprise that while the child was sick, it was worth appealing to God in the hope of changing the divine mind but, now that the child is irreversibly dead, fasting is of no use since nothing can bring him back to life (2 Sam 12:21–23). In effect, David has mourned in advance. His behavior blurs the boundaries between supplication and grief. However, his ability to cease grieving the instant he hears his son has died shocks the servants—and perhaps the reader.

David's lack of emotion at the loss of his child is extraordinary; even in tragic circumstances where one is helpless at the loss of a child, one experiences grief, rage, loss, guilt. David's pragmatism and rationality under these circumstances are more revealing of the flaws in his private character than volumes of anti-David polemic could possibly be. David's pragmatic acceptance of the death of the child resonates with his pragmatic condemnation of Uriah to death. Has he learned nothing from Nathan's parable? We understand more starkly now the hard lesson implicit in Nathan's oracle: David is to learn the value of human life the hardest way there is to learn it. We who know what is to come hear in David's laconic acceptance of this child's death a raw contrast with the inconsolable cry of the grieving father, בני אבשלום בני בני אבשלום 'O my son Absalom, my son, my son Absalom!' (2 Sam 19:1–5).

From a literary point of view, the dead child is the product of the forbidden adulterous union and thus its symbol. With the death of the child, David puts behind him any guilt or shame for what he has done. He picks himself up off the ground and washes his hands of the grime and the crime simultaneously. That done, he can ask after his dinner (2 Sam 12:20).

A clue to the literary significance of the eating events in this text is the language surrounding David's preparations for his meal.[97] The series of words for washing, anointing, and eating are used together elsewhere in accounts of banquets throughout the biblical text. Seeing the series of banquet expressions in this context, where mourning is expected, draws the reader's attention to the eating act, associating it linguistically with feasting and festivities. This linguistic association heightens the contextual dissonance inherent in the reversal of conventional expectation expressed explicitly in this text by the servants in reaction to David's shocking behavior. David's behavior foreshadows that of Jehu in 2 Kings 9, who sits down to a meal after Jezebel is pushed to her death, and only when he is finished does he inquire

---

97. On sequence of actions and language relating to banquet, see Lichtenstein, *Episodic Structure*, 136–60.

about her burial arrangements. Just as Jezebel's death and the igno-
minious disposition of her remains fulfill an oracle and signal payment
of the price God exacts for her transgressions, so the death of this
child signals for David the fulfillment of an oracle and payment of the
price of his sins.

One possible result of the reversal of conventional expectation of
the king's eating or not eating as expressions of grieving or not grieving is to mirror the reversal of other conventional expectations in
these chapters. Many conventions have been flouted by this king: the
sacral character of marriage, respect for human life, and the expected
sequence of marriage, conception, and childbirth. The reversals surrounding eating or not eating serve as a literary device linking these
ideas rhetorically, inviting the reader to look at other reversals suggested by the text and allowing a deeper comprehension of the significance of what has ocurred in terms of what is to come.

Supplication.   Supplication is defined as the action of humble or
earnest petition or entreaty or a humble prayer addressed to God.[98] It
is the expression of an intensification of the relationship between the
supplicant and God. Supplication is represented in the Bible by a
wealth of different gestures. Fasting, a reversal of eating and drinking,
is a variable of supplication, as are weeping, praying, sitting in the dust,
and wearing sackcloth. Each of these actions symbolizes a shedding of
distractions by the supplicant, indicating a sharpening and narrowing
of focus from things of this world to God alone. That some of these
supplicatory gestures are also associated with death and mourning underlines the supplicant's renunciation of worldly distraction and his or
her humility and vulnerablility.

Going without food and water is a powerful symbol of human renunciation of the world and focus on the divine. The only personal detail recorded of Moses during his 40 days on the mountain is that he
ate no bread and drank no water while he received the Ten Commandments (Exod 34:28). This intensification of focus through austerity is
made explicit in Deut 29:4–5, in Moses' final address to the people,
when he refers to the austerity of the wilderness journey: "Bread (לחם)
you did not eat and wine or strong drink (יין ושכר) you did not drink in
order that you would know that YHWH is your God."[99]

---

98. William Little, H. W. Fowler, and J. Coulson, *The Shorter Oxford English Dictionary* (rev. C. T. Onions; Oxford: Clarendon, 1933) 2086.

99. I am indebted to my colleague Stephen P. Garfinkel, member of the Department of Bible and Dean of the Graduate School at JTS, for pointing these references out to me.

There are many examples of supplication in the Hebrew Bible that do not involve fasting. David's prayer for mercy after his transgression in ordering a census in 2 Samuel 24 is almost exactly paralleled by the account in 1 Chronicles 21; fasting is not mentioned. During the dedication of the Temple in parallel accounts in 1 Kings 8 and 2 Chronicles 5–6, Solomon's appeal to God for future mercy when the people are in need is framed in a prayer, and the means for communicating the people's distress to God is also by means of prayer. Fasting is not mentioned.

Hezekiah successfully petitions for divine aid twice. Fasting is not mentioned in either case. First, in 2 Kgs 19:1–4 and the parallel account in Isaiah 36–37, Hezekiah is dismayed by the coercive rhetoric of the Rabshakeh. Hezekiah and his chief scribes and priests rend their clothes and don sackcloth. The king also offers an effective letter-prayer (2 Kgs 19:14–20), and the danger is averted.[100] Prayer, in combination with weeping, is also effective in securing an extension of Hezekiah's life when he falls ill, as reported in 2 Kgs 20:1–6. Clearly, fasting is not universally required in the Hebrew Bible in order to make divine supplication.

However, fasting as an act of supplication does occur several times in Hebrew biblical narrative. I exclude examples from prophetic poetry, where fasting is so well known in its association with supplication that mention of the one evokes the other, as in Joel 1:14 and 2:15–17.[101]

Fasting is associated with supplication in Nineveh's appeal for a divine reprieve in Jonah 3; Esther's preparation to appear, unsummoned, before Ahasuerus in Esther 4; the Babylonian king's appeal for Daniel's well-being in the lion's den in Daniel 6; Ezra's petition for divine protection on his pilgrimage of return to Jerusalem in Ezra 8; his plea for divine forgiveness when he finds out about the foreign wives in Israel's midst; and his determination to correct this transgression in Ezra 9–10.

Some of the other elements that occur as variables of supplication, such as tearing garments and wearing sackcloth, also evoke images of mourning as well as supplication. This overlap of expression and re-

---

100. For possible ancient Near Eastern parallels to this incident, see William W. Hallo, "The Royal Correspondence of Larsa, I: A Sumerian Prototype for the Prayer of Hezekiah?" *Kramer Anniversary Volume* (AOAT 25; Neukirchen-Vluyn: Neukirchener Verlag, 1976) 209–24.

101. On the significance of this and other non-recurring doublets for the unity of authorship of Joel, see David Marcus, "Non-recurring Doublets in the Book of Joel," *CBQ* 56 (1994) 56–67.

sulting ambiguity enrich the expression and interpretation of texts in which they occur. For example, Nehemiah fasts, weeps, prays, and sits in mourning for days when he hears about conditions in Jerusalem (Neh 1:4). Is his reaction one of grief or supplication? Here, there is a blurring of the lines between mourning and petition, as there is in the imagery of prophetic poetry. The traditional gestures of grief precede a long prayer that ends with a plea for divine support for 'your servant's success' (והצליחה־נא לעבדך היום ותנהו לרחמים לפני האיש הזה, 1:11), most likely in making his petition to the Persian potentate for a leave from the king's service that is the subject of the following chapter, Nehemiah 2. Like Ezra's plea for a safe pilgrimage to Jerusalem in Ezra 8, Nehemiah's request is favorably received.[102]

The advocacy by the Deuteronomist of prayer as a means of communication with the divine is well known,[103] and this bias may account for the absence of other gestures, including fasting, in supplication narratives in the Deuteronomic History. It is interesting that most examples of supplication that include the element of fasting come from later biblical literature and that the element of fasting is absent in supplication accounts in the earlier biblical texts. It is tempting to speculate that the convention in literary prophecy associating fasting and supplication might account for this phenomenon.

A variety of gestures contribute to the expression of supplication in biblical narrative. Some of these cluster in patriarchal or Deuteronomic histories, and others occur more often in postexilic biblical books. Fasting in SUPPLICATION is just one variable of that constant.

---

102. See Edward L. Greenstein, "Autobiographies in Ancient Western Asia," in *Civilizations of the Ancient Near East* (ed. Jack M. Sasson et al.; New York: Scribner's 1996) 4.2421–32.

103. See the classic study by Moshe Weinfeld, *Deuteronomy and the Deuteronomic School* (Oxford: Oxford University Press, 1972; repr. Winona Lake, Ind.: Eisenbrauns, 1992) 32–52, 195–270, and passim.

CHAPTER FOUR

The Unexpected Absence of Eating and Drinking

The Absence of Eating and Drinking

At the beginning of the previous chapter, I made the case that eating and drinking are literary devices when they occur in biblical narrative: whenever everyday actions such as eating, sleeping, elimination, or fornication occur in biblical narrative, they carry meaning with them beyond the mundane. The inverse is true as well: even in circumstances where eating and drinking can be presumed to have occurred, they are not mentioned in the text unless they have specific literary significance. In the vast majority of descriptions of life-cycle occasions such as birth, circumcision, weaning, marriage, and others, references to eating and drinking are entirely absent from biblical narrative. This general absence heightens the significance of eating and drinking when they do occur on life-cycle occasions.

Eating and Drinking on Life-Cycle Occasions

The life-cycle events that I consider here are annunciation, weaning, espousal, blessing, commissioning, and death and resurrection. The number of eating and drinking events associated with all such occasions in the entire Hebrew Bible is relatively small—fewer than twenty. The paucity of textual references to such feasts suggests that when they do occur they are literarily significant. I have found, in fact, that in such cases a larger pattern is present that calls for viewing the function of EATING and DRINKING as a constant. I discuss these patterns in chapters 5 and 6.

For now, I will show that eating and drinking are not a required element to mark life-cycle events represented in the Bible. Within the analytical framework I have established so far, eating and drinking are variables within the constant category of LIFE-CYCLE EVENTS. Thus, when they do occur in such texts, they beg for further analysis to determine their specific literary function.

For each category of LIFE-CYCLE EVENT, I will adduce examples that occur in the context of an eating or drinking occasion as well as examples in which the same life-cycle event occurs in the absence of an eating or drinking context. This approach will demonstrate that eating and drinking are variables of that occasion and not a requirement, literarily or otherwise, for the description of each life-cycle event.

Annunciation, Birth, and Circumcision

Significant events surrounding conception, pregnancy, and childbirth in biblical narrative occur in a variety of settings, none of them necessarily an eating or drinking context. I will survey them very briefly here.

Three birth annunciations in the Hebrew Bible occur in conjunction with eating and drinking: the annunciation of the birth of Isaac in Genesis 18; the annunciation of the birth of Samson in Judges 13; and the annunciation of the birth of Samuel in 1 Samuel 1. Each of these three annunciations comes by word of a messenger. The annunciation of Jacob and Esau to Rebekah is different from these in several ways. Instead of coming by messenger, the annunciation occurs in an ORACLE in Gen 25:20–26. The precise nature of Rebekah's inquiry and the type of ORACLE are not mentioned, and any eating or drinking reference is completely absent from this text. The text is silent about any gift Rebekah might bring, or any offering she might make.

From a literary point of view, the textual evidence shows that annunciation may come by means of either messenger or oracle; the conventions associated with annunciation in Hebrew biblical narrative do not appear to require that annunciation only occur in a context that includes eating and drinking.[1]

---

1. For a discussion of "annunciation" type scenes, see James G. Williams, "The Beautiful and the Barren: Conventions in Biblical Type-Scenes," *JSOT* 17 (1980) 107–19, especially p. 110; Robert Alter, "Biblical Type-Scenes and the Uses of Convention," *Critical Inquiry* (1978) 355–68, especially p. 359; and idem, "How Convention Helps Us Read: The Case of the Bible's Annunciation Type-Scene," *Prooftexts* 3/2 (1983) 115–30.

Analogies may be useful in clarifying the distinction between the type scene as noted here and morphological patterns discussed in section 3 of this study. Professor Murray Lichtenstein of the Department of Classical and Oriental Studies at Hunter College, City University of New York, has suggested privately that the relationship may be analogous to the relationship of a single bead (type scene) to a pattern of beads strung on a necklace (structural morphology).

As for other events surrounding pregnancy and childbirth in the Hebrew Bible, eating and drinking do not appear to be necessary to these: birth, naming, or circumcision. In no case is eating or drinking connected to any biblical report of the birth of a child. Following their births, children are named, and often the reason for choosing a particular name is given, although not always—Samson's name is not explained, for example in Judg 13:24—but no eating or drinking is ever mentioned in connection with the naming of a child.

Circumcision is only noted a few times in the Hebrew Bible, and only twice does it apply to a newborn or to a child: to Isaac in Gen 21:4 and, enigmatically, to Zipporah's son in Exod 4:24–26. Every other time circumcision occurs, it is in the context of extraordinary circumstances, and adolescents or adults are the subjects: Abraham and his household, including Ishmael, in Genesis 17; the men of Shechem in Genesis 34; and the Israelites at Gilgal in Joshua 5. None of these circumcisions occurs in an eating or drinking context. At Gilgal, however, immediately following the circumcision that takes place, perhaps, on or after the tenth day of the month (reading together Josh 4:19 and 5:2), the text reports that the first Passover in the land is celebrated on the fourteenth day of the month (Josh 5:10). The text separates the Passover celebration itself (and its concomitant eating of the fruits of the land and the cessation of manna) from the rite of circumcision that precedes it (Josh 5:9–10). Taking all of the evidence together, we see that eating and drinking are apparently not required for the literary depiction of biblical practices surrounding the LIFE-CYCLE occasions of childbirth, naming, or the act of circumcision. When eating and drinking occur, they are variables in these categories and may also bear some other literary significance.

Weaning

Weaning, by its very nature, has to do with eating and drinking: it represents a transition between one means of nourishment, appropriate for infants and young children, and another, appropriate for older children and adults. As such, it is a major rite of passage for both mother and child and might be expected to be accompanied by a feast symbolizing the new relationship between the child and the adult world. Yet only once in the Hebrew Bible is weaning (the Hebrew root גמל) unambiguously accompanied by a feast: Isaac's weaning in Gen 21:1–8. This text is significant in many ways, and its uniqueness in terms of the context of a feast is just one indication. I analyze this narrative in great detail in chapter 5.

Other weanings are noted without any reference to feast, banquet, or any other eating or drinking event. These include Gomer's weaning of her daughter Lo-ruhamah (Hos 1:8) and the weaning of Hadad's son Genubath, borne by the sister of Tahpenes, in 1 Kgs 11:20.[2]

One narrative is ambiguous with respect to weaning. Jochebed nurses Moses until he is grown (Hebrew root גדל), at which time she presents him to Pharaoh's daughter, who names him (Exod 2:10). The text makes no specific mention of weaning and does not define what age Moses has attained at his presentation. No eating or drinking is noted either. Hannah's weaning of Samuel (1 Sam 1:23–24) is ambiguous with respect to eating and drinking. Are the commodities she brings with her and her son on their pilgrimage to Jerusalem part of a gift to the sanctuary accompanying the dedication of Samuel to the Lord's service, or are the sacrificial provisions she prepares part of the process connected with the weaning of her child? Either way, it would appear that the text does not regard eating and drinking as essential to the description of weaning in the Hebrew Bible, and so from a literary perspective eating and drinking are variable elements within the LIFE-CYCLE category of weaning.

Espousal

There are only three wedding feasts noted in the Bible: Jacob's marriages to Leah and Rachel in Genesis 29, Samson's wedding feast in Judges 14, and Esther's wedding banquet in Esth 2:18. Certainly, wives are taken without descriptions of formal ceremonies, as for example with Esau more than once, in Gen 26:34 and 28:9. In Gen 24:67, the text notes that Isaac brings Rebekah into the tent of his mother, Sarah, and follows this immediately with the statement that he took Rebekah as his wife (ויבאה יצחק האהלה שרה אמו ויקח את־רבקה ותהי־לו לאשה). If there is a ceremony or feast associated with this process, it is not reported.[3] Rebekah is espoused to Isaac at a meal in Genesis 24, but the original purpose of the meal is not to celebrate a betrothal but to offer hospitality to Abraham's servant. The feast is spread before the servant

---

2. The Septuagint reads ἐξέθρεψεν 'reared' (Hebrew root = גדל) for 'weaned' (Hebrew root = גמל) in the Masoretic text.

3. There has been much discussion, however, about the betrothal type scene, which does not appear to require an eating or drinking event, although it seems to take place at the well where flocks are watered. See Robert C. Culley, *Studies in the Structure of Hebrew Narrative* (Philadelphia: Fortress / Atlanta: Scholars Press, 1976) especially pp. 41–43; and studies built on his work, including Williams, "The Beautiful and the Barren," especially p. 109; and Alter, "Biblical Type-Scenes and the Uses of Convention," especially pp. 359–65.

has stated his business, and the servant refuses to partake in the meal until he has discharged his mission (Gen 24:31–33).

The distinguishing gesture for espousal does not appear to be a feast or other celebration but the symbolic action of spreading one's skirts over the intended (פרשׂ כנף), performed by the male partner. Even so, this gesture is not reported in every instance of espousal. This is a gesture well known from Ruth's plea to Boaz on the threshing floor in Ruth 3 and known, as well, from the allegory of God's espousal of Jerusalem in Ezek 16:8. An allusion to this gesture occurs in a legal context in Deut 23:1, where the prohibition against exposing the father's skirt (לא יגלה כנף אביו) refers to the carnal taking of a woman whom one's father has espoused.[4] Eating and drinking are variables within the constant LIFE-CYCLE element of espousal.

Blessing

Only once in the Hebrew Bible is the blessing of one's children associated with eating and drinking, and that is Isaac's blessing of Jacob and Esau in Gen 27:1–28:5. Nowhere else in the Bible do we have the practice of eating associated with such an event. Jacob blesses Joseph's children in Genesis 48, for example, and his own children in Genesis 49 without any mention of an eating or drinking context. As I have stated, this unique occurrence of blessing in conjunction with eating is the key to my understanding of the Patterns of Destiny, which is the main subject of this book, and I discuss this text, too, in great detail in chapter 5. For now it is clear that an eating and drinking context is not required for the blessing of children in the Hebrew Bible.

Blessings may contain references to food, as in the promise of abundance in Isaac's blessings and in the images of rich bread and royal sweets in Jacob's blessing of Asher in Gen 49:20 and Jacob's blessing of Joseph as a fruitful bough, with the blessings of the deep, of the breasts, and of the womb in Gen 49:22–26. Food and drink may also be used metaphorically, either positively, as in Jacob's blessing of Judah with teeth white with milk and garments washed in wine (Gen 49:11–12), or with negative associations, as in Jacob's blessing of Benjamin as a ravening wolf devouring prey in Gen 49:27. But the content

---

4. A reversal of the gesture of covering with a skirt may be intended in the reference to divorcing a woman as stripping her or sending her out naked (see Hos 2:5, 11–12). Among other discussions of this practice in Hosea, see H. L. Ginsberg, "Hosea, Book of," *EncJud* 8.1010–24; and also Yochanan Muffs, *Love and Joy: Law, Language and Religion in Ancient Israel* (New York: Jewish Theological Seminary of America, 1992), 49.

of such blessings need not have anything to do with the literal acts of eating and drinking, making these a variable element within the constant LIFE-CYCLE element of blessing.

Commissioning

I include commissioning among life-cycle events for purposes of discussion, and on the analogy of annunciation. Like annunciations, commissioning does not occur in every character's history, but military call, royal anointing, and prophetic commissioning usually occur when the individual is of an age to discharge the associated responsibilities; and when commissioning does take place, it represents an important watershed in a person's life. As in annunciation accounts, when the Bible reports on commissioning events, the individual is marked for some special mission.

Only five examples of commissioning in the Hebrew Bible occur in an eating or drinking context. One is a military call: Gideon is summoned to service by a divine messenger, to whom he offers hospitality in Judg 6:11–24. One is a prophetic appointment: Ezekiel's call involves the symbolic eating of a scroll in Ezek 3:1–9. Three are the designations of kings: the anointing of Saul in 1 Sam 9:1–10:16, the covert anointing of David in 1 Sam 16:1–13, and the accession of Solomon in 1 Kgs 1:1–49. Solomon's accession is also reported in 1 Chronicles 28–29, a text that I discuss further in chapter 6, along with the other commissioning texts referred to here that do include eating.

Eating and drinking are not required for any of these. Military leaders are summoned where no eating or drinking is reported, as in Deborah's mobilization of Barak in Judges 4; the prophets Hosea, Joel, Amos, Obadiah, Jonah, Micah, Nahum, Habakkuk, Zephaniah, Zechariah, and Malachi begin to deliver the word of the Lord without any reference to eating or drinking, literal or symbolic. Isaiah (Isaiah 6) and Jeremiah (Jeremiah 1) are also designated without any explicit eating, although God does put words into Jeremiah's mouth (Jer 1:9 and 15:16), and Isaiah's mouth is touched by a burning coal and cleansed before he volunteers for a divine mission (Isa 6:6–8). Jehu is anointed king of Israel without the benefit of a feast (2 Kgs 9:1–14). In addition, there are several reports of kings' succeeding one another without a report of either anointing or celebration, as when Jehoahaz succeeds his father, Jehu, in 2 Kgs 10:35.[5] In commissioning narratives, as in the

---

5. Raphael Patai reviews published literature on the structure of coronation rites as they are expressed in modern cultures of the Near East and similarly analyzes coronation rituals in the Bible in his article "Hebrew Installation Rites," *HUCA* 20

other LIFE-CYCLE stages, eating and drinking are variable elements of the constants.

Death and Resurrection

Unambiguous evidence for funerary meals or mortuary banquets is completely lacking in biblical narrative. The allusion to "sacrifices of (or to) the dead" associated with Baal Peor in Ps 106:28 (ויאכלו זבחי מתים) occurs in a poetic, not narrative, context and refers to a clearly condemned pagan practice. Moreover, this poetic reference lacks any hint of the term usually associated by scholars of the Near East with such eating and drinking: *marzeaḥ* (מרזח). This term, which occurs twice in the Bible, once in Jer 16:5 and once in Amos 6:7, probably has to do in its biblical usage with a cry—of joy, based on the context in Amos; of lament, from the context in Jeremiah.

There has been much scholarly hypothesis based on art and inscriptions about the nature of the institution of the *marzeaḥ* in the ancient Near East and, by extension, in the Bible.[6] However, its limited and

---

(1947) 143–225. Significantly, he finds that, when eating and drinking events are associated with these festivities, the eating and drinking occur not before but after the coronation and anointing in every pattern listed. This reinforces the observation made in the present study that the mention of eating and drinking events is not required for royal succession or for consecration and that the Patterns of Destiny discussed in this study are distinct from any coronation or installation pattern, since in the Foundation and Doom Patterns the EATING or DRINKING event occurs at the beginning of the expected sequence.

6. Just some of the scholarship published on this subject over the past thirty years: Eleanor Ferris Beach, "The Samaria Ivories, *Marzeaḥ*, and Biblical Text," *BA* 56/2 (1993) 94–104; Elizabeth M. Bloch-Smith, "The Cult of the Dead in Judah: Interpreting the Material Remains," *JBL* 111 (1992) 213–24; and idem, *Judahite Burial Practices and Beliefs about the Dead* (JSOTSup 123; Sheffield: Sheffield Academic, 1992); William W. Hallo, "Royal Ancestor Worship in the Biblical World," in *"Sha'arei Talmon": Studies in the Bible, Qumran, and the Ancient Near East Presented to Shemaryahu Talmon* (ed. M. Fishbane, E. Tov, and W. W. Fields; Winona Lake, Ind.: Eisenbrauns, 1992) 381–401; Karel van der Toorn, "Funerary Rituals and Beatific Afterlife in Ugaritic Texts and in the Bible," *BiOr* 48 (1991) 40–66; Susan Ackerman, "A Marzeaḥ in Ezekiel 8:7–13?" *HTR* 82 (1989) 267–81; Theodore J. Lewis, *Cults of the Dead in Ancient Israel and Ugarit* (HSM 39; Atlanta: Scholars Press, 1989); Philip J. King, "The Marzeah Amos Denounces—Using Archaeology to Interpret a Biblical Text," *BARev* 15/4 (July/August, 1988) 34–44; Richard D. Barnett, "Assurbanipal's Feast," *ErIsr* 18 (Nahman Avigad Volume; 1985) 1–6; N. Avigad and J. C. Greenfield, "Bronze Phiale with Phoenician Inscription," *IEJ* (1982) 118–28; Jean-Marie Dentzer, *Le Motif du banquet couché dans le Proche-Orient et le monde grec du VIIe au IVe siècle avant J.C.* (Rome: École Française de Rome, 1982) 529–58; Marvin H. Pope, "The Cult of the Dead at Ugarit," in *Ugarit in Retrospect: Fifty Years of*

ambiguous occurrence in biblical texts, and the necessarily hypothetical nature of even scholarly discussion on the subject, renders further examination of this elusive topic speculative and outside my objective here.

Three instances of resurrection are reported in the Hebrew Bible, one associated with Elijah (1 Kgs 17:17–24) and two with his disciple Elisha (2 Kgs 4:18–37 and 13:20–21). In none of these cases is eating or drinking directly associated with the process of resuscitation, although in two of the instances (in 1 Kings 17 and 2 Kings 4) the relationship between the resurrecting prophet and the mother of the dead child is one of a history of hospitality provided by the woman for the miracle-worker. In the third instance (2 Kings 13), there is no relationship at all: an anonymous corpse comes to life after contact with the dead bones of Elisha. Eating and drinking are clearly not required for descriptions of the LIFE-CYCLE element of resurrection in the Hebrew Bible.

Eating and Drinking in Celebration

Eating and drinking events accompany many kinds of joyful occasions in the Bible. As I noted earlier, some of these celebrations are cultic. Cultic celebrations include the removal of the ark to Jerusalem in 2 Sam 6:1–19 and its parallel account in 1 Chr 13:5–14, and the Passover celebration following permission to build the Second Temple, as recounted in Ezra 5–6. There is also a cultic celebration at the dedication of the wall of Jerusalem in Neh 12:43, featuring offerings (זבח) and rejoicing (שׂמח). One other celebration occurs in a cultic/covenant context in 2 Chronicles 15, where Asa and the people rejoice with shouting and shofar blast at the conclusion of a covenant ceremony. Other celebrations occur in life-cycle events and include Solomon's accession in 1 Kgs 1:1–49 and Esther's wedding banquet in Esth 2:18. In each category of examples we have seen that similar events are narrated in the Bible without references to eating and drinking, signifying that eating and drinking are variables within these other constants and are not required for these events to take place.

Ugarit and Ugaritic (ed. G. D. Young; Winona Lake, Ind.: Eisenbrauns, 1981) 159–79; Paolo Xella, "Sur la nourriture des morts: Un aspect de l'eschatologie mésopotamienne," in *Death in Mesopotamia: Papers Read at the XXVIe Rencontre Assyriologique Internationale, 1979* (ed. B. Alster; Copenhagen Studies in Assyriology 8; Copenhagen: Akademisk, 1980) 151–60. On ancestor veneration and worship, including ritual repasts for the departed, see Herbert Chanan Brichto, "Kin, Cult, Land and Afterlife: A Biblical Complex," *HUCA* 44 (1973) 1–54.

What about eating and drinking as a natural part of other kinds of celebrations? In fact, there is only one celebration involving eating and drinking in the Hebrew Bible that occurs in a text that does not clearly belong to a category I have already identified as a constant: the celebration by the Jews of their victory over their foes in Esth 8:1–9:32.

In no other biblical text is a victory in battle celebrated with rejoicing as described in this text. Most victories are not commemorated at all, even though on occasion mention is made of the division of spoil, as it is with Abraham and the kings in Genesis 14, the Children of Israel versus Midian in Numbers 31, and David rescuing Ziklag in 1 Samuel 30. The defeat of Canaan in Judges 4 is celebrated with a victory song in Judges 5. Other victories are commemorated by proscribing the spoil, thus dedicating it to God: Hormah in Num 21:3 and Jericho in Josh 6:26.

Only in Esther 8–9 is victory celebrated with feasting and celebration, and only here is an *anticipated* victory celebrated with gladness, joy, feasting, and holiday (Esth 8:16). The uniqueness of this instance invites further examination.

In this example, no sacrifices are ordered or offered, no priest is present, or sanctuary designated. Yet the description of the Jews' triumph over their foes in these chapters of Esther and of the order for annual remembrance of their victory throughout the generations is strongly reminiscent of the tone, language, and syntax of the similar charge to future generations to remember and observe the momentous liberation of God's people recorded in Exodus 12.

Compare, for example, the messages in Esther 8–9 and Exodus 12. The celebration by the Jews described in Esth 8:16–17 anticipates actual victory, as does God's prescription for observing the liberation of the Israelites in Exodus 12. Esth 9:28 and Exod 12:14 share the charge to commemorate (Hebrew verbal root זכר) the events for future generations (Hebrew noun דור). Esth 9:28 mentions that the celebration is to be observed family by family, evoking the family divisions for the eating of the Paschal lamb ordered in Exod 12:3–4.

The institutionalization of the festival of Passover is essentially cultic in nature; the institutionalization of the feast of Purim is essentially secular in nature.[7] However, at least from a literary perspective, the narrative ordering the institutionalization of the festival of Purim is

---

7. As Carey Moore takes pains to point out in his commentary on this book, "men, not Yahweh, delivered the Jews." See Carey A. Moore, *Esther: A New Translation with Introduction and Commentary* (AB 91; Garden City, N.Y.: Doubleday, 1988) 91. Also see Gillis Gerleman, *Esther* (BKAT 21/1; Neukirchen-Vluyn: Neukirchener Verlag, 1970) 22.

modeled on the text ordering the cultic institutionalization of the central myth of the earlier Hebrews and later of the Jews: the Exodus from Egypt. The secularity of the second takes on the sacred, cultic garb of the first through the fact and manner of the ordering of an annual festival. Through its tone and content, this celebration places itself among cultic events.

In the Hebrew Bible it seems that when eating and drinking occur at a celebration, this celebration is most often in a cultic context, rarely in a life-cycle or covenant context and never in the context of celebration for its own sake. Celebration, then, is not a constant on its own but is itself a cluster of variables consisting at different times of song, feasting, cultic dedication (חרם), and so forth. These variables occur in constants I have already identified, such as CULT, LIFE CYCLE, or COVENANT.

Summary of Eating and Drinking as a Variable within Other Constants

My goal in chapter 3 and in this chapter was to account for all of the examples of eating and drinking in the biblical corpus that do not fit into my morphology for Foundation and Doom. In the Patterns of Destiny that I have identified, EATING and DRINKING function as constants. In all other patterns, eating and drinking must function as variables within other constants.

I began by identifying eating and drinking as literary elements that occur frequently in the Hebrew Bible. I sketched briefly the constant functions for the elements in which eating and drinking occur: CULT, MIRACLE, SYMBOLIC ACTION, DREAM, ETIOLOGY, MILITARY LEADERSHIP, PERFIDY, MISFORTUNE, MOURNING, SUPPLICATION, and a variety of LIFE-CYCLE events. Among these I examined examples where the direction is reversed either for the constant itself or for the variables of eating and drinking and concluded that in every case, eating and drinking operate as just two of the variables that occur within these constants in biblical narrative, whatever their direction.

Thus far, Propp's methodology has successfully accounted for those examples of eating and drinking that do not fit into the Pattern for Foundation and Doom that I have identified. This is an essential step in proving the usefulness of morphological analysis. The next step, in chapters 5 and 6, is to apply Proppian analysis to the cases in which EATING and DRINKING appear in a specific sequence with other constants within a structural pattern that defines a genre—that is, those cases in which EATING and DRINKING function as morphological constants.

CHAPTER FIVE

Patterns of Destiny

Eating and Drinking as Constants within the Establishment/Foundation Genre

Morphology and Genre

Propp showed that structural patterns define story type: in his terms, morphology defines genre.[1] In thinking about the story of Isaac blessing Jacob and Esau, I noticed that many biblical episodes and some from ancient Near Eastern literature, regardless of the many different story lines or plots, began with an EATING or DRINKING event and proceeded through some kind of encounter that included an ORACLE and, often, to an AFFIRMATION of that ORACLE. This pattern recurred so often in such a variety of literature, always exhibiting the same elements in the same sequence, that I decided to apply Proppian analysis to each example in order to determine whether I had indeed identified a genre-defining morphology. This chapter describes what I found.

I begin with a sample morphological analysis of a biblical text and continue with a demonstration of the Patterns of Destiny revealed by this analysis, an explication of texts sharing the morphology of the Foundation Pattern and its paired opposite, the Doom Pattern, demonstrating how these operate in biblical narrative. I examine the role of EATING AND DRINKING when they themselves function as constant elements within specific morphological patterns.

Methodological Considerations and Sample Analysis

According to Propp's definition, two characteristics determine whether an element is a constant in a morphological pattern: first, whether it appears to be stable across different tales; and second,

---

1. Vladimir Propp, *Morphology of the Folktale* (2d ed.; ed. L. A. Wagner; trans. L. Scott; Austin: University of Texas Press, 1968) 14–24.

whether it occurs in the same sequence with respect to other constants in those tales.[2] Once a constant has been identified, its function is determined according to its consequences, that is, by what follows the occurrence of that constant in a particular sequence.[3] This process of testing and retesting to make sure an element fulfills its anticipated role is very similar to the process of reading as defined by contemporary reception theory.[4]

As Vladimir Propp has shown, the elements making up a tale fall into patterns made up of a limited number of constant elements that he calls "functions." Not every possible constant will occur in each text, but when it does occur it will fall in the same sequence relative to the other constants.[5] Although there are many variations of these elements and many possible additional intervening components, they must occur in a particular order. Victory may not precede struggle; return may not precede departure; a hero's adventures and triumph must precede reward, and so forth. Even the youngest child recognizes that every fairy-tale begins with some event that disturbs the equilibrium of "once upon a time" and that there then follows a series of adventures culminating in success, victory, or other triumph over adversity, resulting in a restoration of equilibrium.[6]

My investigation applies Propp's method to biblical narratives containing eating or drinking events. I have shown in chapters 3 and 4 that very often eating and drinking may operate as variables of several

---

2. Ibid., 20–21.

3. Ibid., 67.

4. See also Peter J. Rabinowitz, "Reader Response Theory and Criticism" and Geert Lernout, "Reception Theory" in *The Johns Hopkins Guide to Literary Theory and Criticism* (ed. Michael Groden and Martin Kreiswirth; Baltimore: Johns Hopkins University Press, 1994) 606–9 and 609–11, respectively; and see the references I cite in chapter 3, n. 1 (p. 40).

5. Propp notes, "We observe that actually, the number of functions is quite limited. [For the Russian fairy-tale] only some 31 functions may be noted. The action of all tales included in our material develops within the limits of these functions. The same may also be said for the action of a great many other tales of the most dissimilar peoples. Further, if we read through all of the functions, one after another, we observe that one function develops out of another with logical and artistic necessity. We see that not a single function excludes another. They all belong to a single axis" (Propp, *Morphology*, 64).

6. This language of equilibrium and disequilibrium is used by Claude Brémond, whose studies flow out of Propp's but whose level of analysis is several grades of abstraction removed from his. See, for example, his article "The Morphology of the French Fairy Tale: The Ethical Model," in *Patterns in Oral Literature* (ed. H. Jason and D. Segal; The Hague: Mouton, 1977) 49–76.

Sample Morphological Analysis: Genesis 18:1–19

Initial Situation	18:1 Yнwн appeared to him by the oaks of Mamre, while he was sitting at the opening of his tent in the heat of the day.[a]
Arrival of guests	18:2 He raised his eyes and looked: now three men were standing before him. When he saw them, he ran to greet them from the opening of
Greeting	the tent and bowed to the earth.
EATING event: Summons/Invitation	18:3 Then he said, "My lords, please, if I have found favor in your sight, please do not pass by your servant.
	18:4 Please, a little water will be brought; wash your feet, then recline under the tree
	18:5 while I bring a bit of bread, so you may refresh your hearts. Then, afterward, you may pass on—since you have already passed thus far to your servant."
Acceptance	They said, "Do just as you have spoken."
Preparation	18:6 Then Abraham hastened to the tent, to Sarah. He said, "Haste! Three measures of fine flour! Knead and make cakes!"
	18:7 Next, to the herd Abraham ran. He brought a calf, tender and good; he gave it to the servant-boy; he hastened to prepare it.
Service	18:8 Then he brought curds and milk and the calf that he had prepared, and he put it before them, and he stood by them under the tree while they ate.
ENCOUNTER/CHALLENGE	18:9 Afterward, they said to him, "Where is Sarah your wife?" And he said, "Here, in the tent."

a. The translation of this passage is my own. See *BHS*; Everett Fox, *In the Beginning: A New English Rendition of the Book of Genesis* (New York: Schocken, 1983); NJPSV; RSV.

ORACLE
  Promise/
  Blessing
	18:10 Then he said, "I will certainly return to you as this time recurs, and here! A son to Sarah your wife!"

[information connective]	Meanwhile, Sarah was listening at the opening of the tent behind him.
[information connective]	18:11 Now Abraham and Sarah were old, advanced in years; it had ceased to be for Sarah as the way of women.

ENCOUNTER (cont.)
  Challenge:
    Skepticism expressed
	18:12 So Sarah laughed within herself, saying, "After I am worn out, is there pleasure for me? And my lord is old!"

Response:
  Challenge
  acknowledged/
  Unmasking
	18:13 YHWH said to Abraham, "Why is it that Sarah laughed, saying, 'Is it really true that I shall give birth, now that I am old?'

Promise reiterated	18:14 Is anything too wonderful for YHWH? At the set season I will return to you, as this time recurs, and Sarah shall have a son."

Withdrawal:
  Challenge denied
  Challenge affirmed
	18:15 But Sarah dissembled, saying, "I did not laugh," for she was afraid. But he said, "No, but indeed you did laugh."

DEPARTURE	18:16 Then the men rose up from there, and they looked toward Sodom; and Abraham went with them to see them off.
(START OF NEXT MOVE)	18:17 Meanwhile, YHWH thought, "Shall I hide from Abraham that which I am about to do?
AFFIRMATION OF ORACLE	18:18 For Abraham shall certainly become a great nation, and numerous, so that in him all the nations of the earth shall be blessed.
	18:19 For I know him well, and on account of that he shall command his children and his household after him, and they will keep the way of YHWH to do righteousness and justice, in order that YHWH might bring to Abraham all that was spoken about him."

different constants. In this chapter, I identify patterns in biblical narrative within which EATING and DRINKING themselves operate as constant functions. These cases meet the criteria of Propp's definition of a constant: structural patterns in some Hebrew Bible narratives in which an EATING and/or DRINKING event is stable across different narratives, and also falls in the same relative position within a specific sequence of other constant elements.

The patterns revealed by Proppian analysis define a genre of narrative that embodies in its structure significant meaning for an audience, in the same way that "once upon a time" signals meaning for contemporary readers. These patterns constitute a biblical genre that signals the divine establishment or condemnation of an entity. I call these *Patterns of Destiny.*

I found that Patterns of Destiny begin with an EATING and DRINKING event at which there is an encounter of some kind. This encounter contains or results in an ORACLE that may be positive or negative. The text generally concludes with an AFFIRMATION of the ORACLE.

In all Patterns of Destiny, divine will is expressed in either a blessing or a curse, both of which are the positive and negative variable elements in the constant function of ORACLE associated with these patterns. The morphological structure constituting these patterns reflects explicit divine will that some culturally significant entity be either established and maintained or else condemned and overthrown. These Patterns of Foundation or Doom embody within their structure a clear theological message that reinforces or counterpoints the message conveyed on the surface or plot level of individual narratives: adherence to divine will results in divine providence; opposition to divine will results in catastrophe.

Before I discuss the many biblical examples of these patterns, perhaps it would be useful to demonstrate my analytical approach on a sample text. I begin with a morphological analysis of Gen 18:1–19, the annunciation of Isaac's birth (see pp. 120–21 for analysis).

Discussion of Morphological Analysis.   In this analysis, I apply Propp's method of morphological analysis to biblical texts but do not force these texts into Propp's model, which defines the genre of the Russian fairy-tale.[7] Thus, although I use Propp's terminology wherever it applies to the naming of the constants or functions in the patterns I find, where his terms do not apply I designate new ones that fit the biblical corpus.

───────────────

7. See my discussion throughout chapter 2.

The *Initial Situation* for this biblical pericope is set forth in Gen 18:1. Propp identifies this element in the Russian fairy-tale this way: "A tale usually begins with some sort of initial situation. The members of a family are enumerated, or the future hero (e.g., a soldier) is simply introduced by mention of his name or indication of his status. Although this situation is not a function, it nevertheless is an important morphological element."[8] This definition appears to hold for the biblical text as well.

The Arrival of Guests in 18:2 is the event that upsets the stasis established by the initial situation and sets the plot in motion. Perhaps this element can be said to be the inverse of and analogous to the function "absentation" of some member of the family that can occur in what Propp terms the "preparatory sequence" in the Russian fairy-tale.[9] In Propp's schema, the "preparatory sequence" of functions precedes the actual beginning of the plot but follows the setting of the initial scene.[10] In the biblical text, the arrival is immediately followed by the Greeting, signaled by the Hebrew phrase וישתחו ארצה 'then he bowed to the ground'. This is a sequence that is typical of hospitality in ancient Near Eastern literature.[11]

The EATING sequence itself follows in 18:3–8 with the activities of: Summons or Invitation to a repast; Acceptance of the invitation by the guests; Preparation of the food items, the catalog of which signals that a banquet is at hand; and finally, Service of the meal, with the host setting the food before the guests and standing by to attend their needs. In some cases, the task of seating the guests appropriately is part of this sequence, as it is in the Sumerian text "Enki's Journey to Nippur" (lines 104–9), where Enki seats the major gods in their appropriate

---

8. Propp, *Morphology*, 25.

9. Ibid., 26.

10. Ibid., 31.

11. On the sequence of elements making up the "banquet complex" in ancient Near Eastern literature, including arrival, greeting, preparation, foods served, and so on, see Murray H. Lichtenstein, *Episodic Structure in the Ugaritic Keret Legend: Comparative Studies in Compositional Technique* (Ph.D. diss., Columbia University, 1979) 44–59; and his article "The Banquet Motifs in Keret and in Proverbs 9," *JANES* (1968) 19–31. On the formulaic uses of the expression וישתחו, see Frank H. Polak, "וישתחו: Group Formulas in Biblical Prose and Poetry," in *"Sha'arei Talmon": Studies in the Bible, Qumran, and the Ancient Near East Presented to Shemaryahu Talmon* (ed. M. Fishbane, E. Tov, and W. W. Fields; Winona Lake, Ind.: Eisenbrauns, 1992) 81*–91* [Heb.]. On the uses of השתחוה as part of a formula of greeting, see chapter 5 of the study by Mayer Irwin Gruber, *Aspects of Non-verbal Communication in the Ancient Near East* (Studia Pohl 12; Rome: Pontifical Biblical Institute, 1980).

places;[12] in CTA 3:A of the Baal cycle, where Kothar is seated at Baal's right hand;[13] and in Gen 43:33, where Joseph's brothers are amazed that such a high Egyptian official is wise enough to seat them in order of seniority.

During the course of the meal, or perhaps after the guests have eaten, an ENCOUNTER occurs. In this text, the ENCOUNTER begins at 18:9 and runs through 18:15, just before the guests depart. This sequence of ENCOUNTER and [DEPARTURE] is a common juxtaposition in biblical narrative, as well as across the literatures of the ancient Near East.[14] The function of ENCOUNTER may be physical or verbal and can

---

12. A. A. Al-Fouadi, *Enki's Journey to Nippur: The Journeys of the Gods* (Ph.D. diss., University of Pennsylvania, 1969); transliteration, p. 75; translation, pp. 83–84; see also Samuel Noah Kramer, *Sumerian Mythology: A Study of Spiritual and Literary Achievement in the Third Millennium B.C.* (2d ed.; New York: Harper, 1961) 62–63.

13. For a discussion of the seating trope in Northwest Semitic banquet sequences, see A. J. Ferrara and S. B. Parker, "Seating Arrangements at Divine Banquets," *UF* 4 (1972) 37–39.

14. This juxtaposition is a major component in the patterns of biblical narrative that I address in this chapter. Many studies dealing with the banquet in the literature of the ancient Near East may be found. In addition to the studies already cited, just a few of the most pertinent include: E. Lipiński, "Banquet en l'honneur de Baal: CTA 3 (V AB), A, 4–22," *UF* 2 (1970) 75–88; J. B. Lloyd, "The Banquet Theme in Ugaritic Narrative," *UF* 22 (1990) 167–93; and Matitiahu Tsevat, "Eating and Drinking, Hosting and Sacrificing in the Epic of AQHT," *UF* 18 (1986) 345–50. Several studies are based on graphic rather than textual evidence, including: André Parrot, "Les peintures du palais de Mari," *Syria* 18 (1937) 325–54; M. Mellink, "Hittite Friezes and Gate Sculptures," in *Anatolian Studies Presented to Hans Gustave Güterbock on the Occasion of His 65th Birthday* (ed. K. Bittel et al.; Istanbul: Nederlands historisch-archäologisch Institut, 1974) 201–14; Richard D. Barnett, "Assurbanipal's Feast," *ErIsr* 18 (Nahman Avigad Volume; 1985) 1–6; Jean Bottéro, "The Cuisine of Ancient Mesopotamia," *BA* 48 (March 1985) 36–47; and Jean-Marie Dentzer, *Le motif du banquet couché dans le Proche-Orient et le monde grec du VIIᵉ au IVᵉ siècle avant J.C.* (Rome: École Française de Rome, 1982).

Many scholars have noted that some kind of encounter often marks meals in ancient Near Eastern literature as well. M. E. Vogelzang, in an article concerning Akkadian dispute literature, notes: "In Mesopotamian epic literature (and in epic literature in general) this is a common feature: all kinds of things happen during or after a peaceful and joyful meeting like a banquet or a feast, or during a more general meeting of the gods or the elders of a town. It forms the setting of stories like, for instance, *Lugal-e, Nergal and Ereshkigal, Anzu,* and during important turning points of the epic of *Gilgamesh*." She draws a conclusion, however, that I do not think tells the whole story: "So we may perhaps conclude, that this feature characterizes a small reflection of the intellectual and cultural life at the Mesopotamian royal court and of the literary activities of Mesopotamian scribes in their Edubba" (Marianna E. Vogelzang, "Some Questions about the Akkadian Disputes," in *Dispute*

take many forms: challenge, negotiation, task, contest, trick, petition, interrogation, attack, disputation, and so forth.

In this text, the ENCOUNTER begins indirectly with the guests inquiring after Abraham's wife in 18:9 and continues with an ORACLE predicting the birth of a son in due course, 18:10a. The narrative conveys by means of an [information connective] that Sarah overhears the ORACLE (18:10b), and by means of another [information connective] (18:11) the narrative explains the reason for her reaction to what she overhears. In the analysis of a narrative, it is sometimes useful to distinguish between information conveyed directly to the reader (or audience) and information conveyed by characters to one another within the narrative. When this is the case, information conveyed by the narrator to the reader/audience may be termed an [information connective], and information conveyed by one character to another within the text may be termed [information mediation].[15] Although these are useful, even indispensable, to characters or audiences, information exchanges occur on the surface level of the text and do not exist on the structural level: they are not themselves actions and do not move the plot forward. Nevertheless, it is still useful to label them in order to

---

Poems and Dialogues in the Ancient and Mediaeval Near East [ed. G. J. Reinink and H. L. Vanstiphout; Orientalia Lovaniensia Analecta 42; Leuven: Peeters, 1991] 57). I am indebted to my friend and colleague Sarah Diamant for calling this reference to my attention.

J.-J. Glassner also notes the literary phenomenon of a banquet followed by an encounter and suggests that this is a means by which the outsider may become integrated into the group, a sociological insight that he puts forward in his article "L'Hospitalité en Mésopotamie ancienne: Aspect de la question de l'étranger," *ZA* 80 (1990) 60–75, especially pp. 63–65. H. L. J. Vanstiphout also comments on this phenomenon, in "The Banquet Scene in the Mesopotamian Debate Poems," in *Banquets d'Orient* (ed. R. Gyselen; Res Orientales 4; Bures-sur-Yvette, France: Le Groupe pour l'Étude de la Civilisation du Moyen-Orient, 1992) 9–21.

15. Vladimir Propp termed information conveyed between one character and another in a tale a "mediation" (*Morphology*, 36) and apparently disregarded (for morphological purposes) information conveyed between the narrator and the reader or audience. Heda Jason terms all descriptive information, whether between one character and another within a tale or between narrator and reader/audience, "connectives" and distinguishes among connectives of time, place, and other information ("A Model for Narrative Structure in Oral Literature," in *Patterns in Oral Literature* [ed. H. Jason and D. Segal; The Hague: Mouton, 1977] 104–6). I make a further distinction by combining Propp's and Jason's two terms and calling information conveyed by the narrator for the benefit of the reader/audience "information connective" and information conveyed by one character to another within the text "information mediation." This level of distinction is not always necessary, but sometimes it is useful in the course of narratological analysis.

distinguish the role of every segment of the narrative under analysis. For purposes of this discussion, I have placed them in square brackets.

The encounter continues after the two [information connectives]. In a pattern of Challenge, Response, Withdrawal, Sarah expresses skepticism to herself (18:12) and is distressed when the guest, whom the narrator designates as YHWH, appears to read her mind, interpreting her lack of faith as a challenge to divine omnipotence (18:13). God affirms the ORACLE of the promised son, but the ENCOUNTER continues: Sarah withdraws her skepticism by denying that she laughed (18:15a), but the Lord does not back down and has the last word in this encounter: לֹא כִּי צָחָקְתְּ 'No, but indeed you did laugh' (18:15b).

The indication of omniscience on the part of the guest in 18:13 and the narrator's designation of the speaker as YHWH are the first indications in this narrative that one guest, at least, is not the casual traveler he initially appears to be. This is a case of implied concealment and unmasking, which is common in biblical narrative as well as in literature across the ancient Near East.[16]

Continuing with the text in Genesis, the guests then take their DE-PARTURE, and the next move begins. A move, according to Propp, has a beginning (VILLAINY or LACK) and a conclusion (VILLAINY REVERSED,

---

16. Propp has two categories, which he calls *Unrecognized arrival* of the hero and *Recognition* of the hero, that may be analogous to the categories noted here (Propp, *Morphology*, 60–62); as in the Genesis 18 text, the fairy-tale hero's identity is sometimes revealed by his deeds and/or abilities.

I note here just a few examples of texts in which concealment is a factor in biblical narrative: in Genesis 29, when Jacob marries Leah; in Genesis 42 and 43:1–45:16, when Joseph encounters his brothers in Egypt; in 1 Samuel 28, when Saul visits the Wise Woman of Endor; in 1 Kgs 14:1–18, when Jeroboam's wife inquires of the prophet about her son's illness; and in 1 Kings 22 and the parallel text in 2 Chronicles 18, when Ahab prepares himself for what proves to be his final battle.

The phenomenon of concealment also occurs among the cultures of the ancient Near East. In Egyptian literature, in at least one episode from the Judgment of Horus and Seth, Isis, widow of Osiris and mother of Horus, arrives disguised at a remote location where the gods are picnicking before rendering judgment in this drawn-out dispute (see Miriam Lichtheim, *Ancient Egyptian Literature, Volume II: The New Kingdom* [Berkeley: University of California Press, 1976] 216–18). Concealment and disguise are also important elements in the Tale of Two Brothers (see ibid., 203; and S. Hollis, *The Ancient Egyptian Tale of Two Brothers* [Cambridge: Cambridge University Press, 1990]). In Hittite literature, Telepinu, son of the storm-god, disappears in a pique, hides himself on the moor, and is ultimately unmasked by a tiny bee dispatched by the mother goddess Hannahanna (Harry A. Hoffner, Jr., *Hittite Myths* [Society of Bibilical Literature Writings from the Ancient World; Atlanta: Scholars Press, 1990] 15–20).

LACK LIQUIDATED).[17] Tales may be composed of one or more moves, and one move does not have to be completed for another one to begin with a new act of VILLAINY or a new LACK.[18] Thus, additional moves may be sequential, or they may be wholly or partially embedded in a preceding move. In the Genesis 18 text, for example, the move dealing with the destruction of Sodom begins before the narrative under discussion is quite finished, so the beginning of the next move is embedded in the initial text. The challenge, as biblical scholars have often noted to their chagrin, is in defining with precision the beginning and end of a narrative within a larger whole.

For reasons that will become clearer in my discussion of specific morphologies, the narrative boundary for our sample text includes vv. 17–19, where God goes even further than merely affirming the ORACLE by reiterating it as in 18:14; here, God affirms the ORACLE by taking action *as though the events predicted by the oracle have already occurred.* In 18:17–19, God decides to discuss with Abraham the divine plan for Sodom as though Abraham's future role as the progenitor of a nation were already a reality. Here, God articulates the divine decision to take a specific action in the present based upon circumstances that will not exist until a future time when the ORACLE is actually fulfilled. This behavior on God's part is the strongest possible AFFIRMATION of the divine ORACLE. I found in my analysis that the function of AFFIRMATION is often found in narratives participating in this pattern.

In Genesis 18, the line of Abraham is being established through Sarah. The plot of the narrative is undergirded by a structural support: a Foundation Pattern containing a positive ORACLE that is affirmed by no less an authority than God. In the discussion of life-cycle events in chapter 4, I showed that annunciations do not require an eating and drinking context. Here, where an annunciation does take place at a meal, a morphological analysis reveals that it is no accident that, of all possible variables, an eating and drinking event appears in this text.

---

17. Propp, *Morphology*, 58–59. On these paired functions marking the beginning and end of a tale, summarized by Propp in the function category LACK/LACK LIQUIDATED and including VILLAINY or MISFORTUNE/VILLAINY or MISFORTUNE LIQUIDATED, see ibid., p. 53.

18. Propp discusses the complexities of multiple moves, embedding, assimilation, and other phenomena in chapter 9 of his study, especially in section A of that chapter, "The Ways in Which Stories Are Combined," *Morphology*, 92–96. See also Heda Jason, *Ethnopoetry: Form, Content, Function* (Forum Theologiae Linguisticae 11; Bonn: Linguistica Biblica, 1977) 74–75; and idem, "A Model for Narrative Structure in Oral Literature," 99–140, especially pp. 114–17.

Although they may be a variable in annunciations in general, EATING and DRINKING are structurally essential for Patterns of Destiny. Here, at the momentous juncture where the descendants of Abraham are being established through the line of his wife, a Foundation Pattern is called for—and therefore an EATING and DRINKING event is required.

It is important to note that the entity being established is a line of descent *through Sarah*. As I will show later on in this chapter, Abraham's line of descent through Hagar is established in its own narrative, reinforced by its own Foundation Pattern, as is Isaac's through Rebekah. On a structural level, the matriarchs are the essential subjects of the Patterns of Foundation for the Children of Israel and the Children of Ishmael.

Patterns of Destiny: Establishment and Condemnation

When many biblical texts containing an eating or drinking event are analyzed in the same way that I have just examined Genesis 18 and the results are compared, a pattern emerges that follows the same morphology: an EATING or DRINKING event occurs at which there is an ENCOUNTER that includes an ORACLE; often the ORACLE is AFFIRMED. The structure is identical whether the ORACLE is positive or negative. Within the morphology of Patterns of Destiny, blessing and curse and foundation and doom are variables within the constant element of ORACLE.

This structural identity is highlighted by the juxtaposition of a Foundation Pattern with a Doom Pattern in chapters 18 and 19 of Genesis.[19] The Foundation Pattern underlying Genesis 18 is signaled by a positive ORACLE. A Doom Pattern signaled by a negative ORACLE underlies the destruction of Sodom in Gen 19:1–29.

The text may be summarized and analyzed this way: The angels arrive in Sodom and are welcomed by Lot, who invites them to share his hospitality. After some urging, they agree, and Lot prepares a feast for them, which they eat (EATING, Gen 19:1–3). Then follows an ENCOUNTER among Lot, the strangers, and the townspeople that is resolved by supernatural means (Gen 19:4–11). The visitors, who have sufficiently investigated the extent of wickedness in Sodom as suggested in Gen 18:20–21, announce the impending destruction of the city (a negative ORACLE, Gen 19:12–13). Lot's family does not believe them, and Lot

---

19. Many scholars have drawn attention to the similarities among the texts discussed here. See Stuart Lasine, "Guest and Host in Judges 19: Lot's Hospitality in an Inverted World," *JSOT* 29 (1984) 37–59; and Robert C. Culley, *Studies in the Structure of Hebrew Narrative* (Philadelphia: Fortress and Scholars Press, 1976).

himself delays acting until the visitors bodily remove Lot, his wife, and his daughters from the city (DEPARTURE, Gen 19:14–22). The ORACLE receives AFFIRMATION with the annihilation of Sodom once Lot and his family are safe (Gen 19:23–29).

The structural pattern is identical in both texts, except that a negative ORACLE in Genesis 19 makes its Pattern of Destiny one of Doom. The pattern for both Foundation and Doom Accounts consists of [PILGRIMAGE or JOURNEY]; EATING/DRINKING; [ENCOUNTER]; ORACLE; [AFFIRMATION]. I have put elements in square brackets that are often present in these narratives, but are not necessary for the morphology to be identified as a Foundation or Doom Pattern. Elements in small capitals are constants, essential to the Foundation or Doom morphology.

Each of the texts sharing this pattern in biblical literature and also in the various literatures of the ancient Near East deals with the establishment or condemnation of an entity of major significance to the culture that is retelling the story. I term each of the texts sharing this pattern a Foundation Account, or a Doom Account, and together these narratives share the morphological structure I call Patterns of Destiny, which defines the category or genre of these accounts.

These Foundation Accounts and Doom Accounts tell how the observed world order—or nation, people, city-state, family, or similar cultural element—either came to be powerful or ascendant, or came to its ruin or anathema; they describe the divine establishment or condemnation of social or national units.

Although the patterns observed in the sample texts exhibited five constant elements in common, comprehensive examination of biblical texts in which EATING and DRINKING occur reveals that only two of these functions are both necessary and sufficient in order to define the genre of Foundation Accounts: an EATING or DRINKING event and an ORACLE. Although other functions—such as ENCOUNTER, DEPARTURE, AFFIRMATION, and others that occur in the examples I examine below— are *often* present along with these two constants in biblical narratives, no other functions are *always* present. EATING/DRINKING and ORACLE must always be present in order for a particular narrative to be categorized as either a Foundation Account or a Doom Account.

There are many biblical narratives that exhibit this structure. Each of the 22 biblical examples and all of the ancient Near Eastern examples of the Foundation Pattern discussed in this book contain both of these elements, as do 22 biblical examples of the Doom Pattern. Out of all of these, 14 of the biblical and 13 of the ancient Near-eastern examples of the Foundation Pattern also contain the fuller pattern of elements (EATING, ENCOUNTER, ORACLE, and AFFIRMATION), as do 20 of the biblical and 7 of the ancient Near Eastern examples of Doom Accounts.

In this chapter, I will look first at clear examples of the Foundation Pattern containing a positive ORACLE and then at clear examples of the Doom Pattern containing a negative ORACLE. I will begin by looking at the earliest examples of the Foundation Pattern found in ancient Near Eastern literature, from the third millennium B.C.E., and then briefly survey the wide distribution of this morphology over more than two thousand years across Mesopotamia and the Levant. This examination will offer a clue to the origin and development of the morphology of these Patterns of Destiny in the civilizations surrounding Israelite culture. Then I will turn to the rich biblical development of these morphologies of establishment and condemnation. Wherever possible, I will introduce examples of ancient Near Eastern parallels as I present clear biblical examples of both the Foundation Pattern, containing a positive ORACLE, and of the Doom Pattern, containing a negative ORACLE.

The Foundation Pattern in Ancient Sumer

The oldest Patterns of Destiny that I have discovered are Foundation Accounts. The Foundation Account narrative pattern—a core of EATING/DRINKING and ORACLE often accompanied by other functions, such as PILGRIMAGE, ENCOUNTER, DEPARTURE, or AFFIRMATION—is found throughout the literatures of the ancient Near East. It may be seen most clearly in the Sumerian stories that are classified by Sumerologists among the hymns recounting the "Journeys of the Gods."

The Sumerians were a non-Semitic, non-Indo-European people based in what is today southern Iraq. They were the dominant cultural group of the entire region from about 4000 B.C.E. to about 1500 B.C.E. Their ethnic and linguistic affiliations are still unclassifiable, although they invented the first writing system, wedge-shaped cuneiform, adopted by nearly all of the peoples of the Near East.[20] The Sumerians developed religious and spiritual concepts that profoundly influenced the entire Near East, including the later Hebrews and Greeks, and, through them, modern Western culture as well.

Journeys of the Gods.   The noted University of Pennsylvania Sumerologist Åke Sjöberg was the first to note that among Sumerian compo-

---

20. Kramer, *Sumerian Mythology*, vii.

sitions are several texts that deal with the travels of the gods to
sanctuaries beyond their cultic areas. These texts date to the third millennium B.C.E. or even earlier and deal with the journeys for which the
sanctuaries of the great Babylonian gods Enlil and Enki are significant.[21] Sjöberg classified the texts according to two criteria: first, texts
in which an entire journey is described, in contrast to texts in which
such a journey is merely alluded to; and second, texts that appear to refer to annual or repeated journeys, in contrast to texts that appear to
treat of a unique occurrence.

In the past 25 years, scholarly attention has been paid to text edi-
tions of these hymns, among them A. J. Ferrara's publication of
"Nanna-Suen's Journey to Nippur" and Al-Fouadi's study of "Enki's
Journey to Nippur," both owing much to Sjöberg's pioneering work.[22]

Many scholars have noted the thematic similarities of these compositions to one another and also the presence of a banquet in each one,
but no one has yet undertaken a systematic morphological analysis of
these works with a view to demonstrating the possible existence of a literary "genre." Interest, until now, has been primarily linguistic and
philological. When it has gone beyond these concerns, scholarship has
focused on understanding the cultic and ritual implications of these
works in light of nonliterary evidence.[23] While these studies are important and also illuminating, a literary approach might offer additional
insights not available by other means.

---

21. Sjöberg dates the "Journeys of the Gods" to the Old Babylonian period, with
the most reliable texts dating from the later Neo-Sumerian period at the end of the
third millennium B.C.E. (Å. W. Sjöberg, "Götterreisen," in *RlA* 3.480–83).

22. A. J. Ferrara, *Nanna-Suen's Journey to Nippur* (Studia Pohl, Series Maior 2;
Rome: Pontifical Biblical Institute, 1973); Al-Fouadi, *Enki's Journey to Nippur*. For
an overview of the texts and allusions participating in this pattern, see Sjöberg,
"Götterreisen," 480–83. For a wider context, see, for example, idem, *Der Mondgott
Nanna Suen in der Sumerischen Überlieferung* (Stockholm: Almqvist & Wiksell, 1960).
For nonliterary parallels, see also H. Sauren, "Besuchsfahrten der Götter in Su-
mer," *Or* n.s. 38 (1969) 214–36.

23. See ibid., especially pp. 217–34, on the nonliterary evidence for cultic and
ritual journeys of Sumerian divine images and emblems. Frankena discusses the
takultu ritual and notes (on p. 129 of his English summary) that it concludes with a
ritual blessing in which "all the gods who have been regaled are entreated to give
abundant blessing to the giver of this meal, the king of Assur, in exchange for the
royal entertainment; and with this the real reason of the takultu-ceremonial is laid
bare, for on the welfare of the king depends the prosperity of the land" (R. Frankena, *Takultu: De sacrale Maaltijd in het Assyrische ritueel, met een overzicht over de in
Assur vereerde Goden* [Leiden: Brill, 1954]). For some of the many other works on
ancient Near Eastern ritual and on possible biblical parallels, see the bibliography.

Among the texts describing complete journeys that Sjöberg takes to be of annual or repeated frequency are the following compositions:

1. Nanna's Journey to Nippur
2. Nininsina's Journey to Nippur
3. Ninurta's Journey to Eridu[24]

Sjöberg suggests that through these annual visits, old cultic relationships or connections were regularly renewed, and notes that the most significant theme of these compositions is the assurance of abundance through the blessing of the senior god. In at least one composition, the text also makes clear that this fruitfulness is to be secured through the determination of a favorable fate for the city by Enlil.[25]

These interconnected ideas of destiny and blessing are also important to the Patterns of Destiny that are the subject of this book.

Two other compositions are noted by Sjöberg:

4. Inanna's Journey to Eridu
5. Enki's Journey to Nippur

According to Sjöberg, each of these last two reports a unique occurrence, describing a divine journey for a different purpose. Whatever the cultic relationship of this second group is to the first, from a literary point of view all five compositions share a morphological pattern in which the same episodes follow one another in sequence although, as Sjöberg noted, there are indeed variations among the texts, some of which may also be of literary significance, as we shall see below.

---

24. See Daniel Reisman, "Ninurta's Journey to Eridu," *JCS* 24 (1971) 3–8.

25. Sjöberg makes this connection explicit, reading one text in terms of the other. He writes:

A Journey of the God Nininsina to Nippur is the subject of KAR 15 = KAR 16. The content of this bilingual composition is as follows:

Nininsina steps out of her cell/room; she draws over to the marketplace of the city of Isin, and following her is her consort Pabilsag, her children, protective spirit, and the residents of the city. At the head of the procession is her emblem (ŠU-NIR = ŠURINNU). The goddess travels as far as the Euphrates, and she travels from the wharf in Isin by ship to the "wine quay" in Nippur.

The chief theme is the determination of fate [destiny] by Enlil. The section in which this determination is contained is, however, not preserved. Wherein these consisted, we may, however, see from the composition of "Nanna's Journey to Nippur."

This excerpt taken from Sjöberg, "Götterreisen," 481 (English translation mine).

A summary of one of these hymns will help to illustrate the general morphology.

Nanna's Journey to Nippur. In order to obtain Enlil's blessing for his patron city of Ur, the moon-god, Nanna-Suen, resolves to take a journey to visit his father, Enlil, at the cult center of Nippur. Nanna-Suen constructs and loads a *magur*-boat with an inventory of gifts. He embarks for Nippur, stopping en route at five intermediate locations. When he finally arrives before the gatekeeper of Enlil's É-KUR shrine at Nippur, he gains admittance by listing the wonderful gifts he has brought to Enlil, and a banquet is prepared and enjoyed by guest and host. Nanna-Suen requests Enlil's blessing (possibly so that such offerings may continue to be brought to Enlil), and the blessing is granted.[26]

A similar pattern obtains in the other hymns classified as divine journeys, mentioned above.

This synopsis shows that the Sumerian texts exhibit the same morphological elements seen earlier in the biblical examples, in substantially the same order. These hymns follow the pattern of [PILGRIMAGE] or [JOURNEY] in order to participate in a banquet, an EATING event at which there occurs an ENCOUNTER, including a PETITION for blessing followed by the granting of that BLESSING or other DESTINY ORACLE, and [DEPARTURE] for the return home, after which the fulfillment of the blessing or ORACLE is AFFIRMED.

It is apparent that the texts classified as Journeys of the Gods are also part of the literary genre I define here, exhibiting a morphology consistent with the Patterns of Destiny. Specifically, they fall into the category of Foundation Accounts, each of which explains the establishment or ascendance of the city that is the subject of the hymn. Within this genre, many begin with a [JOURNEY], and each hymn contains an EATING event, a feast or banquet, followed by an ENCOUNTER that includes an ORACLE or BLESSING. The texts conclude with a [DEPARTURE] and an AFFIRMATION of the ORACLE or blessing.

Scholars of the literatures of the ancient Near East do not always classify these texts by their morphological category, defined here as Patterns of Destiny, whether Foundation Accounts or Doom Accounts. Instead, scholars are in the habit of grouping them by some motif that

---

26. See the outline of this structure listed in Ferrara, *Nanna-Suen*, 12–13. The fact that the blessing is integral to the hymn and not just tacked on is apparent in the frequency with which the securing of the blessing is the objective of a story and in the fact that the successful achievement of this goal ends the hymn (see Sjöberg, "Götterreisen," especially p. 481).

occurs, such as the Sumerian "Journeys of the Gods" or by the name of the main character, as in the Hittite "Illuyanka Tales."[27] Such classification obscures the literary function of these tales, which is to tell of the foundation of significant cosmic, cultural, and theological components of a people. Such classification also inhibits the comparative or contrastive analysis of these stories in terms of one another in order to gain a deeper understanding of any common significance and the implications of any variation from or elaboration upon the expected pattern.

Grouping these texts by structure rather than by subject allows for their classification within a single genre of age-old literary roots. The biblical pattern, containing a meal and dealing with the ascendance of its subject people, originated as part of an ancient literary convention of foundation events signaled by an initial EATING or DRINKING event and incorporating an ORACLE of blessing bearing upon the fate of the ORACLE's subject. When compared with Doom Accounts, which as a group are relatively smaller in number and later in date in ancient Near Eastern literature, the large number of early Foundation Accounts found in the Near East suggests strongly that the original pattern is the Establishment Pattern and that the morphology of Doom evolved as a variation of the basic morphology and had its richest development in biblical literature.

The Foundation Pattern Elsewhere in the Ancient Near East

The morphology of the Foundation Pattern is found in other major literatures of the ancient Near East. Very often, the accounts mark the establishment of cultural institutions similar to cultural institutions marked by Patterns of Destiny in the Hebrew Bible. Here I will give a very general survey of the incidence of the Foundation Pattern in the ancient Near East in order to indicate its range of distribution. I note in these examples where structural parallels exist with the Hebrew Bible, and I will also incorporate other Near Eastern examples throughout the book as they are relevant to the biblical discussions. I will deal most extensively with Sumerian and Semitic literature throughout my discussion, but the Foundation Pattern may also be found in the Homeric literature of ancient Greece, in late Egyptian literature, and in the Christian Scriptures. Although a systematic analysis of these three corpora must await a different forum, I can bring an example or two from each to demonstrate the richness and pervasiveness of the Patterns of Destiny in the literature of the ancient world.

---

27. Hoffner, *Hittite Myths*, 11–14.

Akkadian Literature.   Foundation Patterns occur twice in the Akkadian creation myth, *Enūma Eliš*. In both cases, the structure of the Foundation morphology underlies the establishment of entities of major significance. The first occurs during the banquet at which Marduk is acclaimed supreme god, after which he establishes the observed world order.[28] Following is a morphological summary.

By the end of tablet 1, Marduk and the younger gods who are his cohorts are aroused to action by a threat from Tiamat, their mother, who is stirring things up and planning to vanquish them in retaliation for their having murdered their father, Apsu. Tiamat names Qingu as her general. He is elevated to chief, with the right to declare destinies at a council of Tiamat's cohort divinities. This council is notably lacking a banquet or other eating and drinking event in its initial introduction and in its multiple repetitions: the assembly is initially called in tablet 1, line 131 and lines 151–61, and the lines are repeated several times as the messenger is commanded, the council is convened, their plans are made known to their opponents, and so forth. The absence of any reference to a feast is an indication that eating and drinking are variables and not essential to the morphology of an assembly of the gods. This is a clue that when a banquet does occur in such a context, its function merits closer examination.

Tablet 2 begins when Ea (who is also called Enki) hears of Tiamat's plan and is stricken with fear, even though it was he who struck the final mortal blow in subduing Apsu. Ea's son Marduk begs for a chance to vanquish Tiamat and her awesomely armed retinue. Marduk urges Ea to call an assembly of the gods (tablet 2, lines 120–29), which he does. In his instructions to the messengers, Ea stresses repeatedly that the gods are to be called to an assembly that includes a banquet with festive bread and wine, at which the gods will be asked to elevate Marduk to supremacy by declaring his destiny (tablet 3, lines 1–10).

At this banquet assembly, the gods enter the hall, greet one another, and converse as they eat festive bread and pour the wine (EATING).[29] When they become languid and their spirits rise, they do fix Marduk's fate as supreme among them (first ORACLE, tablet 3, lines 131–38). Marduk must pass a cosmic test as part of this ENCOUNTER with his fellow gods. They test Marduk's cosmic fitness by setting him to make a

---

28. See E. A. Speiser (trans.), "The Creation Epic," *ANET*, 60–72. A more recent translation may be found in Benjamin R. Foster, *Before the Muses: An Anthology of Akkadian Literature* (2 vols.; Bethesda, Md.: CDL, 1993) 1.351–402. See *Enūma Eliš*, tablet 3, line 1 through tablet 4, line 34 for the primary pattern.

29. For a structural analysis of the banquet sequence itself, see Lichtenstein, *Episodic Structure in the Ugaritic Keret Legend*, 37–56.

constellation disappear and reappear (tablet 4, lines 19–26). The pattern closes with an AFFIRMATION of the first ORACLE, when the gods acclaim Marduk and restate his mission to destroy Tiamat (second ORACLE, tablet 4, lines 27–34). The other gods invest Marduk with the trappings of power, he assembles his awesome weapons, and goes off to encounter Tiamat, his grandmother and his foe, whom he succeeds in vanquishing (AFFIRMATION of second ORACLE, tablet 4, lines 27–132).

The presence of two oracles is a clue to the structural complexity of this episode. The first ORACLE, Marduk's fate, is positive, elevating him as supreme among the gods. The morphology associated with this OR-ACLE is a Foundation Pattern. Intertwined with this pattern is the condemnation of Tiamat, signaling a Doom morphology that makes use of the same EATING and DRINKING event as the Foundation Pattern. Structurally, the message is that Marduk's glorious destiny is inextricably bound up in the Doom of Tiamat—a message that reinforces the surface level of the plot.

The epic goes on to describe Marduk's disposition of Tiamat's remains, out of which he fashions the observed universe, including times, seasons, and the assignment of temples and spheres of influence for each of the other divinities (the remainder of tablet 4 and tablet 5, lines 1–76). The Foundation Pattern underlying the elevation of Marduk to supreme god is affirmed in this account of his wisdom in crafting the world order following his defeat of Tiamat. Marduk concludes his creative tour de force by directing Ea in the proper creation of humankind from the blood of the rebellious Qingu, thus freeing the gods from hard labor (tablet 6, lines 1–38). The Foundation Pattern signaling Marduk's ascension marks the creation of the known world.

Egyptian Elaborations on Patterns of Destiny.   Foundation and Doom Patterns often occur in stories where the surface narrative is elaborately developed but, in spite of the ornate detail on the plot level, the structural level still exhibits a clear morphology. Two late Egyptian wisdom tales are good examples.[30] In these texts, while the tale-teller's art results in a profusion of detail and repetition, the basic morphology occurs in the order associated with Patterns of Destiny. Also, rather than deal with the foundation of the cosmos, nation, people, or city-state, both of the Egyptian episodes summarized here speak of the establishment of an international reputation for wise men and miracle workers.

---

30. See Miriam Lichtheim, *Ancient Egyptian literature, Volume III: The Late Period* (Berkeley: University of California Press, 1980) 90–94.

Two late Egyptian tales, "The Legend of the Possessed Princess" and "The Tale of Setne-Khamwas II," are notable for exhibiting the core pattern of EATING followed by ORACLE and AFFIRMATION, although other elements may be inverted, doubled, or trebled.

"The Legend of the Possessed Princess" is of Persian or Ptolemaic date, although the copy is made to appear as a monument belonging to Ramses II of the thirteenth century B.C.E.[31] In this text, the daughter of a foreign power, the king of Bakhtan, appears to be possessed by a demon. Her elder sister is Queen Nefrure, Great Royal Wife of the Pharaoh of Egypt, so it is natural that when none of Bakhtan's wise men can help her, her father sends to the king of Egypt for help (PILGRIMAGE). The messenger finds the pharaoh at a feast (EATING), where he petitions for help (ENCOUNTER). The king sends his royal scribe to investigate, who sends word that a cure for the princess is possible but requires the intervention of an Egyptian divinity. The pharaoh seeks an ORACLE from the great god who expels disease demons and receives divine approval for the dispatch of a divine image to save the daughter of the king of Bakhtan. The statue is dispatched (PILGRIMAGE #2) and effects a cure after negotiating with the possessing spirit (AFFIRMATION). The spirit asks for a feast to be celebrated by the king of Bakhtan in his honor (ORACLE #2), before he will dispossess the princess (ENCOUNTER #2). The king of Bakhtan agrees to the spirit's terms, the festival is celebrated (EATING #2), the demon abandons the princess, and all rejoice (AFFIRMATION #2). The consequence is that the foreign king acknowledges Egypt's superiority in matters of wisdom, magic, and religion.

The pattern may be summarized, accounting for doublets and elaborations, as: PILGRIMAGE, EATING, ENCOUNTER, ORACLE, PILGRIMAGE #2, ORACLE #2, ENCOUNTER #2, EATING #2, AFFIRMATION, RETURN. In spite of this tale's apparent differences from the other Foundation Accounts" we have considered, the core constants—the functions of EATING, ENCOUNTER, ORACLE, AFFIRMATION—occur in the order associated with the Foundation Pattern. This Foundation Pattern is, however, elaborated with another pattern embedded in the sequence: PILGRIMAGE #2, ORACLE #2, EATING #2, ENCOUNTER #2. The elaborate structural framework serves to communicate a nationalistic/theological message confirming the superiority of the wisdom and power of the gods of Egypt over those of her neighbors.

Another late Egyptian text exhibits a similar purpose. "The Tale of Setne-Khamwas II" occurs in a copy dating from the Roman period.[32]

---

31. Ibid.
32. Ibid., 138–51.

The king of Egypt is sad because he cannot meet a Nubian challenge to read a document without opening it (LACK/DESIRE). He refuses to eat or drink.[33] The son of Setne-Khamwas, the pharaoh's wise man, assures the king that he can accomplish this task (ORACLE). In anticipation of success, the three Egyptian leaders banquet happily (EATING). The banquet is followed by the miraculous reading of the document by the wise man's son (ENCOUNTER). The document when read reveals the perfidy of the messenger, who is magically eliminated. Egypt's reputation for wisdom, as well as her standing among the surrounding nations (especially the Nubians), is confirmed and enhanced (AFFIRMATION). The pattern here is LACK/DESIRE, ORACLE, EATING, [MIRACULOUS] ENCOUNTER, and AFFIRMATION.

The sequence of pattern elements in this late Egyptian narrative varies somewhat from the order of elements in the Foundation narratives we examined at first, reflecting a literary elaboration upon, or allusion to, the original template. In these tales, the structural morphology of the Foundation Pattern is pressed into service toward a cultural goal that reflects the cultural focus of the tale-teller's time and place. The establishment of Egypt's reputation for wisdom by means of the Foundation Pattern in "The Tale of Setne-Khamwas II" and "The Legend of the Possessed Princess" reflects the late-period preoccupation with magic and wisdom and Egypt's concern in that period for its international standing. Transformations of these Patterns of Destiny reflecting evolving cultural emphases also occur in Hebrew biblical narrative, as I shall show in chapter 7.

Homeric Literature.   The entire action of Homer's *Odyssey* begins with a Foundation Account.[34] The *initial situation*[35] is described by the

---

33. The refusal to eat or drink, a reversal of the EATING event, is often a clue to something amiss. See the examination of Genesis 24 earlier in this chapter and, especially, my interpretation of the aftermath of the deaths of Nadab and Abihu in light of other biblical instances of cultic meals in chapter 3 above.

34. I am grateful to Professor Murray H. Lichtenstein of the Department of Classical and Oriental Studies at Hunter College, City University of New York, for this reference, taken from Homer, *The Odyssey* (LCL; Cambridge: Harvard, 1984; orig. pub., 1919) 1.12–27. For a recent cross-cultural comparison of Greek myth to the myths of Mesopotamia, see Charles Penglase, *Greek Myths and Mesopotamia: Parallels and Influence in the Homeric Hymns and Hesiod* (London: Routledge, 1994).

35. In this work, I italicize elements of the morphological analysis that are not part of the sequence of elements that make up the pattern under discussion but that nevertheless merit attention as part of the discussion; see above, my discussion of the sample analysis of Genesis 18, pp. 120–27. Propp begins his own analysis with an "initial situation" whose equilibrium is upset in some way by LACK/DESIRE;

bard, outlining how all of the gods but one pity poor Odysseus, whose journey home from the Trojan War is beset with onerous obstacles (1.1–19). Poseidon alone is implacably angry with Odysseus, but the pitiless divinity is off feasting among the far Ethiopians, who do him honor (EATING, 1.22–26), and while he is distracted the other gods assemble in the halls of Zeus to consider Odysseus's case (ENCOUNTER, 1.26–75). Zeus is convinced that it is up to the assembled gods to see that Odysseus is allowed to return home (ORACLE, 1.76–78), and his pronoucement is confirmed by Athena, who immediately proposes practical measures to implement the Assembly's decision (AFFIRMA-TION, 1.80–95).

The Foundation Pattern that initiates the action of the entire *Odyssey* undergirds a narrative that expresses divine volition. It is the will of the gods that Odysseus return home, expressed structurally by means of the Foundation morphology and textually by means of an account of the decision taken by the Assembly of the gods. Here, Homer is reinforcing the surface message of the plot by building it on the framework of a Pattern of Destiny. The audience is certain that the hero will return; it only remains to discover how this predetermined outcome is to be achieved.

Later in book 1, Odysseus's son Telemachus is also vouchsafed a Foundation Pattern, this one reinforcing the adventure he undertakes at Athena's urging in order to learn more of his father's whereabouts. The servants are preparing a feast in the home of Telemachus and his mother, Penelope (EATING, 1.110–43), in order to feed the horde of suitors that has taken up residence in the belief that Odysseus is dead and his presumed widow an attractive object of matrimony. Athena appears, disguised as an old friend of Odysseus, and she and Telemachus sit down to the meal at a remove from the other guests so that they can have a private conversation. An ENCOUNTER ensues among the rowdy suitors (1.144–77), during which Athena manages a private word with Odysseus's son. Athena predicts the safe return of Odysseus (ORACLE, 1.200–205) and urges Telemachus to implement her plan in the guise of giving him sound advice (1.206–318). AFFIRMATION takes several forms, as the ORACLE is repeated in Telemachus's mind after Athena's departure (1.320–22), and Telemachus acts upon Athena's advice immediately (1.337–72), reassuring his reluctant nurse, whom he presses into service, that his dangerous plan was not made without

---

by italicizing these words, I wish to draw attention to the initial situation as a unit without giving it as much weight as the constant elements of the genre-defining pattern. Not every narrative discussion includes this element, nor does it need to.

the protection of a god (1.372). Both father and son are assured of Odysseus's safe return, and their adventures proceed under the aegis of divine protection. In both of these cases, Foundation Patterns function as literary devices to counterpoint the tribulations of the various heroes and to signal to the audience that a positive outcome is divinely ordained.

Christian Scriptures.   The Foundation Pattern is also present in the Christian scriptures, most clearly in the Synoptic Gospel accounts of the Last Supper, which takes place on the festival of Unleavened Bread, the Passover feast.[36] Common to Matthew 24, Mark 14, and Luke 22 is a Foundation Pattern associated with Jesus' establishment of the Eucharist. In all three, this basic sequence occurs: Jesus and his disciples are EATING the Paschal meal,[37] and they engage in an EN-COUNTER about what is to come.[38] Following the breaking of bread, Jesus utters the ORACLE establishing the Eucharist.[39] This ORACLE is AF-FIRMED when Jesus repeats a variation of it during the cup of wine.[40]

The Foundation Pattern functions in the Christian scriptures to underline an essential theological message on the eve of the Crucifixion. The Foundation Pattern in these texts underscores on a structural level the narrative message of the divine establishment of a new covenant through Jesus and the coming of the Kingdom of God.

This same narrative also contains a Pattern of Doom in its structural framework. Both Patterns of Destiny hinge on a single EATING and DRINKING event, the Paschal feast of the Last Supper.

The two Patterns of Destiny are placed one following the other, joined by the EATING account of the Last Supper in each of the Synoptic Gospels.[41] The negative ORACLE associated with the Doom Pattern in every case is Jesus' prediction of his betrayal at the hands of one of his disciples.[42] In each Gospel, the betrayal is predicted and the Doom of the human Jesus is affirmed.[43] In each Gospel, the negative ORACLE

---

36. Matt 26:17–29, Mark 14:12–25, Luke 22:7–34.
37. Matt 26:26–27, Mark 14:22–24, Luke 22:19.
38. Matt 26:20–26, Mark 14:17–22, Luke 22:14–23.
39. Matt 26:28–29, Mark 14:25, Luke 22:29–30.
40. Matt 26:27–29, Mark 14:23–25, Luke 22:20–22.
41. Matt 26:17–29, Mark 14:12–25, Luke 22:7–34.
42. Matt 26:20–26, Mark 14:17–22, Luke 22:14–23.
43. Matt 26:20–25 (EATING, 20–21; ENCOUNTER 21–22; ORACLE, 23–24; AF-FIRMATION, 25); Mark 14:17–21 (EATING, 17; ORACLE, 18; ENCOUNTER 19; AFFIRMATION, 20–21); Luke 22:14–18 (EATING, 14–15; ENCOUNTER, 15; OR-ACLE, 16; DRINKING, 17; AFFIRMATION [repetition] 18).

is followed by the Foundation Pattern associated with Jesus' establishment of the institution of the Eucharist, with its promise of a new covenant and the establishment of the Kingdom of God. Negative ORACLE precedes positive ORACLE, and both are connected through the Paschal meal. The underlying structural morphology reinforces the theological message of the scriptural narrative: the Paschal sacrifice is Jesus, whose passion must precede resurrection, just as sin and betrayal must precede salvation.

Although much further work remains to be done, these examples from a variety of Near Eastern, Greek, and other literatures testify to the widespread use of the morphology of Doom and Foundation all across Mesopotamia and the Levant from the third millennium B.C.E. through at least the first century C.E. The occurrence of these patterns in biblical narrative emerges from and participates in this deeply rooted tradition.

Patterns of Destiny: Establishment

The Foundation Pattern that I observed in Genesis 18 also occurs in Genesis 21, Isaac's weaning feast. In both of these examples, there are *five* common features that occur in sequence.

First, there is a feast, an EATING event, for the three visitors in Genesis 18 and for Isaac's weaning in Genesis 21.

Second, at the feast there is an ENCOUNTER that includes the *third* element, an ORACLE or BLESSING. In Genesis 18, a son's birth is foretold, Sarah doubts and laughs, and a skeptical Sarah is reassured by an angel that the divine prediction will come to pass. In Genesis 21, Sarah demands Ishmael's banishment, and a reluctant Abraham is divinely reassured that Ishmael, too, will become a nation.

Fourth, the encounter is followed by a DEPARTURE, by two of the angels in Genesis 18, and by Hagar and Ishmael in Genesis 21.

Finally, an AFFIRMATION of the ORACLE is articulated by the text. In Gen 18:17–19, God explicitly decides to confide the divine plan for Sodom to Abraham because of Abraham's future status as the father of a great and mighty nation, acting upon the ORACLE as though it had already come true. In Gen 21:17–18 the divine ORACLE is repeated to Hagar, the boy's mother, and his well-being is emphasized in vv. 20–21, where Ishmael's divine protection is explicitly noted, followed by the AFFIRMING report of his coming to manhood and taking a wife.

The Foundation Pattern embedded in Genesis 21 establishes Ishmael, the descendant of Abraham through Hagar, as a great nation. The ORACLE is given to Abraham and affirmed to Hagar. This account is parallel to and symmetrical with the Foundation Pattern for Abraham's line through Sarah. Abraham will be the father of many nations, as God promises, but the key to the establishment of each nation is through the mother.

This insight is reinforced by the conversation between God and Abraham in Gen 17:16–21. God promises Abraham seed through Sarah, who at that time is 90 years old. Abraham throws himself on his face, laughing at the very idea, and begs God to consider Ishmael. God agrees to make Ishmael a great nation for Abraham's sake but insists on maintaining the divine covenant with Isaac, Sarah's son to be (Gen 17:21). God repeats the identity of Isaac, Sarah's son, as the divinely favored descendant again in Gen 21:12–13 and repeats the promise to make the son of the slave woman Hagar a nation too, for Abraham's sake. Twice, in the context of lines of descent, both boys are identified in terms of their mothers, and this emphasis on the maternal line is reinforced on the structural level as each nation descending from a specific mother is established with its own Foundation Pattern. Abraham is to be the father of many nations, but the divine foundation of each is structurally established through the maternal line.

Foundation Accounts in the Bible.   Both an elaboration of and variation upon this pattern occur in the narrative of Genesis 24, which deals with the betrothal of Rebekah to Abraham's son Isaac. Here, the PILGRIMAGE or JOURNEY of Abraham's servant ends at the well where Rebekah gives water to him and his camels (DRINKING event, 24:18–20). He reveals that he is a messenger from her kinsman, and when her family is informed of these events, the servant is then invited to partake of her family's hospitality (ENCOUNTER, 24:22–32). The camels are fed, and the servant and his retinue wash, but he refuses to take any food or drink himself until he has told his tale (EATING REFUSED or DELAYED, 24:32–33). He tells it at great length ([information mediation/doubling],[44] 24:34–49), and his request for Rebekah's hand on behalf

---

44. On the meaning of this kind of repetition in narratives, termed *doubling* or *trebling*, depending on the case, see Propp, *Morphology*, 74–75, where he refers to "trebling"; see also Axel Olrik, "Epic Laws of Folk Narrative," in *The Study of Folklore* (ed. Alan Dundes; Englewood Cliffs, N. J.: Prentice-Hall, 1965) 129–41; and his recently reprinted work *Principles for Oral Narrative Research* (trans. Kirsten Wolf and Jody Jensen; Folklore Studies in Translation; Bloomington: Indiana University Press, 1992; orig. pub., 1921). Olrik terms this phenomenon "doubling" and, like Propp, believes that a duplicated element should be counted once for morphological purposes.

of his master is accepted (24:50–51). Betrothal gifts are distributed (ENCOUNTER #2, 24:53), and only then do the servant and his retinue EAT and DRINK and spend the night (24:54). In the morning, an objection is raised against his immediate departure with the intended bride, who is consulted as to her wishes and consents to accompany him (EN-COUNTER #3, 24:55–58). They send her off with an ORACLE in the form of a blessing for myriad progeny who will prove successful against their adversaries.

In Genesis 18, the narrative structure confirms that Sarah is the conduit through which God's promise to Abraham will be fulfilled. In Genesis 21, the structure confirms the promise of great nationhood through Hagar's son, Ishmael. In Genesis 24 the structural focus on the matriarchs continues in spite of the variation of EATING refused and the elaboration of the retelling of the tale. The core pattern of EATING followed by ORACLE underlies this narrative and reinforces the structural focus on the progenitrix: the line of Abraham through Isaac is to be continued via Rebekah.

The Foundation Pattern in Ugaritic Legends. The establishment of lines of descent is a central concern in the Northwest Semitic epics of King Keret and of Aqhat.[45] As in the biblical examples, Foundation Patterns underlie these narratives of progeny.

The pattern in the Keret legend begins with a dream granted to him by El when Keret has wept himself to sleep; in the dream, Keret is given instructions on how to proceed to secure progeny. The structural pattern underlying the first part of the Keret legend is: EATING/DRINKING (Keret is commanded to and does prepare an offering to Baal consisting of at least one of a lamb, kid, fowl, and wine or honey); he is told to and does prepare provisions for a long [JOURNEY/PILGRIMAGE] to seek a bride; in an ENCOUNTER with the king, he demands and

---

45. H. L. Ginsberg (trans.), "The Tale of Aqhat," *ANET*, 149–55, tablet A, col. 1, lines 25–end; and col. 2. The legend of King Keret has several motifs that are echoed in the patriarchal narratives: the hero despairs of an heir; the hero undertakes a divinely commanded journey; a wife is secured from afar; the hero secures the promise of a line of progeny at a banquet, where blessing is received from on high. See the "Legend of King Keret," KRT A, cols. i–vi, and KRT B, cols. i–iii:24; and Ginsberg's translation in *ANET*, 143–49. See Claus Westermann, *The Promises to the Fathers: Studies on the Patriarchal Narratives* (Philadelphia: Fortress, 1980) 166–86; and, more recently, R. Hendel, *The Epic of the Patriarch: The Jacob Cycle and the Narrative Traditions of Canaan and Israel* (HSM 42; Atlanta: Scholars Press, 1987) 33–98; and Simon B. Parker, *The Pre-Biblical Narrative Tradition* (SBLRBS 24; Atlanta: Scholars Press, 1989), especially pp. 225–32.

receives the king's daughter for his wife; he returns home and (OR-ACLE) is blessed by the leading gods with sons and daughters who are eventually born (AFFIRMATION).

The pattern in Aqhat is: Danel provides food and drink to the holy ones for seven consecutive days, in hopes of incubating a dream (EAT-ING/DRINKING); in the dream, Baal pleads with El that Danel be granted progeny (ENCOUNTER); El takes Danel by the hand, blesses him with vigor, and promises him progeny (ORACLE); a messenger tells Danel the good news, and Danel laughs and proclaims his soul at ease (AFFIR-MATION). This pattern is virtually doubled as Danel returns home, pre-pares a seven-day banquet for the "skillful ones" and "daughters of joyful noise" (EATING), after which his wife conceives (ENCOUNTER), and Danel counts the months of her pregnancy (AFFIRMATION). The text is broken, but a son is apparently born, whom Danel names Aqhat.

Like the biblical texts establishing the two lines of Abraham that I outlined above, both of these Ugaritic texts open with a leader's lack of progeny and continue with an ORACLE predicting that this lack will be liquidated, which it eventually is. The morphology in both Keret and Aqhat, as it is for the establishment of Abraham's two lines and for Isaac through Rebekah, is EATING/DRINKING, ENCOUNTER, ORACLE, and AFFIRMATION.

Foundation of the Israelite Nation. In the Hebrew Bible, each stage of the formation of the Israelites as a people and as a nation is accom-panied by a story that includes an EATING or DRINKING event followed by an ORACLE or a blessing. Aside from the patriarchal narratives mentioned already, the establishment of the Israelites as a nation be-gins with the command to prepare for the first Passover, in Exodus 12, and directions for future generations to memorialize the saving act of the Exodus about to take place. The EATING of the Paschal meal is to precede the Exodus (12:1–13), and an ORACLE predicting divine salvation is affirmed by God's command for future observance of the not-yet-performed miraculous rescue (12:14–20). Moses emphasizes the certainty of the fulfillment of these and other divine promises in his repetition of the divine command to the elders (12:24–27). As with the annunciation of Isaac, AFFIRMATION takes the form of God's acting as though the ORACLE has already been fulfilled by commanding what is to be done in generations to come, long after the people have been saved from Egypt and installed in the land of promise. These com-mands are followed by performance by the Israelites (12:28) and the Exodus from Egypt (12:28–42).

Foundation of the Israelite Monarchy. Biblical accounts of the establishment of the Israelite monarchy also participate in this pattern.[46] There is a Foundation Pattern associated with every stage of its development, from the idea of an Israelite monarchy to the anointing of David.

The shift in paradigm from charismatic leadership by judges to leadership by an Israelite king is foreshadowed by the structural patterns underlying the opening chapters of 1 Samuel. A Foundation Pattern undergirds the narrative of the birth of Samuel, anointer of kings. It opens with an EATING event in 1 Samuel 1, followed by an ENCOUNTER with Eli the priest, and culminating in his blessing of Hannah, predicting that her prayers will be answered. This ORACLE is AFFIRMED by the narrative report that the boy is born in due time. Samuel's birth and destiny of service to God are established structurally as well as narratively.

In contrast to the Foundation Account of Samuel's birth and dedication to God is the condemnation of Eli and his house, which immediately follows in 1 Sam 2:12–36. The message on the surface level of the narrative is reinforced by the underlying structure of a Doom Pattern. In this Doom Account, the *initial situation* is noted, namely, that Eli's sons are scoundrels (1 Sam 2:12). Their sin concerns impiety in their treatment of the food offerings (EATING/DRINKING) and is described in great detail (1 Sam 2:13–17). Samuel's situation and that of his natal family complete the recounting of the initial situation. The ENCOUNTER is between Eli and his sons, in which Eli berates them for sexual transgressions, which bear no apparent relationship to the EATING impieties already mentioned. In contrast to the detailed account of the food transgressions, the sexual improprieties are only hinted at in passing (1 Sam 2:22–25a). An *information connective* contrasts the intransigence of Eli's sons with the approbation of Samuel and attributes the situation to divine will (1 Sam 2:25b–26). An ORACLE follows in which a man of God predicts the demise of Eli's house and the end of his priestly hegemony (1 Sam 2:27–36). While the punishment is spelled out in great detail, the transgressions of Eli's house are noted only generally and seem to include only the impieties concerning sacrificial offerings (1 Sam 2:29). The ORACLE specifies a sign that will AFFIRM the prediction: both of Eli's sons will die on the same day (1 Sam 2:34), which they eventually do (1 Sam 4:11, 17). Another AFFIRMATION of the Doom of Eli's house

---

46. For a discussion of the structure of the rituals surrounding anointing and enthronement, see R. Patai, "Hebrew Installation Rites," *HUCA* 20 (1947) 143–225.

takes place in 1 Samuel 3, this one very general regarding both transgression and punishment (3:11–14).

The Patterns of Destiny that open the book of 1 Samuel foreshadow this change in the world order and signal at whose hand these changes will take place. In every case, the divine will is the motivator, but human behavior is the means of execution. The juxtaposition of the structural patterns reflects the change in Israelite leadership from judges to a monarchy and also hints that God's choice can be revoked—as it is when Saul is rejected in favor of David.

The link among these ideas is the person of Samuel, who in his youth is a positive counterexample to Eli's wicked sons, personifying the succession of the newly favored one and the rejection of the previously chosen line. Later in his career, Samuel acts as an agent of the changes foreshadowed in his youth: he initiates monarchy by anointing Saul as Israel's first king; later, after Saul is rejected, Samuel also anoints David, Saul's supplanter. With Patterns of Foundation and Doom so closely juxtaposed, the structural level of the text reinforces the change in the world order that is to come to Israel at the hand of Samuel. Samuel's dual role as symbol and as agent of change is unique: he is the only person in the biblical account of Israelite history to anoint two kings. In this case, the structural Patterns of Foundation and Doom support the narrative and symbolic levels of the text.[47]

Kingship itself is established in Israel in a narrative supported by a Foundation Pattern. It begins with a JOURNEY/PILGRIMAGE by Saul and a servant to look for Saul's father's lost asses with no success (1 Sam 9:3–5). A series of [connectives] informs Saul and the reader that a man of God has arrived in town and might be available to help with their inquiry (1 Sam 9:6–14). Samuel is expecting them. He welcomes them and invites them to a feast (EATING/DRINKING), at which Saul is offered an honored place and a choice portion (1 Sam 9:19–25). Samuel talks with Saul on the roof that evening, and at dawn Saul and Samuel continue their ENCOUNTER (1 Sam 9:25–10:8) as they walk and talk and the seer anoints the first king of Israel. Samuel offers Saul a positive ORACLE, complete with signs (1 Sam 10:1–7),[48] establishing Saul as

---

47. For an insightful discussion of the symbolic and metaphoric relationships between Samuel's early life and the history of the Israelite monarchy, see Robert Polzin, *Samuel and the Deuteronomist—A Literary Study of the Deuteronomic History, Part Two: I Samuel* (New York: Harper & Row, 1989), especially pp. 18–79.

48. E. Tov, *The Text-Critical Use of the Septuagint in Biblical Research* (Jerusalem Biblical Studies; Jerusalem: Simor, 1981) 4, 52–53. For purposes of the discussion in this book, structural analysis will transcend these later text divisions as required.

king of Israel. The text reports that all of the forecast signs were fulfilled that same day (1 Sam 10:9–13).

Israel's second king is also heralded in an episode that is undergirded by a Foundation Pattern, but the surface narrative of David's anointing is very different from the surface narrative of Saul's anointing. The Foundation of the Davidic dynasty is recounted with some ambivalence on the narrative level; structurally, however, the Foundation Pattern is intact. Tension between the unambiguous structural messages, representing divine volition, and the ambivalent narrative messages, signifying the human element, reflects the polarities that permeate the Deuteronomic history.

David is anointed covertly in 1 Sam 16:1–13. A very reluctant Samuel JOURNEYS to Bethlehem at God's suggestion, bringing a sacrifice termed זבח in 16:2–3,[49] as Samuel's "cover story," to protect him from Saul's potential wrath. Samuel invites Jesse and his sons along with the elders of the city to purify themselves and join him in the sacrificial feast (זבח, EATING, 16:4–5). As the guests arrive, Samuel surveys each of the sons of Jesse, and one by one each is rejected by God (ENCOUNTER, 16:6–10). Impatient with this errand that he has undertaken only halfheartedly, Samuel asks if Jesse has any other sons,[50] and David is produced (16:11). God tells Samuel that this is the one (ORACLE, 16:12), Samuel anoints him in the presence of his brothers, the spirit of the Lord grips David from that day on (AFFIRMATION), and Samuel returns to Ramah without any further mention of the sacrificial meal (16:13).

Samuel's haste in this case contrasts sharply with his behavior on the occasion of Saul's anointing, just a few chapters earlier. In 1 Samuel 9,

---

49. As noted in chapter 3 (p. 50 n. 14) above, this term denotes a well-being sacrifice, or שלמים, in the eating of which the offerer and his guests participate. A meal is understood. See, for example, Leviticus 3 and 2 Chr 30:22.

50. The precise Hebrew meaning of כי־לא נסב עד־באו פה is unclear. The word נסב is problematic in v. 11. It is usually translated 'sit down' and is generally considered to have the connotation of beginning something. The sense here would be that David must be produced before the company can sit down to the feast. Henry Preserved Smith, in *A Critical and Exegetical Commentary on the Books of Samuel* (ICC; Edinburgh: T. & T. Clark, 1977; orig. pub., 1898) 145–47, suggests that perhaps סבב is used of going around an altar, hence beginning a sacrificial feast; the Syriac Peshitta uses the root *hpq* 'to return', apparently understanding the Hebrew as שוב 'to return'; Jewish commentators read הסבה 'leaning' as the customary way to eat a meal (Rashi, Metzudat Zion, R. Joseph Kara, ad loc.).

It is possible that the implication is to sit or to recline around a table at a meal, based on readings in the Targum, the Septuagint, and the Vulgate. See S. R. Driver, *Notes on the Hebrew Text and the Topography of the Books of Samuel* (2d ed.; Oxford: Clarendon, 1966; orig. pub., 1913) 134.

a sacrificial feast, a זבח, is prepared in advance according to divine instructions (9:12–15). When Samuel sees Saul, God tells him majestically, 'Behold the man about whom I told you, "this one will govern my people" ' הנה האיש אשר אמרתי אליך זה יעצר בעמי (9:17). In contrast, when Samuel sees David, God tells him briefly, 'Come, anoint him, for that's he' קום משחהו כי־זה הוא (16:12b). Saul is seated at the head of the table and given a choice portion reserved for him alone (9:23–24). Nothing whatever is said of the sacrificial feast after David's hasty anointing; Samuel leaves Bethlehem immediately to return to his home (16:13). In 1 Samuel 9–10, on the other hand, Samuel takes time to talk with Saul and give him advice, both before and after his anointing (9:26–10:8).

On the narrative level, Samuel's effort on behalf of his first anointing contrasts with his apparent distaste for the second anointing. Samuel's affinity to Saul and ambivalence about David conflicts with God's decision to reject Saul, and God expresses divine impatience with Samuel (1 Sam 15:35–16:1). This ambivalence is absent on the structural level. Morphologically, both anointings faithfully exhibit the full Foundation Pattern: JOURNEY, EATING, ENCOUNTER, ORACLE, AFFIRMATION, DEPARTURE. Israelite monarchy is duly inaugurated in Israel in 1 Samuel 9, and the Davidic kingship is duly established in 1 Samuel 16.

Establishment of Israelites in the Land of Promise. Like the establishment of the monarchy, the establishment of the Israelites in the land of promise also reveals a Foundation Pattern. Joshua 5–6 tells of the Israelites at Gilgal and establishes Israelite hegemony in Canaan. This account in Joshua of the establishment of Israel on the land represents fulfillment of the biblical ideal for settlement and conquest. After the first Passover observance and the first EATING of the produce of the land, the manna ceases (5:10–12). Joshua has an enigmatic ENCOUNTER with an angel reminiscent of Moses at the burning bush (5:13–15). Next, Joshua receives an ORACLE regarding the conquest of Jericho that incorporates the command and performance of a symbolic action seven times (a formulaic number, 6:2–5). After the battle (6:6–21) and the redemption of the promise made in Joshua 2 to Rahab (6:22–25), the ORACLE and its conditions are AFFIRMED (6:26–27). Establishment of Israel in the land of promise is divinely ordained and of enormous national significance, meriting a Foundation Pattern in its recounting.

Establishment of the Israelite Cult. The Foundation of a third national institution, the Israelite cult, is described in Exod 24:1–25:8, just after the covenant has been cut between God and the people, with Moses as intermediary. This text begins with the divine summons of

Moses, Aaron, Nadab, Abihu, and the 70 elders of Israel to ascend the mountain (Exod 24:1–2). There, they witness a theophany and share a meal (Exod 24:11b): ויחזו את־האלהים ויאכלו וישתו 'they beheld a vision of God, and they ate and drank'. This meal operates on one level as a literary hinge, linking the covenant that has just taken place with the establishment of the cult that is about to happen. EATING and DRINKING are followed by an ENCOUNTER between God and Moses that lasts a formulaic 40 days and 40 nights (Exod 24:12–18).[51] The ORACLE is embodied in the divine command to solicit gifts from the people, out of which Moses is to supervise the construction of the tabernacle, which is to be the focus of the divine presence in the midst of the people. God promises that if they build it, God will dwell among them (Exod 25:8): ועשו לי מקדש ושכנתי בתוכם.[52] The essential elements of the Foundation Account are present here in the expected sequence: EATING and DRINKING followed by ORACLE.

It is significant that, although a Foundation Pattern underlies the establishment of the Israelite cult, there is no Foundation Pattern in the structure of the biblical account of creation in Genesis 1. The establishment of the cult is the defining moment of Israelite nationhood, received by Moses on Sinai, as are the Ten Commandments.

---

51. On formulaic numbers in tales, see, for example, Jason, *Ethnopoetry*, 93.

52. The peak encounter with God is interrupted by the people's apostasy. Moses returns to find the people worshiping the golden calf, which he destroys utterly (Exod 32:20), seizing it, burning it, grinding it, and strewing it. An Ugaritic parallel to this biblical sequence is Baal's discussion of his temple design during a banquet celebrating his victory over Yam (tablet 2, col. 4). While the order of tablets for the Ugaritic epic is uncertain (Ginsberg, "Legend of King Keret," 143; and R. J. Clifford, "Mot Invites Baal to a Feast: Observations on a Difficult Ugaritic Text [CTA 5.i = KTU 1.5.1]," in *Working with No Data: Semitic and Egyptian Studies Presented to Thomas O. Lambdin* [ed. D. M. Golomb and S. T. Hollis; Winona Lake, Ind.: Eisenbrauns, 1987) passim, especially the concluding paragraph on p. 64), it appears that Baal's pride in his new edifice leads somehow to his reckless defiance of Mot. Mot captures Baal, ensnaring at the same time earth's abundance. Baal's sister, Anat, attacks Mot, described in a verbal sequence echoed in Moses' annihilation of the golden calf, in which she seizes, cleaves, winnows, burns, grinds, and strews Mot, thereby restoring Baal (and abundance) to the world. Following Moses' annihilation of the calf, the children of Israel are also restored to their earlier relationship in covenant with their God. These correspondences were seen and discussed by Samuel E. Loewenstamm, "The Making and Destruction of the Golden Calf," *Bib* 48 (1967) 481–90, reprinted and enlarged in the two collections of his essays, the earlier *Comparative Studies in Biblical and Ancient Oriental Literatures* (AOAT 204; Neukirchen-Vluyn: Neukirchener Verlag / Kevelaer: Butzon & Bercker, 1980) and the more recent publication, *From Babylon to Canaan: Studies in the Bible and Its Oriental Background* (Jerusalem: Magnes, 1992).

Establishment of the Cult of Marduk.   The context of the Foundation Pattern establishing the Israelite cult is strikingly similar to that of the establishment of the cult of Marduk. The foundation of the cult in both cultures is treated separately from the creation of the universe. In the Akkadian account, following Marduk's victory over Tiamat, *Enūma Eliš* recounts the establishment of temples and worship for the Semitic pantheon. The establishment of cultic practice merits a Foundation Pattern separate from the Foundation Pattern underlying Marduk's creation of the universe, as does the establishment of the Israelite cult in the biblical account.

This second occurrence of the Foundation Pattern in *Enūma Eliš* marks the establishment of cultic relationships among the gods, including the ritual supremacy of Marduk and his shrine of Babylon. Following Marduk's masterwork of creation, the other divinities laud his wisdom and propose to build him a temple for his abode. The dedication takes place at a banquet (tablet 6, lines 49–80).

The gods assemble and are seated for a feast at the newly constructed shrine of Babylon, Marduk's temple and dwelling place (EATING/DRINKING, tablet 6, lines 46–76). They declare themselves happy with the stations and tasks that Marduk has assigned. Anu places Marduk's bow as a sign in heaven and determines its destiny (ENCOUNTER, tablet 6, lines 77–91). In the Hebrew Bible, God's bow is placed in the heavens to mark the re-creation of the world after the Flood, as a sign of God's commitment to Noah and to the present world order. Here, as in the biblical Flood story, the bow acts as a sign sealing the creation of the known universe by the divinity. In both cases, the weapon of the divinity is hung as a sign of the cessation of hostilities and a commitment to the new order—in Marduk's case, the end of internecine wars among the gods and their acceptance of Marduk as their new supreme deity; in Noah's case, the end of the destruction of creation by God and the divine commitment to the Noahide covenant.

Marduk is seated, and the great gods prostrate themselves before him and declare his destiny the highest (ORACLE, tablet 6, lines 92–120). The gods then pronounce Marduk's 50 sacred names, recapping Marduk's history[53] and concluding with an adjuration to invoke Marduk's name in every rite (AFFIRMATION, tablet 6, lines 121–end; tablet 7, lines 1–162). This Foundation Pattern marks the establishment of cultic relationships among the gods and ritual prescriptions for their worship.

There are two items of note here: first, that the structural framework of the Foundation Pattern is associated with the establishment of

---

53. See Foster, *Before the Muses*, 388.

rituals and rites of worship in both Akkadian and Israelite literature; and second, that a separate Foundation Pattern occurs for creation and cultic worship in each. These two together indicate that the proper ordering of relationships between the human world and the sphere of the divine is perceived in both cultures as separate from the creation of the material universe and is of such major cultural significance for both of these ancient civilizations that it warrants separate morphological emphasis.

A Northwest Semitic fragment gives an account of the construction of a divine abode in an episode in the Ugaritic epic of Baal, when Baal's temple design is decided at a banquet. In this account, Baal eats a meal with his vizier and builder, Kothar-wa-Ḫasis (EATING); Baal proposes to build a palace, in which Kothar-wa-Ḫasis wishes to put windows. Baal opposes this design feature, apparently to thwart his old rival Yamm (ENCOUNTER). The text is broken, but Kothar-wa-Ḫasis predicts that Baal will come to see it his way (ORACLE), a prediction that comes to pass after Baal conquers a series of many towns and, upon his return, indeed calls for the opening of a window in his palace. Kothar-wa-Ḫasis crows with glee when his prediction comes true (AF-FIRMATION). At a minimum, the Foundation Pattern underlies this episode in order to underscore the significance of the establishment of Baal's long-sought abode.[54] A similar function attends the Foundation Pattern for the biblical tabernacle in Exodus 24–25.

A reconsecration of the holy Temple also incorporates into its structure a Foundation Pattern. I showed earlier in my discussion of cultic variables in chapter 4 above that the act of ritual consecration in the Bible does not require an eating or drinking event. Therefore, the

---

54. Because of the broken nature of the lines, it is difficult to tell the significance of this Foundation Pattern beyond the establishment of Baal's palace. See Ginsberg's translation in "Poems about Baal and Anath," *ANET*, 134, where the relevant passages are designated as tablet II AB, col. v, line 106–col. vii, line 41; and G. R. Driver, *Canaanite Myths and Legends* (Old Testament Studies 3; Edinburgh: T. & T. Clark, 1976), where the relevant passages are designated as tablet II, col. 5, line 44–col. 7, line 44. Since the order of the tablets relating to the Baal cycle is still a matter of scholarly dispute, it is difficult to make any judgments regarding the sequence and pattern underlying more than texts we have received as discrete units. See Richard J. Clifford, "The Temple in the Ugaritic Myth of Baal," in *Symposia Celebrating the Seventy-Fifth Anniversary of the Founding of the American Schools of Oriental Research (1900–1975)* (ed. F. M. Cross; Zion Research Foundation Occasional Publications; Cambridge, Mass.: American Schools of Oriental Research, 1979) 137–45; idem, "Cosmogonies in the Ugaritic Texts and in the Bible," *Or* 53 (1985) 183–201; idem, "Mot Invites Baal to a Feast," 55–64; and B. Margalit, *A Matter of Life and Death: A Study of the Baal-Mot Epic (CTA 4–5–6)* (AOAT 206; Neukirchen-Vluyn: Neukirchener Verlag, 1980).

EATING event accompanying the reconsecration of the Temple by Hezekiah in 2 Chronicles 29 and 30 invites further study. In 2 Chronicles 29 and 30 there is an episode that is absent from the books of Kings and unique to the Chronicler: the reconsecration of the Temple and its cult by Hezekiah. The structure of chapter 30 is a Foundation Pattern.

The narrative opens with Hezekiah's desire to implement the Passover and his summons of the people, via proclamation and the dispatch of messengers (30:1–13). Many people undertake a [PILGRIMAGE] and assemble for the offering and EATING of the Paschal sacrifice (30:13–18a). In the ENCOUNTER that follows, Hezekiah successfully intercedes for the people who ate of the sacrifice even though they were in an unclean state (30:18b–20). Seven days of joyous festivities are observed twice (formulaic number, doubling, 30:21–26), and the chapter concludes with a BLESSING/ORACLE by the Levites and AFFIRMATION that their voice was heard in heaven (30:27).

This text, taken in context with the previous chapter recounting the reconsecration of the Temple cult, signifies the reestablishment of the priestly service in the Jerusalem Temple. The narrative structure is that of the Foundation Pattern, with the unspecified blessing by the Levitical priests in v. 27 taking the morphological place of ORACLE, complete with AFFIRMATION noted in the second half of the same verse. The presence of the Foundation Pattern underscores the significance that the Chronicler accords to Hezekiah's reform as a reestablishment of the Israelite cult according to the will of God.

CHAPTER SIX

Patterns of Destiny

Eating and Drinking as Constants within the Condemnation/Doom Genre

Now that I have discussed several clear examples of the Foundation Pattern and demonstrated that it underlies the establishment of the essential elements constituting the nationhood of Israel, I would like to turn to the most important variation of the Foundation Pattern. As I showed in the earlier discussion of Genesis 19, the Doom Pattern exhibits the same morphology as the Foundation Pattern, but the variable in the ORACLE slot is negative, consisting of curse, condemnation, adverse prophecy, unfavorable prediction, and so forth.

Accounts of Doom in the Hebrew Bible

A paradigmatic illustration of the Doom Pattern occurs in Dan 5:1–30, which recounts the divine condemnation of King Belshazzar, heir to the throne of his father, Nebuchadnezzar. Belshazzar hosts a great banquet at which he becomes drunk (EATING/DRINKING, 5:1). In his inebriated state, Belshazzar orders the gold and silver vessels that were captured from the Jerusalem Temple to be brought and used by the nobles at his profane feast (beginning of ENCOUNTER, 5:2–28). The nobles are drinking from the holy vessels, praising their pagan gods as they do so, when the king is alarmed by the sudden appearance of the fingers of a human hand writing on the wall of his palace (ORACLE, embedded in the ENCOUNTER, 5:5). In a familiar wisdom trope, the ENCOUNTER continues with a vain effort to decipher the writing on the part of the king's wise men, the offering of rich rewards to the successful interpreter, the calling of Daniel, the king's charging him with the

153

task, Daniel's rejection of material gifts, and his undertaking of the interpretation (5:7–17).[1]

Daniel interprets the omen in the context of Belshazzar's failure to learn from his father's folly the necessity of glorifying the Lord of Heaven. Instead, Belshazzar's contempt for the Lord's holy vessels has earned him divine condemnation: Daniel interprets the handwriting on the wall as the doom of Belshazzar and his kingdom (5:18–28). The text gives no indication that this ORACLE is taken seriously by the king. Instead, the text underlines the king's frivolity with irony: as though the ORACLE and its interpretation were part of elaborate entertainment, Daniel is rewarded for his successful decipherment with what is certainly an ephemeral appointment to the troika of rulership of the doomed kingdom. The chapter closes with a terse AFFIRMATION of the first part of the ORACLE: Belshazzar is murdered that very night (5:30).[2]

The pattern of this text may be summarized as an EATING/DRINKING event at which there occurs an ENCOUNTER in which is embedded an ORACLE and its interpretation; the narrative closes with AFFIRMATION of the ORACLE. The ORACLE, however, is not the blessing found in the Foundation Pattern; instead, here in Daniel 5 and in the Doom Pattern throughout the Bible the ORACLE consists of a curse or condemnation of a person (here, the king) and/or an entity (here, his united kingdom).

Doom of King and Dynasty

Another king and dynasty are also condemned in narratives exhibiting the Pattern of Doom. The Hebrew Bible leaves no doubt about its

---

1. On the motif of the wise man as savior and the subtype Disgrace and Rehabilitation of a Minister, especially as it occurs in the Bible and the literature of the ancient Near East, see Donald B. Redford, *A Study of the Biblical Story of Joseph (Genesis 37–50)* (VTSup 20; Leiden: Brill, 1970) 96–97. For an analysis of such stories that takes into account pattern and sequence in addition to shared motifs, see Susan Niditch and Robert Doran, "The Success Story of the Wise Courtier: A Formal Approach" (*JBL* 96 [1977] 179–93), in which they rightly criticize the approach of W. Lee Humphreys as set out in "A Lifestyle for Diaspora: A Study of the Tales of Esther and Daniel" (*JBL* 92 [1973] 211–23). Humphreys ignores the importance of sequence in his discussion of isolated motifs in these texts. See idem, "The Motif of the Wise Courtier in the Book of Proverbs," in *Israelite Wisdom: Theological and Literary Essays in Honor of Samuel Terrien* (ed. John G. Gammie et al.; New York: Union Theological Seminary, 1978) 177–90. The motif of a disgraced and rehabilitated minister also occurs in the story of Ahikar. For the various versions of this tale, see F. C. Conybeare, J. Randel Harris, and Agnes Smith Lewis, *The Story of Ahikar* (Cambridge: Cambridge University Press, 1913).

2. The next move of the narrative continues in Daniel 6, where the first verse of that chapter affirms the final judgment of the ORACLE: Darius the Mede receives the kingdom after Belshazzar's demise (6:1).

view of the Northern king Ahab, one of only two leaders in the Hebrew Bible to be subjects of multiple Doom Patterns. Jeroboam, the first king of the North, is the other; the narratives concerning him are discussed at length in chapter 7 below.

There are three oracles against Ahab in the book of Kings: 1 Kgs 20:42, after Ahab's treaty with Ben-hadad of Aram; 1 Kings 21, after his appropriation of Naboth's vineyard; and 1 Kings 22, Micaiah's prediction of Ahab's defeat and death in battle. However, only one of these, 1 Kings 21, features a Doom Pattern. A fourth ORACLE against Ahab appears in 2 Chronicles 18 and features Micaiah's prediction of Ahab's demise in contrast to the prediction of victory offered by the 400 prophets of Samaria, who are misled by a lying spirit sent by God for just this purpose. Each of these narratives and the relationship among them merit further discussion.

In Ahab's first Doom Pattern, in 1 Kings 21, the vineyard episode supplies an EATING and DRINKING event that fills the appropriate morphological slot: Ahab desires Naboth's vineyard and sulks when Naboth will not sell his patrimony, refusing to eat (EATING reversed, 1 Kgs 21:4–6). A series of ENCOUNTERS follows (1 Kgs 21:7–16). Jezebel, in Ahab's name, writes letters to elders and nobles commanding them to proclaim a fast (EATING reversal #2) and secure false witnesses to accuse Naboth of blasphemy. The kangaroo court culminates in Naboth's murder. Jezebel's success in procuring Naboth's vineyard precedes the ORACLE of Doom pronounced upon Ahab by Elijah in 1 Kgs 21:20–24. The doubling of EATING reversals underlies the unsavory outcome on a structural level. The bearing of false witness at the order of the monarch foreshadows the divinely dispatched lying spirit that overtakes the prophets of Samaria in 1 Kings 22 and 2 Chronicles 18. A lone prophet in each case—Elijah or Micaiah—speaks the truth.

This Doom Pattern precedes an account in 1 Kings 22 of the lying spirit of prophecy sent to mislead the kings of Israel and Judah. The episode in 1 Kings 22 does not exhibit a Pattern of Doom in its underlying structure. The Doom morphology is not required, since Ahab has already been duly condemned in the preceding chapter. However, 2 Chronicles lacks the episode of Naboth's garden and so is missing the Doom Pattern for Ahab that would be contained in it.

Chronicles does have an episode parallel to 1 Kings 22, however, with one significant addition. The parallel episode in Chronicles contains the same elements as 1 Kings 22 except that it is prefaced by a sacrificial feast (זבח) shared by the kings of Israel and Judah on the eve of their battle against Aram. The EATING event required by the Doom morphology is supplied by the Chronicler's account of a sacrificial feast shared by Ahab and Jehoshaphat, preceding the episode featuring Micaiah's ORACLE of Doom. This additional EATING event, absent from 1 Kings 22, is followed by the same ORACLE as in 1 Kings 22. Thus, the underlying structure in 2 Chronicles 18 is Ahab's second Doom Pattern,

The story of Naboth's vineyard is completely absent from the account of Ahab's reign in 2 Chronicles. The sacrificial feast is completely absent from the parallel account of this episode in 1 Kings 22. Both the Chronicler and the Deuteronomist apparently felt that Ahab's demise deserved to be preceded by a Doom Pattern, requiring an EATING or DRINKING allusion followed by an ORACLE; each found a way to incorporate this pattern into the episode preceding Ahab's demise.

Condemnation of the North and the South

Readers who come to recognize the Doom Pattern expect to find it underlying two major destructions in the history of Israel, the destruction of the Northern Kingdom and the captivity of Judah. These readers are not disappointed. The Northern Kingdom is the subject of several texts exhibiting an underlying Doom Pattern. In chapter 7, I shall discuss the episodes in which Northern idolatry is condemned in 1 Kings 12–13 and 14. Here, I address the narrative in 1 Kgs 19:1–18, where God condemns Northern idolators, followed by two accounts condemning Josiah of Judah.

Doom of the Northern Kingdom. In 1 Kings 19, Elijah is twice fed miraculously following his flight from Jezebel after slaying 450 of her prophets of Baal. This doubled EATING/DRINKING event is followed by a doubled ENCOUNTER between Elijah and God in which Elijah twice complains that Israel has slaughtered the prophets of the Lord and now seeks his own life. The divine response is an ORACLE, in which the Northern idolators are condemned to their fate at the hands of the three agents God instructs Elijah to deputize: Hazael of Aram, Jehu ben Nimshi of Israel, and Elisha ben Shaphat, successor to Elijah (1 Kgs 19:15–18). This ORACLE is AFFIRMED in 1 Kgs 19:19–21, in which Elisha ben Shaphat becomes Elijah's attendant and is the first to be deputized. The language of this text reflects the principle of מידה כנגד מידה 'measure-for-measure'. As Elijah and the other prophets of God suffer by the sword in the hands of Northern idolators, so Northern idolators will suffer by the sword in the hands of God's agents.

Doom of David's House. David's ultimate decline is precipitated by his affair with Bathsheba in 2 Samuel 11 and his murder of her husband, Uriah. David's punishment for the murder and for his adulterous union with Bathsheba is predicted in an ORACLE delivered by Nathan in 2 Samuel 12. God is displeased with David's sinful behavior and sends Nathan with a parable to David. The parable contains the EATING/DRINKING event in which the rich man appropriates the poor man's sheep for his feast (2 Sam 12:1–4). In the ENCOUNTER that follows between David and Nathan, David comes to realize that he himself has behaved reprehensibly (2 Sam 12:5–9). Nathan delivers the divine curse (2 Sam 12:10–14): in a "measure-for-measure" ORACLE, Nathan predicts that the sword will never depart from David's house on account of David's murder of Uriah and that David's own wives will be publicly taken by another. David acknowledges his guilt, and Nathan reports that, although David merits death for his transgressions, God has ameliorated the penalty: David will live, but the child of the adulterous union will perish. The ORACLE receives AFFIRMATION in the events of 2 Sam 12:15–24: as predicted by the ORACLE, the child of David's adultery dies.[3]

Doom of Judah and Jerusalem.   Judean trespasses do not go uncondemned in the Hebrew Bible. The demise of Judah and Jerusalem is predicted in 2 Kgs 23:21–30, even as that great reformer Josiah renews the neglected covenant and cleanses the defiled Temple. The EATING event is Josiah's Passover (2 Kgs 23:21–23); the ENCOUNTER that follows is Josiah's campaign against ghosts and familiar spirits, idols, and fetishes (2 Kgs 23:24). But all of Josiah's zeal is insufficient to blot out the stain of his grandfather Manasseh, and in an ORACLE of Doom, the Lord pronounces the exile of Judah and the destruction of Jerusalem (2 Kgs 23:26–27). Perhaps an AFFIRMATION of this ORACLE is Josiah's early death (2 Kgs 23:29–30), in a demise that foreshadows the fulfillment of the ORACLE in 2 Kings 25, which recounts the fall of Judah. Whether the ORACLE predicting Judah's downfall is organic to the chapter or added by a later redactor, its placement in the sequence of events so as to underpin the text with a Doom morphology argues that this pattern was indeed a widely recognized literary convention.

A less morphologically ambiguous condemnation is reserved for Josiah by the Chronicler in 2 Chronicles 35. Here we have an explicit Doom Pattern, complete with an EATING event (Josiah's Passover, 2 Chr 35:1–19), an ENCOUNTER (between Josiah and the king of Egypt, 2 Chr 35:20), and a divine ORACLE (from the unlikely mouth of Pharaoh

---

3. This episode is treated in great detail in chapter 3 above, in my discussion of mourning and supplication.

Necho, 2 Chr 35:21) that is AFFIRMED (by the text and by the tragic events that follow, 2 Chr 35:22–27). Significantly, this is the only Doom Pattern reserved for a Judean king in the Hebrew Bible. Solomon's idolatry results in the end of the United Kingdom, but his own fate is unaffected; the warning to Judah to heed God's commandments in the second episode of 1 Kings 13 is, as I shall show in chapter 7, coded metaphorically and does not mention anyone by name, let alone a specific Judean monarch. Perhaps this fact can be taken as additional evidence of the Chronicler's recognized bias against Josiah and toward Hezekiah, as the most righteous of monarchs.[4]

Elaborated but Clear Morphological Examples

As with any well-known device, accretions, elaborations, and creative development enrich the Destiny Pattern's use. In the rest of this chapter, I will offer examples of elaborated but otherwise clear examples of Foundation and Doom Patterns in biblical and Near Eastern literature. In the following chapter, I will consider more subtle examples.

Jacob: Ascendance through Guile

The example that triggered my discovery of these patterns is an especially interesting elaboration on the expected Foundation Pattern in Genesis 27, where Isaac's blessing of his children establishes Jacob's ascendancy over his brother Esau. Isaac sends Esau in pursuit of game so that the patriarch can enjoy savory venison before blessing his elder son. The EATING event is not apparently tied to the overt or stated purpose of the story, which is Isaac's blessing of his sons. Nowhere else in the Bible is the practice of eating associated with such an event. As I noted in the introduction, Jacob blesses Joseph's children in Genesis 48 and his own children in Genesis 49, without any mention of an eating or drinking context.

In addition, Isaac's focus on eating wild hunted food is unique in biblical narrative.[5] An examination of "banquet language" in biblical

---

4. For a survey and analysis of the Chronicler's ideology, see Sara Japhet, *The Ideology of the Book of Chronicles and Its Place in Biblical Thought* (Frankfurt am Main: Peter Lang, 1989). Japhet makes this point about the Chronicler's relative attitudes toward Josiah and Hezekiah on p. 489.

5. See Clifford, "Mot Invites Baal to a Feast," 55–64. Especially suggestive is the discussion on pp. 57–60, where the author contrasts the banquet produce of cultivated herd and field—the environment watered by Baal—with Mot's "feast" of the wild ox, the hind, the wild ass, and Mot's comparison of his appetite to that of the

texts reveals that the expected food would be from the domesticated herd and flock,[6] as it is when Abraham prepares the messengers' meal in Genesis 18--the kind of food that Isaac does, in fact, eat, although he is not aware of it at the time. The practical effect on the level of plot of Esau's hunting trip is to get him out of the way so that the "right" son receives the blessing, and the ascendance of the apparently less powerful progenitor of the Israelites is established. But Esau's mission does not have to involve food or eating in order for this plot function to be served. Saul meets his destiny searching for his father's lost asses in 1 Samuel 9, and Joseph meets his fate conveying his father's greeting to his brothers in Genesis 37.

If eating and drinking are not necessary in order for Isaac to bless his children, which is the stated purpose of the story, or in order to get Esau out of the way, setting in motion the plot of the story, then why is eating made so much of in this narrative?

The answer is that the morphology of the genre of the story requires it. An eating or drinking event is necessary to the structure of the kind of story represented here, the "genre" or "type" story of a benchmark in the formation of the Israelite tribes—a Foundation story of the Children of Israel. I have already shown in Genesis 18 and 21 the Foundation Pattern underlying the establishment of two of Abraham's lines, through his sons, Isaac and Ishmael, respectively. Here, the first of these two lines is singled out for special treatment. These narratives are more than just a family story. Jacob, who later earns the eponym Israel, is a type of the people who bear his name.[7] His blessing is a foundational event of national proportions: Jacob's establishment as the inheritor of Isaac's blessing speaks of Israel's establishment as a people of special blessing as well. The Foundation Pattern underlying Jacob's acquisition of his father's blessing reinforces this message.

---

lion and of the "snorting creature of the sea." Clifford makes the point that all of these associations with Mot are "instances of powers beyond humans' capacity to observe and control" (p. 59).

6. See Lichtenstein, *Episodic Structure*, 106–34, 166, 180–208; and idem, "Banquet Motif," 19–31. See especially the discussion in which Lichtenstein outlines the internal structure of banquet sequences in Genesis 18 and 19; 1 Sam 28:24–25; and Judg 6:19 ("Episodic Structure," 180–83) and compares banquet formulas in the ancient Near East to the catalog of animals used in the banquet in 1 Kgs 5:3 and in Deut 14:4–6 (ibid., 200–208). The general topos of the banquet is discussed, ibid., 106–34 and 166.

7. Stephen A. Geller, "The Struggle at the Jabbok," *JANES* 14 (1984) 37–60, especially pp. 50–59; and idem, "The Sack of Shechem: The Uses of Typology in Biblical Covenant Religion," *Prooftexts* 10 (1990) 1–15.

Inanna: Ascendance through Guile

Evidence from the ancient Near East supports the thesis that an EAT-
ING or DRINKING event is required by the genre defined by Patterns of
Destiny. Even the variations from the expected pattern have Near East-
ern parallels. The EATING event is marked by deception in Genesis 27.
An interesting parallel from Sumerian literature, "Inanna's Journey to
Eridu," has Inanna, one of the younger Sumerian divinities, securing
divine ordinances by deception at a private dinner party with Enki so
she can bestow them on her patron city of Uruk.[8]

The *initial situation* opens with Inanna contemplating her own
womanly splendor in the sheepfold. She is delighted with herself and
wishes to honor Enki, the god of wisdom, at his abode in the Abzu. She
sets off alone, without further preparation ([PILGRIMAGE]), and Enki,
who knows all things, anticipates her arrival. He instructs his vizier to
prepare buttercake, cold water, and beef for Inanna, who is to be
greeted at the "table of heaven" (EATING). Enki and Inanna drink vast
quantities of beer together and then more beer. They toast and challenge each other (ENCOUNTER).

In his cups and feeling good, Enki offers the boons of high priest-
hood, godship, and the throne of kingship to Inanna. She replies, "I
take them!" He continues to offer her additional boons, including 14
divine ordinances necessary for rulership (ORACLE). Inanna accepts
them all, securing them for herself and for her patron city of Erech/
Uruk. Inanna then recites a list of all of the powers given to her by
Enki (AFFIRMATION). It consists of all of the womanly qualities, political, social, and religious power, and all of the trades, crafts, and other
elements necessary for civilization. Inanna loads these treasures onto
the Boat of Heaven and pushes off for her city with Enki's blessing for
her safety (DEPARTURE).

When Enki regains his senses, he realizes that all of the holy objects
are gone. He sends his minions to pursue Inanna to retrieve the boat
and its booty. Inanna is outraged that Enki is going back on his word
and manages to evade him at every city along the route from Eridu,
where Enki dwells, to Erech/Uruk, her destination. When she arrives
home safely, Enki acknowledges Inanna's possession of the divine ordinances for her city, and there is much jubilation in Erech/Uruk.

A full Foundation Pattern underlies this text, recognizable in spite
of much narrative embellishment. The Sumerian story, like Genesis 27,

---

8. Samuel Noah Kramer, *Sumerian Mythology: A Study of Spiritual and Literary
Achievement in the Third Millennium B.C.* (2d ed.; New York: Harper, 1961) 64–68;
Å. W. Sjöberg, "Götterreisen," in *RlA* 3.480–83, section 5.

is etiological, explaining the ascendance of Inanna's patron city over the other city-states of Sumer, just as the biblical account explains the ascendance of Jacob's children over Esau's.

Each account bears mythico-historical implications for its culture: the ascendance of the city's goddess, the ascendance of the eponymous ancestor of Israel. Both stories raise by implication the question of what it means for a cultural entity—a people, a city—to have as its eponymous ancestor or patron a youth of relatively low status who gains ascendancy by means of the deception of a disadvantaged elder.

Ruth: Establishment of the Line of David

Just as the patriarchal line of Israel's eponymous ancestor is established in a text featuring the structural framework of a Foundation Pattern, so the line of Israel's greatest king is established morphologically as well as narratively. In David's case, the maternal and paternal forebears both merit a Foundation Account.

In chapter 2 of the book of Ruth, the expected Foundation sequence EATING/DRINKING followed by BLESSING/ORACLE occurs twice; each time, a different one of the three key characters bestows or receives blessing. In the first (2:8–13), Boaz offers Ruth a DRINK, which is followed by an ENCOUNTER in which Boaz BLESSES Ruth that she may receive full recompense from God for her kindness; she responds with gratitude. In the second, Boaz invites Ruth to share the workers' lunch, which she EATS and has part of left over (2:14). Ruth then gleans more food for herself and Naomi, returns home to share her bounty with Naomi, and tells of her good fortune (ENCOUNTER, 2:15–19). When Naomi sees the great abundance that Ruth has brought home from the fields of her kinsman and hears of his kindness to Ruth, she BLESSES Boaz (2:20).

From its very beginnings in the Sumerian hymns of divine journeys, the Foundation Pattern is associated with a deep concern for the establishment of agricultural abundance. The pattern in Ugaritic and biblical patriarchal narratives adds to its association a deep concern with the establishment of lines of progeny. In the book of Ruth, both sets of concerns are linked through the medium of blessing and fulfillment.[9] In this chapter of the book, both ancestors of the house of David are blessed, each separately, within a context of agricultural abundance. By the end of the book, fulfillment comes within the context of the establishment of a line of progeny: the birth of Obed and the genealogy

---

9. See Barbara G. Green, *A Study of Field and Seed Symbolism in the Biblical Story of Ruth* (Ph.D. diss., Graduate Theological Union, 1980) 105–23.

from Boaz to David. On the structural level, the genealogy of King David is associated with both kinds of abundance, linking David with the twofold promise to Abraham of land and seed in Genesis 15.

Haman: Doom of a Villain

An elaboration of the Doom Pattern underlies the central chapters of the book of Esther (Esth 5:1–7:10). The pattern itself occurs in the expected sequence and is clear once one knows what to look for. However, the narrative context includes doublings, embedded and overlapping episodes, and other literary elaboration. There is a doubling of the EATING element, as Esther invites the king and Haman to one drinking party (מִשְׁתֶּה) and then to another (5:1–8). There are multiple ENCOUNTERS with Haman at the center, as first Haman is slighted by Mordecai and then shares his annoyance at the Jew with his wife and other advisers, who counsel him to do away with all Jews (5:9–14). An elaborate information mediation interrupts this encounter (6:1–3), when the king is reminded that he has failed to reward Mordecai for foiling a conspiracy against the royal life. The ENCOUNTER resumes (6:7–14) with Haman's misguided suggestion for rewarding a man whom the king wishes to honor. Haman's unavoidable humiliation is taken as a sign of things to come by his wife and his advisers, who predict Haman's impending ruin in the literary form of an ORACLE (6:12–13).[10] The ORACLE is confirmed at the drinking party the next day, at which Haman is accused by Esther and then convicted by his own impetuosity (7:1–8). AFFIRMATION of the ORACLE is complete when Haman is impaled high on the stake he has prepared for his rival, Mordecai.

In this story, the morphology of Doom functions in a literary environment to foreshadow on the structural level the doom of the villain, which takes place on the narrative level. Structural foreshadowing can

---

10. The language in v. 13b of the Hebrew text suggests an oracular pronouncement: אִם מִזֶּרַע הַיְּהוּדִים מָרְדֳּכַי אֲשֶׁר הַחִלּוֹתָ לִנְפֹּל לְפָנָיו לֹא־תוּכַל לוֹ כִּי־נָפוֹל תִּפּוֹל לְפָנָיו 'If this Mordecai before whom you have begun to fall is from the seed of the Jews, then you shall not prevail over him; rather, you shall surely fall before him'. The structure of the statement, protasis followed by apodosis, is the standard form of omens in the ancient Near East (see A. L. Oppenheim, *Ancient Mesopotamia: Portrait of a Dead Civilization* [Chicago: University of Chicago Press, 1964] 206–27 for a discussion of Akkadian omens; and R. D. Biggs [trans.], "Akkadian Didactic and Wisdom Literature," *ANET*, 605 for an Akkadian example). The use of the infinitive absolute form in the apodosis of the statement, an archaization in this late text, recalls the divine commands in the Pentateuch. The repetition of the root נפל 'to fall' and the alliteration of the twice-repeated לפניו reinforces on the rhetorical level the ominous nature of this pronouncement.

occur whether the ORACLE is positive or negative. Earlier, I showed that the structure predicts a positive outcome in Homer's *Odyssey*, in which two Foundation Patterns underlie book 1, forecasting the return of the hero. Here, the doom of an enemy of Israel is anticipated in the very framework of the narrative.

Sennacherib: Doom of an Enemy of Israel

The doom of another enemy of Israel is also confirmed on a structural level. A Doom Pattern underlies the condemnation of Sennacherib of Assyria in 2 Kings 18–19, an episode paralleled in Isaiah 36–37. Hezekiah, praised by the text for resisting Assyria and clinging to the Lord (2 Kgs 18:1–8), is nonetheless intimidated into submission by two Assyrian campaigns: Shalmaneser's siege and capture of Samaria followed by the deportation of its inhabitants (2 Kgs 18:9–12), and the assault on the fortified towns of Judah by Sennacherib (2 Kgs 18:13–16). Assyria is not satisfied with Hezekiah's capitulation, however, and a delegation of Assyrian officials is sent to Jerusalem (2 Kgs 18:17–18). In an ENCOUNTER with Judean officials, the Rabshakeh of Assyria urges the surrender of Jerusalem to Sennacherib's demands and taunts the Judeans with a mock ORACLE accusing them of idolatry and suggesting that Assyria is a punitive scourge ordered by the Lord personally, who therefore cannot be relied on to save the people (2 Kgs 18:19–25).

When the Judean officials, horrified that the Rabshakeh is speaking the plainly understood Judean language in the hearing of the people, beg him to speak instead in the diplomatic tongue of Aramaic, the Rabshakeh raises his voice and continues in Judean. He presses his argument in an extended discourse, later repeated to Hezekiah, that is replete with EATING and DRINKING references, several of them reversed (2 Kgs 18:26–37). Among these reversals are a reference to EATING dung and DRINKING urine because of siege-induced famine (2 Kgs 18:27b), and a reference to Assyria as a land much like their own, of grain and vine, of bread and wine, of olive oil and honey, of life and not death (2 Kgs 18:32). This last reference evokes the designation of Egypt as a land of milk and honey by Dathan and Abiram in Num 16:13–14. Dathan and Abiram's ill-advised reference to Egypt was followed by divine retribution, implemented by means of prophetic mediation. With this example in mind, we may anticipate disaster for the Rabshakeh's side. In fact, when Isaiah the prophet is called in by a frantic Hezekiah (2 Kgs 19:1–4), the Rabshakeh's oracle-style oration is contradicted by the prophet in a genuine ORACLE (2 Kgs 19:5–7).

Before this ORACLE can be affirmed, the ENCOUNTER between Assyria and Judah continues (in a doubling, 2 Kgs 19:8–19). Sennacherib sends a letter threat to Hezekiah, which Hezekiah places before the

Lord with a heartfelt prayer for deliverance. The ORACLE is doubled as well, as Isaiah informs Hezekiah that his prayer has been heard and answered and predicts the doom of Assyria (2 Kgs 19:20–34). The sign Isaiah gives that the ORACLE is true is a positive reference to EATING the produce of their own land: in the first and second years, EATING what grows of itself, and in the third, sowing, reaping, planting, and EATING of the fruit (2 Kgs 19:29). This sign appears to be a metaphor for the surviving remnant of the house of Judah (2 Kgs 19:30–31).[11] There is no record in the biblical text that this sign ever came to pass, but AFFIRMATION of Isaiah's ORACLE dooming Sennacherib (2 Kgs 19:32–34) follows immediately, with tidings of disease striking down 85,000 in the Assyrian camp and murder striking down Sennacherib as he worships his god in Nineveh (2 Kgs 19:35–36).

In the dreams of Joseph in Genesis 37 and of Pharaoh in Genesis 41, doubling has the effect of expressing divine determination (Gen 41:32). Here in 2 Kings 19, the doubling of the Pattern of Doom is a literary device that suggests that God has firmly determined the doom of Sennacherib. It is odd that the sign that Isaiah's prophecy is true is never confirmed, given the well-documented concern of the Deuteronomist with fulfillment of prophecy. Nevertheless, the unconfirmed sign serves an important structural function: an EATING reference is required by the morphology of the Doom Pattern undergirding the narrative, and so this reference to EATING the fruits of the land is essential here whether it is later confirmed or not. In spite of the many elaborations that embellish this narrative, the underlying Patterns of Doom are unmistakable, confirming the condemnation of an enemy of Israel.

The Doom Pattern in Accounts of Paradise

In every culture, all paradise myths must end in doom, since no culture in the world is perfect or without its struggles, and paradise myths account for how this state of events came to be.[12] It is significant that

---

11. On the concept of the surviving remnant, see G. Hasel, *The Remnant: The History and Theology of the Remnant Idea from Genesis to Isaiah* (Andrews University Monograph 5; Berrien Springs, Mich.: Andrews University, 1972).

12. I am indebted to Professor Tamara M. Green of the Department of Classics and Oriental Studies, Hunter College, City University of New York, for this insight, personally communicated, June 1994. See Barbara C. Sproul, *Primal Myths: Creating the World* (New York: Harper & Row, 1979); and Louis Derousseaux (ed.), *La Création dans l'Orient ancien* (Paris: Du Cerf, 1987).

Expanded and developed discussions of many of the ideas in this section are available now in my essay "The Doom of Paradise: Literary Patterns in Accounts of

the doom of the state of paradise in the Hebrew Bible contains an EAT-ING event. The entire Doom morphology is present in this narrative.

The Paradise Account in the Hebrew Bible

A Pattern of Doom closes the first episode of the primeval history in Genesis 3. The EATING of the fruit of the tree (Gen 3:1–7) is followed by an ENCOUNTER among Eve, the serpent, God, and Adam (Gen 3:8–13), culminating in an ORACLE dooming the serpent and humankind to mutual enmity, and dooming both men and women to hard labor (Gen 3:14–19). The ORACLE receives AFFIRMATION in the expulsion of Adam and Eve from the garden (Gen 3:22–24).

Although other ancient cultures have paradise myths in which an ideal situation is ill-fated, the Patterns of Destiny are by no means universally present. This pattern is absent, for example, from Greek paradise myths. The Greek myth of Pandora, as it is told in Hesiod's "Works and Days," blames the present unpleasant state of the world on female curiosity, and no eating event is in evidence.[13] In fact, this and

---

Paradise and Mortality in the Hebrew Bible and the Ancient Near East," in *A Feminist Companion to Genesis, Volume II* (ed. Athalia Brenner; Feminist Companion to the Bible 2/2; Sheffield: Sheffield Academic Press, 1998) 53–80.

13. Hesiod "Works and Days" lines 42–107, in Hesiod, *The Homeric Hymns, and Homerica* (trans. H. G. Evelyn-White; LCL; Cambridge: Harvard University Press, 1982; orig. pub., 1914) 5–10. "Works and Days" ascribes the creation of Pandora to Zeus's desire to exact from mankind a heavy price for the fire that was brought to them by Prometheus against Zeus's will. Lines 90–93 describe the state of men before Pandora's unleashing of the plagues contained in the casket she unwittingly opens: "For ere this the tribes of men lived on earth remote and free from ills and hard toil and heavy sicknesses which bring the Fates upon men" (p. 9). Rather than fitting into a Foundation Pattern, however, this tale fits into a category defined by a pattern of INTERDICTION (men may not have fire) / INTERDICTION VIOLATED (men secure fire through the intervention of Prometheus) / PUNISHMENT (Pandora is created and presented to mankind along with a casket of plagues, which she unleashes unsuspectingly) / MITIGATION (but Hope remains). This pattern is suggested by Propp (*Morphology*, 26–28) and discussed further by Alan Dundes (*Morphology of North American Indian Folktales* [Folklore Fellows Communications 195; Helsinki: Suomalainen Tiedeakatemia / Academia Scientiarum Fennica, 1964] 64–72 and passim).

An eating event does precede another version of the creation of Pandora in Hesiod's "Theogony" lines 536–616, 118–25 in the same Loeb Classical Library volume. Zeus is bested by Prometheus in a trick explaining why the gods receive the bones and fat of a sacrifice and people may eat the meat. In his anger, Zeus withholds fire from mankind, and Prometheus defies him by bringing the gift of fire to them anyway. Prometheus is punished for bringing fire to mankind by having his regenerating liver devoured daily by an eagle, and mankind's "price for the blessing

other related Greek myths exhibit a morphology different from that of the Patterns of Destiny, one that does not require an eating event as a constant element. These texts exhibit the morphology of INTERDIC-TION/INTERDICTION VIOLATED.[14] This phenomenon, which occurs frequently in the Hebrew Bible, has already been noted in biblical studies.[15]

A Sumerian Account of Paradise

The Doom Pattern does occur, however, in several Mesopotamian paradise accounts. The Sumerian paradise myth, "Enki and Ninhursag," exhibits the Doom Pattern on its structural level, although on the level of plot it appears to be quite different from the biblical account.[16] It takes place in Dilmun, the Sumerian Eden, which is filled with sweet water at the command of Enki. There then follows a series of ENCOUN-TERS in which Enki proceeds to impregnate the goddess Ninhursag, "Mother of the Land," who gives birth to a daughter, whom Enki also impregnates, and who also gives birth to a daughter. Enki impregnates a total of three or four succeeding generations of his female progeny,[17] but the pattern is finally broken by his great-granddaughter Uttu, who, apparently on the advice of her great-grandmother Ninhursag, refuses to cohabit with Enki until he brings her cucumbers, apples, and grapes (lines 128–67). When he does, the fruit of their union appears, under

---

of fire" is "the beautiful evil" of woman, since all women are descended from the beautiful but guileful Pandora (lines 585–89, 122–23). There is no Foundation or Doom Pattern present in this account either. This episode does, however, exhibit the INTERDICTION/INTERDICTION VIOLATED/PUNISHMENT pattern noted for the earlier account of Pandora's creation.

A study of the parallels between the Greek Pandora and Prometheus and the Sumerian Enki may be found in Charles Penglase, *Greek Myths and Mesopotamia: Parallels and Influence in the Homeric Hymns and Hesiod* (London: Routledge, 1994) 197–229.

14. See Propp, *Morphology*, 26–28; and Dundes, *North American Indian Folktales*, 64–72.

15. Biblical examples of this pattern, though he does not use these terms, are noted and discussed by Culley in *Studies in the Structure of Hebrew Narrative*, 100–115. Culley bases his structural analyses on the work of Parry and Lord on oral traditions and therefore does not use Proppian morphological analysis or terminology in his work.

16. This text was first published by Samuel Noah Kramer as *Enki and Ninhursag: A Sumerian "Paradise" Myth* (BASOR Supplement 1; New Haven: American Schools of Oriental Research, 1945); see idem, "Enki and Ninhursag: A Paradise Myth," *ANET*, 37–41.

17. Lines 109–27; the number of generations depends on the variant read; see ibid., *ANET*, 37 n. 5.

the influence of Ninhursag, to be the sprouting eight plants (lines 165–95). Enki angers Ninhursag by EATING each of these plants in turn (lines 196–217), and Ninhursag curses Enki (ORACLE) and disappears. Enki begins to sicken, and the great gods grieve for his condition. A fox volunteers to find Ninhursag, and he is promised a reward to bring her back so that she can heal Enki (lines 221–49). Enki is healed by Ninhursag in what appears to be a symbolic rebirth and the healing of each of his affected organs (equal in number to the plants he has eaten) by means of the engendering of newborn deities from his afflicted members (lines 250–68).

The essential elements of EATING and ORACLE/CURSE associated with the Doom Pattern are present in this Sumerian myth. They are followed by an amelioration of the curse that is not present in the biblical account of the expulsion from Eden but that does occur in other biblical stories.[18]

An Akkadian Account of Paradise Lost

The Pattern of Doom observed in Sumerian and biblical paradise stories also occurs in other ancient Near Eastern literature. The Akkadian epic of Gilgamesh contains episodes in which a state of paradise is lost, EATING events are present, and the underlying structure features Patterns of Destiny. Two episodes containing EATING events mark Enkidu's transition to a civilized state. One is an EATING and DRINKING event in the wild; the other is a paradigm of the acculturated banquet.

The first pattern opens with Enkidu's feeding on grass and drinking at watering places in the wild (EATING/DRINKING),[19] followed by Enkidu's meeting with the hunter from whose traps he frees his friends, the wild animals of the steppe (ENCOUNTER). The hunter seeks advice, first from his father and then from Gilgamesh, who advises him that once Enkidu has been seduced by a cult-prostitute/harlot,[20] he will be repudiated by his feral companions and will no longer be a threat to

---

18. See, for example, Cain's mark of divine protection after his punishment is pronounced in Genesis 4. For a brief survey of the parallels between this Sumerian myth and the biblical paradise narrative, see Samuel Noah Kramer, *History Begins at Sumer: Twenty-Seven "Firsts" in Man's Recorded History* (Garden City, N.Y.: Doubleday, 1956) 143–49.

19. Assyrian version, tablet 1, col. 2, lines 39–41.

20. Two terms are used as synonyms, *ḫarīmtu* and *šamḫātu*, sometimes written *šamkātu*. The second may be the woman's name or her profession. These can mean 'harlot' or 'prostitute', usually connected with temple or cult. See CAD Ḫ 101–2, Š/1 311–12.

the hunter (ORACLE).[21] All proceeds as Gilgamesh predicts: Enkidu is seduced and is subsequently rejected by the wild animals who had been his companions (AFFIRMATION).[22]

For Enkidu, this episode signals the end of his primeval state. The structure underlying this episode, telling of the end of Enkidu's state of paradise, is a Doom Pattern. He has lost the paradise of his initial feral existence and has not yet become fully human. However, the equivocal nature of this pattern is apparent in the structure underlying the episode immediately following this one.[23] The doom of Enkidu's existence in harmony with the wild is immediately juxtaposed with a variation of the Foundation Pattern underlying the account establishing Enkidu as a civilized human being.

Enkidu is devastated by the animals' rejection of him and turns to the harlot, who describes for her eager listener the glories of Uruk as a perpetual festival, in a possible allusion to EATING and DRINKING. Best of all, Uruk is the home of Gilgamesh, a fit companion for the lonely Enkidu.[24] The harlot describes dreams that Gilgamesh has received predicting the arrival of Enkidu (ORACLE),[25] but before he is fit for the culture of Uruk, Enkidu must become acculturated.

The socialization of Enkidu begins with his learning to eat and drink as people do (EATING/DRINKING). She leads him to the shepherd-hut, where Enkidu masters the EATING of cooked food and the DRINKING of strong drink. He is transformed by this process into a human being who anoints himself with oil, puts on clothing, and protects the flocks from the wild animals that were so recently his companions.[26] Enkidu, now fully initiated into cultural boundaries, embarks for Uruk, where Gilgamesh is reported to be exceeding his bounds. The ENCOUNTER between Enkidu and Gilgamesh ends in a draw, and, as predicted by the double dreams, the two become fast friends, ready to embark on the adventures before them (AFFIRMATION).[27]

---

21. Assyrian version, tablet 1, col. 2, line 42 to col. 4, line 45.

22. Assyrian version, tablet 1, col. 3, lines 46–51, col. 4, lines 1–29.

23. For a biblical example of this equivocation, expressed on the structural level, see the discussion in chapter 7 below of the juxtaposition of inverted Foundation and Doom Patterns in the establishment of Solomon and the doom of Adonijah as successors to David in 1 Kings.

24. Assyrian version, tablet 1, col. 4, lines 30–47; col. 5, lines 1–22.

25. Assyrian version, tablet 1, col. 5. lines 23–end; col. 6, lines 1–30.

26. Old Babylonian version, tablet 2, col. 2, lines 31–end; col. 3, lines 1–end.

27. Old Babylonian version, tablet 2, cols. 4–6. For a slightly different formulation of the equation of culture with death, see, for example, G. S. Kirk, *Myth: Its Meaning and Functions in Ancient and Other Cultures* (Berkeley: University of California Press, 1970) 132–53, especially p. 151.

The Foundation Pattern in this episode features a transposition of the elements of ORACLE and EATING/DRINKING, although all other elements associated with this pattern are present and in their expected sequence. The double pattern in the Akkadian epic implies that it is not enough to lose paradise in order to become human. The variation on the Foundation Pattern in the structure suggests that once the state of paradise is lost (Doom Pattern), a state of civilization must then be established (Foundation Pattern).

Akkadian Accounts of Human Mortality

A major question in ancient Near Eastern texts is why humankind is mortal and whether it is possible for ordinary people to attain immortality. The biblical story of the expulsion from Eden explains human mortality, since measures are taken specifically so that humankind will not be able to return to paradise—there, perhaps, to have an opportunity to eat from the tree of life. A Doom Pattern underlies the biblical narrative. Doom Patterns underlie several myths and legends treating the issue of mortality in Akkadian literature as well.

The message that civilization is a mixed blessing is reinforced by the episode in which Enkidu comes to realize he is fated for an early death resulting from his adventures with Gilgamesh. Here, in addition to transposing the ORACLE and EATING/DRINKING, this pattern, which begins as a variation of the Doom Pattern, is transformed midway into a Foundation Pattern.

Enkidu begins by cursing the harlot and the blandishments of civilization that lead to his early death (ORACLE).[28] Shamash intervenes (ENCOUNTER), reminding Enkidu of the pleasures of civilization to which the harlot introduced him, citing especially the food fit for the gods, the wine fit for kings, noble garments, and the friendship of Gilgamesh (EATING/DRINKING).[29] Enkidu is convinced by Shamash and transforms his curse into a blessing of the harlot, even though his own mood is still morose.[30] Far from being affirmed, Enkidu's first ORACLE is reversed by means of his own words. The question is whether civilization brings about humanity's establishment or humanity's undoing. On both the narrative level and the structural level, this episode appears to recognize the equivocal nature of human culture.

---

28. Assyrian version, tablet 7, col. 3
29. Ibid., lines 33–48.
30. Assyrian version, tablet 7, col. 4, lines 1–12.

Enkidu's demise is foretold in an episode underpinned by a Doom Pattern.[31] Ishtar is furious that Gilgamesh and Enkidu have killed the Bull of Heaven sacred to the goddess.[32] Gilgamesh, however, jubilantly shows off his trophy, and his praises are sung upon his triumphant return to Uruk.[33] Gilgamesh and his companions feast in celebration (EATING)[34] and then retire for the night. Enkidu sees the gods in council in a dream, where, in spite of a spirited defense by Shamash (ENCOUNTER), it is determined that Enkidu must die for the murder of the Bull of Heaven (ORACLE).[35] The ORACLE is doubled as a second dream confirms the negative omen, and Enkidu does sicken and die (AFFIRMATION).[36] Enkidu's transformation from feral to mortal man is complete. Together, this Doom Pattern underlying Enkidu's death and the Foundation Pattern that underlies his socialization at the beginning of the epic bracket Enkidu's story, underlining further the equivocal role of civilization in human mortality.

Gilgamesh's search for immortality is the subject of the section that follows the death of Enkidu. Gilgamesh finds that one human couple has indeed achieved immortality through divine intervention and demands the same divine consideration for himself.[37] In an episode that exhibits an elaboration of the Doom Pattern, Utnapishtim asks who will call a divine assembly on Gilgamesh's behalf and shows that Gilgamesh cannot even defeat sleep, death's poor imitation (ENCOUNTER: Test/Test failed).[38] Upon the urging of his wife, the immortal Utnapishtim tells Gilgamesh of a plant that rejuvenates the eater (ORACLE).[39] Gilgamesh dives into the deep and secures the plant (Task set / Task achieved).[40] Gilgamesh postpones eating the plant until he has returned to Uruk, a delay that proves fatal (EATING reversed).[41] A serpent sniffs the fragrance of the plant, carries it away, and sheds its skin (AFFIRMATION of ORACLE).[42] The hope of Gilgamesh for even the

---

31. Tablet 6, lines 150–end, and tablet 7, cols. 1–4; see E. A. Speiser, "The Epic of Gilgamesh," *ANET*, 72–90.

32. Tablet 6, lines 150–65.

33. Ibid., lines 166–83.

34. Ibid., line 187.

35. These two functions are found in tablet 7, col. 3, lines 1–16.

36. Tablet 7, col. 4.

37. Old Babylonian version, tablet 11, lines 1–7.

38. Ibid., lines 197–233. For this function in the Russian fairy-tale, see Propp, *Morphology*, 39–46.

39. Old Babylonian version, tablet 11, lines 258–70.

40. Ibid., lines 271–79.

41. Ibid., lines 280–286.

42. Ibid., lines 287–289.

appearance of immortality, rejuvenation, is usurped by the serpent. The failure of Gilgamesh to pass the initial challenge to conquer sleep, death's imitator, is reiterated in his failure to eat the plant of rejuvenation. The futility of even this hero's effort to find immortality is reinforced by the underlying structure of the epic, a Pattern of Doom.

Another Akkadian text, the story of Adapa, treats the subject of human mortality.[43] The role of Adapa, who bears the epithet *atraḫasīsa* 'exceedingly wise', is to provide food offerings for the gods (EATING/DRINKING).[44] One day, when he is out fishing to provide for these offerings, his boat is capsized by the south wind. Adapa "breaks the wing" of the south wind, preventing it from blowing for seven days, thus bringing his action to the attention of Anu, the chief god, who demands that Adapa be summoned before him (ENCOUNTER).[45] Enki advises Adapa on his comportment on high (ORACLE). Enki predicts that Adapa will be offered food and drink, which Enki advises Adapa to refuse (EATING/DRINKING reversed), and oil and garments, which Enki advises him to put on.[46] Thus it comes to pass: Adapa refuses the food and drink, and puts on the oil and garments (AFFIRMATION). However, the reversal of EATING/DRINKING implied in Adapa's refusal of food and drink foreshadows an unexpected outcome. When Anu demands that he tell why he refused the food and drink that would have bestowed immortality upon humanity, Adapa must confess that his protector, Enki, has given him misleading advice.[47] Anu, delighted at Enki's success in keeping immortality from humankind, apparently releases Enki's city Eridu (from feudal obligations?) and offers humanity amelioration for its failure to achieve immortality, in the form of healing for certain maladies.[48]

The essential elements of EATING, ENCOUNTER, ORACLE/CURSE and AFFIRMATION associated with the Doom Pattern are present in this myth in the appropriate sequence. However, following the AFFIRMATION there is an [AMELIORATION] of the curse. This element of [AMELIORATION] occurs in three of the Near Eastern paradise texts that I

---

43. See E. A. Speiser, "Adapa," *ANET*, 101–3. See now Shlomo Izre'el, *Adapa and the South Wind: Language Has the Power of Life and Death* (Mesopotamian Civilizations 10; Winona Lake, Ind.: Eisenbrauns, 2001).

44. Tablet A, lines 10–20.

45. Tablet B, lines 1–13.

46. Ibid., lines 14–34.

47. On this tale as it relates to deception, see O. H. Prouser, *The Phenomenology of the Lie in Biblical Narrative* (Ph.D. diss., Jewish Theological Seminary of America, 1991) 177–79.

48. Tablet B, 66–end, and tablet D, entire.

have discussed so far: in the Sumerian myth in which Ninhursag turns each of Enki's agonies into a healing divinity; in Enkidu's curse, which was changed to a blessing of the *harīmtu* in the Gilgamesh epic; and in the healing arts given by Anu to Adapa in place of the immortality he missed out on by refusing food and drink.

This element of [AMELIORATION] also occurs in the biblical text of Genesis 3. After the expulsion from Eden, God makes garments of skin for Adam and Eve, ameliorating their exposure to harsh daily life.[49] The [AMELIORATION] constant appears to function within the subgenre of paradise myth as an element that offers comfort to those bereft of the ideal state.

Even without taking the element of [AMELIORATION] into account, we see that Patterns of Destiny compose the framework of paradise myths, as they do the Establishment and Condemnation of other essential cultural phenomena. In chapter 7, I will show how knowledge of the morphology of these Patterns of Destiny can add new levels of meaning to narratives in which the structural elements are less clearly apparent.

---

49. See above, n. 18 (p. 167).

CHAPTER SEVEN

Patterns of Destiny:
Variations and Adaptations

Ellipses, Transpositions, and Reversals in
Patterns of Destiny

In this chapter, I will begin to explore the value of morphological analysis in recognizing the messages encoded on the structural level of texts in which the Patterns of Destiny are not fully present. Instead, allusion, nuance, inversion, reversal, and other variations obscure the clear framework of Foundation and Doom that have been fully accessible in the examples I have examined until now.

Vladimir Propp recognized that morphologies with inverted or transposed constants still retained their morphological identities. The inversions or transpositions represented only fluctuations of the fundamental pattern and not new entities. He also saw that on occasion an incomplete form of the pattern could present itself. If a function was absent, he noted, the structure of the tale was maintained by the remaining functions. Propp also allowed for the doubling of constants and the elimination of functions through assimilation.[1] At one time or another, the structure of biblical narrative reflects all of these transformations in Patterns of Destiny. In this chapter, I will examine a variety of these.

First I will look at cases where one of the constants in the morphology of Doom or Foundation is implied or altered in some way, but the reference to these patterns is still strong enough to be recognized readily by readers familiar with the genre. Then I will move on to more subtle examples.

---

1. Vladimir Propp, *Morphology of the Folktale* (2d ed.; trans. Laurence Scott; Austin: University of Texas Press, 1968) 107–9.

An Allusion to the Foundation Pattern

Gen 8:18–9:1, in which a new order is unveiled following the re-creation of the world after the flood, contains a Foundation Pattern that reinforces the reestablishment of seasons and civilization. Corre-spondences have long been noted between the biblical account of the flood and its aftermath and the flood stories of the ancient Near East, especially the epic of Gilgamesh and the myth of Atraḫasis.[2] In many ways, Noah's actions when he descends from the ark resonate with these more ancient texts, by means of both similar and contrasting elements.

Upon God's command to Noah to descend from the ark, Noah builds an altar to God. He takes a number of the clean animals and of-fers burnt offerings on the altar (8:18–20). YHWH smells the pleasing odor and resolves never again to curse the earth on account of human-ity, noting that the inclination of the human heart is evil from its youth. God further resolves never again to smite all life (8:21). The sea-sonal order is affirmed (8:22), and God blesses Noah and his sons, re-iterating the first blessing and mandate offered in Genesis, to be fruitful and multiply and fill the earth (9:1).

---

2. In the epic of Gilgamesh, see especially tablet 11; in the Atraḫasis myth, see especially tablet 3 and following. Translations of the former may be found in E. A. Speiser, "The Epic of Gilgamesh," *ANET,* 72–99; translation of the latter may be found in Benjamin R. Foster, *Before the Muses: An Anthology of Akkadian Literature* (2 vols.; Bethesda, Md.: CDL, 1993); translations of both may be found in Stephanie Dalley (trans.), *Myths from Mesopotamia: Creation, the Flood, Gilgamesh and Others* (Oxford: Oxford University Press, 1982). The following are just some of the studies treating similarities and differences among the ancient Near Eastern and biblical flood accounts: A. T. Clay, *A Hebrew Deluge Story in Cuneiform* (New Haven: Yale University Press, 1922); Alan Dundes, *The Flood Myth* (Berkeley: University of California Press, 1988); Sir James George Frazer, *Folk-Lore in the Old Testament: Stud-ies in Comparative Religion Legend and Law* (abridged ed.; New York: Tudor, 1923); Tikva Frymer-Kensky, "The Atraḫasis Epic and Its Significance for Our Under-standing of Genesis 1–9," *BA* 40/4 (December 1977) 147–55; Alfred Gottschalk, "The Image of Man in Genesis and in the Ancient Near East," *Maarav* 7 (1991) 131–40; William W. Hallo, "Information from before the Flood: Antediluvian Notes from Babylonia and Israel," *Maarav* 7 (1991) 173–81; Alexander Heidel, *The Gilgamesh Epic and Old Testament Parallels* (Chicago: University of Chicago Press, 1946); I. M. Kikawada and A. Quinn, *Before Abraham Was* (Nashville: Abingdon, 1985); W. G. Lambert and A. R. Millard, *Atra-Ḫasis: The Babylonian Story of the Flood* (Oxford: Clarendon, 1969); J. H. Tigay, *The Evolution of the Gilgamesh Epic* (Phila-delphia: University of Pennsylvania Press, 1982).

Ancient Near Eastern Parallels

There are two Akkadian accounts of the flood, each generally similar to the other, though with important differences. One account occurs in tablet 11 of the Gilgamesh epic, after Gilgamesh has traveled long and wide in his quest for immortality and has finally discovered the remote abode of the Akkadian flood survivors, Utnapishtim and his wife. Utnapishtim tells Gilgamesh the story of the flood and explains that the gods have granted the couple immortality on account of their thoughtfulness in providing sacrifices to the gods immediately after debarkation from their boat. The starving gods are portrayed as hungrily sniffing up the smoke of the sacrifices, which are their nourishment and which had ceased during the destruction caused by the flood.[3] The gods had resolved, for reasons unspecified in this text, to bring about a flood.[4] Enlil is enraged that anyone has managed to escape his decree.[5] Enlil is prevailed upon by the other gods, especially by Enki, to reward the human couple instead of punishing them.[6] Utnapishtim and his wife are granted immortality: both are banished from the land of mortals, to dwell far away at the source of rivers.[7]

In Atraḫasis, a reason is given for the flood. Enlil orders the destruction of humanity because humans make too much noise, and he wishes to silence their clamor.[8] Less drastic measures such as plague and famine have proved ineffective.[9] Like Utnapishtim, Atraḫasis, who will be the survivor of the flood in this account, is warned by Enki to build a boat to escape the coming deluge.[10] Afterward, Atraḫasis also offers a sacrifice after debarkation, and the divinities in this account also cluster around like flies to inhale its aroma.[11]

But there are important differences between these two accounts. In Atraḫasis, the gods starve during the flood, with no human beings to bring offerings.[12] They resolve never again to destroy humankind on account of their practical need to ensure their own sustenance, and

---

3. Gilgamesh, tablet 11, lines 155–61.
4. Ibid., lines 11–19.
5. Lines 170–173.
6. Lines 177–186.
7. Lines 189–196.
8. Atraḫasis, tablet 2, col. 1, lines 1–10.
9. Ibid., cols. 1–6.
10. Atraḫasis, tablet 3, col. 1, lines 15–37.
11. Ibid., col. 5, lines 30–35.
12. Col. 3, lines 30–31.

they devise other means of population control to limit noise pollution.[13] In Gilgamesh, Enki argues for alternatives to a great flood to punish wrongdoers, but no decision by Enlil or the divine assembly is recorded.[14] The only divine action reported in Gilgamesh is the resolution to reward Utnapishtim and his wife with immortality.[15]

In spite of these differences on the surface level of plot, the structural pattern in both Gilgamesh 11 and Atraḫasis 3 is the same: a Foundation Pattern associated with the aftermath of the flood. It begins with the divinities sniffing the offering (EATING),[16] followed by an ENCOUNTER among the gods as they argue about whose fault it is that there has been such mass destruction and who is responsible for the survival of humanity.[17] Each account then has a different positive ORACLE—in Gilgamesh, to reward the human couple and not to punish them; in Atraḫasis, the resolution not to destroy all life at once and to find other means of population control.[18] Each ORACLE is followed by an AFFIRMATION—in Gilgamesh, Utnapishtim and his wife are made immortal and transported to their new faraway abode; and in Atraḫasis, the alternate means of population control are defined and implemented.[19] In both Akkadian flood stories, the Foundation Pattern occurs in full on the structural level of the texts.

Biblical Allusion to Ancient Near Eastern Parallels

At first glance, the biblical flood episode does not show a complete Foundation Pattern. The constant function of EATING appears to be missing. Although, like the Akkadian divinities, God inhales the agreeable fragrance of Noah's sacrifice, the God of the Bible does not need sustenance, and there is no hint in the text itself that the pleasing odor, ריח הניחח, is a divine meal.

However, there is a long cultural history of regarding sacrifice to the divine as food for the gods, and the element of the starving gods inhaling the fragrant first postdiluvian sacrifice occurs in each of the extant ancient Near Eastern flood stories. In this context, the biblical sacrifice and divine inhalation is an allusion to an EATING event (Gen

---

13. Col. 6, lines 1–50.

14. Gilgamesh, tablet 11, lines 179–88.

15. Ibid., lines 189–94.

16. Ibid., lines 155–61; Atraḫasis, tablet 3, lines 30–35.

17. Gilgamesh, tablet 11, lines 170–76; Atraḫasis, tablet 3, col. 5, lines 36–51; col. 6, lines 1–15.

18. Gilgamesh, tablet 11, lines 176–94; Atraḫasis, tablet 3, col. 6, lines 16–50.

19. Gilgamesh, tablet 11, line 196; Atraḫasis, tablet 3, col. 6, lines 41–50, col. 7, lines 1–7.

8:20), part of an ENCOUNTER during which God resolves never again to destroy all life and affirms the seasonal order [ORACLE, Gen 8:21]. This ORACLE is AFFIRMED in Gen 8:22 and also in the following passage, Gen 9:1–3, promising agricultural abundance, which is dependent on seasonality. The structure underlying the narrative describing the world reconstituted after the flood contains the core elements of the Foundation Pattern, EATING followed by an ORACLE. This structure accords with, and reinforces, the message of the biblical text. It is also the only biblical Foundation Pattern associated with an act of temporal creation or re-creation—neither the creation of the universe in Genesis 1 nor the second creation of humanity in Genesis 2 exhibits this infrastructure. This is consistent with the idea that the state of paradise is always and necessarily doomed. Only the state of the present world order, with its times and seasons, warrants the structural reinforcement of a positive Pattern of Destiny.

Allusions and References to the Doom Pattern

I move now from cosmic establishment to mortal condemnation. These are instances in which the Doom Pattern does not appear as fully as in the narratives so far examined; nevertheless, enough of the elements occur in the expected relationship to one another that a Pattern of Doom is suggested.

Condemnation of Noah

Noah's sacrifice triggers the allusion to the Doom Pattern underpinning the re-creation of the world after the flood, and the very next episode reminds the reader of what God has learned the hard way, that human nature is inclined to evil. God's anger was already kindled and the flood was triggered by the divine observation that human nature is evil from its youth (Gen 6:5). After the flood, however, God recognizes that human nature is the same as it was before, but now he resolves never to destroy the world again. Instead, he sets up laws to curb the evil of human inclination (Gen 9:4–6).[20]

As soon as God has made a divine covenant with Noah, Noah plants a vineyard and becomes drunk on his own wine (Gen 9:20–21). Noah's son Ham sees his father's nakedness, and tells his brothers, who cover their father (Gen 9:22–23). Noah is enraged at Ham's action when he awakes and learns of it (Gen 9:24) and curses Ham's son, Canaan, condemning him to be a slave to his brothers. At the same time, Noah blesses his sons Shem and Japheth.

---

20. Frymer-Kensky, "The Atraḫasis Epic."

There are many strange things in this text. The two most often discussed are the nature of the sin that would warrant such eternal condemnation and the reason for Canaan's being the object of the curse instead of Ham.[21] The answers to these questions may never be known, but the structural level confirms the narrative message that eternal fates are being decided. Morphologically, the structural framework of the text consists of one Doom Pattern and two Foundation Patterns. Canaan is condemned to serve his brothers, while Shem is blessed by God, and Japheth is to dwell in the tents of Shem and increase.

A DRINKING event (9:20) leads to an ENCOUNTER among the unconscious Noah and his three sons (9:22–24), as a result of which Noah pronounces a curse on Canaan, son of Ham (ORACLE #1, 9:25), and a blessing on Shem and Japheth (ORACLE #2, 9:26–27). No AFFIRMATION of these oracles follows in the text, but the ascendance of Israel over the Canaanites in the promised land may be a clue to the ultimate affirmation, at least from a biblical perspective.

Condemnation of Jeroboam, First King of the North

The Northern Kingdom is the subject of several Doom Accounts. Its first king, Jeroboam, is the subject of two of them. In 1 Kgs 14:1–18, Jeroboam's dynasty is cut short, his line condemned. Abijah, son of Jeroboam, falls ill. Jeroboam sends his wife on a PILGRIMAGE/JOURNEY to Shiloh in disguise to inquire of the blind prophet Ahijah whether the boy will live or die. She prepares and takes with her a gift of food (EATING): ten loaves of bread, crackers or biscuits (נקדים), and a jar of honey (14:1–4). In an [information mediation], God warns the blind prophet of her mission and identity, and Ahijah duly acknowledges her true identity when he hears her footsteps at the door (ENCOUNTER and [unmasking], 14:5–6).

The prophet delivers the ORACLE that God has ordained (14:7–16): because Jeroboam has worshiped other gods in preference to the God who placed him on the throne of Israel, God has condemned the

---

21. For a summary of the midrashic interpretation of this enigmatic episode as well as a discussion of the comparative traditions, see Albert I. Baumgarten, "Myth and Midrash: Genesis 9:20–29," in *Christianity, Judaism and Other Greco-Roman Cults: Studies for Morton Smith at Sixty* (ed. Jacob Neusner; SJLA 12; Leiden: Brill, 1975) 55–71. Baumgarten evaluates the proposition that the heavily edited biblical account suppresses some sexual transgression such as castration or homosexual rape. I am grateful to Dr. David Marcus of the Jewish Theological Seminary for directing me to this source.

house of Jeroboam to an evil fate (רעה, 14:10). All males will be cut off, and the dead will lie exposed for the dogs to eat in the city and the birds to eat in the field. As for the child, Abijah, he will die when his mother's feet reenter the city. Ironically, Abijah will be the only one of Jeroboam's house to be mourned and properly buried. The ORACLE continues with a condemnation of Northern Israel on account of the idolatry of the people following Jeroboam's example. The AFFIRMA-TION of part of the ORACLE comes in 14:17–18 with the death, burial, and mourning of Abijah.

There are two variations in this narrative that bear comment. First, in a reversal of expectations—both the readers' and the characters'—the food that Jeroboam's wife prepares and carries to the prophet as a "fee" for his services is never delivered, nor is it eaten. This is not unusual in biblical narrative; there are several occasions when reference is made to paying a fee for the services of a seer or prophet, though in the narrative event it is not actually paid. One example is Saul's desire to pay the seer for information on his lost asses in 1 Samuel 9, and another is Elisha's refusal of Naaman's gift when he is healed of leprosy in 2 Kings 5. In each of these cases, the unanticipated eventuality of the gift's not being received is matched by the unexpected nature of the ORACLE. Saul does not expect to be anointed king of Israel, nor does Naaman expect to be told to dip seven times in the muddy Jordan. Jeroboam also does not expect the ORACLE he receives, though he is given more than he bargains for. The prophet offers the information he seeks—the fate of his languishing son—and gratuitously adds the doom of Jeroboam's house and of the Northern Kingdom as well.

Second, the AFFIRMATION of the ORACLE differs slightly from the OR-ACLE itself. In 1 Kgs 14:12, the prophet predicts that the child will die when his mother's feet enter the city: בבאה רגליך העירה ומת הילד. But in 14:17, the child dies when his mother comes to the threshold of the door: היא באה בסף הבית והנער מת. This minor difference in one aspect of the ORACLE's fulfillment is reflected in the minor difference in the fulfillment of another aspect: in 1 Kgs 15:25–30, where the slaughter of Jeroboam's house is consummated by the usurper Baasha, the colorful curse of the exposure of the slain to beast and bird in city and field is not noted, although these graphic details are certainly included in other narrative instances, some of which I shall examine later on in this chapter.

This example of the Doom Pattern is incomplete and inferential. By means of allusion to the well-known pattern, the text speaks to the discerning audience who is already familiar with and understands the literary reference to the morphology of Doom.

Condemnation of Ben-hadad of Aram

A structure similar to the structure of 1 Kings 14 appears in a strange story condemning Ben-hadad of Aram in 2 Kgs 8:7–15. Ben-hadad, king of Aram, has fallen ill. He hears of the arrival of Elisha in Damascus and, as Jeroboam does in 1 Kings 14, he sends a messenger bearing a gift to inquire of the prophet whether he will recover. In 2 Kgs 8:9, Ben-hadad dispatches Hazael with a gift of 'every good thing of Damascus, forty camel-loads' כל־טוב דמשק משא ארבעים גמל.

This reference to 'every good thing' is an EATING allusion. The formula טוב [+ place reference] is frequently used in the sense of 'blessing' in the Hebrew Bible, often with the explicit meaning of 'good things to eat' or in a context where comestibles are clearly represented among the 'good things' to which the phrase refers.[22] Explicit EATING references include Isa 1:18–19, Jer 2:7, Ezra 9:12, and Neh 9:36, where the noun טוב 'good thing' is used with the verb אכל 'to eat'. Contexts in which the meaning is agricultural abundance include Deut 6:11 and Neh 9:25, where the reference is to houses full of 'all good things', followed by an agricultural catalog of such comestibles as vine, olive, and fruit trees.

In Gen 45:18–23, the expression with טוב occurs several times in a context in which Joseph is trying to persuade his brothers to bring his father down to Egypt to weather the remaining famine years. Joseph's message to his father juxtaposes 'the good things of the land' טוב ארץ מצרים with an explicit reference to eating: he promises that he will give them 'all the good things of Egypt, and you shall eat the fat of the land' ואתנה לכם את־טוב ארץ מצרים ואכלו את־חלב הארץ. He tells them not to bother to bring their utensils or household goods because they will have access to all the best things of Egypt: כי־טוב כל־ארץ מצרים לכם הוא. Joseph sends his father ten asses laden with the best things of Egypt, עשרה חמרים נשאים מטוב מצרים, and ten asses carrying foodstuffs for the road—grain, bread, and provisions. Two out of these three references are explicitly linked to comestibles, strengthening the association of the expression 'good things' with food and eating.

In addition to this philological evidence, support for reading an allusion to EATING/DRINKING in this phrase in 2 Kings 8 arises from the similarities it exhibits to 1 Kings 14 in both structure and plot. Although gifts to seers are variable and include money (1 Samuel 9) and

---

22. For comparative Semitic evidence, see *mn'm* (the Phoenician semantic equivalent of the Hebrew טוב) in the Azitawada inscription (*KAI* no. 26, lines 5–6), F. Bron, *Recherches sur les Inscriptions Phéniciennes de Karatepe* (II Hautes études orientales 11; Geneva: Droz, 1979) 43–44; J. Gibson, *Textbook of Syrian Semitic Inscriptions*, volume 3: *Phoenician Inscriptions* (Oxford: Clarendon, 1982) 46–47.

garments (2 Kings 5), in both 1 Kings 14 and in 2 Kings 8, the gift sent to the prophet is explicitly food. This parallel combined with the weight of philological evidence suggests strongly that a reference to food may be read in the expression כל טוב דמשׁק 'all good things of Damascus'. This reference fills by allusion the EATING slot in the Doom Pattern indicated here.

During their ENCOUNTER, Elisha offers the strange reply that Hazael is to reassure Ben-hadad that he will certainly recover, even though God has shown the prophet that Ben-hadad will surely die (ORACLE, 8:10). The ORACLE continues, as Elisha expresses to Hazael his own anguish at the havoc Hazael will wreak upon the Children of Israel when he becomes king in Ben-hadad's place (8:11–13). The ORACLE is AF-FIRMED, as it is in Daniel 5, with the murder of the king (8:15). Here the treachery is committed by Hazael, who, perhaps emboldened by the prophet's words, undertakes on his own initiative to bring the ORACLE to fulfillment.

Structurally, the morphology of this narrative is complex, beginning with an allusive EATING constant that is not made explicit and continuing with the multifaceted ORACLE. The three-part ORACLE implies three Patterns of Destiny—two of Doom and one of Establishment. The Doom Patterns concern Ben-hadad, condemned to death by murder at the hand of Hazael, and Israel, doomed to the devastations of war, also at the hand of Hazael. Hazael is the agent of destruction in both cases, and, ironically, the very ORACLEs of Doom for Ben-hadad and Israel are the ORACLEs of Foundation for Hazael: they establish him as the next king of Aram and victor over Israel. From Elisha's perspective (and also Israel's), Hazael's ascendance is disaster, even if divinely ordained. The Foundation Pattern underlying the ORACLE predicting his rise is surrounded on all sides by morphologies of Doom. The complex nature of this narrative is hinted at by the morphological intricacy of the structural level of the text.

In this example, as in the story of Jeroboam's son, the expected pattern is incomplete, with some elements present only by implication or completely absent. Nevertheless, it seems apparent that an entity is being condemned on the surface level of the text, and the underlying structure may reinforce that message with references to the Pattern of Doom.

Saul: Doom of Dynasty and Condemnation to Death

Saul's dynasty is doomed in a narrative underpinned by a clear Doom Pattern. The morphology underlying the later prediction of Saul's own death, however, is rich with variations and allusions.

In 1 Sam 13:8–14, a Doom Pattern condemns Saul's dynasty early in his reign. Saul, impatient on account of the people's defection as he waits for a delayed Samuel in order to begin sacrifices at Gilgal, undertakes to sacrifice the burnt offering himself and is about to undertake the שלמים, the well-being sacrifice shared by the people (EATING, 1 Sam 13:8–9a), when Samuel arrives at the scene and demands to know what Saul is up to (ENCOUNTER, 1 Sam 13:9b–12). Saul defends himself to no avail. Samuel condemns his dynasty in an ORACLE, which tears the monarchic line from Saul and promises to appoint as ruler someone else (1 Sam 13:13–14). AFFIRMATION of this ORACLE comes in 1 Samuel 16 with the anointing of David.

Later, in 1 Sam 28:3–25, Saul's death is predicted with a variation of the Doom Pattern. Saul's anointer and sometimes harsh mentor, Samuel, has died. God does not answer any of Saul's conventional queries, and a desperate Saul seeks unconventional advice on the eve of his battle with an overpowering force of Philistines at Gilboa (1 Sam 28:3–6). Disguising himself, Saul undertakes a JOURNEY to a spiritualist at Endor (1 Sam 28:8–10), where he begs for and receives an ENCOUNTER with the ghost of Samuel. During this encounter, Saul is unmasked as the king of Israel (1 Sam 28:11–16) and, in an ORACLE, Samuel predicts the deaths of Saul and his sons in battle the next day (1 Sam 28:17–19). Saul, weak with hunger, faints with the shock of Samuel's words and is eventually persuaded to take a bit of nourishment (EATING, 1 Sam 28:20–24). The visit ends with his hasty DEPARTURE (1 Sam 28:25).

In this example, the EATING event is displaced to the end of the story (1 Sam 28:20–25). This structural displacement is reinforced on the narrative level by the incongruity of the king's being nurtured by an outlawed spiritualist, who feeds him essentially the same meal that Abraham fed the messengers of God in Genesis 18. We are told in v. 20b that Saul has not eaten anything all day and all night, implying that an EATING reversal (suggesting a negative outcome) has in fact occurred in its accustomed sequence preceding the ORACLE; yet the text presents it out of sequence. Saul at first refuses anything to eat (v. 23), although we have seen him fainting from weakness. Saul's poor judgment, expressed repeatedly in his biblical history, has manifested itself before in inappropriate eating and fasting. Here, on the eve of his death, we are shown on the levels of structure and narrative that the king's powers of judgment are still out of joint.

Solomon's Anointing and the Doom of an Attempted Accession

In chapter 5 above, I showed that the inauguration of the Israelite monarchy with Saul's anointing and of the Davidic dynasty with David's anointing both exhibit the Foundation Pattern. Only one other narrative, Solomon's accession as recounted in 1 Chronicles 28–29, exhibits this structural pattern at the anointing of a king. However, in the case of Solomon the pattern is inverted.

The account of Solomon's accession in 1 Kings 1 is without a feast for Solomon; instead, his half-brother Adonijah holds a feast in premature anticipation of his own succession. The account in 1 Chronicles is quite different. Here, there is no sign of conflict with David's other sons. Solomon has his own accession banquet (EATING event, 1 Chr 29:21–22) and is not anointed as he is in the 1 Kings account. The ORACLE in 1 Chr 28:9–10 concerns Solomon's mission to build the Temple. However, there is an inversion in this pattern: the OR-ACLE, embedded in an ENCOUNTER, precedes the EATING event.

The pattern in 1 Chronicles is as follows: ASSEMBLY of the people by David (28:1); ENCOUNTER, in which David makes a long speech outlining the history of his royal house and his desire, denied by God, to build a temple (28:2–5); ORACLE, which takes the form of the word of God, placed in the mouth of David, choosing Solomon to succeed him and to build God's house according to plans that he has provided (28:6–21); the ENCOUNTER continues, with David requesting and receiving freewill offerings from the people for building the Temple, which he dedicates in a long speech of blessing (29:1–20); then there is the EATING and DRINKING of vast quantities of sacrifices (זבח) and libations, followed by the AFFIRMATION of Solomon as David's successor, his anointing, and the anointing of Zadok as high priest (29:22). The narrator concludes that Solomon successfully took over the throne of his father, David, that all Israel accepted him, and that God blessed him with regal majesty (29:23–25).

Propp's method allows for inversion of elements along with other predictable variations. Thus, the variation in the expected pattern found in 1 Chronicles 28–29 is still a valid expression of the Foundation morphology. However, as the only account of an anointing in which the core functions of EATING and ORACLE are inverted, the text may be expressing on a structural level the equivocal message of Solomon's accession: this may be obtained by reading 1 Chronicles 28–29 in terms of the much more ambivalent account in 1 Kings 1.

Indeed, the structural patterns underlying Solomon's accession to the Davidic throne at the expense of his half-brother Adonijah in 1 Kgs

1:1–49 foreshadow the Bible's ambivalence in evaluating Solomon's rule. On both the level of plot and the level of structure, the narrative in 1 Kgs 1:1–49 exhibits an ambivalent evaluation of Solomon's succession. The juxtaposition of the underlying Patterns of Foundation and of Doom for the same events suggests that Solomon's succession is tinged with the doom attending Adonijah's failed attempt.

On the surface level, in striking contrast to the unalloyed celebration of Solomon's accession in the parallel account in 1 Chronicles 28–29, the narrative in 1 Kings is ambivalent about Solomon's succession to the throne. In 1 Kings 1, the selection of Solomon to succeed David is the product of a concerted effort, not to say conspiracy, to influence the failing king, implemented by David's court prophet, Nathan, and Solomon's mother, Bathsheba.

After establishing David's advanced age and failing health (1 Kgs 1:1–4), the text describes how Adonijah, David's oldest living son and heir apparent, invites his supporters to a sacrificial feast (זבח, EATING/DRINKING, 1 Kgs 1:5–10) at which he plans to announce his succession to his father's throne. When word of this banquet reaches those who oppose him at David's court, a lengthy ENCOUNTER ensues (1 Kgs 1:11–40) involving Nathan, Bathsheba, and David. This interaction results in the ORACLE/BLESSING, pronounced by David and seconded by Benaiah son of Jehoiada, that Solomon will succeed as king (1 Kgs 1:33–37).[23] This ORACLE receives AFFIRMATION when Solomon is anointed by Zadok the priest and acclaimed by the people in a noisy procession (1 Kgs 1:38–40).

This Foundation Pattern, the subject of which is Solomon's accession to the throne, is immediately followed by a Doom Pattern, the subject of which is Adonijah's failure to succeed David to the throne (1 Kgs 1:41–49). The text attempts to express simultaneity in recounting these events.[24]

---

23. 1 Chr 27:5 identifies Jehoiada as a priest, and 2 Sam 23:20 identifies his place of origin as Kabzeel. Benaiah is identified as one of David's mighty men (1 Chr 27:6), whose heroic exploits are noted in 2 Sam 23:20–23. Whether or not Benaiah comes from a priestly family, his role in this narrative echoes the role of Eli the priest of Shiloh in 1 Samuel 1. Both invoke the blessing that it be God's will that the words spoken (by David in 1 Kings 1 and by Hannah in 1 Samuel 1) will come true. This blessing functions as the ORACLE in the Foundation Pattern in both narratives.

24. For a discussion of literary techniques that express simultaneity in the Hebrew Bible, see Shimon Bar-Efrat, *Narrative Art in the Bible* (JSOTSup 70; Sheffield: Almond, 1989). On the simultaneity underlying this episode in 1 Kings 1, see his extensive discussion on pp. 167–69.

Adonijah and his guests, who have just finished EATING, hear the noise of Solomon's anointing celebration (1 Kgs 1:41). Just as they are wondering what it could mean, a messenger arrives, and in a lengthy [information mediation] repeats the story of Solomon's accession, complete with ORACLE/BLESSING and AFFIRMATION (1 Kgs 1:43–49). The ENCOUNTER that follows is enacted by proxy (1 Kgs 1:49–53). The guests flee, and Adonijah escapes to the tabernacle, where he seeks refuge by seizing the horns of the altar. The Doom ORACLE follows as Solomon, informed of this development, promises that Adonijah is only safe if he behaves well; if Adonijah commits any infraction whatsoever, he will die. This ORACLE is affirmed when Adonijah is brought from the altar to bow before the king, who sends him home with his skin provisionally in one piece (AFFIRMATION and [DEPARTURE], 1 Kgs 1:53).[25]

The structural level of this account of the succession of Solomon features a complex of Destiny Patterns associated with Solomon's success and Adonijah's failure to achieve Davidic endorsement of his succession. The Foundation Pattern establishing Solomon as David's successor flows seamlessly into the Doom Pattern condemning Adonijah's attempt to accede to the throne, hinting perhaps at the seamless progression from Solomon's glory to the Doom of the United Kingdom. In a mirror-image inversion, the EATING event is the same in both patterns, functioning as a hinge[26] and suggesting that the difference between a Foundation Pattern and a Doom Pattern really depends on one's point of view.

In many of these examples, there has been a correlation between an unusual morphology on the structural level and an unexpected outcome on the narrative level. It is logical if there is any relationship at all between structure and plot that this should be so.

Inversion and Other Variations

Inversion in the expected order of the elements of a pattern on the structural level often signals an inversion in expectations on the surface level of the narrative. Particularly for the Foundation Pattern, it makes sense to anticipate that something will be wrong with the established entity when something is amiss in the morphology. Several hero narratives foreshadow the idiosyncrasies of their subjects in this way.

---

25. Adonijah, far from behaving well, is guilty of treason and is executed by Solomon when he requests his father's concubine from Bathsheba, in 1 Kgs 2:13–25.

26. I am indebted to anthropologist Mary Douglas for our conversations in New York in April 1993 on the subject of the function of hinge elements in literary and anthropological contexts.

Gideon's Call

An inverted Foundation Pattern underlies Gideon's call in Judg 6:11–23. Gideon is called by an angel of the Lord to a mission similar to Moses' mission: he is to lead an encounter with a foreign oppressor and act as divine conduit for a miraculous victory. In this case, however, the expected sequence of the core functions is inverted: the OR-ACLE (Judg 6:12–16) precedes the EATING event (Judg 6:18–21). In addition, the meal itself is never eaten but is instead transformed from a hospitality banquet reminiscent of Abraham's for the messengers in Genesis 18 (Judg 6:19) to a cultic event, a burnt offering for the Lord (Judg 6:20–21). On a structural level the narrative is telling us that the glory in this case, like the meal itself, belongs completely to God. The inverted structure anticipates Gideon's own character and fate. Gideon is an unlikely hero, threshing wheat in the cave of a winepress and demanding multiple proofs of God's sincerity. Gideon closes his reign in ambiguity, and he is succeeded by an illegitimate son with illegitimate pretensions.

The doom of Gideon's illegitimate son, Abimelech, in Judg 9:16–49 anticipates the close of the cycle begun with the inverted Foundation Pattern in Judg 6:11–24.[27] Abimelech has murdered 70 of his half-brothers and, unconcerned by the curse hurled on him and Shechem by his surviving half-brother, Jotham (ORACLE, Judg 9:16–20), has ruled in Shechem for three years. God sends a spirit of discord between Abimelech and Shechem in order that Abimelech may be punished and his brothers' deaths avenged (AFFIRMATION #1, Judg 9:22–24). An EATING/DRINKING event follows, a festival for the god of Shechem, described by the text (9:27) as taking place in בית אלהיהם 'the temple of their god'. The reference is ambiguous: Who is the god of Shechem? Is this the God of Israel, or a pagan deity? Is this cultic EATING event direct or reversed? This ambiguity concerning cultic legitimacy echoes the ambiguities raised by Jotham (Judg 9:16–21) concerning Abimelech's legitimacy as Gideon's son and as a true leader. Fittingly, the locus of these ambiguities is Shechem, where the narrative plays out and where the ambiguities are ultimately resolved.

The wine of the festival leads to boasting and an extended ENCOUN-TER (9:27–49) in which Gaal ben Ebed challenges the rulership of Abimelech, with dire consequences for all. Abimelech is told of Gaal's

---

27. On the relationship of Judges 6 to Judges 9, see Jan Fokkelman's essay "Structural Remarks on Judges 9 and 19," in *"Sha'arei Talmon": Studies in the Bible, Qumran, and the Ancient Near East Presented to Shemaryahu Talmon* (ed. M. Fishbane, E. Tov, and W. W. Fields; Winona Lake, Ind.: Eisenbrauns, 1992) 33–45.

treason, and battles ensue over the next few days, in which Gaal is vanquished and Shechem and the Tower of Shechem are destroyed: the first is sown with salt; the second is burned. Finally, the ORACLE pronounced earlier by Jotham is fulfilled and AFFIRMED in a battle at the town of Thebez. Abimelech is injured by a woman who drops a millstone on his head and finished off by his armor-bearer, in an echo of Sisera's death at the hands of Jael (Judges 4–5) and a foreshadowing of Saul's begging to be run through by his armor-bearer (1 Sam 31:3-6).

The Doom Pattern in this text exhibits several variations on the expected morphology: the ORACLE precedes the EATING event, and it is affirmed in a direct statement by the text itself before it can be validated by an event or by a character within the narrative. These variations reinforce on the structural level the message of the narrative level that is made explicit in Jotham's fable: beware appearances; things are not always what they seem.

Many intertextual allusions built into the text help the reader to resolve the ambiguities surrounding Abimelech's legitimacy. The divine spirit of discord referred to by the text (Judg 9:23) may be analogous to the lying spirit sent by God as described by Micaiah in 1 Kings 22 and 2 Chronicles 18 and to the prophetic mission to mislead for which Isaiah volunteers in Isaiah 6. Abimelech's death echoes Sisera's at the hand of Jael (Judges 4–5) and foreshadows Saul's (1 Sam 31:3–6) and Sheba ben Bichri's (2 Sam 20:22). These associations place Abimelech firmly in a category shared by condemned kings, usurpers, and transgressors.

It has has been suggested by several scholars that, in spite of refusing the crown offered by his people, Gideon pretended to hegemony.[28] There are several clues to Gideon's secret desire for both royal and religious authority. He names his illegitimate son after his illegitimate ambitions: Abimelech, meaning 'my father is king'. Then, in language reminiscent of the incident of the golden calf, Gideon causes an ephod, a cultic breastplate, to be made of the earrings of eager Israelites. This becomes a snare to Gideon and his household (מוקש, Judg 8:27). An ephod is the divinitory chestpiece of the high priest, who may only be the eldest son of the Aaronid branch of the tribe of Levi. Gideon, youngest son in a minor branch of the tribe of Manasseh (Judg 6:15), may not legitimately make or wear such a ritual object. The text says that Gideon and his family are ensnared by the ephod. Does this refer to Gideon's illegitimate ambitions for himself and his

---

28. See, for example, ibid.; and David Gunn's article "Joshua and Judges," in *The Literary Guide to the Bible* (ed. Robert Alter and Frank Kermode; Cambridge, Mass.: Belknap, 1987), especially p. 114.

family? If so, this first Israelite experiment with dynasty anticipates Saul's failure to found a dynasty, and perhaps it also anticipates the ultimate downfall of the entire dynastic enterprise. The inversions and reversals woven into the framework underlying these troubling final episodes of the story of Gideon and his successor reinforce its unhappy narrative themes of masquerade, illegitimacy, and bloodshed. That these aberrations are structural suggests, perhaps, that these misfortunes will continue to mark the national history of Israel.

Annunciation of Samson's Birth

The annunciation of Samson's birth in Judges 13 shares many similarities with Gideon's call.[29] In a miraculous ENCOUNTER, an ORACLE (Judg 13:3–5) is given by an angel of the Lord to Manoah's wife, predicting the birth of a son whose mission will be to free Israel from a foreign oppressor (the Philistines). However, the annunciation of Samson's birth exhibits its own structural variations, different from those in Gideon's call. An EATING and DRINKING reference is embedded in the ORACLE, in which the angel enjoins Samson's mother from certain kinds of food and drink (Judg 13:4). This ORACLE is doubled in an [information mediation] that is part of ENCOUNTER #2 between the angel and Manoah (Judg 13:11–14). The Nazirite prohibitions are the first of several food reversals in this narrative. In an allusion to Abraham in Genesis 18, Manoah invites the messenger to share a meal, but his hospitality is refused and the meal is transformed into a burnt offering to the Lord (EATING #2, Judg 13:15–16, 19). In these brief verses, hospitality is offered and refused, and a meal set for human consumption is dedicated to God.

The fire of the burnt offering is miraculous, both here and in Gideon's story, as it is in the ever-burning bush of Exodus 3: Gideon's offering is miraculously set aflame by the messenger (Judg 6:21); the angel ascends to heaven in the flames of Manoah's offering (Judg 13:20). We expect the annunciation of Samson's birth to precede the establishment of a hero in Israel, but at the same time, Samson's failure to achieve his heroic promise is foreshadowed by these structural reversals, inversions, and transformations of the Foundation Pattern.[30]

---

29. See Edward L. Greenstein, "The Riddle of Samson," *Prooftexts* 1/3 (1981) 237-60, especially pp. 248 and 258 n. 70; and Yair Zakovitch, "The Sacrifice of Gideon (Jud. 6:11–24) and the Sacrifice of Manoaḥ (Jud. 13)," *Shnaton* 1 (1975) 151–54 [Heb.; Eng. summary, p. xxv].

30. Edward L. Greenstein has suggested a reading of the story of Samson as an archetype of the faith history of the Children of Israel, analyzing the entire narrative in terms of linguistic, rhetorical, and structural "riddles." See his article "The Riddle of Samson."

Morphological Reversals and the
Reversal of Expectations

When I introduced the concept of *reversal* as it applies to variables and constants in chapter 2, I also noted that in some cases the reversal of an expected outcome can be signaled by the reversal of an expected element within the structural pattern of a narrative. This can often be seen when the condition of famine is alleviated or reversed. In these cases, a reversal of context is also being signaled.

Jacob's Descent to Egypt

Earlier in this chapter, I used the language of plenty in Gen 45:21–24 to make the case that an allusion to EATING is present in the Doom of Ben-hadad of Aram in 2 Kings 8. The language of plenty in the Joseph story is startling, given the conditions of famine and rationing that obtain, even in Egypt, during the seven lean years. Joseph's gesture signals a reversal of the famine, at least as it is experienced by his family. In Genesis 45, Joseph sends festal gifts to Jacob in Canaan, to encourage his swift descent to Egypt to join his family, especially his long-lost son. The munificence of these gifts symbolizes the feast conditions that obtain in Egypt in comparison with the famine conditions being experienced by Jacob in Canaan. Joseph also reverses the effects of the famine for the rest of his family, according to the report in Gen 47:11–12.

This language of feasting and abundance functions as an allusion to EATING in a Foundation Pattern, whose subject is the sojourn of the Children of Israel in Egypt. The initial gift of bounty (EATING, Gen 45:17–24) is followed by an ENCOUNTER between Joseph's brothers and father, in which Jacob is urged to descend to Egypt (Gen 45:25–28). At Beer-sheba, as he nears the border between Canaan and Egypt, Jacob offers sacrifices to God and receives a night vision (ORACLE, Gen 46:1–4) in which God promises to go down to Egypt with him and bring him back. The ORACLE is AFFIRMED when Jacob, unquestioning, acts upon it and descends to Egypt with his family (Gen 46:5–7). The ORACLE is later AFFIRMED again, when as further promised Joseph is beside Jacob when he dies (Gen 50:1).

The message that the denouement of this narrative is a fulfillment of divine will is expressed explicitly twice in the Joseph cycle, in Gen 45:7–8 and 50:19–20. The reversal of morphological elements is echoed in the narrative context (Jacob's family is at home among strangers, experiencing plenty in the midst of famine) and signals the power of divine providence in protecting God's chosen and guiding the destiny of Jacob and Joseph and their entire family.

Similar reversals involving plenty in times of famine are operating in 2 Kings 4, though delivered by supernatural rather than human agency. The effect in the Elisha stories is the same as it is in the Joseph cycle: reversal of expected circumstances signals a reversal of expected outcome. In both the Joseph and the Elisha narratives, reversal of the negative situation for a chosen few reiterates the availability of divine providence for God's elect, even though external circumstances might appear to dictate the opposite. Morphologically, in these cases, the reversal of famine constitutes Propp's function of LACK LIQUIDATED, signaling here, as it does in Propp's model, the close of an episode.[31]

Nehemiah Rebuilds Jerusalem

Another narrative, Nehemiah 1–2, exhibits a still more complex expression of the Foundation Pattern. Nehemiah is the cupbearer to King Artaxerxes. In chapter 1, Nehemiah hears of the sorry state in which Jerusalem languishes. He weeps, mourns, fasts (EATING and DRINKING reversed), and prays in supplication. In 1:8–11, Nehemiah prays to God that he might play a part in the reestablishment of Jerusalem and as part of that prayer recapitulates a divine ORACLE in which he reminds God of the divine promise to gather the people in Jerusalem. In 2:1, a still-grieving Nehemiah serves the king wine at a meal (EATING and DRINKING). This juxtaposition represents a reversal reversed, with the EATING reference shifting from fasting to feasting, and the reader can correctly anticipate a reversal in Nehemiah's situation. Nehemiah's long countenance invites the king's inquiry (2:2). The ENCOUNTER that follows gives Nehemiah royal permission to embark on a PILGRIMAGE to Jerusalem, which he successfully undertakes (2:3–9). Nehemiah reconnoiters the ruined city in anticipation of the rebuilding and rallies the inhabitants to the task (2:11–18). He responds to objections with an AFFIRMATION of divine approbation (2:19–20).

This text contains many variations from the expected Foundation Pattern. There is a transposition of EATING and [PILGRIMAGE], for example. There is also an allusion to an ORACLE in 1:8–9 rather than a direct ORACLE or BLESSING, although divine will and divine protection are frequently invoked, notably in 2:4, 8, 12, and 18. The narrative also features a reversal reversed: the fasting event in 1:4, a reversal of EATING/DRINKING that would usually signal dire circumstances, is itself reversed in chapter 2, as the king is served at a feast with his consort,

---

31. Propp, *Morphology*, 53–55.

boding well for the proposed enterprise. In spite of these variations and elaborations, on a structural level this narrative alludes to the morphology of a Foundation Pattern. Such an allusion is appropriate in a narrative whose purpose is to tell us of Nehemiah's success in repairing Jerusalem and reestablishing a Temple cult in Judea. Readers who have the impression from reading this self-justifying memoir that humility is not characteristic of Nehemiah may have expected a fully structured Foundation Pattern rather than an unobtrusive allusion in an autobiographical book. The subtlety of the structural reference may be due either to false modesty or to Nehemiah's reluctance to arouse the suspicions of an overlord, the risks of which are recounted in Neh 6:6–9.

Saul's Reversals

Reversals can work on two levels at the same time, operating as subtle literary devices on the surface level of the narrative and functioning on the structural level to foreshadow shifts of fortune. An example of this dual function operates in 1 Samuel 14. A Doom Pattern condemning Saul's dynasty underpins a narrative that tells how the king's son forfeits his life.

On the day of battle, Saul imposes an oath on his troops to fast until nightfall (ORACLE/CURSE #1, 1 Sam 14:24). This oath incorporates reversals on two levels: structurally, the adjuration to fast is a reversal of EATING, cueing audiences to expect a reversal of expectation to come; narratively, fasting before a battle is counterintuitive, as Jonathan points out (1 Sam 14:29–30).

Following a rousing victory earlier in the day made possible by a diversionary skirmish initiated by Jonathan (14:14–23), the troops come across some honey spilled on the ground but refuse to eat any on account of their oath (ENCOUNTER #1, 14:25–26). Jonathan is ignorant of the king's command to fast on the eve of battle and tastes some honey (EATING #1, direct, 14:27). One of the troops tells him of Saul's interdiction, saying that his father had adjured the troops, cursing anyone who eats anything that day (doubling of ORACLE #1 and [information connective], 14:28). Jonathan, voicing the message of the narrative, condemns his father's judgment, commenting that the reverse of the king's order to fast might have been the wiser military course (1 Sam 14:29–30).

The troops are victorious against the Philistines all day, and the famished Israelites fall upon the spoil, slaughtering sheep and cattle on the ground and eating them without spilling out the blood (EATING #2 reversed, 14:31–32). Saul attempts to correct this violation of cultic ritual after the fact by setting up an altar to which the troops bring the cattle spoil that evening (14:33–35). Wishing to consolidate his victory against the Philistines, Saul proposes a night attack (ENCOUNTER #2, 14:36). The priest insists on inquiring of God first, but no answer is forthcoming (ORACLE #2 reversed, 14:37). Saul suspects God's silence is due to violation of his vow and casts lots to discover that Jonathan is the culprit (14:38–42). Jonathan confesses his transgression and is prepared to die. Saul is prepared to execute him, but the people intervene and Jonathan is spared (AFFIRMATION reversed, 14:43–46).

Two Patterns of Doom make up the framework of this episode. The subject of the first Pattern of Doom is Saul's judgment and, by extension, his competence as a leader of troops, up to now his chief strength. This condemnation of Saul's judgment is articulated by his son Jonathan in 1 Sam 14:29–30, who exclaims that if the troops had eaten of the spoil their victory over the Philistines would have been even greater. Saul's poor judgment is confirmed when Saul wishes to finish off the Philistines in a night raid but does not receive permission from God on account of the violation of the vow. If Saul had not made his rash vow, God would not have been offended, and his troops would have had the strength to fight a night battle. The outcome of this episode is that Saul the father is relieved but Saul the king is humiliated. Morphologically, reversal of an expected EATING function foreshadows reversal of expected outcomes. As a result, the reading of Saul's competence as king and as father are also reversed.

In the second pattern, the core functions of EATING and ORACLE are reversed, as is the AFFIRMATION, foreshadowing the many reversals present on the narrative level. This second Pattern of Doom has as its subject Jonathan himself, whose life is forfeit for violating, however unintentionally, his father's reckless interdiction. Jonathan is prepared to accept the ultimate consequence of his transgression, and Saul, in a reversal of his role of father, is prepared to implement his own royal decree. In another reversal of expectations, although Jonathan is condemned by his father, he is saved by the people (though not, in the end, by God). Morphologically, AFFIRMATION occurs in reverse when the first ORACLE is negated by the acclamation of the people. However, the people can only temporarily set aside the consequences of Saul's curse. In the end, God claims Jonathan's life, which is forfeit under his father's vow. Jonathan's doom confirms the condemnation of Saul's dynasty, foretold by Samuel in 1 Sam 13:13–14. Saul and his three sons fall on the same day in 1 Sam 31:6, and Jonathan's death precedes his father's. Jonathan is not Saul's heir for even one moment.

Doom of the United Kingdom

Reversal also marks the Doom morphologies found on the structural level of narratives condemning such national entities as the
United Kingdom of Israel and the Northern Kingdom.

Idolatry is the cause of the condemnation of Solomon's United
Kingdom in 1 Kings 11. The chapter opens with a description of the
situation in Solomon's court (11:1–8): Solomon loved many foreign
women and, in his old age and under their influence, he is guilty of following foreign gods. The specific action that triggers divine reproof is
Solomon's construction of shrines to Chemosh of Moab and Molech
of the Ammonites: 'and he did the same for all his foreign wives who
offered (incense) and sacrificed (זבח) to their gods' כן עשה לכל־נשיו
הנכריות מקטירות ומזבחות לאלהיהן (11:8).

This narrative allusion to EATING/DRINKING is followed by an EN-
COUNTER between God and Solomon (11:9–13) in which God accuses
the king of violating their covenant and, in an ORACLE, pronounces the
doom of the United Kingdom, not in Solomon's lifetime, but in the
lifetime of his successor. One tribe only will remain in the hands of
Solomon's son. The whole kingdom is not to be torn away from the
house of Solomon only on account of God's relationship with David,
his servant, and his chosen place, Jerusalem. As if to demonstrate the
direct impact of Solomon's fall from divine grace, the narrative immediately begins to recount episodes in which Solomon's authority is
challenged, and Solomon's enemies are succored in foreign courts
(11:14–25). The ORACLE is AFFIRMED explicitly in Ahijah's prophecy to
Jeroboam in 11:29–39.

In this text, the reversal of the cultic element encoded in Solomon's
apostasy is a clue to the negative outcome: the doom of the United
Kingdom. As we have seen, the underlying morphology reinforces this
surface element on the structural level of analysis. Starting from the
peak of Israelite cultic glory, the dedication of the Jerusalem Temple in
1 Kings 8, Solomon sinks to the depths of idolatry and divine repudia-
tion, recapitulating the similar progress of the Children of Israel from
the peak of the Sinai theophany to the apostasy of the worship of the
golden calf.

Doom of the Northern Kingdom

The end of idolatry in Northern Israel is predicted in 1 Kgs 12:25–
13:10, in connection with Jeroboam's first public ritual. Jeroboam
shares with Ahab the distinction of being the subject of multiple narratives that exhibit a Doom morphology on the structural level. In order

to discourage defection from Israel to Judea on account of the Temple in Jerusalem, Jeroboam builds and dedicates sanctuaries on the borders of the Northern Kingdom featuring golden calves and במות ('high places'). He declares a pilgrimage holiday, and the people gather for a feast (EATING, 12:25–33). As he ascends the altar to offer incense, a Judean man of God cries out in the Lord's name (ENCOUNTER, from 13:1–10). The Judean man of God curses the altar, predicts the coming of Josiah to put an end to idolatry and slay the priests of the high places, and offers as a sign that the altar will be torn apart that very day and the ashes poured out (ORACLE, embedded in the encounter, 13:1–3). Jeroboam reaches out to order the Judean's arrest, but his arm withers, and at the same time the altar splits and the ashes pour out, AFFIRMING the sign predicted in the ORACLE of Doom (13:4–5).

The story of the Judean man of God continues beyond this first Doom Pattern. A new move begins with DESIRE/LACK as Jeroboam begs the man of God to intercede for him and heal his arm; the Judean does so, and Jeroboam's arm is restored. The king invites the man of God home with him for dinner and a reward, but the Judean refuses, claiming divine interdiction against EATING or DRINKING in that place. He also may not return the same way he came. This INTERDICTION sets the narrative up for the VIOLATION and PUNISHMENT that take place in the rest of the chapter.[32]

The man of God's refusal to eat is the second reversal of an EATING event so far in this narrative. The first is the reversal of the cultic meal in 12:25–33, signaling the apostasy of an unsanctioned religious feast. The sensitive reader is warned by this initial reversal that no good is likely to come out of these actions. The second reversal, EATING and DRINKING refused (13:7–9), is the result of a food taboo communicated by God directly to the Judean. This metonymic connection of the anonymous Judean with all of Judah is not lost on the reader, especially since the larger context of the narrative is divine condemnation of idolatry.[33] The Judean righteously observes the interdiction in this

32. The functions of INTERDICTION, INTERDICTION VIOLATED, and PUNISHMENT are discussed by Propp among the 31 functions belonging to the Russian fairy-tale (see Propp, *Morphology*, 26–28). This pattern occurs frequently in the Hebrew Bible. Robert Culley has begun to study some of these narratives with a structuralist, although not Proppian, approach; see Robert C. Culley, "Five Tales of Punishment in the Book of Numbers," in *Text and Tradition: The Hebrew Bible and Folklore* (ed. Susan Niditch; Society of Biblical Literature Semeia Studies; Atlanta: Scholars Press, 1990) 25–34.

33. On anonymity as a clue to the metaphorical device of a single individual's standing for the nation as a whole, see, for example, Greenstein, "The Riddle of

instance. However, in the next move he violates the interdiction (13:15–19), reversing the divinely decreed reversal: he allows himself to be deceived and literally led astray. He pays for his failure of vigilance with his life.

In another Doom Pattern mirroring the sequence that opened this narrative, the lying Northern prophet ENCOUNTERs the Judean, who allows himself to be persuaded to eat and drink with him (EATING, 13:19). An ORACLE is pronounced, condemning the Judean for disobeying God's commandment (המצוה אשר צוך, 13:21) and punishing the Judean with death and exile from the resting place of his fathers (13:22). The ORACLE is AFFIRMED by the ensuing events, as the lying Northern prophet is quick to realize (13:24–25).

It may appear initially that the Doom Pattern, generally reserved for the demise of leaders or national entities, is excessive if not redundant in the condemnation of this lone, nameless Judean. The clue to this puzzle is found in the earlier observation about the second EATING reversal, the divine food taboo, that the Judean stands for all Judah and his fate for theirs if God's commandments are not obeyed. The OR-ACLE in 13:21–22, Deuteronomic in its language and sweeping generalization, contributes to this impression, as does the Judean's fate: death and exile. Just as the first part of the narrative (12:25–13:10) is a warning to the North against idolatry, so the second part of the narrative (13:11–25) is a warning to the South to obey God's commandments. The Patterns of Doom bracketing the pericope, each with its reversal, provide the clues to support this interpretation.

The Morphological Message of Hope in Captivity

I have long been troubled by the closing of the saga of Israel at the end of 2 Kings. The story that begins with cosmic creation and the deeds of the patriarchs, that climaxes at Sinai, and that plays itself out in the land of promise, seems to end with a whimper in 2 Kings 25. Parallel accounts in identical language close both the book of 2 Kings and the book of Jeremiah.[34] These accounts describe Jehoiachin's release from prison and his eating in the presence of the king of Babylon all of the rest of his life. Why is Jehoiachin's release from prison given so much weight? An aging Judahite king is given a reprieve from prison and, still in exile, is grateful to be living off the kindness of his captor.

Samson," where he suggests that this metaphoric relationship is a key to one reading of Judges 13–16.

34. 2 Kgs 25:27–30 and Jer 52:31–34.

Surely such a message is a weak ending for the patriarchal narratives and Deuteronomic History, works of such powerful scope and artistry.

From a literary perspective, the double account closing two books in the received collection draws special attention to itself.[35] Perhaps the structural level of these texts will yield a more powerful concluding message. The language in 2 Kings and Jeremiah is identical. For simplicity, I refer here to the account in 2 Kings.

The Babylonian king, Evil-merodach, 'raises the head' (נשא ראש, 25:27, ENCOUNTER) of Jehoiachin of Judah and releases him from prison. He 'speaks good things to him' (וידבר אתו טבות, 25:28) and raises his throne above the thrones of the other captive kings in Babylon (implied ORACLE). Jehoiachin's prison garments are removed, and he 'eats bread perpetually before him' (ואכל לחם תמיד לפניו, 25:29, EATING), that is, Jehoiachin is given regular rations at the command of the king all of the rest of his life.

The reference to EATING as a signifier of the Babylonian king's favor toward Jehoiachin suggests that it is worth checking whether a Pattern of Destiny might be implied in the structure of these texts. If so, the message for an audience familiar with this literary convention would indeed be compelling and full of hope, alluding as it does to the beginning of a new order centered on a Judean heir of the house of David.[36]

---

35. See, for example, I. B. Gottlieb, "*Sof Davar*: Biblical Endings," *Prooftexts* 11 (1991) 213–24.

36. This reading was anticipated, without the benefit of structural analysis, by Gerhard von Rad, in *Old Testament Theology, Volume I: The Theology of Israel's Historical Traditions* (trans. D. M. G. Stalker; New York: Harper & Row, 1962) 343. Montgomery and Gehman are more cautious: "The book is thus concluded with the theme of the continued dignity of the house of David, with what hope in mind we may only surmise" (James A. Montgomery and Henry Snyder Gehman, *A Critical and Exegetical Commentary on the Book of Kings* [ICC; Edinburgh: T. & T. Clark, 1941] 567); Martin Noth (*The Deuteronomistic History* [JSOTSup 15; Sheffield: JSOT Press, 1981] 97) reads a pessimistic ending of judgment fulfilled, as do Cogan and Tadmor, who read these verses as "non-integral to the book of Kings" on linguistic and historiographic grounds and challenge von Rad's theological reading (Mordechai Cogan and Hayim Tadmor, *II Kings* [AB 11; New York: Doubleday, 1988] 329–30). Long, who provides a nice summary of the differing opinions, sides with those who take this text as a message to the survivors to get along with the Babylonians in diaspora (Burke O. Long, *2 Kings* [FOTL 10; Grand Rapids, Mich.: Eerdmans, 1991] 289), especially with Christopher T. Begg ("The Significance of Jehoiachin's Release: A New Proposal," *JSOT* 36 [1986] 49–56). A recent literary reading by Jan Jaynes Granowski relies, as I do in my analysis, on intertextuality and concludes that the ambiguity is purposeful and appropriate ("Jehoiachin at the King's Table: A Reading of the Ending of the Second Book of Kings," in *Reading between Texts: Intertextuality and the Hebrew Bible* [[ed. Danna Nolan Fewell; Literary Currents in Biblical Interpretation; Louisville: Westminster/John Knox, 1992] 173–88).

A divine ORACLE is absent from the text, but the Babylonian king's speaking favorably to Jehoiachin and raising his throne higher than that of the other kings could function as an allusion to a positive OR-ACLE operating in Foundation Patterns. Perhaps reading this text in terms of other similar texts can shed light on whether there is justification in reading on the structural level an allusion to the Foundation Pattern.

The Restorations of Job, Joseph, and Jehoiachin

Jehoiachin was king of Judah when he was taken into captivity eleven years before the fall of Judah. Job 42:10–15 is another narrative that tells of the ultimate restoration of a man who fell from the pinnacle of good fortune to the nadir of distress. Examining Job's restoration can shed light on Jehoiachin's.

The closing chapter of the book of Job contains a puzzling meal (EATING, 42:11). Following the circumstantial statement in the preceding verse (42:10), that God has restored to Job double what he had had before (ORACLE, described as the Lord's BLESSING of Job when the specifics are enumerated in 42:12–15), the text recounts in a series of sequential clauses that all of Job's brothers and sisters and all of his friends who had known him before assemble to eat a meal in his home (EATING, 42:11). They console and comfort him and give him gifts. This sequence is followed by circumstantial clauses confirming the specifics of the Lord's blessing of Job, namely, with sheep, camels, oxen, she-asses, sons, and daughters (AFFIRMATION, 42:12–15).

This narrative is puzzling because the stated purpose of the feast is to console and comfort Job—an odd purpose, considering that the account of the meal is clearly bracketed by the narrative testimony that Job's restoration has already taken place. One may ask what need Job has of comfort, consolation, and the gifts of his friends if he has already been restored by divine providence. Might this puzzle be a clue that the meal in this text has another function?

The substance of the Lord's blessing of Job consists of bounty and progeny, the very blessings that are the central concern of the Foundation Accounts in the Sumerian "Journeys of the Gods" and of the similarly structured biblical patriarchal narratives discussed in chapter 6 above. Job's personal well-being is clearly being reestablished on the narrative level of the text. But on the structural level, through the Foundation Pattern underlying the closing verses of the book, Job's personal restoration is made analogous to the foundation of national and cultural entities elsewhere in biblical narrative and in the literature of its cultural milieu.

It is tempting to read Jehoiachin's personal restoration, with its structural allusion to a Foundation Pattern, in terms of Job's personal restoration, with its structurally explicit Foundation Pattern. In fact, there is one more biblical account of personal restoration that might reinforce such a reading.

Joseph's release from prison in Gen 41:1–46 lends itself to literary association with Jehoiachin's release in 2 Kings 25 and Jeremiah 52.[37] From the perspective of their respective literary contexts, there are several parallels: as young men, both are removed to a foreign prison from positions of authority that they had held, at the whim of a foreign official; both serve prison sentences without hope of release; both are released at the command of a king; upon release, both change their prison clothes; both are then elevated above their peers. The expression 'to lift the head' נשׂא ראשׁ[38] is associated with Joseph's interpretation of the dreams of the butler and the baker just preceding this chapter in Genesis and occurs in both accounts of Jehoiachin's release, further associating the Joseph story with the Jehoiachin story.

Genesis 41 opens with the description of Pharaoh's disturbing dreams, themselves a doubling, both containing references to EATING (reversed, 41:1–7).[39] A double ENCOUNTER follows, first between the butler and Pharaoh and then between Pharaoh and Joseph (41:8–16). The two dreams are repeated for Joseph's benefit in an [information mediation], and Joseph words his interpretation as a divine ORACLE (42:25–31), whose very doubling constitutes an AFFIRMATION. This explicit Foundation Pattern is followed by Joseph's appointment as Pharaoh's second-in-command and the beginning of God's plan for gathering the Israelites together in Egypt and then redeeming them from bondage in the formative and constitutive act of their peoplehood.

The Foundation Pattern Alluded to in 2 Kings 25

Morphological analysis reveals that, structurally, Genesis 41 exhibits the Foundation Pattern, linking it on this level to the Job story and reinforcing my reading of Jehoiachin's release as an allusion to this pattern.[40] This reading subtly suggests hope to those who understand the

---

37. See, for example, Donald B. Redford, *A Study of the Biblical Story of Joseph (Genesis 37–50)* (VTSup 20; Leiden: Brill, 1970) 97; and Granowski, "Jehoiachin at the King's Table," 183–86.

38. On this expression, see David Marcus, "'Lifting up the Head': On the Trail of a Word Play in Genesis 40," *Prooftexts* 10 (1990) 17–27.

39. See my discussion in chapter 3 above, beginning on p. 72.

40. Donald A. Seybold, "Paradox and Symmetry in the Joseph Narrative," in *Literary Interpretations of Biblical Narratives* (ed. Kenneth R. R. Gros Louis, James S.

pattern, much the way that a story ending "once upon a time . . ." would suggest in our culture that the story was not yet over. Reading 2 Kgs 25:27–29 as an allusion to the Foundation Pattern strengthens what appears only on the narrative level to be a weak ending to the Deuteronomic History.

This analysis is an outstanding example of the way that identification of the conventions associated with the basic Foundation Pattern permits the identification of Foundation allusions in biblical texts, where what is being established is not made explicit but may nonetheless be theologically or culturally significant. I expect that, subjected to this kind of analysis, allusions or elaborations of Foundation and Doom Patterns may be identified more systematically and with more certainty, adding an additional level to our understanding of these texts.

Prophetic Adaptations and Transformations

The degree to which the Foundation Pattern persists in biblical literature may be judged by its reuse in prophetic compositions. The prophets Haggai, Jeremiah, and Ezekiel exhibit Foundation Patterns at some point in their missions.

Haggai

The prophet Haggai is charged with inspiring the postexilic returnees to rebuild the Jerusalem Temple. The Foundation Pattern underlies his entire message. Hag 1:6 employs an allusion to EATING and DRINKING reversed, referring to agricultural scarcity (much sown and little reaped) and famine (EATING without satisfaction, DRINKING without fill). The ORACLE follows: God promises that if the Temple is finished, God will look upon it with favor (1:7–8). That divine favor will take the form of abundance is expressed in reversals: God discloses that famine and drought have been brought upon the people on account of their neglect of the Temple, implying that fertility will follow the Temple's rebuilding (1:9–11). The ENCOUNTER appears to involve the prophet in several impassioned exhortations to the governor and the high priest and, through them, to the people (1:12–2:15). The initial implied promise of abundant food and drink is AFFIRMED in 2:15–19, as the ominous reversal is reversed with the statement that beginning with the day that the foundation is laid for rebuilding the Lord's Temple, God will send the blessings of seed, vine, fig tree,

---

Ackerman, and Thayer S. Warshaw; The Bible in Literature Courses; Nashville: Abingdon, 1974) 1.59–73.

pomegranate, and olive tree.[41] The rebuilding of the Jerusalem Temple is morphologically undergirded by an allusion to the Foundation Pattern.

Prophetic Initiation of Ezekiel and Jeremiah

I have shown earlier, in chapter 4, that an eating event is not required for prophetic commissioning. Therefore, when EATING does occur in a minority of cases, the texts must be examined closely to see what message is borne on the morphological level.

The prophets Hosea, Joel, Amos, Obadiah, Jonah, Micah, Nahum, Habakkuk, Zephaniah, Zechariah, and Malachi begin to deliver the word of the Lord without any reference to EATING or DRINKING, literal or symbolic. Isaiah's book begins without any reference to EATING, although the prophet's mouth is touched by a burning coal and cleansed before he volunteers for a divine mission (Isa 6:6–7).[42]

---

41. The idea that abundance is directly related to temple construction is explicit in the Sumerian temple hymn on the Gudea Cylinders and also in the vision of the new Temple described in Ezekiel 40–48. See, for example, J. D. Levenson, *Theology of the Program of Restoration of Ezekiel 40–48* (HSM 10; Missoula, Mont.: Scholars Press, 1976), especially pp. 25–36; and Moshe Greenberg, "The Design and Themes of Ezekiel's Program of Restoration," *Int* 38 (1984) 181–208. For a comparison of the Gudea and Ezekiel Temple accounts, see my "Biblical Parallel to a Sumerian Temple Hymn? Ezekiel 40–48 and Gudea," *JANES* 24 (1997) 1–11. For a general survey of temple ideology in the ancient Near East, see A. Hurowitz, *I Have Built You an Exalted House: Temple Building in the Bible in Light of Mesopotamian and Northwest Semitic Writings* (JSOTSup 115; Sheffield: Sheffield Academic Press, 1992) 33–57, especially pp. 54–57; Daniel Bodi, *The Book of Ezekiel and the Poem of Erra* (Freiburg: Universitätsverlag, 1991) 219–30; Richard J. Clifford, *The Cosmic Mountain in Canaan and the Old Testament* (Cambridge: Harvard University Press, 1972); Michael A. Fishbane, "The Sacred Center: The Symbolic Structure of the Bible," in *Texts and Responses: Studies Presented to Nahum N. Glatzer on the Occasion of His Seventieth Birthday by His Students* (ed. M. Fishbane and P. Flohr; Leiden: Brill, 1975) 6–27; idem, *Text and Texture: Close Readings of Selected Biblical Texts* (New York: Schocken, 1979) 111–20; S. W. Holloway, "What Ship Goes There? The Flood Narratives in the Gilgamesh Epic and Genesis Considered in Light of Ancient Near East Temple Ideology," *ZAW* 103 (1991) 328–55. The classic work on Temple service in ancient Israel is by Menahem Haran, *Temples and Temple-Service in Ancient Israel: An Inquiry into Biblical Cult Phenomena and the Historical Setting of the Priestly School* (Oxford: Clarendon, 1978; repr. Winona Lake, Ind.: Eisenbrauns, 1985).

42. Although some scholars have classified Isaiah 6 as the prophet's commissioning (see George Buchanan Gray, *A Critical and Exegetical Commentary on the Book of Isaiah* (ICC; Edinburgh: T. & T. Clark, 1912] 1.99), other scholars today do not do so, in part because of its appearance so long after the prophet began his mission. The theme of God's purposeful deception of the people is echoed in the narrative

Two prophets of exile, however, do recount EATING events associated with their commissioning, and Patterns of Destiny are present in the structure of both of these episodes. Ezekiel is called by God from the community of exiles in Babylonia. In the beginning of his call, he sees a theophany and throws himself down on his face (Ezek 1:1–28). This ENCOUNTER continues as the voice of God speaks to Ezekiel, sending him to prophesy to the people of Israel, a nation of rebels against God (ORACLE, 2:1–7). God gives Ezekiel a symbolic scroll inscribed with woe and commands him to eat (EATING, 2:8). Ezekiel eats the scroll, and God affirms the earlier ORACLE in which he told Ezekiel that, though he will be unheeded, he is to address the Babylonian community of exiles (AFFIRMATION, Ezek 3:7–11).

In this pattern, the ORACLE and EATING events are transposed, signaling a transposition of the expected outcome. When a prophet is sent by God, the expectation is that his word will be heard by the people. Yet in this case, God tells Ezekiel from the beginning that his word is doomed to fall on deaf ears. The ORACLE consists of multiple segments, suggesting that more than one Pattern of Destiny is present. In the first, divine protection is established for Ezekiel. In the second, Israel is condemned to confront a prophet of doom and not heed his words. This second pattern implies the failure of Ezekiel's mission and, by extension, the doom of the house of Israel.

Similar transformations of the Patterns of Destiny appear to underlie the establishment of Jeremiah's mission. When Jeremiah is first called by God, he objects, as Moses does, that he is inexperienced in public speaking (Jer 1:4–6). This ENCOUNTER continues with a multipart ORACLE consisting first of the promise of divine protection for the prophet (1:7–8), followed by a symbolic allusion to an EATING event, as God puts divine words into the prophet's mouth (Jer 1:9).[43] God follows this gesture with the continuation of the ORACLE, appointing Jeremiah as a prophet "to uproot and to pull down, to destroy and to overthrow, to build and to plant" (Jer 1:10). The rest of the chapter (indeed, the rest of Jeremiah's prophetic book) is an AFFIRMATION of the ORACLE, explicitly expressed in 1:17–19, where Jeremiah is directed to gird his loins and speak to the people. He is not to fear their hostility because he is protected by God.

---

of 1 Kings 22, in which the prophet Micaiah has a vision of a deceptive spirit volunteering to mislead the Northern prophets. See O. H. Prouser, *The Phenomenology of the Lie in Biblical Narrative* (Ph.D. diss., Jewish Theological Seminary of America, 1991), 152–81, especially pp. 157–61.

43. Jeremiah alludes poetically to this event in Jer 15:16.

Again, as it is for Ezekiel, a Pattern of Destiny is present in Jeremiah, featuring multiple oracles, some positive and some negative. Patterns of Doom and Foundation entwine each other at the beginning of Jeremiah's prophetic mission, signifying the doom and hope for redemption that appear throughout Jeremiah's prophecies. Israel is doomed in her current sinful state, but a remnant will be established. The structural underpinning of Jeremiah's call foreshadows this double polarity.

These two major prophets, who both live through the fall of Judah, are forewarned on the structural level during their initial contacts with God. Though God promises each of them protection, the burden of their prophecies will be negative and their missions full of woe. The morphological twining together of Patterns of Doom and of Foundation in the openings of these two texts foreshadows their outcomes.

Patterns of Destiny Transformed into Metaphor

The ultimate transformation of the elements making up the morphology of Patterns of Destiny is the shift from concrete to abstract and back again. That is, for example, actual meals are replaced in a pattern by metaphoric devouring and then shift again to become an EATING reversal. This fluidity is the sign of a literary device that has evolved into mature use, so well understood by its audience that allusions and inversions may substitute for full or literal discriptions.[44] So far in this chapter, I have already shown illustrations of transformations like these. One example remains.

An entire generation is condemned in an allusion to the Doom Pattern heralded by a grisly metaphor that is the reversal of an EATING event in Numbers 13–14. The narrative begins with the selection of the men who will scout the promised land and continues with their dispatch ([PILGRIMAGE/JOURNEY], Num 13:1–22). The EATING function of this morphology is filled by several competing images (Num 13:23–33). First, there is the EATING/DRINKING allusion embodied in the giant cluster of grapes brought from Naḥal Eshcol and held up before the people as an example of the fruit of the land (Num 13:23–24). The image in this verse is still both direct and literal, although exaggerated.

Second, there is the report that the land is flowing with milk and honey (ארץ זבת חלב ודבש, 13:27), an indication that what the Lord has promised is in fact the case. This image of food and drink represents another direct allusion to EATING and DRINKING, this one an echo of

44. H. L. Ginsberg, "A Strand in the Cord of Hebrew Hymnody," *ErIsr* 9 (Albright Volume; 1969) 45–50.

the land of promise first described in Exod 3:8 and repeated in Exod 3:17 and 13:5.

Third, the exaggeration of Num 13:23–24 is transformed into a reversal in Num 13:28–33, when the enormous fruit is seen to foreshadow the ominous size of the inhabitants. It thus becomes a symbol of enormous obstacle rather than a representation of enormous fertility. Finally, there is the grotesque EATING image—building on the size of the grape cluster and the proportionately giant size of the inhabitants—of a land that devours (אכל) its inhabitants (13:32), even figuratively.[45]

The ENCOUNTER is between Moses and Aaron, on the one hand, and, on the other hand, the people, who are distraught in anticipation of disaster (14:1–10). The Lord intercedes on the side of the leaders in a doubling of the ENCOUNTER, this time an encounter between the Lord and Moses. Moses succeeds in dissuading the Lord from destroying the people completely. The punishment is mitigated in an ORACLE predicting the doom only of the Exodus generation (Num 14:20–38), an ORACLE affirmed by Moses, who repeats it to the condemned. AFFIRMATION continues when the people try to take into their own hands control over their entrance into the land of promise and are roundly defeated at Hormah (Num 14:39–45). Thus, the Doom Pattern underlying this text consists of the sequence [PILGRIMAGE], EATING/DRINKING, ENCOUNTER, ORACLE, AFFIRMATION.

The transformation of the scouting mission from the first practical act of conquest to the final doom of the Exodus generation is foreshadowed by the mixed nature of the EATING and DRINKING imagery in the underlying structure. Every direct image of EATING and DRINKING also exhibits a reversal in this narrative: the symbol of fertility is also perceived as a symbol of threat; the land of abundance is also perceived as a land of death. Such a combination of images juxtaposed to one another in the position of an expected EATING or DRINKING event suggests an outcome that is mostly disastrous but possesses seeds of hope.

The reinterpretation of the immense fruit, a symbol of fertility (Num 13:23–24), as a symbol of threat (Num 13:28–33) reflects the transformation undergone by the Exodus generation from their divine election at Sinai to their condemnation for faithlessness in the wilderness of Paran. This connection is made explicit in God's punitive ORACLE in Num 14:20–23. The literary resonance forward and back in the biblical text also applies to the image of the land devouring its

---

45. I am indebted to Dr. Nili Scharf Gold of the University of Pennsylvania for discussing this metaphor with me. For the conventional understanding of this image, see George Buchanan Gray, *Numbers* (ICC; Edinburgh: T. & T. Clark, 1986) 151.

settlers. This allusion anticipates the punishment of Dathan and Abiram in Num 16:27–34 and also suggests an inversion of the metaphor inherent in Lev 18:25 and 28: the threat that the land will vomit out its inhabitants as a punishment for disobedience.

The association of "a land flowing with milk and honey" in Num 13:27 with its antithesis, a land devouring its settlers in Num 13:32, also recalls the Lord's desire to withdraw from personally leading the people to the 'land flowing with milk and honey' ארץ זבת חלב ודבש after the debacle of the golden calf, 'lest I devour you on the way' פן אכלך בדרך (Exod 33:3). The metaphoric allusion in Exodus 33 to a connection between the land of milk and honey and the death of the people on the way is concretized and made explicit in the narrative of Numbers 13–14. But just as Moses intercedes successfully on behalf of the people in Exod 33:12–17, so, too, his intercession in Num 14:11–38 mitigates the Lord's wrath. AMELIORATION in this Pattern of Doom echoes the amelioration in the examples of the Doom of paradise discussed in chapter 6 above. Reflecting the complex nature of the EATING events in this narrative, the outcome, while extremely negative, is not without its message of reassurance: the people of the Exodus generation are doomed, but their children may live to inherit the land of promise.

In this chapter I have reviewed allusions, reversals, and transformations of the Patterns of Destiny as they occur in many different contexts in the Hebrew Bible. The persistence of these patterns in so many contexts suggests that the morphology of Patterns of Destiny is a literary convention, most often associated with the establishment or condemnation of cultural entities but flexible and durable enough to be reused and elaborated on in other contexts.

CHAPTER EIGHT

Summary and Conclusion

Summary

In a broad study relying on the theoretical approach of the Russian formalist Vladimir Propp, I have analyzed the underlying structures of more than 150 texts in which eating and drinking occur in the Hebrew Bible. I noted that the elements of eating and drinking may function on a structural level either as a variable component or as a constant constituent in a predictable sequence in a variety of biblical contexts.

Using the method laid out by Propp, I examined many cases where eating and drinking operate as variables within other constants such as CULT, MIRACLE, DREAM, ETIOLOGY, LIFE-CYCLE EVENTS, and others. I have also shown that structural patterns appear to underlie some biblical narratives that contain eating and drinking events.

I have found that when eating and drinking occur as a stable element across different narratives and fall in sequence with respect to other constant elements, they are part of a pattern portending the establishment or condemnation of a cultural entity. This pattern consists of the elements of EATING/DRINKING, [ENCOUNTER], ORACLE, [AFFIRMATION], and I term such a structure a Pattern of Destiny.

I have shown that this single morphology has two major expressions, depending on whether the oracle is positive or negative. The nature of the oracle determines whether the subject of the oracle is established or condemned. The two subsets of the category are, therefore, Foundation Patterns and Doom Patterns. I have shown how the direction of the eating or drinking event may provide cues for the reading of the structural level against the surface level of the text, operating as a counterpoint, foreshadowing, or reinforcement of the events recounted. Many examples were analyzed showing how these structural patterns may be elaborated, varied, or transformed to function as nuanced literary devices.

Finding the Ancient Reader

I have defined an ancient genre widespread in time and place, ranging from the third millennium B.C.E. to at least the first century C.E., from Mesopotamia and Egypt to the Levant. This genre was obvious enough within the ancient Near Eastern cultural context to allow for permutations and allusions and variations on its basic structure.

The many, many examples of these patterns that occur in a variety of ways throughout biblical narrative and Near Eastern literature testify that they were literary conventions of long standing, whose use, reuse, and transformation of morphology were known and understood by ancient audiences well enough to pick up on allusions, reversals, inversions, and other variations.

Reclaiming an understanding of this genre gives modern readers insights into the text and an opportunity to experience the text in a way that is much more similar to the way that the original audiences would have experienced them than has been possible before now. The Pattern of Destiny is yet another tool that can help us better understand the world view of the ancient reader.

Future Study

My research suggests many further avenues of inquiry. Morphological analysis can be applied in greater depth to the constants identified and sketched out in chapter 3, further refining the morphologies I suggest for such biblical categories as CULT, MIRACLE, DREAM, and so forth, and examining the intertextual implications that are only available upon deeper analysis and consideration. Perhaps other constants may be identified and classified as well. These same categories, or even newly proposed genres, might be explored further in the cognate literatures of the ancient Near East to determine whether my findings can be applied to an even wider cross-cultural matrix.

The Patterns of Destiny that I discuss in depth for biblical literature in chapters 5–7 might be applied in greater depth to other literary corpora. I have reached back into the third millennium B.C.E. for Sumerian examples of this genre, and I have offered sample analyses of Homeric texts and sacred scriptures. I have only sketched the barest beginnings of morphological analysis in these corpora. Yet to be done are thorough studies of Christian Scriptures, Homeric Greek, and other literatures of late antiquity or of the medieval world. It would be interesting to know how far forward these tropes were understood and at what point they were lost to their audiences. My findings might be applied as well to the literatures of later periods and in more widely scattered geographical regions influenced by biblical and Near Eastern cultures to see whether these patterns continued to be used and recognized.

Finding New Theological Meaning

Just as archaeological excavation helps to reconstruct ancient cities, careful analysis of the morphology of literary structures can reclaim levels of meaning in sacred texts, levels of meaning that would have been understood by its earlier auditors but that has been lost to modern readers.

Two essential characteristics of the texts identified as belonging to the genre of Destiny Patterns are essential to classifying their meaning: first, each of the primary texts in this study was sacred to the culture that preserved it; second, the ORACLE element in the Pattern of Destiny is assumed within biblical narrative to be divinely determined. These two qualities signify that a primary meaning emerging from these texts is, by definition, theological. My analysis is thus a powerful tool for reading theological meaning on the structural level of biblical texts, a meaning that would have been obvious to ancient audiences. Comparing the structural messages to the message of the surface narrative can often yield a more nuanced reading: the structural patterns underlying these texts sometimes support and sometimes contrast with the meaning on the surface of the text.

The many insights and intertextual connections made possible only after morphological analysis or confirmed by its findings testify to the productivity of this approach for our greater understanding today of sacred texts and their origins.

Bibliography of Works Cited

Achtemeier, Paul J. (ed.). *Harper's Bible Dictionary*. San Francisco: Harper & Row, 1985.

Ackerman, Susan. "A *Marzeaḥ* in Ezekiel 8:7–13?" *Harvard Theological Review* 82 (1989) 267–83.

Al-Fouadi, A. A. *Enki's Journey to Nippur: The Journeys of the Gods*. Ph.D. dissertation, University of Pennsylvania, 1969.

Alexander, T. Desmond. "Lot's Hospitality: A Clue to His Righteousness." *Journal of Biblical Literature* 104 (1985) 289–91.

Alfrink, B. "L'expression Neʾesap ʾel ʿAmmâw." *Oudtestamentische Studiën* 5 (1948) 118–31.

____. "L'expression Šakab ʿIm ʾAbotâw." *Oudtestamentische Studiën* 2 (1943) 106–18.

Alter, Robert. *The Art of Biblical Narrative*. New York: Basic, 1981.

____. "Biblical Type-Scenes and the Uses of Convention." *Critical Inquiry* (1978) 355–78.

____. "How Convention Helps Us Read: The Case of the Bible's Annunciation Type-Scene." *Prooftexts* 3/2 (1983) 115–30.

Alter, Robert, and Frank Kermode (eds.). *The Literary Guide to the Bible*. Cambridge: Harvard University Press, 1987.

Andrews, James R. "The Rhetoric of Coercion and Persuasion: The Reform Bill of 1832." *Quarterly Journal of Speech* 56 (1970) 187–95.

Apo, Satu. "The Structural Schemes of a Repertoire of Fairy Tales: A Structural Analysis of Marina Takalo's Fairy Tales Using Propp's Model." Pp. 147–58 in *Genre, Structure and Reproduction in Oral Literature*. Bibliotheca Uralica 5. Budapest: Akademiai Kiado, 1980.

____. "The Variability and Narrative Structures of Magic Tales from Universal Models to Describing the Differences between Tales." Pp. 487–501 in *D'un conte . . . à l'autre: La variabilité dans la littérature orale*. Edited by Veronika Görög-Karady and Michele Chiche. Paris: Centre Nationale de la Recherche Scientifique, 1990.

____. "The Variability and Narrative Structures of Wondertales: From Universal Models to Describing the Differences between Tales." Pp. 151–60 in volume 33 of *Studia Fennica: Review of Finnish Linguistics and Ethnology*. Helsinki: Suomalainen Kirjallisuuden Seura, 1989.

Auty, Robert, and Arthur Thomas Hatto. *Traditions of Heroic and Epic Poetry*. 2 volumes. Publications of the Modern Humanities Research Association 9. London: Modern Humanities Research Association, 1980–89.

Avigad, N., and J. C. Greenfield. "Bronze Phiale with Phoenician Inscription." *Israel Exploration Journal* (1982) 118–28.

Aycock, D. Alan. "The Fate of Lot's Wife: Structural Mediation in Biblical Mythology." Pp. 113–19 in *Structuralist Interpretations of Biblical Myth*. Edited by Edmund Leach and D. Alan Aycock. Royal Anthropological Institute of Great Britain and Ireland. London: Cambridge University Press, 1983.

Baldick, Chris. *The Concise Oxford Dictionary of Literary Terms*. Oxford: Oxford University Press, 1990.

Baltzer, Klaus. *The Covenant Formulary in Old Testament, Jewish, and Early Christian Writings*. Philadelphia: Fortress, 1971.

Bar-Efrat, Shimon. *Narrative Art in the Bible*. Journal for the Study of the Old Testament Supplements 70. Sheffield: Almond, 1989.

Barnett, Richard D. "Assurbanipal's Feast." *Eretz-Israel* 18 (Nahman Avigad volume; 1985) 1–6. Jerusalem: Israel Exploration Society.

_____. "Bringing the God into the Temple." Pp. 10–20 in *Temples and High Places in Biblical Times*. Edited by A. Biran. Jerusalem: Hebrew Union College, Jewish Institute of Religion, 1981.

Barthes, Roland. *Image-Music-Text*. Translated and edited by Stephen Heath. New York: Farrar, Straus and Giroux, 1977.

_____. "The Struggle with the Angel: Textual Analysis of Genesis 32:23–33." Pp. 21–33 in *Structural Analysis and Biblical Exegesis: Interpretational Essays by R. Barthes, F. Bovon, F.-J. Leenhardt, R. Martin-Achard and J. Starobinski*. Translated by Alfred M. Johnson, Jr. Pittsburgh: Pickwick, 1974.

Bascom, William R. "Four Functions of Folklore." Pp. 279–98 in *Study of Folklore*. Edited by Alan Dundes. Englewood Cliffs, New Jersey: Prentice-Hall, 1965.

Baumgarten, Albert I. "Myth and Midrash: Genesis 9:20–29." Pp. 55–71 in *Christianity, Judaism and Other Greco-Roman Cults: Studies for Morton Smith at Sixty*. Studies in Judaism in Late Antiquity 12. Leiden: Brill, 1975.

Beach, Eleanor Ferris. "The Samaria Ivories, *Marzeaḥ*, and Biblical Text." *Biblical Archaeologist* 56/2 (1993) 94–104.

Beatie, Bruce A. "The Myth of the Hero: From Mission Impossible to Magdalenian Caves." Pp. 46–65 in *The Hero in Transition*. Edited by Ray B. Browne and Marshall W. Fishwick. Bowling Green, Ohio: Popular Press, 1983.

Begg, Christopher T. "The Significance of Jehoiachin's Release: A New Proposal." *Journal for the Study of the Old Testament* 36 (1986) 49–56.

Ben-Amos, Dan. "Comments on Robert C. Culley's 'Five Tales of Punishment in the Book of Numbers' (Pp. 25–34)." Pp. 35–45 in *Text and Tradition: The Hebrew Bible and Folklore*. Society of Biblical Literature Semeia Studies 20. Atlanta: Scholars Press, 1990.

Ben-Amos, Dan (ed.). *Folklore Genres*. American Folklore Society / Bibliographical and Special Series 26. Austin: University of Texas Press, 1976.

Berger, David. "On the Morality of the Patriarchs in Jewish Polemic and Exegesis." Pp. 49–62 in *Understanding Scripture: Explorations of Jewish and Christian Traditions of Interpretation*. Edited by Clemens Thoma and Michael Wyschogrod. New York: Paulist Press, 1987.

Berlin, Adele. "Ethnopoetry and the Enmerkar Epics." *Journal of the American Oriental Society* 103 (special issue dedicated to Samuel Noah Kramer; 1983) 17–24.

Bland, Kalman P. "The Rabbinic Method and Literary Criticism." Pp. 16–23 in *Literary Interpretations of Biblical Narratives*. Edited by Kenneth R. R. Gros Louis. Nashville: Abingdon, 1974.

Blenkinsopp, Joseph. "Biographical Patterns in Biblical Narrative." *Journal for the Study of the Old Testament* 20 (1981) 27–46.

Bloch-Smith, Elizabeth M. "The Cult of the Dead in Judah: Interpreting the Material Remains." *Journal of Biblical Literature* 111 (1992) 213–24.

_____. *Judahite Burial Practices and Beliefs about the Dead*. Journal for the Study of the Old Testament Supplements 123. Sheffield: JSOT Press, 1992.

Bodi, Daniel. *The Book of Ezekiel and the Poem of Erra*. Orbis biblicus et orientalis 104. Freiburg: Universitätsverlag, 1991.

Bottéro, Jean. "The Cuisine of Ancient Mesopotamia." *Biblical Archaeologist* 48/1 (1985) 36–47.

Bremond, Claude. "The Morphology of the French Fairy Tale: The Ethical Model." Pp. 49–76 in *Patterns in Oral Literature*. Edited by Heda Jason and Dimitri Segal. The Hague: Mouton, 1977.

_____. "The Narrative Message." Translated by A. M. Johnson. *Semeia* 10 (*Narrative Syntax: Translations and Reviews*; 1978) 5–55.

Brichto, Herbert Chanan. "Kin, Cult, Land and Afterlife: A Biblical Complex." *Hebrew Union College Annual* 44 (1973) 1–54.

Bron, François. *Recherches sur les inscriptions phéniciennes de Karatepe*. Volume 2. Hautes Études Orientales 11. Geneva: Droz, 1979.

Buchan, David. *The Ballad and the Folk*. London: Routledge, 1972.

_____. "Propp's Tale Role and a Ballad Repertoire." *Journal of American Folklore* 95/376 (1982) 159–72.

_____. "Talerole Analysis and Child's Supernatural Ballads." Pp. 60–77 in *The Ballad and Oral Literature*. Edited by Joseph Harris. Harvard English Studies 17. Cambridge: Harvard University Press, 1991.

Buchler, Ira R., and Henry A. Selby. *A Formal Study of Myth*. University of Texas, Center for Intercultural Studies in Folklore and Oral History Monograph Series 1. Austin: University of Texas, 1968.

Buttrick, George Arthur (ed.). *Interpreter's Dictionary of the Bible*. New York: Abingdon, 1962.

Bynum, David E. "Samson as a Biblical *Pher Oreskos*." Pp. 53–63 in *Text and Tradition: The Hebrew Bible and Folklore*. Society of Biblical Literature Semeia Studies 20. Atlanta: Scholars Press, 1990.

Byock, Jesse. *Feud in the Icelandic Saga*. Berkeley: University of California Press, 1982.

Calloud, Jean. *Structural Analysis of Narrative*. Translated by D. Patte. Philadelphia: Fortress, 1976.

Camp, Claudia, and Carole R. Fontaine (eds.). *Semeia* 61 (*Women, War, and Metaphor: Language and Society in the Study of the Hebrew Bible*; 1993).

Carden, Patricia. "Fairy Tale, Myth, and Literature: Russian Structuralist Approaches." Pp. 179–97 in volume 9 of *Literary Criticism and Myth.* Edited by Joseph P. Strelka. Yearbook of Comparative Criticism. University Park, Pennsylvania: Pennsylvania State University Press, 1980.

Cazelles, H. "Alliance du Sinai, alliance de l'Horeb et renouvellement de l'alliance." Pp. 69–79 in *Beiträge zur Alttestamentichen Theologie: Festschrift für Walther Zimmerli zum 70. Geburtstag.* Edited by Herbert Donner, Robert Hanhart, and Rudolf Smend. Göttingen: Vandenhoeck & Ruprecht, 1977.

Centre pour l'Analyse du Discours Religieux. *Analyse semiotique des textes: Introduction, théorie, pratique.* Lyons: Presses Universitaires de Lyon, 1979.

Clay, A. T. *A Hebrew Deluge Story in Cuneiform.* New Haven: Yale University Press, 1922.

Clifford, Richard J. "Cosmogonies in the Ugaritic Texts and in the Bible." *Orientalia* 53 (1985) 183–201.

_____. "Mot Invites Baal to a Feast: Observations on a Difficult Ugaritic Text (CTA 5.i = KTU 1.5.1)." Pp. 55–64 in *"Working with No Data": Semitic and Egyptian Studies Presented to Thomas O. Lambdin.* Edited by David Marcus Golomb and Susan T. Hollis. Winona Lake, Indiana: Eisenbrauns, 1987.

_____. "The Temple in the Ugaritic Myth of Baal." Pp. 137–45 in *Symposia Celebrating the Seventy-Fifth Anniversary of the Founding of the American Schools of Oriental Research (1900–1975).* Edited by F. M. Cross. Zion Research Foundation Occasional Publications. Cambridge, Massachusetts: American Schools of Oriental Research, 1979.

Coats, George W. *Rebellion in the Wilderness: The Murmuring Motif in the Wilderness Traditions of the Old Testament.* Nashville: Abingdon, 1968.

Cogan, Mordechai, and Hayim Tadmor. *II Kings: A New Translation with Introduction and Commentary.* Anchor Bible 11. New York: Doubleday, 1988.

Conroy, Charles. *Absalom, Absalom! Narrative and Language in 2 Samuel 13–20.* Analecta biblica. Rome: Pontifical Biblical Institute, 1978.

Conybeare, F. C., J. Rendel Harris, and Agnes Smith Lewis. *The Story of Ahikar.* Cambridge: Cambridge University Press, 1913.

Coote, Robert B. (ed.). *Elijah and Elisha in Socioliterary Perspective.* Atlanta: Scholars Press, 1992.

Couffignal, Robert. "'Jacob lutte au Jabboq': Approches nouvelles de Genese, xxxii, 23–33." *Revue thomiste* 4 (1975) 582–97.

Craigie, Peter C. *The Problem of War in the Old Testament.* Grand Rapids, Michigan: Eerdmans, 1978.

Creed, Robert P. "A Context for the Study of Oral Traditions." *Pacific Quarterly (Moana)* 8/4 (1984) 11–15.

Cross, Frank Moore. "The Divine Warrior in Israel's Early Cult." Pp. 11–30 in *Biblical Motifs: Origins and Transformations.* Edited by Alexander Altmann. Cambridge: Harvard University Press, 1966.

_____. "The Epic Traditions of Early Israel: Epic Narrative and the Reconstruction of Early Israelite Institutions." Pp. 13–40 in *The Poet and the Historian: Essays in Literary and Historical Biblical Criticism.* Harvard Semitic Studies 26. Chico, California: Scholars Press, 1983.

Culler, Jonathan. *Structuralist Poetics: Structuralism, Linguistics and the Study of Literature*. Ithaca, New York: Cornell University Press, 1976.

Culley, Robert C. "Five Tales of Punishment in the Book of Numbers." Pp. 25–34 in *Text and Tradition: The Hebrew Bible and Folklore*. Edited by Susan Niditch. Society of Biblical Literature Semeia Studies 20. Atlanta: Scholars Press, 1990.

_____. "Oral Tradition and Historicity." Pp. 102–16 in *Studies on the Ancient Palestinian World*. Edited by J. Wevers. Toronto: University of Toronto Press, 1972.

_____. *Studies in the Structure of Hebrew Narrative*. Philadelphia: Fortress Press / Missoula, Montana: Scholars Press, 1976.

_____. *Themes and Variations: A Study of Action in Biblical Narrative*. Society of Biblical Literature Semeia Studies 23. Atlanta: Scholars Press, 1992.

Culley, Robert C. (ed.). *Semeia 5* (*Oral Tradition and Old Testament Studies*; 1976).

_____. *Semeia 3* (*Classical Hebrew Narrative*; 1975).

Dalley, Stephanie (trans.). *Myths from Mesopotamia: Creation, the Flood, Gilgamesh and Others*. Oxford: Oxford University Press, 1989.

Dan, Ilana. "The Innocent Persecuted Heroine: An Attempt at a Model for the Surface Level of the Narrative Structure of the Female Fairy Tale." Pp. 13–30 in *Patterns in Oral Literature*. Edited by Heda Jason and Dimitri Segal. The Hague: Mouton, 1977.

Davis, Ellen F. *Swallowing the Scroll: Textuality and the Dynamics of Discourse in Ezekiel's Prophecy*. Bible and Literature Series 21. Sheffield: Almond, 1989.

Deller, K. H. "*'mn Bll* (Hosea 12, 2): Additional Evidence." *Biblica* 46 (1965) 349–52.

Dentzer, Jean-Marie. *Le motif du banquet couché dans le Proche-Orient et le monde grec du VIIe au IVe siècle avant J.C.* Rome: École Française de Rome, 1982.

Derousseaux, Louis (ed.). *La création dans l'Orient ancien*. Paris: Cerf, 1987.

Dorson, Richard M. "The Eclipse of Solar Mythology." Pp. 57–83 in *The Study of Folklore*. Edited by Alan Dundes. Englewood Cliffs, New Jersey: Prentice-Hall, 1965.

Douglas, Mary. "The Abominations of Leviticus." Pp. 100–16 in *Anthropological Approaches to the Old Testament*. Issues in Religion and Theology 8. Philadelphia: Fortress, 1985.

_____. *Implicit Meanings: Essays in Anthropology*. London: Routledge & Kegan Paul, 1975.

_____. *In the Wilderness: The Doctrine of Defilement in the Book of Numbers*. Journal for the Study of the Old Testament Supplements 158. Sheffield: Sheffield Academic Press, 1993.

_____. *Purity and Danger: An Analysis of Concepts of Pollution and Taboo*. New York: Praeger, 1966 / London: Routledge & Kegan Paul, 1978.

Driel, G. van. *The Cult of Assur*. Assen: Van Gorcum, 1969.

Driver, G. R. *Canaanite Myths and Legends*. Old Testament Studies 3. Edinburgh: T. & T. Clark, 1976.

Driver, S. R. *Notes on the Hebrew Text of the Books of Samuel, with an Introduction on Hebrew Palaeography.* Oxford: Clarendon, 1890.

Drory, Rina. "Ali Baba and the Forty Thieves: An Attempt at a Model for the Narrative Structure of the Reward-and-Punishment Fairy Tale." Pp. 31–48 in *Patterns in Oral Literature.* Edited by Heda Jason and Dimitri Segal. The Hague: Mouton, 1977.

Dundes, Alan. *Analytic Essays in Folklore.* The Hague: Mouton, 1975.

_____. *Essays in Folkloristics.* Kirpa Dai Series in Folklore and Anthropology 1. New Delhi: Folklore Institute, 1978.

_____. *Folklore Matters.* Knoxville: University of Tennessee Press, 1989.

_____. "From Etic to Emic Units in the Structural Study of Folktales." *Journal of American Folklore* 75 (1962) 95–105.

_____. *Interpreting Folklore.* Bloomington, Indiana: Indiana University Press, 1980.

_____. *The Morphology of North American Indian Folktales.* Folklore Fellows Communications 195. Helsinki: Suomalainen Tiedeakatemia / Academia Scientiarum Fennica, 1964.

_____. "On Game Morphology: A Study of the Structure of Non-verbal Folklore." *New York Folklore Quarterly* 20 (1964) 276–88.

Dundes, Alan (ed.). *The Flood Myth.* Berkeley: University of California Press, 1988.

_____. *Sacred Narrative: Readings in the Theory of Myth.* Berkeley: University of California Press, 1984.

_____. *The Study of Folklore.* Englewood Cliffs, New Jersey: Prentice-Hall, 1965.

Durand, Xavier. "Le Combat de Jacob: Gn 32, 23–33." Pp. 99–115 in *L'Ancien Testament: Approches et lectures.* Le Point Theologique 24. Paris: Institut Catholique de Paris, 1977.

Eagleton, Terry. *Literary Theory: An Introduction.* Minneapolis: University of Minnesota Press, 1983.

Edmunds, Lowell (ed.). *Approaches to Greek Myth.* Baltimore: Johns Hopkins University Press, 1990.

Eissfeldt, Otto. "Kultvereine in Ugarit." *Ugaritica* 6 (1969) 187–95.

Enelow, H. G. (ed.). *The Mishnah of Rabbi Eliezer, or the Midrash of Thirty-Two Hermeneutic Rules.* New York: Block, 1933. [Hebrew with English introduction]

Erlich, Victor. *Russian Formalism: History–Doctrine.* 3d ed. Slavistic Printings and Reprintings 4. The Hague: Mouton, 1969.

Fenik, Bernard. *Homer and the* Nibelungenlied*: Comparative Studies in Epic Style.* Martin Classical Lectures 30. Cambridge, Massachusetts: Published for Oberlin College by Harvard University Press, 1986.

_____. *Homer, Tradition and Invention.* Cincinnati Classical Studies new series 2. Leiden: Brill, 1978.

Fensham, C. F. "The Wild Ass in the Aramaic Treaty between Bargaʾayah and MatiʾEl." *Journal of Near Eastern Studies* 22 (1963) 185–86.

Ferrara, A. J. *Nanna-Suen's Journey to Nippur.* Studia Pohl: Series Maior 2. Rome: Pontifical Biblical Institute, 1973.

Ferrara, A. J., and S. B. Parker. "Seating Arrangements at Divine Banquets." *Ugarit-Forschungen* 4 (1972) 37–39.

Fewell, Danna Nolan (ed.). *Reading between Texts: Intertextuality and the Hebrew Bible.* Literary Currents in Biblical Interpretation. Louisville: Westminster/John Knox, 1992.

Finnegan, Ruth H. *Oral Literature in Africa.* London: Clarendon, 1970.

_____. *Oral Poetry: Its Nature, Significance, and Social Context.* Cambridge: Cambridge University Press, 1977.

_____. *Oral Traditions and the Verbal Arts: A Guide to Research Practices.* ASA Research Methods in Social Anthropology. London: Routledge, 1992.

Firmage, Edwin. "The Biblical Dietary Laws and the Concept of Holiness." Pp. 177–208 in *Studies in the Pentateuch.* Edited by J. A. Emerton. Vetus Testamentum Supplements 41. Leiden: Brill, 1990.

Fishbane, Michael. *Text and Texture.* New York: Schocken, 1979.

_____. "The Well of Living Water: A Biblical Motif and Its Ancient Transformations." Pp. 3–32 in *"Shaʿarei Talmon": Studies in the Bible, Qumran, and the Ancient Near East Presented to Shemaryahu Talmon.* Edited by Michael Fishbane and Emanuel Tov, assisted by Weston W. Fields. Winona Lake, Indiana: Eisenbrauns, 1992.

Fohrer, Georg. *Die symbolischen Handlungen der Propheten.* Zurich: Zwingli, 1953.

Fokkelman, Jan P. "Structural Remarks on Judges 9 and 19." Pp. 33–45 in *"Shaʿarei Talmon": Studies in the Bible, Qumran, and the Ancient Near East Presented to Shemaryahu Talmon.* Edited by Michael Fishbane and Emanuel Tov, assisted by Weston W. Fields. Winona Lake, Indiana: Eisenbrauns, 1992.

Foley, John Miles. *Immanent Art: From Structure to Meaning in Traditional Oral Epic.* Bloomington, Indiana: Indiana University Press, 1991.

_____. *Oral-Formulaic Theory and Research: An Introduction and Annotated Bibliography.* New York: Garland, 1985.

Foley, John Miles (ed.). *Comparative Research on Oral Traditions: A Memorial for Milman Parry.* Columbus, Ohio: Slavica, 1987.

_____. *Oral Traditional Literature: A Festschrift for Albert Bates Lord.* Columbus, Ohio: Slavica, 1981.

Fontaine, Carole R. "The Deceptive Goddess in Ancient Near Eastern Myth: Inanna and Inara." *Semeia* 42 (*Reasoning with the Foxes: Female Wit in a World of Male Power*; 1988) 84–102.

_____. "Folktale Structure in the Book of Job: A Formalist Reading." Pp. 205–32 in *Directions in Biblical Hebrew Poetry.* Journal for the Study of the Old Testament Supplements 40. Sheffield: JSOT Press, 1987.

Foster, Benjamin. *Before the Muses: An Anthology of Akkadian Literature.* 2 volumes. Bethesda, Maryland: CDL, 1993.

Fox, Everett. *In the Beginning: A New English Rendition of the Book of Genesis.* Translated with commentary and notes. New York: Schocken, 1983.

Frankel, Yonah. *The Ways of Aggadah and Midrash* [Hebrew]. Yad Le-Talmud. Jerusalem: Massada, 1991.

Frankena, R. *Takultu: De Sacrale Maaltijd in het Assyrische Ritueel, met een Over-zicht over de in Assur Vereerde Goden.* Leiden: Brill, 1954.

Frazer, Sir James George. *Folk-Lore in the Old Testament: Studies in Comparative Religion Legend and Law.* Abridged ed. New York: Tudor, 1923.

Frymer-Kensky, Tikva. "The Atrahasis Epic and Its Significance for Our Under-standing of Genesis 1–9." *Biblical Archaeologist* 40 (December 1977) 147–55.

_____. "The Strange Case of the Suspected Sotah (Numbers v 11–31)." *Vetus Testamentum* 34 (1984) 11–26.

Garfinkel, Stephen. "Another Model for Ezekiel's Abnormalities." *Journal of the Ancient Near Eastern Society* 19 (1989) 39–50.

Gaster, Theodor H. *Myth, Legend and Custom in the Old Testament: A Compara-tive Study with Chapters from Sir James G. Frazer's Folklore in the Old Testa-ment.* New York: Harper & Row, 1969.

Gelb, I. J. "Review of D. J. Wiseman, *The Vassal Treaties of Esarhaddon.*" *Biblio-theca orientalis* 19 (1962) 159–62.

Gelb, I. J., and E. Reiner (eds.). *The Assyrian Dictionary of the Oriental Institute of the University of Chicago.* Chicago: Oriental Institute, 1956–.

Geller, Stephen A. "The Sack of Shechem: The Use of Typology in Biblical Covenant Religion." *Prooftexts* 10 (1990) 1–15.

_____. *Sacred Enigmas: Literary Religion in the Hebrew Bible.* London: Routledge, 1996.

_____. "The Struggle at the Jabbok: The Uses of Enigma in Biblical Narrative." *Journal of the Ancient Near Eastern Society* 14 (1984) 37–60.

_____. "Through Windows and Mirrors into the Bible: History, Literature and Language in the Study of Text." Pp. 3–40 in *A Sense of Text: The Art of Lan-guage in the Study of Biblical Literature.* Jewish Quarterly Review Supple-ment Series. Edited by Stephen A. Geller, with contributions by Adele Berlin, Stephen A. Geller, and Edward L. Greenstein. Philadelphia: Cen-ter for Judaic Studies, 1982.

Genest, Olivette. "Analyse semiotique de Gn 22, 1–19." *Science et Esprit* 33/2 (1981) 157–77.

Gerleman, Gillis. *Esther.* Biblischer Kommentar Altes Testament 21/1. Neu-kirchen-Vluyn: Neukirchener Verlag, 1970.

Gibson, John. *Textbook of Syrian Semitic Inscriptions.* Phoenician Inscriptions 3. Oxford: Clarendon, 1982.

Ginsberg, H. L. "Hosea, Book of." Pp. 1010–24 in volume 8 of *Encyclopaedia Ju-daica.* Jerusalem: Keter, 1972.

_____. "A Strand in the Cord of Hebrew Hymnody." *Eretz-Israel* 9 (*Albright Vol-ume*; 1969) 45–50.

Glassner, J. J. "L'Hospitalité en Mesopotamie ancienne: Aspect de la question de l'étranger." *Zeitschrift für Assyriologie* 80 (1990) 60–75.

_____. "Women, Hospitality, and the Honor of the Family." Pp. 71–90 in *Women's Earliest Records from Ancient Egypt and Western Asia: Proceedings of the Conference on Women in the Ancient Near East, Brown University, Novem-ber 5–7, 1987.* Edited by B. Lesko. Brown Judaic Studies 166. Atlanta: Scholars Press, 1989.

Golka, Friedmann W. "Aetiologies in the Old Testament 1." *Vetus Testamentum* 26 (October 1976) 410–28.

_____. "Aetiologies in the Old Testament 2." *Vetus Testamentum* 27 (1977) 36–47.

Gordis, Daniel H. "Lies, Wives and Sisters: The Wife-Sister Motif Revisited." *Judaism* 34 (summer 1985) 344–59.

Görög-Karady, Veronika. "Retelling Genesis: The Children of Eve and the Origin of Inequality." Pp. 31–44 in *Genres, Forms, Meanings: Essays in African Oral Literature*. Edited by Veronika Görög-Karady. Paris: MSH / Oxford: JASO, 1983.

Görög-Karady, Veronika (ed.). *Genres, Forms, Meanings: Essays in African Oral Literature*. With a foreword by Ruth Finnegan. Paris: MSH / Oxford: JASO, 1983.

Görög-Karady, Veronika, and Michele Chiche (eds.). *D'un conte . . . à l'autre: La variabilité dans la littérature orale*. Paris: Centre Nationale de la Recherche Scientifique, 1990.

Gottlieb, Isaac B. "*Sof Davar*: Biblical Endings." *Prooftexts* 11 (1991) 213–24.

Gottschalk, Alfred. "The Image of Man in Genesis and in the Ancient Near East." *Maarav* 7 (1991) 131–40.

Gould, Kent. "*Beowulf* and Folktale Morphology: God as Magical Donor." *Folklore* 96/1 (1985) 98–103.

Granowski, Jan Jaynes. "Jehoiachin at the King's Table: A Reading of the Ending of the Second Book of Kings." Pp. 173–88 in *Reading between Texts: Intertextuality and the Hebrew Bible*. Literary Currents in Biblical Interpretation. Louisville: Westminster / John Knox Press, 1992.

Gray, George Buchanan. *A Critical and Exegetical Commentary on the Book of Isaiah*, volume 1: *Introduction and Commentary on I–XXVII*. International Critical Commentary. Edinburgh: T. & T. Clark, 1980.

_____. *A Critical and Exegetical Commentary on Numbers*. International Critical Commentary. Edinburgh: T. & T. Clark, 1986.

Green, Barbara Gail. *A Study of Field and Seed Symbolism in the Biblical Story of Ruth*. Ph.D. dissertation, Graduate Theological Union, 1980.

Greenberg, Moshe. "The Design and Themes of Ezekiel's Program of Restoration." *Interpretation* 38 (1984) 181–208.

_____. "On Ezekiel's Dumbness." *Journal of Biblical Literature* 77 (1958) 101–5.

Greenfield, Jonas C. "The *Marzeah* as a Social Institution." *Acta Antiqua Acad. Sc. Hungaricae* 22 (1974) 452–55.

Greengus, Samuel. "Sisterhood Adoption at Nuzi and the 'Wife-Sister' in Genesis." *Hebrew Union College Annual* 46 (1975) 5–31.

Greenspahn, Frederick E. *When Brothers Dwell Together: The Preeminence of Younger Siblings in the Hebrew Bible*. New York: Oxford University Press, 1994.

Greenstein, Edward L. "Autobiographies in Ancient Western Asia." Pp. 2421–32 in *Civilizations of the Ancient Near East*. Edited by Jack M. Sasson. New York: Scribner's, 1995.

_____. "Biblical Narratology." *Prooftexts* 1 (1981) 201–8.

_____. "Deconstruction and Biblical Narrative." *Prooftexts* 9 (1989) 43–71.

_____. "Exodus." Pp. 77–150 in *The HarperCollins Study Bible*. Revised edition by Wayne A. Meeks et al. New York: HarperCollins, 1993.

_____. "The Firstborn Plague and the Reading Process." Pp. 555–68 in *Pomegranates and Golden Bells: Studies in Biblical, Jewish, and Near Eastern Ritual, Law, and Literature in Honor of Jacob Milgrom*. Edited by David A. Wright, David Noel Freedman, and Avi Hurvitz. Winona Lake, Indiana: Eisenbrauns, 1995.

_____. "Reader Responsibility: Making Sense and Non-sense of Biblical Narrative." The Aaron-Roland Lecture, Stanford University. Palo Alto, California, 1992.

_____. "The Riddle of Samson." *Prooftexts* 1/3 (1981) 237–60.

Greenstein, Edward L., and David Marcus. "The Akkadian Inscription of Idrimi." *Journal of the Ancient Near Eastern Society* 8 (1976) 49–57.

Groden, Michael, and Martin Kreiswirth (eds.). *The Johns Hopkins Guide to Literary Theory and Criticism*. Baltimore: Johns Hopkins University Press, 1994.

Gros Louis, Kenneth R. R. "Elijah and Elisha." Pp. 177–90 in *Literary Interpretations of Biblical Narratives*. Nashville: Abingdon, 1974.

Gruber, Mayer Irwin. *Aspects of Non-verbal Communication in the Ancient Near East*. Studia Pohl: Series Minor 12. Rome: Pontifical Biblical Institute, 1980.

Gunkel, Hermann. *The Folktale in the Old Testament*. Translated by Michael D. Rutter, with an introduction by John W. Rogerson. Sheffield: Almond, 1987.

_____. *The Legends of Genesis*. New York: Schocken, 1974.

Gunn, David M. "Narrative Patterns and Oral Tradition in Judges and Samuel." *Vetus Testamentum* 24 (1974) 286–317.

_____. "Traditional Composition in the 'Succession Narrative.'" *Vetus Testamentum* 26 (1976) 214–29.

Gunneweg, A. H. J. "Sinaibund und Davidsbund." *Vetus Testamentum* 10 (1960) 335–41.

Hagan, Harry. "Deception as Motif and Theme in 2 Sm 9–20; 1 Kgs 1–2." *Biblica* 60 (1979) 301–26.

Hallo, William W. "Information from before the Flood: Antediluvian Notes from Babylonia and Israel." *Maarav* 7 (1991) 173–81.

_____. "The Origins of the Sacrificial Cult: New Evidence from Mesopotamia and Israel." Pp. 3–13 in *Ancient Israelite Religion: Essays in Honor of Frank Moore Cross*. Edited by Patrick D. Miller Jr., Paul D. Hanson, and S. Dean McBride. Philadelphia: Fortress, 1987.

_____. "Royal Ancestor Worship in the Biblical World." Pp. 381–401 in *"Sha'arei Talmon": Studies in the Bible, Qumran, and the Ancient Near East Presented to Shemaryahu Talmon*. Edited by Michael Fishbane and Emanuel Tov, assisted by Weston W. Fields. Winona Lake, Indiana: Eisenbrauns, 1992.

_____. "The Royal Correspondence of Larsa: I. A Sumerian Prototype for the Prayer of Hezekiah?" Pp. 209–24 in *Kramer Anniversary Volume: Cuneiform*

Studies in Honor of Samuel Noah Kramer. Edited by Barry L. Eichler. Alter Orient und Altes Testament 25. Kevelaer: Butzon & Bercker, 1976.

Hallo, William W., James C. Moyer, and Leo G. Perdue (eds.). *Scripture in Context II: More Essays on the Comparative Method.* Winona Lake, Indiana: Eisenbrauns, 1983.

Halpern, Baruch. "The Artifact and the Text: Two Monologues?" Pp. 311–34 in *The Archaeology of Israel: Constructing the Past, Interpreting the Present.* Journal for the Study of the Old Testament Supplements 237. Sheffield: Sheffield Academic Press, 1997.

Hanson, Paul D. "1 Chronicles 15–16 and the Chronicler's Views on the Levites." Pp. 69–91 in *"Shaʿarei Talmon": Studies in the Bible, Qumran, and the Ancient Near East Presented to Shemaryahu Talmon.* Edited by Michael Fishbane and Emanuel Tov, assisted by Weston W. Fields. Winona Lake, Indiana: Eisenbrauns, 1992.

Haran, Menahem. *Temples and Temple-Service in Ancient Israel: An Inquiry into Biblical Cult Phenomena and the Historical Setting of the Priestly School.* Oxford: Clarendon, 1978. Reprinted, Winona Lake, Indiana: Eisenbrauns, 1985.

Harrop, Peter. "Towards a Morphology of the English Folk Play." *Lore and Language* 5/2 (1986) 63–99.

Hasel, G. *The Remnant: The History and Theology of the Remnant Idea from Genesis to Isaiah.* Andrews University Monograph 5. Berrien Springs, Michigan: Andrews University, 1972.

Hawking, Stephen. *A Brief History of Time.* New York: Bantam, 1986.

Hawthorn, Jeremy. *A Concise Glossary of Contemporary Literary Theory.* London: Edward Arnold, 1992.

Heidel, Alexander. *The Gilgamesh Epic and Old Testament Parallels.* 2d ed. Chicago: University of Chicago Press, 1949.

Held, M. "Philological Notes on the Mari Covenant Rituals." *Bulletin of the American Schools of Oriental Research* 200 (1970) 32–40.

Hendel, Ronald S. *The Epic of the Patriarch: The Jacob Cycle and the Narrative Traditions of Canaan and Israel.* Harvard Semitic Monographs 42. Atlanta: Scholars Press, 1987.

Hendricks, William O. *Essays on Semiolinguistics and Verbal Art.* The Hague: Mouton, 1973.

_____. *Grammars of Style and Styles of Grammar.* North-Holland Studies in Theoretical Poetics 3. Amsterdam: North-Holland Publishing, 1976.

_____. "The Notion of Style." *Language and Style* 13/1 (1980) 35–54.

Henige, David. "Oral, but Oral What? The Nomenclatures of Orality and Their Implications." *Oral Tradition* 3/1–2 (1988) 229–38.

Hesiod. *Hesiod, the Homeric Hymns, and Homerica.* Translated by H. G. Evelyn-White. 1914. Loeb Classical Library. Cambridge: Harvard University Press / London: Heinemann, 1982.

Hillers, Delbert R., and Marsh H. McCall Jr. "Homeric Dictated Texts: A Reexamination of Some Near Eastern Evidence." *Harvard Studies in Classical Philology* 80 (1976) 19–23.

Hirsch, E. D., Jr. "In Defense of the Author." Pp. 11–23 in *Intention and Interpretation*. Edited by Gary Iseminger. Philadelphia: Temple University Press, 1992.

_____. *Validity in Interpretation*. New Haven: Yale University Press, 1967.

Hoffner, Harry A., Jr. *Orient and Occident: Essays Presented to Cyrus H. Gordon on the Occasion of His Sixty-Fifth Birthday*. Alter Orient und Altes Testament 22. Neukirchen-Vluyn: Neukirchener Verlag, 1973.

_____. *Hittite Myths*. Society of Biblical Literature Writings from the Ancient World. Atlanta: Scholars Press, 1990.

Hollis, Martin. *Models of Man: Philosophical Thoughts on Social Action*. Cambridge: Cambridge University Press, 1977.

Holloway, S. W. "What Ship Goes There? The Flood Narratives in the Gilgamesh Epic and Genesis Considered in Light of Ancient Near East Temple Ideology." *Zeitschrift für die alttestamentliche Wissenschaft* 103 (1991) 328–55.

Homer. *The Odyssey I*. Translated by A. T. Murray. Loeb Classical Library. Cambridge: Harvard University Press, 1919.

Huffmon, H. B. "The Exodus, Sinai and the Credo." *Catholic Biblical Quarterly* 27 (1965) 101–15.

Humphreys, W. Lee. "A Lifestyle for Diaspora: A Study of the Tales of Esther and Daniel." *Journal of Biblical Literature* 92 (1973) 211–23.

_____. "The Motif of the Wise Courtier in the Book of Proverbs." Pp. 177–90 in *Israelite Wisdom: Theological and Literary Essays in Honor of Samuel Terrien*. Edited by John G. Gammie et al. New York: Union Theological Seminary, 1978.

Hurowitz, Avigdor (Victor). *Temple Building in the Bible in Light of Mesopotamian and North-West Semitic Writings*. Ph.D. dissertation, Hebrew University, 1983. [Hebrew]

Illman, Karl-Johan. *Old Testament Formulas about Death*. Publications of the Research Institute of the Åbo Akademi Foundation 48. Åbo, Finland: Åbo Akademi, 1979.

Iser, Wolfgang. *The Act of Reading: A Theory of Aesthetic Response*. Baltimore: Johns Hopkins University Press, 1978.

_____. *The Implied Reader: Patterns of Communication in Prose Fiction from Bunyan to Beckett*. Baltimore: Johns Hopkins University Press, 1974.

_____. "The Reading Process: A Phenomenological Approach." Pp. 50–69 in *Reader-Response Criticism*. Edited by Jane P. Tompkins. Baltimore: Johns Hopkins University Press, 1980.

Izre'el, Shlomo. *The Myth of Adapa and the South Wind: Language Has the Power of Life and Death*. Mesopotamian Civilizations 10. Winona Lake, Indiana: Eisenbrauns, 2001.

Jansen, William Hugh. "The Esoteric-Exoteric Factor in Folklore." Pp. 43–52 in *The Study of Folklore*. Edited by Alan Dundes. Englewood Cliffs, New Jersey: Prentice-Hall, 1965.

Japhet, Sara. *The Ideology of the Book of Chronicles and Its Place in Biblical Thought*. Frankfurt am Main: Peter Lang, 1989.

Jason, Heda. "Content Analysis of Oral Literature." Comments by B. N. Colby, R. A. Georges, and P. Maranda. Pp. 261–310 in *Patterns in Oral Literature*. Edited by Heda Jason and Dimitri Segal. The Hague: Mouton, 1977.

_____. *Ethnopoetry: Form, Content, Function*. Forum Theologiae Linguisticae 11. Bonn: Linguistica Biblica, 1977.

_____. "The Fairy Tale of the Active Heroine: An Outline for Discussion." Pp. 79–97 in *Le conte, pourquoi? comment?: Actes des Journées d'Études en Littérature Orale / Analyse des contes—Problemes de methodes, Paris, March 23–26, 1982*. Edited by Geneviève Calame-Griaule, Veronika Görög-Karady, and Michele Chiche. Paris: Centre National de la Recherche Scientifique, 1984.

_____. "Ilja of Murom and Tzar Kalin: A Proposal for a Model for the Narrative Structure of an Epic Struggle." Pp. 47–55 in *Slavica Hierosolymitana: Slavic Studies of the Hebrew University*. Edited by L. Fleishman, O. Ronen, and D. Segal. Center for the Study of Slavic Languages and Literatures at the Hebrew University of Jerusalem. Jerusalem: Magnes, 1981.

_____. "The Lion Slayer and the Clever Princess: Case Study of a Multigenre Folktale." Pp. 110–34 in *Studies in Turkish Folklore in Honor of Pertev N. Boratav*. Turkish Studies 1. Bloomington, Indiana: Indiana University Press, 1978.

_____. "A Model for Narrative Structure in Oral Literature." Comments by C. Bremond. Pp. 99–140 in *Patterns in Oral Literature*. Edited by Heda Jason and Dimitri Segal. The Hague: Mouton, 1977.

_____. "The Narrative Structure of Swindler Tales." *Arv: Journal of Scandinavian Folklore* 27 (1971) 141–60.

_____. "Russian Criticism of the 'Finnish School' in Folklore Scholarship." *Norveg* 14 (1970) 285–94.

_____. "The Story of David and Goliath: A Folk Epic?" Translated by Sara Mishan. *Biblica* 60 (1979) 36–70.

_____. "Structural Analysis and the Concept of the Tale Type." *Arv, Journal of Scandinavian Folklore* 28 (1972) 36–54.

Jason, Heda, and Dimitri Segal (eds.). *Patterns in Oral Literature*. The Hague: Mouton, 1977.

Jobling, David. " 'The Jordan a Boundary': A Reading of Numbers 32 and Joshua 22." Pp. 183–207 in *Society of Biblical Literature 1980: Seminar Papers*. Society of Biblical Literature Seminar Papers 19. Chico, California: Scholars Press, 1980.

_____. *The Sense of Biblical Narrative: Structural Analyses in the Hebrew Bible II*. Journal for the Study of the Old Testament Supplement 39. Sheffield: Sheffield Academic Press, 1987

Jones, Steven Swann. *The New Comparative Method: Structural and Symbolic Analysis of the Allomotifs of "Snow White."* Folklore Fellows Communications 247. Helsinki: Suomalainen Tiedeakatemia, 1990.

_____. "Structural and Thematic Applications of the Comparative Method: A Case Study of 'The Kind and Unkind Girls.' " *Journal of Folklore Research* 23/2–3 (1986) 147–61.

Kaivola-Bregenhoj, Annikki. "Variability and Narrative Context." Pp. 47–63 in *D'un conte . . . à l'autre: La Variabilité dans la littérature orale.* Edited by Veronika Görög-Karady and Michele Chiche. Paris: Centre Nationale de la Recherche Scientifique, 1990.

Keel, Othmar. *The Symbolism of the Biblical World: Ancient Near Eastern Iconography and the Book of Psalms.* New York: Seabury, 1978. Reprinted, Winona Lake, Indiana: Eisenbrauns, 1997.

Kikawada, Isaac M., and Arthur Quinn. *Before Abraham Was.* Nashville: Abingdon, 1985.

Kilmer, Anne Draffkorn. "How Was Queen Ereshkigal Tricked?: A New Interpretation of the Descent of Ishtar." *Ugarit-Forschungen* 3 (1971) 299–309.

King, Philip J. "The *Marzeah* Amos Denounces: Using Archaeology to Interpret a Biblical Text." *Biblical Archaeology Review* 15 (August 1988) 34–44.

Kirk, G. S. *Myth: Its Meaning and Functions in Ancient and Other Cultures.* Berkeley: University of California Press, 1970.

Kirkpatrick, Patricia G. *The Old Testament and Folklore Study.* Journal for the Study of the Old Testament Supplements 62. Sheffield: JSOT Press, 1988.

Kittel, R. (ed.). *Biblia Hebraica Stuttgartensia.* Assisted by A. Alt, O. Eissfeldt, P. Kahle, et al. Stuttgart: Deutsche Bibelgesellschaft, 1990.

Kline, Morris. *Mathematical Thought from Ancient to Modern Times.* New York: Oxford University Press, 1972.

_____. *Mathematics: The Loss of Certainty.* New York: Oxford University Press, 1980.

Kluckhohn, Clyde. "Recurrent Themes in Myths and Mythmaking." Pp. 158–68 in *The Study of Folklore.* Edited by Alan Dundes. Englewood Cliffs, New Jersey: Prentice-Hall, 1965.

Koehler, Ludwig, Walter Baumgartner, and Johann Jakob Stamm. *The Hebrew and Aramaic Lexicon of the Old Testament in English.* Translated by M. E. J. Richardson. 5 volumes. Leiden: Brill, 1994–2000.

Kooy, V. H. "Symbol, Symbolism." Pp. 472–76 in volume 4 of *International Dictionary of the Bible.* Nashville: Abingdon, 1962.

Köpeczi, Béla, and Gyögy M. Vajda (eds.). *Actes du VIIIᵉ Congrès de l'Association Internationale de Littérature Comparée II: Littératures de Diverses Cultures au Vingtième Siècle et Littérature Comparée et Théorie Littéraire.* Stuttgart: Bieber, 1980.

Korosec, V. "Les Hittites et leurs vassaux syriens à la lumière des nouveaux textes d'Ugarit." *Revue hittite et asianique* 66–67 (1960) 65–79.

Kramer, Samuel Noah. *Enki and Ninhursag: A Sumerian "Paradise" Myth.* American Schools of Oriental Research Supplementary Studies 1. New Haven: American Schools of Oriental Research, 1945.

_____. *History Begins at Sumer: Twenty-Seven "Firsts" in Man's Recorded History.* Garden City, New York: Doubleday, 1958.

_____. *Sumerian Mythology: A Study of Spiritual and Literary Achievement in the Third Millennium B.C.* Illustrated ed. Harper Torchbooks. The Academy Library, 1944. Reprinted, New York: Harper & Brothers, 1961.

Krohn, Kaarle. *Folklore Methodology. Formulated by Julius Krohn and Expanded by Nordic Researchers.* Translated by Roger L. Welsch. Publications of the American Folklore Society: Bibliographic and Special Series 21. Austin: University of Texas Press, 1971.

Kutsch, E. "'Bund' und Fest." *Theologische Quartalschrift* 150 (1970) 299–320.

Lambert, W. G., and A. R. Millard. *Atra-ḫasis: The Babylonian Story of the Flood.* Oxford: Clarendon, 1969.

Lasine, Stuart. "Guest and Host in Judges 19: Lot's Hospitality in an Inverted World." *Journal for the Study of the Old Testament* 29 (1984) 37–59.

_____. "Jehoram and the Cannibal Mothers (2 Kings 6.24–33): Solomon's Judgment in an Inverted World." *Journal for the Study of the Old Testament* 50 (1991) 27–53.

Leach, Edmund. *Genesis as Myth and Other Essays.* London: Jonathan Cape, 1969.

Leach, Edmund, and D. Alan Aycock (eds.). *Structuralist Interpretations of Biblical Myth.* Royal Anthropological Institute of Great Britain and Ireland. London: Cambridge University Press, 1983.

Levenson, Jon D. *The Death and Resurrection of the Beloved Son: The Transformation of Child Sacrifice in Judaism and Christianity.* New Haven: Yale University Press, 1993.

_____. *Theology of the Program of Restoration of Ezekiel 40–48.* Harvard Semitic Monographs 10. Missoula, Montana: Scholars Press, 1976.

Levine, Baruch A. *In the Presence of the Lord: A Study of Cult and Some Cultic Terms in Ancient Israel.* Studies in Judaism in Late Antiquity 5. Leiden: Brill, 1974.

_____. "Silence, Sound, and the Phenomenology of Mourning in Biblical Israel." *Journal of the Near Eastern Society* 22 (1993) 89–106.

Lévi-Strauss, Claude. *Introduction to a Science of Mythology.* 4 volumes. Translated by John Weightman and Doreen Weightman. New York: Harper & Row, 1979.

_____. *Structural Anthropology II.* Chicago: University of Chicago Press, 1976.

_____. "The Structural Study of Myth." Pp. 81–106 in *Myth: A Symposium.* Edited by Thomas A. Sebeok. Bloomington, Indiana: Indiana University Press, 1972.

Lewis, Theodore J. *Cults of the Dead in Ancient Israel and Ugarit.* Harvard Semitic Monographs 39. Atlanta: Scholars Press, 1989.

Lichtenstein, Murray H. "The Banquet Motif in Keret and in Proverbs 9." *Journal of the Ancient Near Eastern Society of Columbia University* 1 (1968) 19–31.

_____. *Episodic Structure in the Ugaritic Keret Legend: Comparative Studies in Compositional Technique.* Ph.D. dissertation, Columbia University, 1979.

_____. "The Poetry of Poetic Justice: A Comparative Study in Biblical Imagery." *Journal of The Ancient Near Eastern Society of Columbia University* 5 (1973) 255–65.

Lichtheim, Miriam. *Ancient Egyptian Literature, Volume I: The Old and Middle Kingdoms.* Berkeley: University of California Press, 1973.

_____. *Ancient Egyptian Literature, Volume II: The New Kingdom.* Berkeley: University of California Press, 1976.

_____. *Ancient Egyptian Literature, Volume III: The Late Period.* Berkeley: University of California Press, 1980.

Lind, Millard C. *Yahweh Is a Warrior: The Theology of Warfare in Ancient Israel.* With a foreword by David Noel Freedman and an introduction by John H. Yoder. Scottdale, Pennsylvania: Herald, 1980.

Lipiński, E. "Banquet en l'honneur de Baal: CTA 3 (V AB), A, 4–22." *Ugarit-Forschungen* 2 (1970) 75–88.

Little, William, H. W. Fowler, and J. Coulson. *The Shorter Oxford English Dictionary.* Revised by C. T. Onions. Oxford: Clarendon, 1933.

Lloyd, J. B. "The Banquet Theme in Ugaritic Narrative." *Ugarit-Forschungen* 22 (1990) 167–93.

Lloyd-Jones, Hugh. "Becoming Homer: Composition and Transmission of Ancient Texts—A Review Essay." *New York Review of Books* 39 (5 March 1992) 52–57.

Loewenstamm, Samuel E. *Comparative Studies in Biblical and Ancient Oriental Literatures.* Alter Orient und Altes Testament 204. Kevelaer: Butzon & Bercker. Neukirchen-Vluyn: Neukirchener Verlag, 1980.

_____. *From Babylon to Canaan: Studies in the Bible and Its Oriental Background.* Perry Foundation for Biblical Research in the Hebrew University of Jerusalem. Jerusalem: Magnes, 1992.

_____. "The Making and Destruction of the Golden Calf." *Biblica* 48 (1967) 481–90.

Lohfink, Norbert. "Poverty in the Laws of the Ancient Near East and of the Bible." *Theological Studies* 52 (1991) 34–50.

Lohr, Charles H. "Oral Techniques in the Gospel of Matthew." *Catholic Biblical Quarterly* 23 (October 1961) 403–35.

Long, Burke O. *The Problem of Etiological Narrative in the Old Testament.* Beihefte zur Zeitschrift für die Alttestamentliche Wissenschaft 108. Berlin: Alfred Töpelmann, 1968.

_____. "Recent Field Studies in Oral Literature and Their Bearing on OT Criticism." *Vetus Testamentum* 26 (1976) 187–98.

_____. *Second Kings.* Forms of the Old Testament Literature 10. Grand Rapids, Michigan: Eerdmans, 1991.

_____. "The Social Setting for Prophetic Miracle Stories." *Semeia* 3 (*Classical Hebrew Narrative*; 1975) 46–63.

Lord, Albert B. "Characteristics of Orality." *Oral Tradition* 2/1 (1987) 54–72.

_____. *Epic Singers and Oral Tradition.* Myth and Poetics. Ithaca, New York: Cornell University Press, 1991.

_____. "Formula and Non-narrative Theme in South Slavic Oral Epic and the OT." *Semeia* 5 (*Oral Tradition and Old Testament Studies*; 1976) 93–105.

_____. "The Gospels as Oral Traditional Literature." Reply by C. Talbert, discussion paper by L. Keck. Pp. 33–91, 93–102, and 103–22 in *The Relationships among the Gospels: An Interdisciplinary Dialogue.* Edited by William O. Walker, Jr. San Antonio: Trinity University Press, 1978.

_____. "Patterns of Lives of the Patriarchs from Abraham to Samson and Samuel." Pp. 7–18 in *Text and Tradition: The Hebrew Bible and Folklore*. Edited by Susan Niditch. Society of Biblical Literature Semeia Studies 20. Atlanta: Scholars Press, 1990.

_____. *The Singer of Tales*. Harvard Studies in Comparative Literature 24. Cambridge: Harvard University Press, 1960.

Mackenzie, J. A. Ross. "Symbol." Pp. 1003–7 in *Harper's Bible Dictionary*. Edited by Paul J. Achtemeier. San Francisco: Harper & Row, 1985.

Magonet, Jonathan. "Abraham and God." *Judaism* 33 (spring 1984) 160–70.

Maranda, Pierre, and Elli Kongas Maranda (eds.). *Structural Analysis of Oral Tradition*. University of Pennsylvania Publications in Folklore and Folklife. Philadelphia: University of Pennsylvania Press, 1971.

Marcus, David. "David the Deceiver and David the Dupe." *Prooftexts* 6 (1986) 163–71.

_____. " 'Lifting Up the Head': On the Trail of a Wordplay in Genesis 40." *Prooftexts* 10 (1990) 17–27.

_____. "Non-recurring Doublets in the Book of Joel." *Catholic Biblical Quarterly* 56 (1994) 56–67.

_____. "The Term 'Coffin' in the Semitic Languages." *Journal of the Ancient Near Eastern Society of Columbia University* 7 (1975) 85–94.

Margalit, B. *A Matter of Life and Death: A Study of the Baal-Mot Epic (CTA 4-5-6)*. Alter Orient und Altes Testament 206. Neukirchen-Vluyn: Neukirchener Verlag, 1980.

Martin-Achard, R. "La Nouvelle Alliance selon Jeremie." *Revue de théologie et de Philosophie*, new series 12 (1962) 81–92.

Matthews, Victor H. "Hospitality and Hostility in Judges 4." *Biblical Theology Bulletin* 21 (spring 1991) 13–21.

McCarthy, D. J. "Hosea XII 2: Covenant by Oil." *Vetus Testamentum* 14 (1964) 215–21.

_____. "Three Covenants in Genesis." *Catholic Biblical Quarterly* 26 (1964) 179–89.

McCree, W. T. "The Covenant Meal in the Old Testament." *Journal of Biblical Literature* 45 (1926) 120–28.

McCullough, W. S. "Israel's Eschatology from Amos to Daniel." Pp. 86–101 in *Studies on the Ancient Palestinian World*. Edited by J. Wevers. Toronto: University of Toronto Press, 1972.

Meagher, Robert E. "Strangers at the Gate: Ancient Rites of Hospitality." *Parabola: The Magazine of Myth and Tradition* 2/4 (1977) 10–15.

Mellink, M. "Hittite Friezes and Gate Sculptures." Pp. 201–14 in *Anatolian Studies Presented to Hans Gustave Güterbock on the Occasion of His Sixty-Fifth Birthday*. Edited by Kurt Bittel, P. H. J. Houwink ten Cate, and Erica Reiner. Istanbul: Nederlands Historisch-Archaeologisch Institut, 1974.

Mendelsohn, Isaac. "On the Preferential Status of the Eldest Son." *Bulletin of the American Schools of Oriental Research* 156 (1959) 38–40.

Mendenhall, G. E. "Puppy and Lettuce in Northwest Semitic Covenant Making." *Bulletin of the American Schools of Oriental Research* 133 (1954) 26–30.

Milgrom, Jacob. *Leviticus 1–16: A New Translation with Introduction and Commentary.* Anchor Bible 3A. New York: Doubleday, 1991.

Miller, Patrick D. *The Divine Warrior in Early Israel.* Harvard Semitic Monographs 5. Cambridge: Harvard University Press, 1973.

Mills, Margaret A. "Domains of Folkloristic Concern: The Interpretation of Scriptures." Pp. 231–41 in *Text and Tradition: The Hebrew Bible and Folklore.* Edited by Susan Niditch. Society of Biblical Literature Semeia Studies 20. Atlanta: Scholars Press, 1990.

Milne, Pamela J. "Folktales and Fairy Tales: An Evaluation of Two Proppian Analyses of Biblical Narratives." *Journal for the Study of the Old Testament* 34 (1986) 35–60.

_____. *Vladimir Propp and the Study of Structure in Hebrew Biblical Narrative.* Bible and Literature Series 13. Sheffield: Almond, 1988.

Mindlin, M., M. J. Geller, and J. E. Wansbrough (eds.). *Figurative Language in the Ancient Near East.* School of Oriental and African Studies. London: University of London, 1987.

Montgomery, James A. *A Critical and Exegetical Commentary on the Book of Kings.* International Critical Commentary. Edinburgh: T. & T. Clark, 1951.

Moore, Carey. *Esther: A New Translation with Introduction and Commentary.* Anchor Bible 7B. Garden City, New York: Doubleday, 1988.

Moran, William L. "The Ancient Near Eastern Background of the Love of God in Deuteronomy." *Catholic Biblical Quarterly* 25 (1963) 77–87.

_____. "A Note on the Treaty Terminology of the Sefire Stelas." *Journal of Near Eastern Studies* 22 (1963) 173–76.

Muffs, Yochanan. *Love and Joy: Law, Language and Religion in Ancient Israel.* Introduction by Thorkild Jacobsen. New York: Jewish Theological Seminary, 1992.

_____. *Studies in the Aramaic Legal Papyri from Elephantine.* Leiden: Brill, 1969.

Muilenburg, J. "The Form and Structure of the Covenantal Formulations." *Vetus Testamentum* 9 (1959) 347–65.

Nagler, Michael N. *Spontaneity and Tradition: A Study in the Oral Art of Homer.* Berkeley: University of California Press, 1974.

Nathhorst, Bertel. *Formal or Structural Studies of Traditional Tales: The Usefulness of Some Methodological Proposals Advanced by Vladimir Propp, Alan Dundes, Claude Lévi-Strauss, and Edmund Leach.* Stockholm Studies in Comparative Religion 9. Stockholm: Acta Universitatis Stockholmiensis, 1969.

Neusner, Jacob. *Parashiyyot 34 through 67 on Genesis 8:15 to 28:9.* Volume 2 of *Genesis Rabbah: The Judaic Commentary to the Book of Genesis—A New American Translation.* Brown Judaic Studies 105. Atlanta: Scholars Press, 1985.

Nicolaisen, Wilhelm F. H. "Variability and Creativity in Folk-Narrative." Pp. 39–46 in *D'un conte . . . à l'autre: La Variabilité dans la littérature orale.* Edited by Veronika Görög-Karady and Michele Chiche. Paris: Centre Nationale de la Recherche Scientifique, 1990.

Niditch, Susan. "Legends of Wise Heroes and Heroines." Pp. 167–200 in *The Old Testament and Its Modern Interpreters.* Edited by Douglas A. Knight and Gene M. Tucker. Chico, California: Scholars Press, 1985.

____. "The 'Sodomite' Theme in Judges 19–20: Family, Community, and Social Disintegration." *Catholic Biblical Quarterly* 44 (1982) 365–78.

____. *The Symbolic Vision in Biblical Tradition.* Harvard Semitic Monographs 30. Chico, California: Scholars Press, 1980.

____. *War in the Hebrew Bible: A Study in the Ethics of Violence.* New York: Oxford University Press, 1993.

Niditch, Susan (ed.). *Text and Tradition: The Hebrew Bible and Folklore.* Proceedings from the Conference on the Hebrew Bible and Folklore held April 28–May 1, 1988, at Amherst College. Society of Biblical Literature Semeia Studies 20. Atlanta: Scholars Press, 1990.

Niditch, Susan, and Robert Doran. "The Success Story of the Wise Courtier: A Formal Approach." *Journal of Biblical Literature* 96 (1977) 179–93.

Nielsen, Eduard. "Moses and the Law." *Vetus Testamentum* 32 (1982) 87–98.

Norris, Frederick W. "Black Marks on the Communities' Manuscripts." *Journal of Early Christian Studies* 2 (1994) 443–66.

Noth, Martin. *The Deuteronomistic History.* Journal for the Study of the Old Testament Supplements. Sheffield: JSOT Press, 1981.

Noy, Dov. "The Jewish Versions of the 'Animal Languages' Folktale (AT 670): A Typological-Structural Study." Pp. 171–208 in *Studies in Aggadah and Folk-Literature.* Edited by Joseph Heinemann and Dov Noy. Scripta hierosolymitana 22. Jerusalem: Magnes, 1971.

Olrik, Axel. "Epic Laws of Folk Narrative." Pp. 129–41 in *The Study of Folklore.* Edited by Alan Dundes. Englewood Cliffs, New Jersey: Prentice-Hall, 1965.

____. *Principles for Oral Narrative Research.* Translated by Kirsten Wolf and Jody Jensen. Folklore Studies in Translation. Bloomington, Indiana: Indiana University Press, 1992.

Olsen, Alexandra Hennessey. "Loss and Recovery: A Morphological Reconsideration of Sir Orfeo." *Fabula* 23/3–4 (1982) 198–206.

Oppenheim, A. L. *Ancient Mesopotamia: Portrait of a Dead Civilization.* Chicago: University of Chicago Press, 1964.

____. *The Interpretation of Dreams in the Ancient Near East.* Transactions of the American Philosophical Society new series 46/3. Philadelphia: American Philosophical Society, 1956.

Pappas, Harry S. "Deception as Patriarchal Self-Defense in a Foreign Land: A Form-Critical Study of the Wife-Sister Stories in Genesis [Gen. 12, 20, 26]." *Greek Orthodox Theological Review* 29 (spring 1984) 35–50.

Parker, Simon B. *The Pre-biblical Narrative Tradition: Essays on the Ugaritic Poems Keret and Aqhat.* Society of Biblical Literature Resources for Biblical Study 24. Atlanta: Scholars Press, 1989.

Parrot, André. "Les Peintures du palais de Mari." *Syria* 18 (1937) 325–54.

Patai, R. "Hebrew Installation Rites." *Hebrew Union College Annual* 20 (1947) 143–225.

Patte, Daniel. *The Religious Dimensions of Biblical Texts: Griemas's Structural Semiotics and Biblical Exegesis.* Society of Biblical Literature Semeia Studies 19. Atlanta: Scholars Press, 1990.

Penglase, Charles. *Greek Myths and Mesopotamia: Parallels and Influence in the Homeric Hymns and Hesiod.* London: Routledge, 1994.

Pike, Kenneth L. *Language in Relation to a Unified Theory of the Structure of Human Behavior.* The Hague: Mouton, 1967.

Polzin, Robert. "'The Ancestress of Israel in Danger' in Danger." *Semeia* 3 (*Classical Hebrew Narrative*; 1975) 81–98.

_____. *Biblical Structuralism.* Semeia Supplements. Missoula, Montana: Scholars Press, 1977.

_____. *Samuel and the Deuteronomist: A Literary Study of the Deuteronomic History, Part Two: I Samuel.* New York: Harper & Row, 1989.

Pope, Marvin H. "The Cult of the Dead at Ugarit." Pp. 159–79 in *Ugarit in Retrospect: Fifty Years of Ugarit and Ugaritic.* Edited by G. D. Young. Winona Lake, Indiana: Eisenbrauns, 1982.

Popper, Karl R. *The Logic of Scientific Discovery.* New York: Harper Torchbooks, 1968.

_____. *Objective Knowledge: An Evolutionary Approach.* Oxford: Clarendon, 1972.

Pritchard, James B. (ed.). *Ancient Near Eastern Texts Relating to the Old Testament.* 3d ed. with supplement. Princeton: Princeton University Press, 1969.

Propp, Vladimir. *Morphology of the Folktale.* 2d ed. Edited with a preface by Louis A. Wagner. Translated by Laurence Scott, with an introduction by Svatava Pirkova-Jakobson; new introduction by Alan Dundes. Austin: University of Texas Press, 1968.

_____. "Structure and History in the Study of the Fairy Tale." Translated by Hugh T. McElwain. *Semeia* 10 (*Narrative Syntax: Translations and Reviews*; 1978) 57–83.

_____. *Theory and History of Folklore.* Edited by Anatoly Liberman. Translated by Ariadna Martin and Richard P. Martin. Theory and History of Literature 5. Minneapolis: University of Minnesota Press, 1984.

Propp, William H. *Water in the Wilderness: A Biblical Motif and Its Mythological Background.* Harvard Semitic Monographs 40. Atlanta: Scholars Press, 1987.

Prouser, Ora Horn. *The Phenomenology of the Lie in Biblical Narrative.* Ph.D. dissertation, Jewish Theological Seminary, 1991.

Rabinowitz, Isaac. *A Witness Forever: Ancient Israel's Perception of Literature and the Resultant Hebrew Bible.* Edited by Ross Brann and David I. Owen. Bethesda, Maryland: CDL, 1993.

Rad, Gerhard von. *Old Testament Theology.* Volume 1. Translated by D. M. G. Stalker. New York: Harper & Row, 1962.

Raglan, Lord. *The Hero: A Study in Tradition, Myth, and Drama.* New York: Vintage, 1956.

_____. "The Hero of Tradition." Pp. 142–57 in *The Study of Folklore.* Edited by Alan Dundes. Englewood Cliffs, New Jersey: Prentice-Hall, 1965.

_____. "Myth and Ritual." *Journal of American Folklore* 68 (1955) 454–61.

Redford, Donald B. *A Study of the Biblical Story of Joseph (Genesis 37–50).* Vetus Testamentum Supplements 20. Leiden: Brill, 1970.

Reisman, Daniel. "Ninurta's Journey to Eridu." *Journal of Cuneiform Studies* 24 (1971) 3–8.

Roth, Wolfgang. "Structural Interpretations of 'Jacob at the Jabbok' (Genesis 32:22–32)." *Biblical Research* 21 (1976) 51–62.

_____. "You Are the Man! Structural Interaction in 2 Samuel 10–12." *Semeia* 8 (*Literary Critical Studies of Biblical Texts*; 1977) 1–13.

Ruiz-Montero, Consuelo. "The Structural Pattern of the Ancient Greek Romances and the *Morphology of the Folktale* of V. Propp." *Fabula* 22/3–4 (1981) 228–38.

Sarna, Nahum M. *Genesis*. Jewish Publication Society Commentary Series. Philadelphia: Jewish Publication Society, 1989.

Sasson, Jack M. *Ruth: A New Translation with a Philological Commentary and a Formalist-Folklorist Interpretation*. Biblical Seminar 10. Sheffield: Sheffield Academic Press, 1995.

_____. "The Worship of the Golden Calf." Pp. 151–59 in *Orient and Occident: Essays Presented to Cyrus H. Gordon on the Occasion of His Sixty-Fifth Birthday*. Edited by Harry A. Hoffner, Jr. Alter Orient und Altes Testament 22. Neukirchen-Vluyn: Neukirchener Verlag, 1973.

Sasson, Jack M. (ed.). *Civilizations of the Ancient Near East*. 4 volumes. Edited by John Baines, Gary Beckman, and Karen S. Rubinson. New York: Scribner's, 1995.

Sauren, H. "Besuchsfahrten der Götter in Sumer." *Orientalia* new series 38 (1969) 214–36.

Saussure, Ferdinand de. *Course in General Linguistics*. Edited by Charles Bally and Albert Sechehaye. In collaboration with Albert Riedlinger, translated by Roy Harris. La Salle, Illinois: Open Court, 1983.

Scheub, Harold. "Oral Narrative Process and the Use of Models." Pp. 71–90 in *Varia Folklorica*. Edited by Alan Dundes. The Hague: Mouton, 1978.

Schneider, Monique. "La Maîtrise de la temporalité: Un combat mythique." Pp. 29–40 in *Le mythe et le mythique*. Cahiers de l'Hermétisme / Colloque de Cerisy. Paris: Albin Michel, 1987.

Scholes, Robert. *Structuralism in Literature: An Introduction*. New Haven: Yale University Press, 1974.

Scholes, Robert, and Robert Kellogg. *The Nature of Narrative*. New York: Oxford University Press, 1966.

Schreiber, Stuart. "Biblical Eating Scenes: Callousness and the 'Prisoner' Motif." Unpublished paper, 1983.

Sebeok, Thomas A. (ed.). *Myth: A Symposium*. Bloomington, Indiana: Indiana University Press, 1965.

Segal, Naomi. "[Review of] Meir Sternberg, *The Poetics of Biblical Narrative: Ideological Literature and the Drama of Reading*." *Vetus Testamentum* 38 (1988) 243–49.

Seybold, Donald A. "Paradox and Symmetry in the Joseph Narrative." Pp. 59–73 in volume 1 of *Literary Interpretations of Biblical Narratives*. Edited by Kenneth R. R. Gros Louis, with James S. Ackerman and Thayer S. Warshaw. Bible in Literature Courses. Nashville: Abingdon, 1974.

Sharon, Diane M. "The Doom of Paradise: Literary Patterns in Accounts of Paradise and Mortality in the Hebrew Bible and the Ancient Near East." Pp. 43–74 in *A Feminist Companion to Genesis II*. Edited by Athalya Brenner. Sheffield: JSOT Press, 1998.

_____. "Ezekiel 40–48 and Gudea's Dream: A Biblical Parallel to a Sumerian Temple Hymn." Unpublished Paper Presented at the Society of Biblical Literature, Cognate Literature Group (Session S-127). Anaheim, California, 1989.

_____. "When Fathers Refuse to Eat: The Trope of Rejecting Food and Drink in Biblical Narrative." *Semeia* 86 (1999) 135–48.

Shupak, Nili. "Egyptian Phrases in Biblical Wisdom Literature." *Tarbiz* 54 (1985) 475–83. [Hebrew]

Silberman, Lou H. (ed.). *Semeia* 39 (*Orality, Aurality and Biblical Narrative*; 1987).

Sjöberg, Å. W. "Götterreisen." Pp. 480–83 in volume 3 of *Reallexikon der Assyriologie*. Edited by E. Ebeling, B. Meissner et al. Berlin: de Gruyter, 1971.

_____. *Der Mondgott Nanna Suen in der Sumerischen Überlieferung*. Stockholm: Almqvist & Wiksell, 1960.

Smith, Henry Preserved. *A Critical and Exegetical Commentary on the Books of Samuel*. International Critical Commentary. Edinburgh: T. & T. Clark, 1977.

Smith, W. Robertson. *The Religion of the Semites: The Fundamental Institutions*. 1889. New York: Meridian, 1956.

Soll, Will. "Misfortune and Exile in Tobit: The Juncture of a Fairy Tale Source and Deuteronomic Theology." *Catholic Biblical Quarterly* 51 (1989) 209–31.

Speiser, E. A. *Genesis: A New Translation with Introduction and Commentary*. Anchor Bible 1. New York: Doubleday, 1963.

_____. *Oriental and Biblical Studies*. Edited by J. J. Finkelstein and M. Greenberg. Philadelphia: University of Pennsylvania Press, 1967.

Sproul, Barbara C. *Primal Myths: Creating the World*. New York: Harper & Row, 1979.

Sternberg, Meir. *The Poetics of Biblical Narrative: Ideological Literature and the Drama of Reading*. Indiana Literary Biblical Series. Bloomington, Indiana: Indiana University Press, 1985.

Sydow, C. W. von. "Folktale Studies and Philology: Some Points of View." Pp. 219–42 in *The Study of Folklore*. Edited by Alan Dundes. Englewood Cliffs, New Jersey: Prentice-Hall, 1965.

Syren, Roger. *The Forsaken Firstborn: A Study of a Recurrent Motif in the Patriarchal Narratives*. Journal for the Study of the Old Testament Supplements 133. Sheffield: JSOT Press, 1993.

Talmon, Shemaryahu. "The 'Desert Motif' in the Bible and in Qumran Literature." Pp. 31–64 in *Biblical Motifs*. Edited by Alexander Altmann. Cambridge: Harvard University Press, 1966.

Taylor, Archer. "Folklore and the Student of Literature." Pp. 34–42 in *The Study of Folklore*. Edited by Alan Dundes. Englewood Cliffs, New Jersey: Prentice-Hall, 1965.

_____. "The Biographical Pattern in Traditional Narrative." *Journal of the Folklore Institute* 1 (1964) 114–29.

Thompson, Stith. *The Folktale*. New York: Dryden, 1946.

_____. *Motif Index of Folklore Literature*. 6 volumes. Bloomington, Indiana: Indiana University Press, 1969.

_____. *The Types of the Folktale: Antti Aarne's Verzeichnis der Märchentypen, Translated and Enlarged*. Folklore Fellows Communications 74. Helsinki: Suomalainen Tiedeakatemia, 1928.

Tigay, J. H. *The Evolution of the Gilgamesh Epic*. Philadelphia: University of Pennsylvania Press, 1982.

Toorn, Karel van der. "Funerary Rituals and Beatific Afterlife in Ugaritic Texts and in the Bible." *Bibliotheca orientalis* 48 (1991) 40–66.

Tov, E. *The Text-Critical Use of the Septuagint in Biblical Research*. Jerusalem Biblical Studies. Jerusalem: Simor, 1981.

Trible, Phyllis. *Texts of Terror: Literary-Feminist Readings of Biblical Narratives*. Philadelphia: Fortress, 1984.

Tsevat, Matitiahu. "Alalakhiana." *Hebrew Union College Annual* 29 (1958) 109–36.

_____. "Eating and Drinking, Hosting and Sacrificing in the Epic of AQHT." *Ugarit-Forschungen* 18 (1986) 345–50.

Van Seters, John. *Abraham in History and Tradition*. New Haven: Yale University Press, 1975.

_____. "The Place of the Yahwist in the History of Passover and Maṣṣot." *Zeitschrift für die Alttestamentliche Wissenschaft* 95 (1983) 167–82.

Vanstiphout, H. L. J. "The Banquet Scene in the Mesopotamian Debate Poems." Pp. 9–21 in *Banquets d'Orient*. Res Orientales 4. Bures-sur-Yvette, France: Groupe pour l'Étude de la Civilisation du Moyen-Orient, 1992.

Vogelzang, Marianna E. "Some Questions about the Akkadian Disputes." Pp. 47–57 in *Dispute Poems and Dialogues in the Ancient and Mediaeval Near East*. Edited by G. J. Reinink and H. L. Vanstiphout. Orientalia lovaniensia analecta 42. Leuven: Peeters, 1991.

Weinfeld, Moshe. "Addenda to *JAOS* 90 (1970), Pp. 184ff." *Journal of the American Oriental Society* 92 (1972) 468–69.

_____. "The Covenant of Grant in the Old Testament and in the Ancient Near East." *Journal of the American Oriental Society* 90 (1970) 184–203.

_____. "Covenant Terminology in the Ancient Near East and Its Influence on the West." *Journal of the American Oriental Society* 93 (1973) 190–99.

_____. *Deuteronomy and the Deuteronomic School*. Oxford: Oxford University Press, 1972. Reprinted, Winona Lake, Indiana: Eisenbrauns, 1992.

_____. *Genesis*. Tel Aviv: S. L. Gordon, 1975. [Hebrew]

Weisberg, David B. "Loyalty and Death: Some Ancient Near Eastern Metaphors." *Maarav* 7 (1991) 253–67.

Wellek, Rene, and Austin Warren. *Theory of Literature*. 3d ed. New York: Harcourt Brace Jovanovich, 1984.

Westermann, Claus. *The Promises to the Fathers: Studies on the Patriarchal Narratives*. Philadelphia: Fortress, 1980.

Whitley, Charles F. "Sources of the Gideon Stories." *Vetus Testamentum* 7 (1957) 157–64.

Williams, James G. "The Beautiful and the Barren: Conventions in Biblical Type-Scenes." *Journal for the Study of the Old Testament* 17 (1980) 107–19.

Xella, Paolo. "Sur la nourriture des morts: Un aspect de l'eschatologie meso-potamienne." Pp. 151–60 in *Death in Mesopotamia: Papers Read at the XXCI^e Rencontre Assyriologique Internationale, 1979.* Edited by Bendt Alster. Copenhagen Studies in Assyriology 8. Copenhagen: Akademisk, 1980.

Zakovitch, Yair. *The Concept of the Miracle in the Bible.* Translated by Shmuel Himelstein. Tel Aviv: MOD, 1990.

_____. "The Sacrifice of Gideon (Jud. 6:11–24) and the Sacrifice of Manoah (Jud. 13)." *Shnaton* 1 (1975) 151–54. [Hebrew]

Zimmerli, W. "Sinaibund und Abrahambund: Ein Beitrag zum Verständnis der Priesterschrift." *Theologische Zeitschrift* 16 (1960) 268–80.

Zucker, Moshe. "Towards a Solution to the Problem of the Thirty-Two Rules of the 'Mishnah of Rabbi Eliezer.'" [Hebrew] *Proceedings of the American Academy for Jewish Research* 23 (1954): [Hebrew Section] 1–39.

Index of Authors Cited

Index of Scripture Citations

Hebrew Scripture

Genesis

1	149, 162, 177
2	41, 177
3	165
3:1–7	165
3:8–13	165
3:14–19	165
3:22–24	165
4	91, 93, 167
6:5	177
8:18–20	174
8:18–9:1	174
8:20	176
8:20–9:18	63
8:21	174, 177
8:22	174, 177
9:1	174
9:1–3	177
9:4–6	177
9:9	64
9:18–29	91
9:20	178
9:20–21	177
9:22–23	177
9:22–24	178
9:24	177
9:25	178
9:26–27	178
12	99
12:6	59, 75
12:10	98
12:10–20	75, 93
14	116
14:11–24	84
15	41, 61, 63, 65
15:17–18	63
16:6–15	56, 77

Genesis (cont.)

17	65, 110
17:16–21	142
17:21	142
18	97, 109, 126–28, 138, 141, 143, 159, 182
18:1	123
18:1–19	120, 122, 128
18:2	123
18:3–8	123
18:9	124–25
18:10	125
18:11	125
18:12	126
18:13	126
18:14	127
18:15	124, 126
18:17–19	127, 141
18:20–21	128
18:20–22	94
19	94, 128, 153, 159
19:1–3	128
19:1–29	128
19:4–11	128
19:12–13	128
19:14–22	129
19:23–29	129
19:27–28	100
19:30–38	77
20	74, 99
21	141, 143, 159
21:1–8	110
21:4	110
21:12–13	142
21:17–18	141

Genesis (cont.)

21:17–20	56
21:20–21	141
21:22–34	61, 79
21:27	61
22	58
23:2	101
24	97, 111, 138, 142–43
24:1–9	62
24:2–4	62
24:9	62
24:18–20	142
24:22–32	142
24:31–33	112
24:32–33	142
24:34–49	142
24:50–51	143
24:53	143
24:54	143
24:55–58	143
24:67	111
25:20–26	109
25:22–23	89
25:27–34	91
25:8	100
26	93
26:1–11	99
26:26–33	62
26:34	111
27	1, 42, 89, 158, 160
27:1–28:5	112
28	41
28:9	111
28:10	71
28:16–17	72

2 Samuel (cont.)
16:10 85
16:11 85
17:27–29 84–85, 97
19 97
19:1–5 103–4
19:16–40 85–86
19:23 85
19:32–40 85
20:22 187
21:1–14 100
23:20 184
23:20–23 184
24 100, 106

1 Kings
1 183–184
1:1–4 184
1:1–49 113, 115,
    183–84
1:5–10 184
1:11–40 184
1:33–37 184
1:38–40 184
1:41 185
1:43–49 185
1:49–53 185
1:53 185
2:5–6 91, 102
2:7 87
2:8–9 86, 102
2:13–25 185
2:36–46 86–87
2:45–46 86
3 41, 86
3:4–15 74
3:15 72
3:16–28 86
5:3 159
8 49, 106, 193
8:35–40 99
11 96, 193
11:1–8 193
11:8 193
11:9–13 193
11:11–14 96

1 Kings (cont.)
11:14–25 193
11:20 111
11:26–40 96
11:29–39 193
12–13 156
12:25–13:10 193,
    195
12:25–33 194
13 158
13:1–3 194
13:1–10 96, 194
13:4–5 194
13:7–9 194
13:11–25 195
13:11–34 95
13:15–19 195
13:21 195
13:21–22 95, 195
13:22 195
13:24 95
13:24–25 195
14 156, 180–181
14:1–4 178
14:1–18 126, 178
14:5–6 178
14:7–16 178
14:10 179
14:12 179
14:17 179
14:17–18 102, 179
14:31 100
15:25–30 179
16:1–7 90
16:1–14 90
16:1–28 96
16:15–19 96
17 115
17:1 100
17:6 57
17:7–16 97
17:12–16 58
17:13–16 57
17:17–24 58, 115
17:24 58
18 57

1 Kings (cont.)
18:17–18 100
18:20–41 100
19 156
19:1–18 156
19:15–18 156
19:19–21 97, 156
20 81
20:1–12 81
20:1–13 92
20:7–11 81
20:13–14 81
20:15–20 81
20:16 81
20:21 81
20:22 82
20:23 81
20:27 82
20:28 81–82
20:29–30 82
20:30–43 82
20:42 155
21 90, 155
21:4–6 155
21:7–16 155
22 126, 155–56, 187,
    201
22:34–37 82

2 Kings
2 59
2–4 58
2:16–24 58
2:19–22 58, 68
3:4–25 82
3:9–27 59
4 59, 97, 115, 190
4:1–7 58
4:8–37 58
4:18–37 115
4:38–41 68
4:38–44 58
5 179, 181
6 86
6:8–23 82, 92, 97
6:24–7:16 82

Job (cont.)
42:10   197
42:10–15   197
42:11   197
42:11–17   98
42:12–15   197

Ruth
1:1   99
2   98
2:8–13   161
2:14   161
2:15–19   161
2:20   161
3   112
3:7–11   69

Esther
1   92
2:18   111, 115
4   106
5:1–8   162
5:1–7:10   162
5:9–14   162
6:1–3   162
6:7–14   162
6:12–13   162
7:1–8   162
8–9   116
8:1–9:32   116
8:16   116
8:16–17   116
9:28   116

Daniel
1–6   24
1:5–16   92, 96
2   71–72
2:1   72
3   93
5   154, 181

Daniel (cont.)
5:1   153
5:1–30   153
5:2–28   153
5:5   153
5:7–17   154
5:18–28   154
5:30   154
6   92, 106
10   71–72
10:7–8   72

Ezra
5–6   115
6:15–22   47
8   106–7
9–10   106
9:12   180

Nehemiah
1–2   190
1:4   107, 190
1:8–11   190
1:8–9   190
1:11   107
2   107
2:1   190
2:2   190
2:3–9   190
2:4   190
2:8   190
2:11–18   190
2:12   190
2:18   190
2:19–20   190
6:6–9   191
8:1–12   66
8:10–12   67
9:25   180
9:36   180
12:43   48, 115

1 Chronicles
13:5–14   50, 115
15:1–16:3   50
15:16–24   50
15:26   50
15–16   50
16:3   51
21   100, 106
27:5   184
27:6   184
28:1   183
28:2–5   183
28:6–21   183
28:9–10   183
28–29   113, 183–84
29:1–20   183
29:21–22   183
29:22   183
29:23–25   183

2 Chronicles
5–6   49, 106
5:12–13   49
12:16   100
15   115
15:9–15   64
18   126, 155–56, 187
29   50, 152
30   152
30:1–13   152
30:13–18   152
30:18–20   152
30:21–26   152
30:22   50, 147
30:27   152
34:29–32   66
35   157
35:1–19   157
35:20   157
35:21   158
35:22–27   158

Christian Scripture

Matthew		Mark		Luke	
24	140	14	140	22	140
26:17–29	140	14:12–25	140	22:14–18	140
26:20–25	140	14:17–21	140	22:14–23	140
26:20–26	140	14:17–22	140	22:19	140
26:26–27	140	14:22–24	140	22:20–22	140
26:27–29	140	14:23–25	140	22:29–30	140
26:28–29	140	14:25	140	22:7–34	140